Reel Exposure

How To Publicize and Promote Today's Motion Pictures

REEL EXPOSURE

HOW TO PUBLICIZE AND PROMOTE TODAY'S MOTION PICTURES

STEVEN JAY RUBIN

Broadway Press
Shelter Island 1991

First printed January 1992

Manufactured in the United States of America

Publisher's Cataloging in Publication
(Prepared by Quality Books Inc.)

Rubin, Steven Jay.
  Reel exposure : how to publicize and promote today's motion pictures / Steven Jay Rubin.
    p. cm.
    Includes index.
    ISBN 0-911747-20-6

  1. Motion pictures--United States--Marketing--Textbooks I. Title.

PN1998.R8 1991   791.437
                                  QBI91-1716

Broadway Press
12 West Thomas St. Box 1037
Shelter Island, NY 11964
516-749-3266 (voice) 516-749-3267 (fax)

Dedication

To the publicist—the unsung hero of motion pictures today!

ACKNOWLEDGMENTS

This book was inspired by questions: What does a publicist do? What's the difference between a studio publicist and a unit publicist? How do you get the jobs? How do you become successful? If not for these questions, the answers would not have become the foundation of this book. So I must thank the people who, over the years, asked me these questions.

I would particularly like to thank my publisher, David Rodger of Broadway Press, for believing in the value of this material and nurturing it through the many editing processes. He also inspired me to make this the first and best possible tome on the field of motion picture publicity today.

I also wish to thank my fellow members of Local 818 of the Publicist's Guild of America—the cream of today's movie publicists. The Guild is the one organization which supports the dignity of publicists and educates the industry on the services we provide. You cannot work at one of the major studios today unless you are a member of the Publicist's Guild. Novice publicists should learn about this organization and keep the Guild's number handy: (818) 905-1541.

Although this book will provide many answers, it will also raise a lot of questions. I would appreciate hearing from people who have further questions or comments on topics covered in this book. Please don't hesitate to contact me through Broadway Press. A continuing dialogue among people in the motion picture community, students and veterans alike, would benefit us all.

Finally, I would like to thank my mother, Eve Rubin, who inspired me from the beginning with her great love of movies and continues to inspire me today on my various "gigs;" and my father, Joseph Rubin, with whom I shared many cinematic adventures—from *The High and Mighty* to *Patton*.

Thanks, everyone!

CONTENTS

INTRODUCTION

Ideally, when you crack open the cover of this book you should hear Ethel Merman singing those immortal lyrics, "There's no business like show business." Roll out that red carpet, turn on those searchlights, polish those dancing shoes, crank up the soundtrack. Sing out a welcome to an unsung arena of show business.

Practically every endeavor in the film business, from acting to screenwriting, from directing to makeup, has its own "How to" book. But there are no books on publicity and promotion. An occasional mention here, a chapter there, but no complete study of a very complicated discipline.

While more and more colleges and universities offer curriculum on film production, there is no degree in film publicity and promotion. Thousands of students go out into the world each year, bravely and gamely, to write their scripts and prepare their short films, but, for the most part, they have no idea how to sell them, or how the motion picture marketing process works.

The skills of the Hollywood publicist/promoter were once learned and perfected in the P.R. factories of the big studios like MGM, Fox or Warners. Today, publicity departments at the major studios are a shell of what they used to be, and, the training ground has virtually disappeared for film publicists.

This book is not going to be the last word on film publicity. But it's the first to take a long and careful look at the day to day tasks every publicist must accomplish. I've tried to give an accurate portrait of what the job entails. The "do's and don'ts" you learn here are based on my own experience. There are of course, the basics: how to coordinate a press junket on location, which media outlets you have to contact first, how to deal with temperamental actors, what to include in an effective press kit. And I've also tried to give as many case histories as possible to give you a feel for the real life conditions of the job.

You're still going to have to get that first job. And you're still going to go out and learn the basics under battlefield conditions, but I hope this book can be a trusted manual to guide you through the early days of your career.

Future publicists are not this book's only targeted audience. *Reel Exposure* is also expected to help any filmmaker—amateur or professional—who wants to know how the publicity and promotion business works. Whether your budget is $40,000 or $40 million, this book has useful information for you.

Whatever your interest, *Reel Exposure* will shed new light on a very guarded subject. Hopefully, the spotlight will be enlightening. Publicity and promotion are evolving disciplines. Just as cameramen develop new devices to make better pictures, we must conduct research and development to ensure more effective publicity and promotion campaigns. Better campaigns will benefit the professional standing of the publicist. More qualified publicists will make the journalists who cover the movies happier. Qualified publicists will impress film producers and executives and I won't have to work so hard justifying the existence of my department on every job. That's my real hope.

A word about how this book is organized. There are chapters covering every aspect of the publicity and promotion business. These chapters are grouped into three sections. Part One, "Definitions and Qualifications," covers the basics of publicity and promotion, including the actual personal qualifications one needs to survive in this business. Part Two, "Production Publicity," demystifies the role of the unit publicist during the actual production of a motion picture. Part Three, "Pre-Release Publicity," covers just that, the publicity work which goes on between the end of shooting and the actual release of the film. I've concluded the book with two more chapters; one provides a few guidelines on evaluating your own effectiveness after you've finished a job, and a final chapter looks briefly into the future to forecast new developments looming on the horizon.

I hope you enjoy the book.

Steven Jay Rubin

Summer 1991

1

WHAT IS PUBLICITY?

Publicity builds awareness for a new motion picture. When the filmgoer sees or hears a story about a movie or an actor—a publicity break—hopefully something sticks in his mind. Then when the motion picture advertising campaign kicks in a few weeks before the film opens, that same person will remember the publicity break and think, "I've heard of that movie." An important connection is established! That's what publicity does.

Quality aside, a film's box office success is determined by how many people see it. The person responsible for getting all those bodies into the theatres is the studio marketing executive. Their worst fear is for a filmgoer to open his Friday newspaper and see a full page advertisement for a new movie and say to himself, "Never heard of it," especially if there's another film on the next page he has heard of! Awareness, in such a situation, can be the key factor influencing which movie is seen and which movie is not.

Awareness studies prior to the release of a film are now commonplace. Market research firms send representatives into shopping malls across the country and present a list of films to the average citizen. The citizen is then asked whether he or she has heard of the movies. From this data, an awareness percentage is established. The sequel to a major blockbuster like an *Indiana Jones* or a *Batman* might reveal 90% awareness prior to release—figures that indicate a potentially tremendous opening weekend at the box office. However, other films on the list could be given a very low awareness figure like 20%. Low numbers are not harbingers for big success.

The point of all this is that before paid advertising kicks in, publicity is a prime awareness builder. And the publicity machines of today have come a long way from the columns of Hedda Hopper and Louella Parsons. Today publicity is an all-media event: super interviewer Barbara Walters interviews Sylvester Stallone on national television;

Entertainment Tonight visits the set of Steven Spielberg's latest extravaganza; NBC Network Radio does a five part segment on violence in American film; *Premiere* magazine debuts with 75 pages on American movie stars of today; and the *New York Times* raves about Meryl Streep's latest film.

As we see these "breaks," we begin to familiarize ourselves with a new product. Pre-advertising campaign awareness is crucial to a movie's success. While huge conglomerates like Proctor and Gamble and Lever Brothers can afford to spend millions of dollars in advertising over many months to build awareness for a new product, the typical movie company normally advertises a new film for two weeks! If the movie fails to perform at the box office, it's gone. That's the law of this jungle.

There are examples of films that opened with very little awareness and rode a wave of word-of-mouth to success. 20th Century Fox's *Breaking Away* was a word-of-mouth picture; so was that same studio's *Big* with Tom Hanks. But they are the exceptions.

To ignore an effective publicity campaign in today's film marketplace is suicidal. Next to sex, movies are the most popular conversation subject in America. And the number of media outlets today devoted to the film medium is unprecedented. Many of them are clamoring for new stories. The appetite of the fan magazines now extends to television shows like *Entertainment Tonight*, programs on E! Entertainment Channel and the morning talk shows. Film magazines such as *Premiere* are becoming increasingly powerful. Daily newspapers and magazines are devoting more space than ever to the movie scene.

Often, the persuasiveness of the publicist isn't even a factor. The outlets want raw publicity materials and they want them now. If press information, slides, stills and video clips are sent on time, they'll be used. But those materials must be available. Many good films have died before they deserved to because of the absence of publicity materials. And such a faux pas can have a chain reaction effect on the future life of a film—through its video and pay cable release.

"I've heard of that movie!" It's the money phrase that indicates success or failure in today's movie marketplace.

2

WHAT IS PROMOTION?

Promotion is another important tool in the motion picture marketing campaign to build awareness for a new movie. Unlike publicity which generally involves a direct relationship between the publicist and the media, promotion introduces a third party or separate event which helps spread the word. Let's cite some quick examples:

■ The bicycle industry supports a bicycle racing movie by taking out advertisements in their trade publications and setting up in-store displays in bicycle shops nationwide.

■ A local morning DJ gives away tickets to a special advance screening of a new movie. He announces the ticket giveaway several times a day over a five day period prior to the film's release.

■ A major fast food restaurant chain ties in with the a new animated film from one of America's top filmmakers. Printed images of the film appear on food wrappers and the fast food companies national TV commercials tout the new movie project.

■ A local newspaper features a full page advertisement promoting a movie. The public is urged to clip the ad, take it to a retailer in a shopping mall and get free tickets to an advance screening.

■ To promote the opening of a new movie about American teenagers sneaking across the Finnish border into Russia, a convoy of Soviet army vehicles are rented, along with costumed Russian troops and marched down Hollywood Blvd in an ersatz parade.

Promotion involves a detail-oriented step by step approach that is akin to walking through the proverbial mine field. Obstacles are presented at every step and if the publicist/promoter doesn't perfectly present his product, the promotion can explode in his face. Third parties are introduced that have an entirely new list of guidelines and priorities.

The third party could be a major corporation that has a special timetable for spending promotional dollars—a timetable that doesn't take into account the unusual distribution patterns of today's films. In other words, they might not be very happy about a movie touted as a national release, that suddenly opens in only one market. Or they might not understand that a film's release date can change—even after careful promotional plans and schedules have been prepared. It's no wonder that most of the major corporate/movie tie-ins are accomplished by the major film companies which carry their own clout in the marketplace and can deal directly with the special needs of third parties.

Movie promoters are much more than navigators of the corporate mine field. They need to have a little bit of the hucksterism of P.T. Barnum, marching down unpaved main streets of every small town in America with elephants, jugglers and acrobats parading behind him. Barnum's extraordinary efforts to reach average consumers on their own turf is a kind of promotion which may seem unsophisticated today, but it should not be forgotten that it worked.

The true showmanship preached by Barnum is a specialized talent that has not been nurtured in Hollywood. When the studios broke up and Hollywood was taken over by the bankers, lawyers and MBAs, the showmanship acumen of the old moguls was seldom carried forth. Today there are very few showmen in the tradition of Alfred Hitchcock, C.B. DeMille, William Castle and Samuel Bronston. And because of this dearth of promoters, the field is open to the creative and the spirited who can create "sumpin' from nuttin." I am reminded of one of the great classics, *The Three Stooges Meet Hercules* in which the famous comedians stood out in front of a Greek amphitheater touting the upcoming contest between their friend, Schuyler, who was impersonating Hercules and the many-headed Hydra monster. As Larry sells his programs, he says "Get your programs, without them you can't tell one head from another!" Now that's promotion.

3

WHAT DO YOU NEED TO BECOME A MOVIE PUBLICIST?

The student headed for medical school knows that he must be proficient in mathematics and chemistry. Similarly, the young publicist of tomorrow must be aware of the prerequisites he will need to be successful. Those considering a career change will also benefit from a discussion of the qualities every good publicist must have. You would be surprised at the confusing, unprepared answers given to the question, "What makes a good publicist?" This chapter looks at nine skills and personality traits which I have discovered are common to all good publicists.

The Importance of Personality—
being talkative, outgoing, people-oriented.

When it comes to movie publicity, wallflowers need not apply. The publicist must be a standout—an outgoing, personable talker who loves people and interaction. A publicist should be prepared to make a speech on a moment's notice. In a crowded movie theater with 500 restless souls, the publicist must step to the forefront and explain why the film is being delayed. In fact, that same publicist might be asked to keep the audience company until the film begins. During such times, you become the world's most spontaneous comedian.

Many times I have compared the publicist to a combination cheerleader and court jester. No, I don't bring pom-poms and tricolored, bell-laden caps to the film set, but they are there nonetheless. A publicist with a likable personality is able to work well with the various personality types found on the film set. There are many varieties, some quite disagreeable. Don't flinch. Deal directly with disagreeable people. Figure out a way to break them down, to win them over, to put them on your side.

I've never had an argument with an actor or a writer in my life. They don't pay me to have arguments. My job is to prevent arguments, to make everyone feel happy. Again, think of the prize fight, I've got to separate the opponents, make sure they fight clean. If they're entangled, I've got to figure out a way to untangle them without getting slapped myself. And you get slapped, sometimes repeatedly.

The Publicist As Diplomat.

In a nutshell, as a publicist you're paid not to antagonize anyone. Your job is to develop the best possible relationships with all entities—cast, crew, studio, media, corporations, government figures, civilians. Movie making is such a pressure cooker at times, an enterprise so devoid of etiquette and patience, that cast and crew never develop the poise to deal with problems diplomatically. The fact that millions of dollars are being spent to make a movie probably has something to do with it. Under financial pressures, people lose their cool very quickly.

As I mentioned earlier with the heavyweight boxing match analogy, the publicist must have the strength to grapple with two opposing parties and make them "fight" cleanly. If a writer comes to a set to interview an actor and the actor suddenly doesn't want to do the interview, it's your job to remedy the situation.

It's not going to solve any problems for you to walk into the actor's dressing room and start saying, "You have to do this interview." Actors, particularly the "stars" of our time, don't have to do anything. They're so pampered by the time they reach a certain star status that they no longer feel compelled to perform certain tasks.

So what do you do? You put on your diplomatic cap, the one you borrowed from Henry Kissinger, and you figure out a way to explain to the actor the importance of the interview and how vital it is to the selling of the picture.

Sometimes, the actor has a problem with a specific writer. They may have had a bad interview in the past, a previous story might have been inaccurate, or the actor simply doesn't like the interview process. I always give my actors plenty of notice about upcoming interviews. I also brief them on who is going to do the interview. If there are problems with a specific writer, find out about them before the writer comes to the interview.

On the first day of shooting, one of the youthful stars of *Pretty in Pink* walked up to me and categorically laid down the law. "I don't speak to teen magazines." He was simple, direct and vehement. The same thing happened on *Desert Bloom* when a certain top actor approached me on the first day of shooting and said, "I don't do interviews during filming." I thanked him for the information.

Arm twisting doesn't work, but as you develop relationships with people, they come around. The *Desert Bloom* actor was a first-rate professional who later did interviews on the set. I just learned that they had to be fairly important ones and he needed plenty of notice.

Actors are moody race horses at times. They need to be coddled, babied, mothered. They have many problems, insecurities, concerns. And because they are "stars," those problems are enormously magnified on the set. If you innocently bump into a "star" in the hallway at MGM, normally a simple "excuse me" or "I'm sorry" will suffice. On the set, a literal or figurative bump can cause you hours, days, weeks of frustrating explanations and apologies.

Knowing the personalities of your cast and crew and their place in the hierarchy of power can help solve problems. Sometimes if an interview is important and the actor is unwilling, you can go to a third party to mediate the situation. When Israel and Egypt weren't talking, Kissinger introduced the U.S. to mediate. The U.S. on the movie set could be the producer, or even one of the other actors. Producers can be effective because they sign the checks. They also have the most to lose if the marketing campaign is hurt by a star's lack of cooperation with the media.

Remember that while you're accommodating the actor, you have to make sure the press person is happy too. Members of the media have their own stellar personalities. Their egos can be bruised just as easily as the actors. Sometimes they also have different priorities than you. You might bring a writer to the set to interview a director and find out about the movie. His editor might have asked him to "dig up some dirt" on a relationship between the director and his top actor—a topic that could lead to fireworks on the set.

To avoid fireworks, do your homework. Prior to any interview, set up some rules about sensitive topics. In pre-release marketing strategy, it is now common for the publicist to come up with a list of a film's publicity strengths and weaknesses. The strengths become the pitching angles, the weaknesses are topics to avoid, topics to steer the media away from.

If Mr. Superstar has repeatedly told you and everyone else that he won't talk about his personal life, you have to communicate that to the press person you bring to the interview. Pre-briefing the media at least affords you the opportunity of telling Mr. Superstar later that, even though the media asked a sensitive question, they had been warned.

One phrase that you must strike from your publicist's vocabulary is, "I forgot." Like the elephant, the publicist never forgets. At my first publicity job, I kept hearing the acronym C.Y.A. whenever certain sensitive tasks were discussed. I soon discovered that C.Y.A. stands for "Cover your ass."

As crude as this phrase is, it's a key to performing successful publicity campaigns. It means you must anticipate problems and be ready to offer solutions. Never tell anyone you forgot to do something. But more importantly, don't forget. It only takes a couple mistakes like that, and your chances of accomplishing your job, or, for that matter, getting another job in the future, are over.

Develop positive relationships and anticipate problems. A movie cast and crew depends on the publicist to make the necessary but often irritating task of promoting the movie as painless as possible. Their job is to make the movie, your job is to promote it.

Love of Movies.

You don't have to love a movie to publicize it. In fact, I've worked on more bombs than I care to talk about. Your job is the same whether you're promoting *Gone With The Wind* or *Bonzo Goes to College*. It's not the individual movies that need love, it's the art form itself.

I'm not interested in developing an average publicist's checklist. I would like to provide information and tips that can lead you to a career as one of the top publicists in Hollywood. I believe that a certain love affair with the movies is key.

The movie business is founded on love for the art form. The first showmen—Griffith, DeMille, Goldwyn, Mayer, the Warner brothers— loved movies and their enthusiasm for the art form showed in their work and how they built an industry. For the most part, that golden age of movie making is long gone. The people who run the business today are technocrats—lawyers, MBAs, advertising executives, businessmen—people who are always looking at the "bottom line," or "how much is this movie going to make?"

You won't find sawdust in the shoes of today's studio execs, the thrill of the circus in their souls, the spirit of showmanship that was so much a hallmark of their predecessors. The rise of the technocrats, the bottom liners, the money people, makes it more essential today that the artists and the craftspeople who actually make the movies, love them.

I like to think the publicist is one of these artists. But even if I were uninspired, my job is to create excitement. The public is not excited by budgets, schedules and interoffice memos. They want to know about the glamour, the gossip, the intensity, the personalities. These are the things you must love so you can communicate them.

Your enthusiasm for the art form can get you a job. Remember the people who hire publicists are often producers who have a lot of money riding on their film. Would you hire someone who walked in with a slight handshake, a monotone voice and a lackluster attitude toward the business—in other words a publicity wallflower? No!

The producer wants someone to dance into his office and glow. Someone who is going to carry his movie pennant to the top of Iwo Jima, someone who is going to sneak up behind Roger Ebert and yell, "Have I got a movie for you!" Even the toughest, most demanding producers I have ever worked for complimented me on my enthusiasm. Going back to my cheerleader analogy: Movie people, consumed by the overwhelming demands of their work, look to you for a boost. A news clipping, a television break, a magazine that's interested—these are items that tend to cheer up producers and studio executives.

When you're speaking to a member of the media, a love for film will spill out of you. You can discuss the actors and their careers, the incredible locations, the director's cinematic touch, the costumes, the makeup, the special effects, the stunts and everything else with a certain glimmer in your voice.

If you have to be a salesperson in this life, the best product in the world to sell is movies. Everyone loves to talk about movies and when it's your job to talk about them, people are all ears. I've sold other items—sweaters, underwear, McDonalds hamburgers, magazines—but there's nothing like the movies. Hey, remember those famous lyrics, "There's no business like show business, like no business I know." It's true and I'm very excited to be a part of it. I hate to think of what I would do if I wasn't in the movies.

Awareness of Film History.

When you work in the film industry you instantly become part of a rich history that has an amazing significance to the media. You'd think that the life of an actor was less important, say, than a major political figure, or an inventor or a great novelist. But how many American school children can remember the names of all the novels written by Sinclair Lewis, or the political offices of James Madison or the invention inventory of Thomas Edison? Ask those same children to list the movies of Dan Akroyd or Chevy Chase.

The dream machine of the movie industry has always fascinated the public and that dream was supplied by the publicist—the keeper of the historical flame. For, while there are hundreds of film historians who write the movie history books and comment on historical trends in today's film making, it is the publicist who churns out the biographies and feature stories that tie today's cinema to its historical roots.

The very nature of film publicity allies it to the past. One of your first jobs on a new project is to identify the players and maximize their involvement in the film. The producer's decision to cast a name actor is based partly on talent and name value. It's your job to translate that name value into publicity value.

How do you do that? First, become familiar with the actor's history—his credits, his background, his reputation. Your press kit demands an up to date readable biography and you have to research it. Researching a bio involves delving into Hollywood history, identifying key film projects and tieing the new film to a rich legacy.

One of my favorite tasks is journeying to the library of the Academy of Motion Picture Arts and Sciences in Beverly Hills where there are files of clippings on every film ever made and every actor who ever appeared in those films. And, more importantly, for your task at hand, they usually have the actor's last bio on file. Thus, you generally don't have to start from scratch asking the actor where he was born and where he went to school—questions that drive veteran actors crazy and discredit the publicist in their eyes.

The publicist must be part historian. On the film set, where history is being made, you are the chronicler. If something exciting happens, your pen is the first to describe it to the world. Imagine a Columbia Pictures unit publicist sitting near the river in Sri Lanka (then Ceylon) where the bridge on the river Kwai is about to be blown up. Or the Paramount publicist who is watching a makeup artist stuff cotton into the mouth of Marlon Brando in *The Godfather*. Or the publicist watching actress Karen Allen stare at a floor full of snakes on *Raiders of the Lost Ark*.

The filming of key movie scenes has, today, as much historical interest for the public as certain global news events. I often think of publicists as news correspondents reporting from their respective bureaus. Instead of Morley Safer on location in Pleiku, South Vietnam, it's Steve Rubin on the set of "Rocky 9" in Philadelphia. I can call up the entertainment desk at the *New York Times* and tell them I'm working on "Rocky 9" and get their immediate attention. I may not sell a story idea, but I know they're going to listen to me. Movie making is history making.

Don't underestimate the value of movie history. Your awareness could determine whether a producer gives you the job. I remember a few years ago reading in the trade papers about a movie going into production called *War is Heck*—an *Airplane*-like spoof of World War II movies. I wanted that job.

One of my first book projects was an historical look at World War II movies called *Combat Films: American Realism 1945-1970*. I began interviewing filmmakers who had been involved with those films and I gathered some great stories and anecdotes. I also became somewhat of an authority on the genre. It didn't hurt one iota to walk into the first interview with the *War is Heck* producer with a copy of my book under my arm. Combined with my rush of enthusiasm for the project and a fair amount of ideas, I got the job. I was so proud of myself. Unfortunately, the studio went through an administrative change, and the project was jettisoned from the production schedule. Still, my knowledge of history had a place in getting me employment.

You don't have to write a book to get a publicist's job in Hollywood, but it does help to know your film history. It's not as if you were being asked to brush up on molecular biology or applied physics. Film history is fun.

If you weren't in Korea, you're not going to immediately identify with a book on the Korean War. Movie books are different. If you weren't present at the filming of *Gone With the Wind*, you're still going to be interested in its filming because you saw the film. When you see a movie, especially the classics, you establish a relationship with the screen which builds over the years on repeat showings. Some of us know screen characters better than we know the presidents of our country or our greatest inventors.

If you're not an expert on film history, don't fret, you can learn enough quickly to conduct an intelligent conversation. First, go to the Academy library, get comfortable there. Check out a few files on your favorite films and learn about them. Pick up a few celebrity biographies and start to read. Larry Edmonds Movie Book Shop in Hollywood and the Samuel French chain are well stocked with books on show business. Buy a few history books and build your own library. Develop an expertise if you can. Producers like publicists who can quote filmographies. You become their personal almanac. When a producer is giving an interview to the New York Times and he's comparing his film with a classic, he might turn to you and ask for the name of that movie. You score enormous points for having the answer.

Quoting film history in your production notes and biographies also helps present your new movie to the media. But make sure your facts are right. If you have an inaccuracy, the first person to notice it will probably be columnist Robert Osborne. He might even mention it in his column, so beware.

Today the publicist is an accepted part of film history. Unit publicists get their names regularly mentioned in the credits, an immortality once reserved for key cast and crew only. When artists accept their Academy Awards, they often thank their publicists. You should find it inspiring that some of the great moments in film history were chronicled by your predecessors in biographies, press notes and releases that were written probably before you were born. You can be the chronicler of tomorrow's classic films.

Writing Ability.

Keep your words of wisdom short and to the point. Publicity writing is closer to advertising copy than the feature article.

Publicity writing is a blend of colorful descriptive prose delivered in a precise, up-tempo, crispy style. What does that mean? In the simplest terms it means write like you were telling a story, like you were talking to your reader.

The longer I work in this industry the shorter the press kits seem to be. I was looking at a kit for the Steve Martin/John Candy comedy, *Planes, Trains and Automobiles* which Paramount had produced. It was very short, probably no more than twenty five pages, including bios.

Having started out as a journalist, my first press kits from the set were voluminous. The bios I wrote were painstakingly detailed, showcasing every important aspect of the actor's life, even the unknown actors. My behind the scenes descriptions read like feature articles describing the highlights of the shooting in fast moving descriptive prose. I had separate feature articles on specialty topics like effects, stunts, and whatever was native to the picture. These pages, sometimes 50-75, were later cut, slashed, and brutalized by studio editors who turned them into 20-30 pages of crisp writing.

Publicity writing really begins to look like ad copy when you discuss how to present the film. This type of writing comes into play in your first press releases, in the paragraph descriptions that the ad department may ask for, or on the first page of the press kit.

If you work as a unit publicist on the set, your copy will be the first to present the film to the media and, thus, to the public. Like a delivery room nurse, you will be the first to get a good look at the newborn and when you walk outside you will be the first to describe the baby to the expectant father.

Positioning paragraphs are fully discussed by producers, writers, studio executives, even the director before they are dispersed to the media. It is one aspect of publicity writing that is agonizing. However, once you have your paragraph it has a thousand uses.

But the press kit is not your only responsibility as a writer. In movie publicity, memo writing occurs more often and has a much more lasting effect on your superiors. When you write your press kit at the end of shooting, or prior to the release period, you turn it in and the job is over. Memo writing can be a weekly job. It is the most important form of communication between you and your superiors. An excellent memo writer is able to translate good work into a strong reputation as a publicist.

Why? Because you're not hesitating to tell your superiors what you're doing. An unqualified publicist, and there are many, keeps to himself, running an independent operation with very little supervision or interference. He thinks he knows what he's doing, goes about it and doesn't let anyone else in on the details. Sure, he'll drop a line occasionally if a break occurs, or a crew comes to the set or if a photo shoot turns out especially nice, but for the most part, the communication is kept to a minimum. I think this is a mistake.

A publicist is a communicator, just as Ronald Reagan was a communicator. Mr. Reagan could always make something positive out of the worst situations. People respected him even when he was giving out bad news. A publicity memo keeps everyone informed. It is like a newspaper article that reminds you about something. Producers love memos because they show that someone is doing some serious work on their movie. Studio executives love memos because they can tell their own superiors that someone is hard at work on the project. Even the Chief Executive Officer loves a memo because it shows that the system is working.

My memos are a kind of ersatz diary of my work. If anything happens in relation to the movie I am working on, I always document it on a computer file. After a number of events are documented, I translate the information into a memo. These memos give my superiors a running commentary on the progress of the publicity campaign. They also make everyone a part of that campaign.

I learned at one of the major studios that people expect to be kept informed and yet very few publicists were writing memos. After coming back from the field on *Desert Bloom*, I was applauded for my consistent, informative memos. Nobody remembered exactly which breaks we got on the film, or how the press kit turned out, or what kind of still coverage we got, but they did remember my memos. We'll discuss the exact format of memo-writing in a later chapter.

Organizational Ability.

A publicist must stay organized. Too many people are depending on you to get the job done. Writers must come and interview the actors and behind the scenes personnel. The interview subjects must show up on time. Television crews have to film and then rush back to their news desks. Producers must be kept informed so that production isn't disrupted. Phone interviews have to occur at a precise moment or deadlines are missed. You must remember to bring press notes for the journalists. You have to keep the writer away from a young ingenue who is not to be interviewed. The director wants to be briefed before he gives an interview. Someone has to be at the airport to pick up an arriving journalist. Another journalist has to be called fifteen minutes before the interview as a reminder. Get the picture?

Publicity is often a series of appointments, arranged and conducted flawlessly. What happens when things go wrong? You have to remember your diplomacy skills. Otherwise, dangerous precedents are set. The writer misses the interview—he's upset. The actress isn't given the correct time of arrival—she's upset. The director isn't informed when the TV show will run—she's livid. The studio misses a photo opportunity—they're incensed. And these events have a tendency to linger in the minds of your associates. When something goes wrong for the publicist, everyone finds out. That's why problem solving and soothing is so much a part of the publicist's makeup.

Without being a worry prone fanatic, I double check and triple check myself. It doesn't hurt to let your parties know several times about appointments. Bothering them with your reminders is nothing compared to missed opportunities.

Document everything you do. If you write a pitch letter, make a copy. If you call a press person, document it on your computer. Again, if your boss asks you if you did something, never say "I forgot." It makes you look bad. When everything is organized and documented, the publicist has time to think and plan ahead.

Oral Communication Skills.

Remember the carnival barker, the guy in the straw hat and ugly pinstripes who used to say something like "Step right up, see the marvel of the ages..." The midways of America's carnivals used to be full of these pitchmen—promoters all who could lure you inside with the turn of a syllable. The quality of their voice, their body language, their enthusiasm, all these elements contributed to your excitement for the show. The carnival barker's pitch is a vivid memory, as much so as the sawdust on the ground, the cotton candy and the fat lady with the beard.

If you're uncomfortable in the role of "pitchman," then you should not be in film publicity. On my first publicity job, I was sent around the country to science fiction conventions—the Trekkie-type conclaves—carrying with me a photograph display, a slide projector and giveaway items.

My assignment was to tell the science fiction subculture about the remake of *Invasion of the Body Snatchers*. It was fun. I would sit at my display table most of the day showing slides, answering questions, passing out bumper stickers with the name of the film emblazoned on them, and then once or twice I would go to the ballroom or auditorium and give a 30 minute speech with slides describing the dynamics of the movie.

Hundreds of young people would visit my booth—I think I had a serious advantage over the other exhibitors because I had a new movie based on one of the all time classics and one of the stars was their hero—Leonard Nimoy.

When I got the job, it was described as a "promotional coordinator." Eventually, I thought of myself as an "advance publicist." However, one day I was reading an article about the film in *Variety* and they mentioned that someone was on the road promoting the movie at science fiction conventions just like *Star Wars* had done. I read with interest. At the end of the story they described me as a "pitchman." And that was what I was. I was "pitching" a new movie to an eager public.

In addition to being comfortable in front of a crowd, you have to, in today's vernacular, "give good phone." Ninety-nine percent of your work takes place on the good old telephone.

I must confess that I started out after college working as a telephone operator in a hospital. My job was to page doctors and speak to nurses and families all day long. Under those conditions, your job depends on your phone manner and your ability to respond to emergencies quickly and efficiently. My work as a telephone operator prepared me well for the publicity world.

What kinds of oral communication skills are crucial? I would rate conciseness at the top. The media, because of the nature of their job and the time constraints they face, usually gives the publicist very short shrift, that is until a relationship develops. However, even after years, I have discovered that some of my favorite contacts are time pressed and can't just chat about new movies. Given these time constraints, you must be able to spit out your pitch quickly and efficiently. No hemmings and hawings, no uhs and but uhs, no pauses and racing for thoughts. If you don't know what you're talking about, don't make the call because you'll embarrass yourself and your project. Come directly to the point: "Hi, this is Steve Rubin with Paramount Pictures (the identification). We're releasing a film in January called "The Godfather Part III." (the reference to the movie). It's the latest chapter in Francis Ford Coppola's epic study of an

American crime family. (the angle). I would like to interest you in an interview with our director, Mr. Coppola (the pitch)."

In four sentences you've basically said everything you need to say. The press person can then make up his mind about how to handle the pitch. Concise information has been provided. What will the response be? Positive: "Yes, I would like to schedule an interview next Thursday, is Mr. Coppola available?" Negative: "I don't think so, we don't have the space and we're working on the Marlon Brando retrospective. But thanks for calling." or Neutral: "It's an interesting story but I'm right in the middle of something. I would like to see the movie first, or some more background material before I make up my mind."

You get more neutrals than positives or negatives. Your job is to turn neutrals into positives. As more materials become available, the press person has a clearer idea what the movie is about and its intrigue factor hopefully increases. If materials can't seem to swing the attitude, then there is always the finished movie, which is usually your last resort. Some writers and editors will not make up their mind regarding coverage until they actually see the movie. In other words, they want to see if it's any good before they devote space or time to it. But that's part of your job too, making materials available to them so that they can make a proper decision.

All of this begins with the pitch so it had better be an effective one. Also, remember that when one person hears your pitch, he's generally going to talk to others about the film. Media word-of-mouth has its own weight. If you have a particularly interesting movie pitch, its message is going to be passed around the office or newsroom. Conversely, if you're blowing the pitch, the negative energy's going to move faster than you can stop it. It might come right back to your boss. You don't want your boss to hear, "Do you know how Steve is describing your movie?"

Put some personality in your voice if you can. Nobody wants to hear a monotone speaking like a computer. Remember you're also competing with the eleven other publicists who call today, some of whom might have wonderful voices and fascinating pitches. You have an obscure art film about French painters living on a Greek Island. You might follow someone pitching *Batman* or the sequel to *Gone With The Wind*. Make your pitch as wonderful as possible.

By all means have fun on the phone. You're not selling cemetery property. I've said this before. If you have to sell, sell movies. People are going to want to talk to you. Movies are news. Don't be too serious. If you have a movie about axe murderers inside a fast food franchise, don't treat it like heavy drama. It's garbage. You know it's garbage, the media knows it's garbage. But you don't have to call it "garbage." It should be easy to come up with an angle, an off the wall pitch that will make a fun story. If the pitch is just right, the press person will get off the phone and yell out, "And I thought I'd heard everything."

Don't fight the media on the phone. Never get into an argument about your movie's merits. You don't win arguments like that. If your pitch gets a negative response, go to your secondary campaign—more material, a screening. You can always rely on a screening to get a journalist to consider a positive "down the line." But don't embarrass yourself by pleading. It denigrates your professionalism and upsets the media. Besides, you have at least 199 other calls to make.

Oral communication skills occasionally extend to live engagements. You may suddenly be called in front of the producers, studio marketing executives, P.R. agency partners, and others to describe the merits of a particular movie and the angles you've isolated. Again, be concise, upbeat and enthusiastic. You may have to employ the same skills in front of the local Kiwanis Club.

Appearance. I mention appearance as a criteria not because I want to be the next Mr. Blackwell categorizing the Best Dressed and Worst Dressed publicists in the land, but because when you're working as a publicist in Hollywood, you are continuously on display. You're having lunch at a fashionable restaurant; you're visiting marketing executives in their high rise office suites; you're dropping off photographs at a star's Bel Air mansion; you join a fellow publicist for lunch in the studio commissary.

People are continuously noticing and evaluating you. Many of these people will be future employers and co-workers, people you want to impress. Hollywood is a small village, smaller than you think. The gentleman standing next to you in the elevator at the Chateau Marmont Hotel could be the head of marketing for Paramount Pictures. The woman pacing in front of the Acura dealership on Wilshire Blvd, debating a car purchase could be a movie producer you would like to work with.

As you become familiar with job hiring practices, nepotism and relationships in Hollywood, you realize that it's important to meet people on a daily basis and, by all means, make a good impression. How many times lately have you heard the phrase "Dress for Success"? I believe it.

I'm not advocating that we all run around like Cary Grant and Grace Kelly wining and dining on the French Riviera. It's going to be difficult to wear suits and dresses on the rugged location of a new western. But it is important to maintain a neat, stylish appearance—dress not only for success but to impress. You won't regret it.

Comfort in Travel.

Although it's possible to get a job working in one city—LA or New York—many publicity jobs are short-term freelance positions that involve travel. Movie people are circus people. They put on a show and then they fold up their tents. You learn how to work out of a suitcase. Film publicity can thoroughly disrupt your life. If you work on a movie that is shot on location, then you are away from your home for as much as 2-3 months at a time. You're not alone, everyone on a film is in the same freelance boat—from executive producer to production assistant. People are assembled because of the film—just like a military campaign in World War II France—and when the film is over, they move on to the next film.

Personally I love to travel and explore new lands. I especially like to do it when someone else is footing the bill. The nice thing about location work is that you don't spend any money. Not only do they pay your salary, but they give you something wonderful called "per diem"—living expenses.

Movie people are a tough breed—just like circus people. The traveling life plays havoc with personal relationships. You're taken away from your home environment, family, friends, pets, and your life style is thoroughly disrupted. It's a penalty you pay to work in the movies.

So you must be a comfortable traveler. A publicist who only wants to work in Los Angeles or New York is going to find limited job opportunities, whereas a well-trained publicist who is available to travel is a valuable commodity in Hollywood.

4

GETTING THE JOB

An article in *Daily Variety* noted that in 1989 the Publicist's Guild—the Hollywood union for publicists—had its highest unemployment rate in history—21%.

When it comes to hiring publicists, employer enthusiasm is underwhelming. Remember those big studio P.R. departments back in the 1930s and 1940s where dozens of publicity experts ran around turning freckle-faced farmer's daughters into movie stars? They're gone now. Studio publicists are becoming an endangered species.

Paramount, Warners, Fox, Universal and Disney may be exceptions, but with most of the major studios going through restructuring and nearly all the independent companies barely surviving, there is the general feeling that one publicist on any feature film is plenty. I have friends all over the publicity map who are feeling the pressure to perform without the support they are accustomed to and which they sorely need. To land a job in this tough market, you're going to have to be creative and persistent. What follows are a few ideas and some inside advice.

Contacts and Ability.

Before you ever get a job, before you start sending out resumes, you have to get into the habit of reading the trade papers—the *Hollywood Reporter* and *Daily Variety*—every day. Why? Because they are your tip sheet, your racing form, your scorecard. The "trades" are where you learn the names of the key players in Hollywood today, many of whom will be your future employers.

A publicist is an information specialist. People hire you because of your contacts in every field, especially media. But you must know what is going on in Hollywood at all times. And it's not the kind of information you learn from the shoe shine person at the Beverly Hills Hotel. Job information—what pictures are going into production, who is hiring, what kind of turnover rate is occurring at the companies—can usually be found somewhere in the trades. Just as actors read

Dramalogue for tips, publicists should consider *Daily Variety* and the *Hollywood Reporter* as their job tip sheet.

Getting a job in publicity depends on A) contacts and B) ability. You can be the most talented publicist in the world and still be wearing out your sofa waiting for the phone to ring. Conversely, you can have all the great contacts, but if you're not qualified to do a great job, those contacts will soon be as cold as a forgotten cup of coffee.

Networking.

You must go out and meet people. Hang out with movie people. Develop a resource group—people who can tell you what's going on. Attend industry seminars—not just the few publicity oriented ones but all types of seminars. It doesn't hurt for you to know a little about producing, directing, distribution, writing. If you can afford it, attend a fund raiser. Get to know people when they're relaxed.

Other ways to meet the key people? How about a phone call to the head of a publicity department or a P.R. agency? Always introduce yourself first in a short, very well written letter. As a publicity executive I occasionally get letters from neophytes explaining their situation and requesting an "audience." It can be flattering to get such a request, especially if it's respectful. But be prepared to get lots of responses like, "too busy" and "I never give interviews."

What do you do if the executive says "yes"? You thank your lucky stars and get to the meeting on time. Perhaps a lunch is impossible, perhaps you only get five minutes with the big cheese, but you must make an impression, a positive one. It's not going to happen very often. P.R. executives, like everyone else, are overworked. But occasionally a senior executive is going to take pity on the neophyte's Catch 22 quandary and offer an invite. Look into it. But remember the rules of diplomacy? Don't take rejection personally and don't beat a dead horse. If it's "no," come up with another idea. I hate having to say "no" five times.

If the executive says "too busy" and yet says "keep in touch"—that means call back in 6 weeks. Maybe you should drop a line in a month if you get a job and you want to share the experience. But don't outstay your welcome. An occasional bit of communication is fine until you've found your niche. You will also find that once you do have a job and you're working in the business, it will be easier to call the P.R. executive because you are now a "colleague."

Public Relations Classes.

Film making is a special craft taught in only a few places. Film publicity is an important, but very specialized part of film making and you're lucky to find one or two classes taught, even at the big universities with established film schools. In Hollywood where film related seminars are a weekly occurrence, the P.R. related ones are few and far between and are often a disappointment.

Why disappointing? Because the ones I'm familiar with emphasize the anecdotal approach—veteran P.R. executives telling stories about their experiences—rather than the step-by-step method of teaching the skills required to be a P.R. professional.

Don't let the quality of the classes dissuade you, however. Classes can be an excellent way for you to "get your feet wet." If you see a P.R. class offered at your local college, take it. It doesn't matter whether the class is entertainment related or not, all P.R. skills are important. If you happen to be in Hollywood, P.R. classes are another networking arena for you. It's difficult to actually meet P.R. professionals in the course of your day, so a chance to interact with them in a classroom environment should be considered a positive experience. I've been in P.R. classes where the instructor actually told the class that he was looking for an intern.

An Agency or Studio Internship.

I often tell new publicists to look into internships—in other words get experience by offering free services. The response I usually get is similar to actor Paul Dooley's outraged comment in the classic *Breaking Away* when his son suggests he refund a purchase on his used car lot: "Refund! Refund!" "Work for free! Work for free!" they say.

Let's face it. Hollywood, union or non-union, is most often a closed door. There are simply too many people and not enough jobs. Under those conditions, one must develop a novel approach to career success. That means either breaking rules or going around them.

To get your foot in the appropriate door, you have to offer a service that can't be refused (remember Marlon Brando's comment in *The Godfather*?). An internship is thus an excellent idea. It simultaneously opens previously locked doors and allows a neophyte to gain valuable experience in the proper professional environment. But in most cases, be prepared to invent your own internship program.

Internships are common in other fields, why not apply them to publicity. Unfortunately, since the collapse of the old studio system internship programs have been ignored or abandoned by key service industries, including marketing. Occasionally, the major studios will contact the local university and develop a summer internship program, sometimes with a basic pay scale. Most of the time, the independent companies and the agencies have to be forced to develop their own internship plans and most have not. It's now up to the future publicist to activate an internship.

First, determine your financial situation. Can you afford to work for free for up to six months? Your ultimate goal is to turn your internship into a full time position. To achieve that you have to a)offer a free service to get into that door and then b)impress the socks off your boss so that he won't want to let you go. He'll open his checkbook and offer you a paying job! A risk? Sure. But if you don't like risks, stay out of the movie business!

To get the ball rolling, assemble a list of studio publicity departments, independent company P.R. departments and P.R. agencies. All are potential employers. Obtain the list either from the library—there are several movie reference books including the *Hollywood Blue Book*, the *Studio Directory* and the *Publicist's Guild Membership Directory*. The latter is the best because it lists names—P.R. directors, agency owners, etc. Never send a letter without addressing a specific person. Otherwise your letter will be trashed. Write a short but direct letter to the P.R. executive. Something like this:

Dear Mr. Smith,

I am very interested in a possible internship position with your company. I believe I have developed important skills that could be of benefit to your daily workload. I can type 60 wpm, take dictation and I have my own car for messenger work. I also have an excellent phone manner.

My background includes a Bachelor's Degree in Communications and I was a staff writer for my college newspaper. I would eventually like to work full time for an agency or studio. For now, I am very willing to work for free to gain the valuable experience I need to secure full time employment.

I will contact your office in the next few days. Perhaps we can set up an appointment at your convenience.

Thank you for your time and I look forward to meeting you.

Sincerely,

Jane Doe
1234 Maple Dr.
Orange, CA 90678
(213) 555-1212

Maybe you're not sure if you even want to be a movie publicist. You think you'd like the job, but you don't know enough about it. An internship could be ideal. There's nothing like diving into the deep end to find out if you're really in the mood for a swim. Since you're most likely working for free, there is less pressure on you to immediately like or understand your surroundings. You have time to make an intelligent decision.

If you get a positive response to one of your letters and you get the appointment, go in and make a strong impression. Charm your potential employer. P.R. executives are always interested in increasing company productivity and efficiency. There are always long range research projects that need to be implemented, but due to under staffing, many of these projects (i.e. developing a new mailing list or updating an old one) are not completed. In these offices an intern would be welcome.

Don't assume that there is no money for the internship. There may be a modest stipend as well as expense money for use of your car. However, if it is a gratis position, accept the consequences and go out and work hard.

Be a sponge. Get to know everyone in the department. Personal relationships are key. You never know when the boss of the company is going to ask one of your fellow employees about you. You want a favorable response. "She's great. We should look into hiring her full time" would be the perfect phrase. Make that a goal.

However, if after putting in a few months, you learn that a position is not going to open up right away, then you have a decision to make. If it's a financial burden to continue working gratis, then go to your boss and find out if any money is available. If the funds don't exist, then you have to change positions. At least, you now have experience in your field. Your resume is a little longer. Hopefully, a money job may pop up at one of those studios or agencies and you can get a crack at it.

Starting At the Bottom.

Employment prospects in your field are looking bleak. There are no jobs, internships, field assignments available. You're staring at a brick wall—a common sight in the movie business. What to do? Do you shift career goals? Do you get a "survival job" waiting tables or bar tending?

What about taking a job as a secretary or receptionist in a publicity company? Somehow, I hear Paul Dooley again. Refund! Refund! Secretary! Receptionist! No way! I didn't get a master's degree in English literature to work as a receptionist. Secretarial work is beneath my dignity. I am executive material. I should be at high level marketing meetings, not taking dictation.

I hear all of these laments when I mention starting at the bottom. But like many businesses, in fact all businesses, you have to pay some dues, often major dues to get anywhere. You'd be amazed at how many top publicists—vice presidents, for that matter—have started in the secretary pool.

My theory is that it's always easier to get a job when you're on the inside—privy to office secrets and politics. If Jane is leaving to have her baby and the office needs a junior publicist for six months, who's going to know about it first? If Roger is transferred to 20th Century Fox next week, who's going to know about it first? Secretaries and receptionists are sitting in the fox holes of the publicity battle. When job hiring takes place, this inside information can prove valuable. "Oh, Mr. Johnson, may I have a word with you about that new publicity position."

Secretarial and receptionist positions not only allow access to key company information and turnover, they put you to work in the publicity business. You're suddenly working for Rogers and Cowan or 20th Century Fox or Paramount. You're in the building, on the lot, amongst your peers in publicity. You've got your foot in the door. Every day, you're going to come to a place where people are actively doing what you want to do. You're either going to be inspired, or you're going to decide that this business is not for you.

Being on the inside you will quickly see the pressures of being a publicist. You'll see how others handle the job. You may be working for one of them.

Secretaries are vital to the movie business, particularly publicity. There are lists of hundreds of media contacts to update, mailings to be sent out, screenings and interviews to be planned with precision. This requires tremendous dedication to detail and follow through that cannot be accomplished by one person. As a secretary you will be a part of a welded team of professionals.

I love the team atmosphere of a company, especially in the publicity field. Because of the pressures and the exhilarations, it's nice to share the experience with others. When you're in the thick of a campaign, when the hours are long and tempers short, when everything depends on actor A getting an interview with Writer B, it's great knowing that you have people in the next room rooting you on, championing your cause, helping you achieve success.

If you're truly good at your job as a secretary, if you pour your energy into it, I believe that there's room for advancement. There are companies where secretaries are stone walled. But if you're as good as you say you are and you've shown a mastery of publicity skills by keeping your eyes and ears open, then there's hope. Ambition plus superlative skills equal advancement in my book.

Secretarial skills shouldn't be pooh-poohed either. The ability to type rapidly, take dictation, answer the phone correctly, organize files, work on the computer and maintain an orderly office are skills with inestimable value. These are skills you can always take with you. And when you're between jobs, you can always utilize these skills in another company.

Working A Low Budget Film.

It's the same old problem. If you want to become a unit publicist (a publicist assigned to a specific film, usually in a freelance capacity), you need to have worked on a film. However, if you haven't worked on a film before they're not going to hire you. Hollywood is the land of Catch 22s.

Unit work, what I consider one of the best jobs in Hollywood today, is tremendously competitive. A few jobs each year for a small group of top, talented, very experienced unit people. How do you break into such a unique cadre, especially if you haven't even been on a set before?

Work on a low budget film first and get your feet wet. Okay, you'll probably have to go back to that hell of hells, no pay, but low budget publicity work is a great training ground.

Every day in Los Angeles, new low budget movies go into production with very little fanfare. Producers can barely raise production costs, let alone have enough money to hire a publicist. These producers are targets of employment opportunity for you. They're needy and if you present yourself well, you might be assigned to develop important publicity materials for a film—and begin the process of working as a unit publicist. You might even get some money out of them.

Unit work becomes easier and more understandable when you've done it. And you can get that experience on the low budget set. You'll see how a director works, how the crew functions, how the actors appear off camera. You'll begin to be comfortable around all of these curious movie creatures.

How do you find these low budget producers? There are three principle sources—the Tuesday edition of the *Hollywood Reporter*, the Friday edition of the *Daily Variety* and the weekly edition of *Dramalogue*. All three publications list films going into production in chart form. Usually there is a production company with a telephone number. If not, try directory assistance using the company's name.

Whether it's a low budget film, a student film, or even a play, the producer is going to need a viable press kit, a good set of photographic stills and any number of press releases, advertising copy, brochures, and other writing materials that you can supply to him. If he finishes his production with none of these materials then his process of selling the film either to a studio or to the public will be crippled.

If you walk in the door offering to provide these materials and supervise the publicity on the set for a reasonable fee (or no fee) he's not going to throw you out the door. Unlike the 100 young film school graduates who want to be production assistants on his film, you're offering a valuable service.

As a publicist you are a specialist. You perform a specific function on the film set. Your services are needed just as much as the assistant director, the costume designer and the makeup person. And your efforts can have a positive effect on the film's marketing. All of these arguments should persuade the producer to grab you and employ you on the production.

If there is no money available, you still need that experience. So work for no money (if you can afford it). Also remember when you're working gratis, you have more freedom to make up your hours. So, technically, you could take a second job in the evenings or weekends, to keep yourself alive while you learn.

With a low budget film under your belt, you've started to master the skills that will eventually lead you toward a paying position on a movie—the most important goal of all.

Taking a Publicist to Lunch.

"Go right to the source and ask the horse...Talk to Mr. Ed." No, I don't mean a palomino with the gift of gab. Take a publicist out to lunch and go brain picking. One of the problems neophytes face is that they have had virtually no contact with members of their chosen profession. You know doctors, lawyers, construction foremen and scientists. How many publicists do you know? When I was offered my first assignment as a unit publicist which involved a three month location trip to Wyoming, I decided that I needed to do some immediate research. This was back in 1981 and there were virtually no books on motion picture publicity and the rules of conduct in the field.

My only hope was that I could learn something directly from my fellow publicists. I contacted a prominent unit publicist and asked him out to lunch. I told him I had been offered my first unit assignment and that I needed some help, and luckily he was happy to oblige.

We met at the MGM commissary on a Friday afternoon. For the next hour, I probed his mind. Unless you know the publicist personally, you'll find that normally he is loath to discuss his trade secrets. Publicists are often very proprietary toward their knowledge and experience.

I learned only a few things that Friday afternoon, but even those few tidbits were a giant step away from total ignorance. One piece of advice has stuck to this day. He said, "Never schedule an interview on location before the lunch break." It was a simple rule, but it had important implications. Location etiquette is a set of rules that are most often learned the hard way. I was grateful for the tip which might help me avoid embarrassment on my first assignment.

Fortunately, you now have this book in front of you. I'm going to let you in on all the secrets of location etiquette, down to the most specific behavior. I didn't have the luxury. But my publicist luncheon date helped.

Writing Your Way Into Publicity Work By Starting on the Media Side.

I broke into publicity work through my writing ability. In 1978, I was a staff writer for *Cinefantastique Magazine*, the Chicago-based science fiction film journal. Even though I was one of their top staff writers, the pay was so miniscule that I supplemented my income by selling the magazine at science fiction conventions, you know, the "trekkie" conclaves.

I would purchase table space next to the guy selling miniature starships and wookies, set up my display and spend the day selling magazines, autographing the articles I had written. My knowledge of the circuit came in handy when the following advertisement appeared one day in the *Hollywood Reporter*:

HELP WANTED

PROMOTIONAL COORDINATOR
Science Fiction expert needed to help promote
major studio science fiction film. Must
know convention circuit. Travel essential.

I wrote to the P.O. Box address and received an immediate call from one of Hollywood's top P.R. firms. They were coordinating the publicity for the *Invasion of the Body Snatchers* remake which had just been filmed and was due out in ten months. The director, Phil Kaufman, was friends with George Lucas whose *Star Wars* had just taken the country by storm.

Lucas had sent a gentleman named Charles Lippincott into the field for months before the release of *Star Wars*, plumbing the science fiction convention circuit with a colorful audio visual presentation that got the kids charged. Lucas reasoned that every kid who attended a science fiction convention would pass the word on an exciting new movie to his group of friends. The campaign obviously helped open the picture and then the all important "word-of-mouth" kicked in.

Now United Artists wanted someone to follow in Lippincott's footsteps and do the same job for *Body Snatchers*. I got the job, not only because I knew the circuit, but I was able to impress the publicists and the producers with my science fiction articles for *Cinefantastique*. I was demonstrating an enthusiasm for the genre which they felt was an important quality in a "pitchman" headed for the circuit. I spoke "trekkie" fluently.

My second opportunity to utilize my writing ability to get a publicity job came a year later after I finished my assignment on *Invasion of the Body Snatchers*. Through a friend, I heard that a small entertainment public relations agency was looking for a staff writer/publicist. Even though I had cut my teeth on a film, I knew nothing about publicity writing. I had never been asked to write a single word of copy on *Body Snatchers*.

However, I had just published a two page article in the *Los Angeles Times* Sunday Calendar entitled: "What Ever Happened to the James Bond Women?" Selling an article to the *Times* is very difficult, so I knew I had an ace up my sleeve when I walked into the interview with the P.R. agency. Quicker than Wyatt Earp, I whipped out the article and placed it on the desk of the agency president. I was hired on the spot.

My writing ability also helped me get my first studio publicity job writing the press kit for the Bo Derek *Tarzan* movie in 1981. Following that, I won my first unit publicity assignment on *Endangered Species*—the Robert Urich/Jobeth Williams starrer about a plague of cattle mutilations in the rural southwest. Again, I knew little about unit publicity work, but the producers were looking for a publicist with strong writing ability who could create some feature stories about a decade long mystery. Even though I had never done a unit before, the producers were impressed enough with my writing ability and enthusiasm to give me the job. I would spend three months in Wyoming on the picture.

A writing career is an excellent jumping off point for motion picture publicity work especially if you've written in any way, shape or form about the movie business. Not only have you demonstrated a knowledge of film, but you've gained valuable insight into the idiosyncrasies of the journalist—information that will help you become an effective publicist. Such knowledge of both sides of the street can be exploited in the job market. The publicist candidate with writing experience will always have an edge.

Developing Your Contacts—Friends, Family Members.

As you determine the course of your publicity career, don't keep it a secret. You're about to become part of a very high profile business. You must develop a high profile too. You never know when your mother or second cousin is going to be in an elevator with Mr. Superstar. It would help if they knew you were looking for a job. And the possibility always exists that Mr. Superstar happens to be looking for a publicist.

Hollywood is also a very small community. If you read the trade papers everyday you will begin to realize that there are a limited number of companies, with a limited number of movie projects at any given time and a small group of people who are in charge of hiring publicists. Everyone of importance knows everyone else of importance. If you're lucky enough to get your name mentioned in an important circle, the odds are good that someone else is going to hear it too.

Although alerting your friends and family is important, it might also be a waste of time if they travel in the wrong business circle. My family for instance is totally devoted to the distribution of wire rope. Their offices are in Compton, California which is the other side of the planet from Hollywood. And even though the company often sells cable to movie studios for special effects or construction work, there is really no social mingling, no contact development that could benefit my career. I have to rely on other people to spread the word.

Build up your contacts by attending industry functions. Every day the trade papers announce seminars, classes, benefits, screenings and various events that are open to the public. This is where your enthusiasm for the movie business comes in very handy.

It also helps if you have a special interest. I benefited from my enthusiasm for science fiction films. My knowledge of the convention circuit won me my first job in publicity. If you happen to love Greta Garbo movies and you've seen every one 22 times, you might not be as crazy as you think. There could be other Garbo fans in the city and your enthusiasm could endear you to them. By all means, cultivate your motion picture eccentricity for all it's worth.

Getting the Interview.

Building contacts is one thing, getting interviews is another. Potential interviewers usually fall into four classifications: 1) studio staff publicists; 2) independent company staff publicists; 3) agency publicists; and 4) producers.

Studio staff publicists work for the major companies—Disney, Paramount, Columbia, Warner Bros., 20th Century Fox, Universal and Tri-Star. Working for a "major" is everyone's goal. In a business where there is generally no stability, where people roam from job to job, life at the major studios can be pretty stable—compared to life on the outside. Since everyone is under a union contract (the Publicist's Guild), the pay is substantial. Major companies have their down times and staff publicists are vulnerable but for the most part everyone wants a job with the majors.

Unfortunately, getting a job with a major company is nearly impossible. There are some things you can do however. Get to know the names of the key staff publicity executives—directors and vice presidents. Drop them a line with your resume attached, particularly if you happen to meet them in a social environment. Keep them posted on what you are doing in the publicity field, particularly if you get a job in the independent or agency environment.

It's easier to get in to see an independent staff publicist (they're not behind as many closed doors), but don't expect them to be any more eager to hire you. Usually, because of the unstable nature of the independent film world (many more bombs than bombshells) these publicists are holding onto their jobs by the skin of their teeth. However, since they're always under-staffed and over-worked, it might be possible to get an internship in such a company or even part-time work helping on a specific film project. Such opportunities could lead to staff work, especially if the company is doing well. Add the names of the independent publicity staff directors to your roster.

The public relations agency is by no means an open shop. The very nature of the agency—keeping clients, finding new ones, fighting overhead—keeps their staff down. However, some agencies have a high turnover rate with agency publicists going to independent companies or the majors, or even off to production jobs. There is no question that the agency is the ideal training ground for the publicity profession.

P.R. agencies come in all sizes. Get to know the names of the agency partners. These are the publicists with the true hiring power.

In addition to getting your resume on a regular basis, they should also know about your specialities. If you have great writing ability and, perhaps, some published work, they should be made aware of it. If you are an expert on fashion and you have great contacts with the fashion publications, let them know. They might have an assignment which needs a specialist in that field.

Even though I love movies, the first P.R. agency I worked for assigned me to non-entertainment accounts. I publicized tractor auctioneers, tour groups, makeup artists and hypnotists. But the skills I developed publicizing these acts held me in good stead when it came time to work on entertainment accounts. So if an opening pops up in a non-entertainment related P.R. agency, don't immediately rule it out. What happens if you're not working. You must take something in a related field, right? Any agency work is good work, especially in the eyes of the studios, independents and producers.

Producers are another potential hiring group. They hire all types of publicists. If they have their own production company and there's a lot of activity, they might hire a staff publicist to build awareness for the entire slate of pictures. If they have a film going into production, they might be looking for a unit publicist. If they have a film going into release and they're not entirely satisfied with the publicity campaign mounted by the distributor (major or independent), they might hire a publicity consultant to supplement the campaign.

Simply because there are many more producers in Hollywood than staff or independent publicity directors, you have a better chance with them. Pick up a copy of the Studio Blue Book and you'll see that there are hundreds of production companies operating in Hollywood. Each of them should receive your resume on a regular basis (every six months, especially if it contains new and appropriate experience) and you should try to interview with as many as possible. Remember even though you don't get the job, you've made a contact. You'll bump into these people again and they'll start mentioning your name.

5

THE PUBLIC RELATIONS ENTITIES

In the beginning there was the studio. Whether it was a tiny office in Gower Gulch or a power suite in MGM's Thalberg Building, in the "Golden Age" publicity and promotion were concentrated in the hands of professionals who were a welded part of a huge machine.

Like steel factories and textile manufacturing plants, the motion picture studio cranked the films out. The major studios—Paramount, MGM, Fox, RKO, Universal, Columbia and Warner Bros. owned the stars, the writers, the directors, the back lots, and the theaters. And they controlled every inch of a motion picture's life. Contract stars were groomed like race horses.

There was a science to the publicity machine in those days. It employed many of the methods of the famous P.T. Barnum because the moguls who ran the studios between the 1920s and 1950s were showmen in the Barnum mold. They understood the value of publicity and promotion long before the era of "marketing," "awareness studies," and gross ratings points. Consequently, the studio publicity and promotion departments were given a great deal of support and respect. Armies of publicists—at home, in the field and overseas— spread the word on new movies. They cranked out publicity material to support the movie machines of Hollywood.

I remember researching the history of *The Bridge on the River Kwai* at the Academy of Motion Picture Arts and Sciences library. The epic adventure was released in 1957 toward the end of mogul Harry Cohn's career. In the production file on "Kwai" were over 50 press releases! Every facet of this film was documented and distributed for media consumption. The actors were true stars and they were promoted like royalty.

Royalty is a good word to describe the actors of the Golden Age. Before television, satellite broadcasts and live media events, the public saw their actors in newsreels, heard them on the radio, and read about them in the movie columns—Hedda Hopper, Louella Parsons, Sheila Graham. Actors were not everyday people. They lived in a magical world—a Hollywood fantasy land—much of which was fabricated by studio publicists. Grooming, the choice of parties and escorts, classic portrait photography, public appearances, charity benefit involvement—virtually all aspects of an actor's public life was controlled by the carefully orchestrated maneuvering of the studio publicist. To present these "royal" personages to the public, royal protocol was in order. Although publicists of the era did not wear white gloves and drive around in carriages, there was a certain reverence for the profession and its responsibilities. The publicist was a vital part of the winning team.

Change came gradually. The studios were forced to sell their theaters. No longer would they control the distribution pipeline. The publicists and promoters who planned local events at the movie house were no longer studio employees. The theaters, no longer in the palm of the moguls, planned their own strategies and established their own priorities. Conflicts developed, loyalty to the studio on a publicity level disappeared.

Actors, writers and directors began to leave the fold, too. The era of the independent filmmaker dealt a blow to the studio machine. Following in the footsteps of United Artists, which had always been the sole independent of consequence, the filmmakers and the actor superstars created their own companies. The contract system, the assembly line of Hollywood, was disappearing fast.

As the motion picture went into a period of decline following the birth of television, the studios themselves began to slim down. Backlots were sold off to developers. Many departments were disbanded. Special effects, wardrobe, art, makeup, props and other studio institutions "went independent." Freelancers formed their own independent outfits and sold their services to the studios who were suddenly favorable to subcontractors.

The decline bottomed-out in the late 1960s when some of the studios were virtual ghost towns.

The publicity and promotion machine changed too. As the power of the independent actor grew, along with agent and manager, so emerged the independent publicist. The era of the agency publicist was born. The major studio publicity and promotion machines were still in place, but their operations were much smaller and their power had diminished. Without the contract system and its rigid control of an actor's life, the fate of a film and its potential success often belonged to the actor and his personal publicist. In the past, an actor was given his marching orders, his list of media appointments and what he could or could not say. No more. Now, an actor's involvement in the marketing of his picture is open to negotiation.

Today, the studio system of the moguls is gone. There are still studios. The logos of Paramount, Disney, Warner Bros., Fox,

Universal and Columbia still dominate the business, but the nature of the game is different. In order to successfully publicize and promote movies today, you must become familiar with how the game is played today. Let's take a look at the players and their power.

The Agency/Talent Publicists.

When the studio publicity departments began to slim down in the late 1960s, the agency publicists took over. Every major star suddenly had his own personal publicist. Being a movie star today still requires the careful career grooming process that shapes a star's public life, however the power has shifted considerably. The studios no longer control the star's life. The stars today control their own destiny.

■ **The Agency As Training Ground.** There is no better training ground than that of the public relations agency. On a daily basis, you learn the strategies of dealing with the talent and the media.

I started my career in a publicity agency. I was hired as a staff writer. My job was to compose the actor's biographies, the behind the scenes stories, all of the material that went into a press kit. And then, starting slowly, I began to pitch the media. I wrote the pitch letters, assembled the materials and began to make my phone calls. Simultaneously, I, being the low person on the totem pole, was sent along to hold the hand of the actor/client during their public appearances. It was called "covering." I went down to the Merv Griffin Show and sat in the blue waiting room while the actors waited for their time on camera. If the actor wanted anything or had any questions, I was there to help out. And I saw how comforting my presence was. Many actors are terrified of the interview process. They like to have their "entourage" present to support them.

"Covering" publicists keep a ready supply of P.R. materials at hand. If the producer loses a film clip or needs an extra set of press notes or bios at the last minute, the publicist is there with the backup materials. The actor would never supply such a thing and shouldn't. An actor should concentrate on what he's going to say, not the location of the correct film clip.

It was also good P.R. for the agency to have a representative on hand. It increased the agency's visibility. Gradual name reinforcement kept the producer supposedly "on our side," so the next time someone from the agency called that producer he or she would hopefully say, "Good to hear from you, we had a great time with so and so, didn't we?" This was opposed to calling up, introducing yourself on the phone, and hearing the producer say, "Who?"

■ **The Agency Pressure Cooker.** Agency publicists are pressured by their clients to perform. That daily pressure becomes a fact of life, part of your body armor. The actor wants a *People Magazine* story. She will be very disappointed if she doesn't get it. She doesn't get it. She makes it very plain that she's very disappointed. She lets your boss know it. He explains to her that the agency tried very hard. He takes half the day to explain. He's very tired at the end of the day. He looks at you and says, "We better do a better job next time, or we're going to lose that client." Now that's pressure.

Agency publicists depend on the monthly retainers their star clients pay. If stars become unhappy, they bolt. And if enough stars bolt, the agency folds. It's as simple as that.

Faced with that pressure, agency publicists are continually courting the media, making friends, developing a personal one-on-one relationship, making sure that the media personage never says the "Who" word. Walk into any trendy industry eaterie at lunchtime in Los Angeles and agency publicists are there courting their contacts. I was one of them—continually matching faces to voices.

Because the agency depends on the star's monthly retainer, the star usually has the final say on what he or she will do. Even the most powerful agency publicists must bow to their client's wishes. This is the major difference between today's agency publicized star system and the old studio system. In the old days, the stars worked for the studio publicity department. Today the agencies work for the stars.

Star power and ego, the pressure to perform, media resistance—these are the daily battlefields of all publicists. Since the agency is the best of all training grounds, it is in the agency confines where these battles are first waged and where a true understanding of motion picture publicity is established.

■ **The P.R. Agency as Adversary?** Don't get me wrong, I respect the agency publicist. I just think their star clients grant them too much power. When a movie goes into production with unknowns or lesser known actors, the studio or independent production company is almost guaranteed the actor's full cooperation. A coordinated publicity campaign in which the actors take part can thus be waged effectively.

When a movie goes into production with major stars, a different scenario can develop. It can't be assumed that the most important actors will be available to help promote the film. It's no longer what the actor will do to support the movie, it's what he won't do. The agency publicist, in doing his job for his client, not the film, can shoo away media people at critical times when the studio is attempting to develop awareness. That's when an adversary relationship begins to develop. It's not that agency publicists square off against studio publicists like enemies across a battlefield. They simply have different priorities. The studio publicist promotes the film, the agency publicist looks after the interests of a single actor.

It is a fact that the number of media outlets covering the movie scene increases every year. *Entertainment Tonight* introduced the show business news show and dozens have followed. Yet, stars do less and less promotion every year, especially personal appearances. Why? Agency publicists call it "over-exposure." "We mustn't show the actor's face too much, the public will grow tired of it." "Remember the great actors of the past, they were mystery characters—Greta Garbo, Charlie Chaplin, Marilyn Monroe, James Dean, even Elvis Presley." The truth is that some of the great actors did lead very private lives, and the public was mystified by them. But the public didn't have instantaneous access to the day's events either. Six news broadcasts a day were unheard of. Daily movie coverage in the newspaper, *People Magazine* cover stories, investigative reporters, *Entertainment Tonight*, cable television movie shows, video magazines, radio syndicates didn't exist in the numbers they do today. Let's face it, the world has shrunk considerably since the Golden Age. So the old "maintaining the mystique and avoiding over exposure" theory doesn't play in the 1990s, especially when $20 million movies are about to open in the marketplace. Just ask the formerly reclusive Warren Beatty who promoted *Dick Tracy* to all media in the summer of 1990. He understood his responsibility to help sell a very expensive project and he did what he had to do. His enthusiasm in doing interviews at a crucial time helped guarantee the film's success.

The Studio Publicity Department.

I remember well my first day at a studio publicity department. After five years as a its unit publicist working on locations around the U.S. I had come back to Los Angeles to take on the tasks of National Publicity Director at one of the large independent studios. I was joining a team.

■ **The Team Approach.** The team concept is important when describing how a studio publicity department functions. When you work in an agency, everyone is generally promoting something different. You all share the same office and the same logo on your business card, but that's about it.

In the studio, everyone has a common goal—"Make Our Movie a Hit." Company loyalty is as natural as rooting for the home baseball team. The list of upcoming releases is your starting lineup. You memorize the stats on all these releases—cast, plot, locations, selling points— and you spend your professional work life touting those dynamics to the media with the enthusiasm of a 12 year old baseball fan.

My first day on the job at the studio was very typical. I didn't sit down the whole day. For 10 hours, I went from meeting to screening to meeting to screening to meeting. I was introduced to my fellow team members and the movies we would publicize and I was off and running.

■ **The Workload.** Studio publicists have their hands full. There are generally too many movies to publicize and not enough hours in the day. You have your daily duties—the preparation of press kits, mailings, returning media telephone calls, screening invitations, RSVPs, photo selection, pitching, preparation of mailing lists, researching new outlets—multiplied by the number of films on your plate.

In the independent studio sector, films that are often picked up for distribution have had virtually no unit publicity. They come to the studio with minimum materials, perhaps a set of still photos and cast and credits sheet. Everything must then be developed by the studio, especially an awareness campaign that was not accomplished during shooting. You're also at the mercy of the distribution department, which determines when that movie goes into theatrical release. Sometimes, a movie comes into the publicity department with no materials and a release date three months away. Then it's really time to scramble.

■ **The Chain of Command.** A full-service marketing department, given the appropriate staffing, breaks down this way: Creative Advertising (responsible for designing prints ads, trailers and TV spots); Media (they purchase the ad space, with a co-op department working closely with the movie theaters); Research (which tests films and ad campaigns); Publicity and Promotion. The larger studios also have a Merchandising and Licensing department.

Publicity is sometimes further divided into electronic (television and radio), print (newspaper) and magazines. Staff publicists usually cover these areas. If the studio has a New York office, the same breakdown may occur on the East Coast. Since most magazines are based in New York City, an East Coast magazine department would be extremely important.

Publicity directors and managers supervise their various areas and develop the strategies for the publicizing and promotion of new films. These same directors may also work closely with a publicity agency that may have been hired to supplement the campaign. It is the publicity director's responsibility to make sure that the agency is doing its job and reporting progress to the studio.

While the director is free to strategize, one of the staff publicists is usually the writing specialist of the team and develops all press kits, announcements and brochures. The staff publicists in their various areas are the pitching geniuses. They talk to the media on a daily basis, just like the agency publicist. They also have expense accounts for taking media people to lunch.

■ **Studio Promotions Department.** One of the many differences between an agency and a studio is that agencies usually don't have full service promotional departments. They seldom get involved in developing product tie-ins and promotions, merchandising items and licensing arrangements. It's an accepted rule that you generally don't ask a publicity agency to set up a radio promotion or a publicity stunt. They're not intensive in this area.

A studio promotions department has one of the most difficult of all jobs—liaison work. When a publicist pitches a story idea to a journalist, once the journalist says yes, the publicist's remaining responsibility is simply to make sure that the journalist gets his interview. When a promotions department gets a yes the job is only beginning. Outside companies have their own guidelines and priorities that are often in conflict with the studio's distribution plans for the film. The promotion specialist has to make sure that every detail is ironed out between the two or more parties before an event is scheduled.

My most difficult job as a promotions director was getting outside companies whose products appeared in our films to commit to a release-period promotion. Sometimes producers are not very careful when placing the products in the film. A little mistake early on can wipe out any chance for promotional benefits. We'll discuss the details of developing effective promotions in a later chapter. Suffice it to say that a promotions department is knee deep in follow-up during most of its existence. Creating a cute T-shirt with the film's logo on the back is one thing, getting McDonalds to coordinate a nationwide contest is another.

The Unit Publicist.

When I first broke into the business as a its writer, I used to buy the trades and read them during lunch. Two or three years of reading the *Hollywood Reporter* and *Daily Variety* and you get an excellent education on the dynamics and key players in the "biz." Since I was a movie buff, I always enjoyed the column that described the new movies that were in production. This usually appeared in Tuesday's *Hollywood Reporter* and Friday's *Daily Variety*. The column gave the film's name, when it had started shooting, where it was shooting, key cast and crew members. I always remembered that the last name always mentioned was usually identified as "P" in *Variety* and "Unit Pub" in the *Reporter*. This was the unit publicist.

However, it was not until I started working in an agency that I met my first unit publicist. She flew in one day with an arm full of stills, some press notes and a few comments to my boss and then she flew out. I gradually came to realize that she was working on the actual set of the film, knew all of the actors and crew personally and was pitching stories and writing press kits entirely on her own.

It's not surprising that it took me so long to identify the responsibilities of a unit publicist. This is a very specialized job. One of the more exciting jobs in motion picture publicity, the unit publicist is a "Jack or Jill of all trades" who applies many skills to a key function in the marketing chain. The unit publicist is the first marketing person on a movie project. The words the publicist uses to describe the movie will be repeated thousands of times over the course of the movie's life. The initial media that are contacted during production, the set visits that take place, the still shoots that are coordinated, the product placement opportunities that are documented—all of these opportunities will determine how successful a film's awareness campaign becomes. Without a unit publicist on the set during production, a producer is doing his film a great disservice. The unit publicist's salary—provided that a professional has been hired—is the best money a producer will ever spend.

The unit publicist is so important to the movie publicity process that I have devoted a large portion of this book to the specific duties inherent in the job. We will examine these later.

The Its Publicity Consultant.

Every field has its specialists. In motion picture publicity and promotion, consultants are very common.

■ **Press Kit Writers.** Some independent companies fail to see the value of hiring a full time unit publicist during production and prefer to bring in a publicist after the fact just to compile a basic press kit. These its publicists are writers and not full-fledged publicists because they're usually not asked to make a single "pitch" to the media.

■ **Last Minute Campaigns.** Sometimes, its publicists are hired at the last minute to create a whole campaign. These "whiz bang" campaigns are very difficult for the freelancer because there usually isn't enough time to effectively court the media. Whereas a studio or agency publicist, given a long enough lead time, can slowly make the national media arena aware of a new film project and its dynamics, a freelancer hired at the last minute is handcuffed and denied effective access to long lead time media, especially magazines, its writers and the feature-oriented television programs.

I'm not saying that a freelancer can't mount an effective campaign. It can be done. But the odds are stacked against the publicist called in as a "fireman" at the last minute.

At the other end of the spectrum from the simple chores of writing and pitching, the its publicity person or consultant is often given a very complex and specialized task. These assignments might include capturing the interest of the college market, the Hispanic market, or the science fiction/Star Trek crowd. He might be given the job of mounting a shopping mall promotion, a radio promotion or an educational liaison campaign. For a feature revival of *Sea Hunt*, a freelancer might be brought in to mount a campaign that reaches all of the nation's skin diving enthusiasts. For a movie on the Middle Ages, a freelancer might be asked to put together a museum exhibition for touring purposes.

■ **The College Marketing Consultant.** The college market involves publicizing the movie through college newspapers and radio stations and possibly creating events on campus. If actors are available, they might be brought to the campus for question and answer sessions after screening film clips. If props, costumes or special effects items are available, these could be toured as well.

In 1983, I sold Columbia Pictures on a 63 day national tour for the 3D science fiction movie *Spacehunter: Adventures in the Forbidden Zone* which starred Peter Strauss and Molly Ringwald. In the movie, Strauss drove an outrageous all-terrain space truck that was continually chased by weird other-worldly motorcyclists and costumed characters (a mix of *Road Warrior* and *Star Wars*). To help promote the film, I suggested we mount the vehicles on a flatbed tractor trailer rig and drive them cross country for exhibition, not only on college campuses where science fiction thrives, but at shopping malls, historic monuments, street fairs, and anywhere where media attention could be drawn. Supplied with original costumes (we would hire college students to put them on and travel through local night clubs), video materials and giveaways, the tour was on the road two months before the film opened and covered over 14,000 highway miles and 12 metropolitan areas. *Spacehunter* opened to $7 million its first weekend in 1983 and was the number one film in the country.

- **Science Fiction Consultants.** Science fiction/Star Trek convention consultants develop materials from new science fiction/horror/fantasy genre films and take them to the monthly conventions where these fans congregate. The work may be as simple as turning on a television monitor and showing a trailer from the new film and passing out free buttons or bumper stickers; or it may involve developing a speech about the film, using slides or film. Elaborate displays beyond a television monitor and tape player are also common. The freelancer in this case is playing the advance "pitchman," traveling the country and spreading the movie "gospel."

- **Hispanic Consultants.** Hispanic publicists deal with the burgeoning Hispanic market. Press kits are translated and sent to Hispanic newspapers, magazines, radio and television stations. Trailers, television spots and newspaper ads are similarly translated. The Hispanic media is also pitched—especially if there are Hispanic actors involved in the project. These specialists insist, though, that there expertise does not have to rely solely on movies with Hispanic actors or specific themes native to the culture. They insist that this market will embrace any highly entertaining motion picture and that by courting the Hispanic market, a high movie-going sector of the populace, the chances for box office success are increased. This is a good argument especially in the sun belt where Hispanics are becoming a majority group.

- **Shopping Mall Promotion Consultants.** For shopping mall promotions, a studio may hire a its consultant to coordinate events on a national basis. Like the Hispanic arena, there are now companies that specialize in shopping mall events. It's not surprising. The shopping mall has become the central focus of many communities nationwide especially when multiplex movie theaters are located within their environs. To attract customers, the marketing departments of your average shopping mall are always looking for interactive events that can get their stores involved and bring excitement to the mall.

- **National Radio Promoters.** Specialists may also be called in to organize national radio promotions. Depending on the film, the trade-off is usually air-time for screenings or giveaways. By providing a screening to a key radio station in New York City, you might get the station to mention the movie 20 times a day for a week. Sometimes you can get the same coverage with 50 T-shirts, or 100 soundtrack albums, or a contest. Radio station promotion directors are generally besieged by movie companies, and they have the advantage of picking and choosing their promotions. Under these circumstances, the major studios have a strong advantage because of the continuity of their product. In order to get a promotion going with the next Eddie Murphy movie, Paramount might ask a station to help out on a lesser known film. The independent companies, often lacking the heavy hitters like Eddie Murphy, Batman or Roger Rabbit, do not have this advantage. Still, a persuasive promoter with the right tools can intrigue any station.

■ **Educational Liaisons.** Educational liaison work involves taking an element of the movie and promoting it to schools and teachers. For a movie like *Meteor*, a special classroom lesson could be prepared on the dynamics of meteors. The students would read up on meteors and, of course, the movie, and the teacher would organize a discussion about the subject. Additional posters and/or giveaways would also be provided. The prospect of promoting films to millions of students nationwide has encouraged many such campaigns dating back to the golden age of movie making. Again, specific companies with educational liaison expertise now exist. Even the major educational publications like the Scholastic Magazine group get involved in film promotion by creating tailored materials for new movies. They charge a large fee but their distribution system is established and they have great credibility amongst teachers. With such a reputation, they have a specific criteria for determining the motion picture projects they will promote.

The Corporate or Product Placement Publicist.

Up until recently, I knew very little about corporate promotional tie-ins, product placement opportunities and "back-end promotions." I did remember the early James Bond movies where the director would show a close-up of a Seiko watch and pay special attention to the newest incarnation of Aston Martin sports car, but I didn't truly understand how these corporate arrangements worked and how they benefited the motion pictures that featured so many products.

■ **Promotional Specialists** Most of the publicists in Hollywood never deal with corporate entities. It's really a promotional specialist's job and because the promotions department is only a full-time function at the majors or larger independent studios, those institutions monopolize the relationship between corporate America and the movie business. It would be very difficult for the average publicist to get the head of marketing for McDonalds on the telephone, let alone get that company to commit to a national promotion. Promotional directors at Disney, Warner Bros. or Universal have the inside tract because their corporate logos are more familiar. Corporate America is intrigued by the prospect of spreading their own product message through the medium of film, especially since the success of the Reese's Pieces association in Steven Spielberg's *ET*, the *Star Wars* merchandising explosion of the mid-1970s, the more recent *Batman* blitz and dozens of other product tie-ins that showcased product to the world. But like any strong relationship, these associations between movies and corporations need to be guided by strong professional hands on both sides. On the movie side, promotional specialists work diligently to get the movie to the attention of the corporations. On the corporate side, marketing executives try to determine the proper film for their product. Increasingly, the relationship is guided by another spin-off of the decentralization of the modern film studio—the product placement company.

- ■ **Product Placement Companies.** Over the past decade, product placement companies have entered the corporate marketplace and cemented relationships with key marketing people at the top companies—companies that market products which could appear naturally and conspicuously in a motion picture scene. These include companies that are in the most competitive of markets such as soft drinks, beer, automobile and consumer electronics.

With contacts assured, a virtual monopoly on the Fortune 500, the product placement companies have developed relationships with Hollywood. They court producers and promotional directors, reading scripts and advising on placements. Keep in mind the fact that motion pictures need all kinds of products for filming. In a Sylvester Stallone action film, the production manager might need 100 motorcycles. Does he pay for them, or does he get them free from Kawasaki? A product placement company often holds the key to answering that question.

Product placement is so vital to some corporations that they maintain full-time offices on the movie lots. This is particularly true of the Detroit auto makers. Many network television shows use automobiles in various scenes. Those cars aren't hired in haphazard fashion but systematically by production managers working with product placement specialists. This system also translates to the motion picture business.

- ■ **Making the Back-end Promotion Viable.** But the product specialists can't do it alone and for the movie company to take full advantage of a product placement, coordination is the key—coordination usually in the hands of a film publicist or promotions specialist. Unfortunately, seldom is there proper coordination down the line. The product placement company might deliver the cars to the production manager, but how will that placement benefit the film during its release? Is Ford going to do a movie promotion in its dealer showrooms? Are they going to use the movie logo in their newspaper and magazine advertisements? Are they going to supply some cars for a national giveaway sweepstakes? These are key questions that fall under the category of "back-end promotion" (or in a more simple phraseology, "what they get, what we get").

Developing awareness through all possible means is the publicist's responsibility. Corporate America's ability to reach the consumer cannot be underestimated. Publicists and promotional specialists should be aware of all the possibilities—most of which are different from typical movie advertising. We will discuss the methodology of product promotions in a later chapter.

6

THE MEDIA ENTITIES

The publicist assigned to D.W. Griffith's *Birth of a Nation* which was filmed in 1915, just like every good publicist since then, had a concise list of contacts who work for newspapers and magazines. Most likely, he was a veteran from Broadway who dealt in news from the stage and probably had the private phone numbers of the top columnists of the day. That publicist's job, no different than that of the modern publicist, was to build awareness for a new film through stories in the press.

A story break in the New York Times was just as important in 1915 as it is today. It gave the film credibility. The public was encouraged to think that if the *Times* was printing a story on *Birth of a Nation* then the movie must be important. And if the publicist could interest other important newspapers in the big cities and a few magazines, an awareness campaign would begin. Nearly eight decades later, the publicist's job has not changed. But the list of media contacts has. We're living in a communications revolution. Today the "media" represents a vast information gathering and dispersal system that affects everyone. Technology has broadened the reach of modern journalism. The term "eyewitness news" was a cute concept in the mid-1960s when it was used as a marketing term to sell local news programs as the "minute men" of journalism—always diligent, always there. But the instantaneous abilities of modern journalism goes beyond the challenge of getting a news truck to a plane crash site. Today journalists are taught to think on their feet and prepare bite-sized news bits that can reach the largest possible audience in the shortest time.

It was a funny moment in *The Big Chill* when actor Jeff Goldblum described his experience as a *People Magazine* correspondent writing stories that people could read during an average trip to the toilet. It was funny, but very true.

However lacking in depth, today's news really is new. Columnists in Los Angeles can type their stories on computers that interact with computers in New York. Laser printing plants connected to satellites in orbit allow major newspapers like the New York Times and USA Today to print local editions that are on the streets of America every day. Those same satellites beam television and radio signals nationwide. You can be driving your pickup truck in the wilds of Alberta, Canada and be listening to talk show host Larry King broadcasting from Washington D.C.

The publicist of 1915 would be shocked at the modern publicist's media list. He couldn't imagine the number of consumer and trade publications that feature movie coverage, the proliferation of television in all its forms, the various radio syndicates and many other forms of "media."

Because of the sheer number of available media outlets, the publicist had better apply a systematic approach to developing an awareness campaign. The days of sitting back and calling Hedda or Louella and getting a "national break" through their columns are long gone. Now the publicist, like the advertising account executive, has to be involved in a specific strategy that can be documented in concise memos that chart activity and progress.

The first step is learning the media players—what they cover, how they operate, and how many people they reach.

The Feature Publicity Writer.

If you pitch a story idea to a *Los Angeles Times* staff writer, and he accepts, then that story appears exclusively in the *LA Times*, a major media outlet. But what if you could pitch a story idea to a writer who could place an article in multiple outlets? Such a coup is possible if you work with the right publicity writers.

I was a journalist before I became a publicist and I still its an occasional film related piece. Free-lancing is no rose garden. There's no regular paycheck and when money comes it comes like molasses through a spigot. Unlike staffers who are guaranteed space in their publications, the freelancer has to compete with other freelancers for space. And when a freelancer approaches a subject with an interview request, he often doesn't get the same respect as a top staff writer.

A sample retort, "Oh, you're free-lancing. Well, do you have a definite outlet or is this on spec?" Staff writers never hear this question. The nature of free-lancing is such that you often will complete an interview and gather research materials before you decide which outlet to pitch. However, freelancers work in many ways. There are freelancers under contract to certain publications (in magazine jargon, they're often called "contributing editors.") There are freelancers who have their own syndicates which submit a single article to dozens of national newspapers. And there are the lone wolfs who are the most independent, pitching their stories to publications with no guarantees.

Multiple Breaks. I like freelancers. I like the way one interview, given to a freelancer can result in pieces appearing in several publications at once. A "nationally breaking" story builds awareness across the continent, and is especially significant when you have a movie opening on a thousand screens at once. It also impresses your superiors when they start seeing tear sheets from papers in different cities all showcasing your movie.

This isn't always true, but I feel that freelancers, if treated fairly and given top cooperation, will be kinder to a film than a staff writer. Freelancers rely on developing solid relationships with the film industry people they interview. Without the guarantee of a steady paycheck, they can't afford to see their contacts dry up and disappear. You'll also find that freelancers are notoriously picky about the subjects they write about and if you do successfully pitch them, they're usually going to be excited about the proposed interview.

Excited enough to write a positive, non-controversial piece? I think so, but I'll also say it depends on the subject.

Switch-Hitters. Freelancers also cross media boundaries. A magazine writer might have a radio talk show. A television talk show host might have a radio column. A magazine columnist might appear on a cable TV show which regularly covers Hollywood. Magazine writers break in newspapers. Newspaper writers break in magazines. Even top national film reviewers may its articles to other outlets (Roger Ebert and Gene Siskel are prime examples, in fact, they've become cottage industries of film coverage.)

How do you compile an effective list of freelancers? Collect top magazines and national newspapers and make your lists of contributors. The Motion Picture Association of America (MPAA) in Van Nuys, California also publishes a yearly directory which lists many freelancers that cover the Hollywood scene. Studio publicity departments will use this directory to compile their screening invitation lists. MPAA "accreditation" is a key to getting studio screening invites.

Newspaper and Magazine Staff Writers and Editors.

Staff writers and editors work exclusively for one publication and they earn a weekly paycheck. They are also a very select group in journalism. Finding a permanent job on the staff of a major publication is very difficult. However, once a job opening does occur, that writer or editor might be associated with the publication for years.

Get to know the names of key staff personnel by perusing the publication and its staff roster. Magazines list their staff usually in the front of the publication. Newspapers don't, and most of the time you have to rely on an independent directory to glean the key names of staff members. There are a number of such publications from companies like Laramie and Nationwide Media Outlets. Check your local library or check with fellow publicists. The directories are usually expensive ($100 is not uncommon) so sharing saves money. They're also supposed to provide you with periodic updates.

- **Developing the One on One Relationship.** Since freelancers are always on the move, I don't schedule a lunch appointment with them very often. Since staff writers and editors have a daily regimen, I find it easier to meet with them. A luncheon rendezvous is appropriate during which I not only pitch a current project, but I try to gauge what the publication is looking for. Generally, editors are happy to discuss their formats because if you know what they're looking for, you won't bother them with the wrong story ideas.

As always, star vehicles and major studio projects get first consideration. Stories with excellent angles and fresh perspectives are also good bets. From there, you simply have to hone your pitch and hope their interest is piqued.

- **When "No" Means "No."** One important point. If the editor or writer says no, then call it a day. I'm not in favor of over-pitching. Developing a relationship with the media, its, staff or otherwise, means understanding what they mean when they say "no thank you." There are publicists out there who treat a no as a challenge. How can I get them to change their minds? I believe that if you are doing your job, defining the appropriate publication, honing your pitch and then pitching, you can get a clear answer. If the answer is negative, get on with your pitching at other publications. The publicist's pitching list is enormous and there's never enough time to get around to all the key publications.

- **When "No" Could Become "Yes."** However, sometimes additional factors can overturn a negative verdict on a story. A staff editor may say no initially then see the movie and change his mind. The publicist should be aware that in motion picture publicity, pitches usually come in two stages—pre-screening and post-screening.

After working in the field for a while, you'll begin to separate those staff people, freelancers, etc. who only determine their story selections after an official screening. This is particularly true of national magazine editors based in New York. Many of these magazines rely solely on their staff reviewers who supply a monthly stream of critiques based on the films they see. The problem: making sure a print of the film is finished in time for them to meet their deadlines.

Bear in mind that national magazines usually work 3-5 months in advance, so if your film is still in post-production a few months before its release, you're going to lose out on showing it to national magazines. Films that are finished months before their release thus have an advantage with this media arena. One other factor can influence a staff writer or editor's attitude toward a story pitch: new developments in the story. Your pitch may suddenly become very topical. In late 1987, I was working on a Tim Curry/Annie Potts comedy called *Pass the Ammo* about a group of latter-day Robin

Hoods who invade the television studio of an evangelist to get their stolen money back.

At one point in the movie, Curry turns to the national TV cameras and says, "I confess, I am a sinner." In the middle of our pitching campaign and months after the Jim and Tammy Bakker scandal had died down, televangelist Jimmy Swaggart was seen on national television uttering the phrase, "I confess, I am a sinner." Suddenly, Curry's comedic speech was hilariously topical. To reinforce that point, we sent video cassettes of that sequence to key publications and television shows.

At my first public relations agency job, I remember working on a book campaign for a novel written by a top national sports writer. The novel was a fictional adventure about a D.B. Cooper-type hijacker who jumped out of a jet airliner and escaped from authorities. This writer had become an expert on Cooper's real-life adventure in the northwest and the mystery surrounding his disappearance. But it was difficult to pitch the book because it was a novel from an unknown writer and the subject was ten years old and stale. I was getting turned down everywhere. Then, amazingly, a flash went out to the media that part of the D.B. Cooper hijack loot had been found on the banks of a river in the northwest. Suddenly, everyone wanted to talk to my author the expert. *Time, Newsweek, LA Times, New York Times*—my phone was ringing off the hook. We had to call a press conference. What a turnaround! It thus pays to keep an eye on the topicality of your movie.

- **Good Intelligence.** Another point to discuss with staff editors and writers is what they are currently working on. Although they often keep mum about the progress on current articles, sometimes because they don't want to be scooped, this information can be extremely valuable to you especially if the article applies to your own project.

The *New York Times* could be working on a general story about female directors or political thrillers or development departments at the independent companies. You can score a lot of points with your superiors when you include relevant information in collage pieces like this. Knowing that the article is being written in the first place is the first step. This question can usually be answered at a comfortable lunch with the staff person. Speaking of meals, unless the staffer says that he must pay his own way, always pick up the media's tab. It's your job and your employer can reimburse you for the expense.

In movie promotion, this is the *ET* generation—and it doesn't have anything to do with Spielberg's extra-terrestrial. No, we're talking about *Entertainment Tonight*, the flashy, up-tempo syndicated entertainment news program that has captured the interest of the American public over the past decade and made household names of people like Mary Hart, Robb Weller, John Tesh and Leeza Gibbons. Not only did *ET* suddenly make entertainment news available to the public on a daily basis, but it introduced behind the scenes movie coverage to the masses. Before *ET*, John Q. Public wasn't familiar with the business side of movie-making. Certainly, there were publications that explored that side—*American Film* magazine was devoted to it, *Time* and *Newsweek* featured an occasional cover story. And specialized mags like *Cinefantastique* and *Starlog* covered the science fiction, fantasy and horror genre.

ET was a whole different experience, though. Like a regular news broadcast with anchors, field reporters and columnists, it gathered an enormous amount of material on all facets of the entertainment industry and presented it in concise news stories, photo features, personal interviews, even trivial bits.

Before *ET*, publicists worked occasionally with the electronic media, bringing local TV crews down to movie sets, setting up an occasional celebrity interview with the New York based morning shows, and preparing film documentaries that were sometimes broadcast on national television. But *ET* increased movie coverage dramatically. Its crews went around the globe, exposing the everyday world of movie making. They interviewed directors, writers and producers, introducing their various skills and responsibilities to the public.

Movie stars were captured on the set, often in costume, discussing the business of filmmaking. In addition to covering the films on location, *ET* anchors reported the news, often quoting stories that had appeared in the entertainment trade papers. Stories on executive shuffles, box office success, marriages and deaths and entertainment industry trends became common.

■ **The TV Camera: Your Best Friend on the Set.** As a publicist, I like *ET* and the many entertainment news reports on TV because these shows are always hungry for new material. You can imagine the burden of *ET's* producers having to produce entertainment news six days a week. These producers are very cooperative with film publicists. Unless you're shooting in outer space or your film is the 87th *Friday the 13th* sequel, *ET* crews are usually interested in a set visit. And one visit could generate a number of stories over the pre-release period.

There's the set visit story, focusing on the filmmaking process which depending on the film and its subject matter could actually become more than one story. If the film is special effects oriented, there could be a set visit piece and separate feature with the special effects team and their particular challenges on this picture. If the picture is based on a famous novel and the author is alive, a separate feature could introduce the background of the movie and highlight an interview with the author. If the film takes place in an exotic location, during an historical period, additional interviews with producers, costume designers, historical consults, even stunt personnel could be highlighted.

- **Additional Stories/Endless Possibilities.** Once the set visit piece is televised (often during production, or shortly thereafter), additional coverage can be planned up through release. If *ET* likes the movie project, it will be on their A list of subjects. What does that mean? Well, when you're covering as much ground as they do, they create a number of collage stories on upcoming film productions, trends and opinions. If a story features five different directors, your director might be one of the interview subjects. If your film was shot underwater, they might feature a story on unusual locations and interview your people. When they feature their summer film roundup, they might include behind the scenes clips from your film. If they're putting together a feature on makeup and hairdressing, they might want to talk to your people as well. The point is that shows like *ET* need plenty of material for their format and if you can get a crew on the set and arrange as many interviews as possible, it's media money in the bank. Also, when the film is released and becomes a hit, all of this previously televised material might suddenly reappear. *ET* recognizes the importance of its tape bank and uses it constantly.

- **The TV Spectrum.** It's amazing how many shows have followed in the *ET* format. There are the pay cable service shows on HBO, Showtime, Cinemax and The Movie Channel. USA Cable has a program called *Hollywood Insider*. MTV has its own entertainment news program, *The Big Picture*. There's the 24 hour movie news service, E! Entertainment Channel, which is extraordinary in the amount of film coverage it needs. There's Group W's *Entertainment Report*. Even the network morning shows—*Good Morning America* (ABC), *The Today Show* (NBC) and *CBS This Morning*—send film crews to location for behind the scenes coverage (B-roll) and interviews.

- **The Electronic Press Kit (EPK).** While we will discuss this area in depth, later, it should be noted here that the success of the entertainment news shows has established the importance of developing the "electronic press kit" (EPK). When these shows cannot visit the set, they are very interested in seeing behind the scenes coverage and interview material. This material is shot by an independently hired EPK company, duplicated onto cassette, added to selected film clips and then sent to the various entertainment news programs. That same material can be sent to regular news editors across the entire country either through hard cassette or satellite delivery.

Even though local news in the smaller cities normally does not produce a regular entertainment news feature a la *ET*, there is a network of local TV stations that are looking for entertainment feature material, especially when it is associated with the bigger star-studded pictures.

An electronic press kit today is far less expensive than it used to be and can be a vital part of the motion picture publicity campaign. The plethora of entertainment news programs available today make it nearly as vital as the standard editorial press kits that have been produced since the earliest days of movies. But whether you create a separate kit or invite the crews to location, dealing with the entertainment news programs is one of your most important responsibilities as a motion picture publicist. No form of media reaches more filmgoers than these programs. They are your bread and butter.

The Columnist.

As I'm writing this chapter, *Hollywood Reporter* columnist Hank Grant announced his retirement. The venerable columnist rested his pen after 35 years. I mention Hank because he was the first columnist I ever met. When I was working for my first public relations agency, my boss used to send me over to the *Reporter* with a written "item." It would always be carefully placed in an envelope with Mr. Grant's name typed on the outside and the capitalized letters HOLLYWOOD REPORTER typed underneath.

In those days, you could walk right in the front door of the *Reporter* and march up to Hank's office, where he would be cranking out his column (you can't do that anymore because they now have a formal reception hall and guard gate—so much for progress). I remember walking up to Hank that first time. He was a very nice man—a big, blustering, big city columnist who had a twinkle in his eye and a gentlemen's demeanor. He knew I was a freshman in the business, but he was polite, accepted the "item" and then offered me a pair of black tennis shoes that didn't fit him. "Take them, kid," he smiled. I was overwhelmed. Hank Grant was giving me a pair of shoes. I couldn't wait to get back to the office and tell my boss.

■ **Horse Trading.** I remember those shoes because they symbolize the relationship between the publicist and the columnist. It's a lot of "horse trading." Columnists are really nothing like magazine or newspaper staff writers, TV producers or coordinators. They have their own style, rules and demeanor. They have their own priorities, idiosyncrasies and viewpoints. More than any other member of the media, they speak a different language, a different dialect and it's up to the publicist to learn that dialect.

The publicist/columnist relationship dates back to the beginnings of organized theater. P.T. Barnum was a column planter. So were all the razzle-dazzle ex-newspapermen who worked for the vaudeville houses and burlesque parlors. Their job was to get their acts in the columns. And it had its darker side. Payoffs, favoritism, blackmail, scandal. Sometimes a columnist could close a show with a bad notice if he didn't get the proper payoff.

During Hollywood's Golden Age, the fate of the movie business was often in the hands of gossip columnists like Sheila Graham, Hedda Hopper, Louella Parsons and Walter Winchell who wielded tremendous power. Column planting achieved art form status during this period. There were newspaper and magazine writers around the country who wrote consistently about the movies, but no one was as powerful as a Hedda or a Louella. If you could break an item in their columns it was considered a tremendous boon to your film.

Today, the columnists are an important media outlet, but they're no longer the number one break. Getting your star on Good Morning America or a cover story in *Premiere* magazine ranks much higher. Still, the value of a break in a column that is nationally syndicated cannot be underestimated.

■ **Trade Paper Columnists.** But let's start with the trade columnists at the *Hollywood Reporter* and *Daily Variety*. The producer of your movie reads the trades every day and is very familiar with Army Archerd's column at *Variety* and Robert Osborne's at the *Reporter*. The fact that their columns appear in the front part of their respective papers is no coincidence—people like to read them first.

I've never asked Army or Bob whether they read each other's column. I don't have to. They know what the other is writing about and if you double plant and it appears, they'll know it. Never give the same item to both of these trade columnists. Oh, it may work some days. But if they catch this practice more than once you could wind up without a contact.

Like elephants, columnists never forget. Remember also, that because of their excellent reputations, columnists are generally never hurting for items. You have to prove to them that your item is more important and pressing than the next person's. Dealing with exclusivity is a tricky business when it comes to items. There are no hard and fast rules but I recommend that if you call the columnist personally with an exclusive (exclusives are never written in), it had better be one.

■ **Generating Items.** Some of your movies are going to be more item intensive than others. If you're working with Mr. Superstar on a film, every breath he takes may be newsworthy. Then again, you might be on a film with unknowns that is item poor. If that is the case, get creative. One area that can breed a slew of column acceptable items is a little historical research. When you're dealing with Robert Osborne at the *Reporter*, this can come in handy because he's the ultimate film historian. But your item better be accurate because if it isn't, Bob will spot it in a minute.

An historical item? Start digging into the backgrounds of your cast, crew and location. You might come up with some amazing discoveries. For instance, you might have an actor who's grandfather was Bela Lugosi. Or your location might have been the site of the original "St. Valentine's Massacre." Your assistant director might be the president's nephew or your makeup supervisor might be married to the head of a major corporation. Now, these aren't guaranteed items, but they will start you on the road to serious research. Also remember that when it comes to item planting, actions speak louder than words.

When you visit your set, don't stand there like a bump on a log. Be an observer. I remember spending a steamy night on a rural location for one of the *Porky's* movies. In one outrageous scene, the leading actor has to "streak" down a country road where he's spotted by a police car. That night, Sherry Lansing, then the head of 20th Century Fox, was visiting the set. The actor, sporting a bathrobe, came over and shook hands with her. It was very formal, until he opened his robe and gave her a big flash. Guess who sent the item to Army Archerd the next day (with her permission of course).

■ **Chain Reaction.** Remember that breaking a trade item can yield additional dividends. You aren't the only one who's reading Army Archerd's column. Other columnists, writers, and movie people read the trades religiously and an item you give to Army or Bob can end up in the *Schenectady Times*. So when your star or producers asks how important the trade columns are or whether they're just industry oriented, you can talk about these dividends. Never underestimate the reach of the trades.

The national columnists operate under similar guidelines and they also appreciate exclusivity. Marilyn Beck in Los Angeles, Liz Smith in New York, Jeannie Williams and Larry King with *USA Today*, and all of the Manhattan based daily columnists are also a vital part of your campaign. Again, you must customize your items. Try to avoid double or triple planting at all costs.

■ **Pacing Yourself.** You don't have to break every column at once. If you're working on a movie set, you usually have two months of shooting. There's no need to hit every columnist at once, it's inefficient. As I will describe in later chapters, you have to structure a publicity campaign that works effectively over a period of many months. If your movie is opening in November and you blow all of your column breaks in June, what kind of news is going to be featured in July, August, September and October. I'm currently working on a film due for release in the month of January. It's currently September. I'm organizing column breaks in every month in a number of outlets. Collectively, they're going to reach many people, who when the film is released, are going to remember the film's title from their readings.

■ **Pitching Materials.** Although I occasionally send written background materials to the trade columnists, I usually pitch them by phone. The national columnists are much more difficult to reach by phone, so you must preface your oral pitch with a written one. Advance production notes are vital or, if you're pitching a particular personality, background on that specific person is needed. Sometimes, a heavy press kit too much in advance of the film's release will be wasted on a columnist. Keep your materials light and organized.

When I'm doing my informational mailings on a new film, I always include the columnists on my mailing list. In this manner, you sometimes get additional column breaks. Also, the columnists become familiar with your movie. They can keep track of the starting date, the cast members, the key behind the scenes personnel and the all important plot elements. Hopefully, when you do call or contact them with your item pitch, they will know something about the project already.

■ **Columnist Set Visits and Phoners.** When you have a particularly interesting location or set, it's wise to consider a columnist for a set visit. Although there are no guarantees, a columnist set visit usually nets a sizable break in one or more columns. You'll also find that while visiting, the columnist will gather additional materials that will break "down the line."

Developing person to person relationships is always vital, not only between you and the columnist but between your cast and crew and the columnist. Writers like to write about people they've met. Make sure the visit is productive for the columnist. I'll have more information on bringing media to the set in a later chapter.

In addition to set visits, you might want to put your star or director on the phone with the columnists. Columnists like "phoners" especially when they're from distant locations. Because of the daily workload, it's often difficult for a columnist to travel. The phone is their work tool. When a film is about to start shooting, a call from the star or director can provide initial readings on the potential and challenge of the production. At the close of production, a second call can focus on the experience and results. Get those phoners done during production because actors and key production personnel have a tendency to leave for all points of the compass when shooting is done.

While many writers and editors are difficult pitching targets, the columnist is usually waiting for your call, waiting for the next hot item that will make the column. Keep it short, interesting and to the point, and you're on your way to a great break and an excellent relationship with a proven source of movie information.

The Trade Journalists.

In any business, a special relationship is developed between company publicists and the industry's trade journals. In the movie industry, filmmakers are aware of the importance of the trades. By "trades," I always mean *Daily Variety* and the *Hollywood Reporter*. There are, to be sure, other trade publications, including *Boxoffice*, *Screen International* and *Movie and TV Marketing*, but only *Variety* and the *Reporter* are read consistently on a daily basis by the majority of film industry professionals. As the *Wall Street Journal* is to the stockbroker, the *AMA Journal* is to the doctor, the trades are to the movie industry.

Ego is such an important element of filmmaking that it often occupies a separate figurative department in most film companies. The publicist is in charge of ego and part of his responsibility is to display that ego in the trades. Primitive chest beating appears frequently in the advertising pages of the trades, usually in the form of full page ads touting new movies going into production, new movies in production, new movies coming out of production and new movies that have grossed $42 million in 35 days (for instance).

But the ads are paid for. The editorial copy that appears in the trades is initiated by publicists who apply the same skills with trade journalists they do with everyone else in the media.

■ **Beats.** The principal beat reporters at both trades are always sniffing for an exclusive, so you don't have to go searching for someone to be interested in your story. If you're working for a specific company—major or independent—you will have a writer assigned to your beat, someone who writes exclusively about your company. Beat writers are your primary contacts at the trades and should be handled with care. When I'm working on staff for a specific company, I try to schedule a lunch every so often just to keep in touch, so that even when I don't have any important news, they keep me in mind. Beat writers cover news stories, but they also deal with the more mundane news items like executive appointments and shuffles. Again, where your appointment story shows up usually depends on exclusivity and the stature of the executive.

Generally speaking, *Daily Variety* will not print a picture of a new executive under the rank of vice president. Even VPs can get shafted in the photo department. The *Hollywood Reporter* places most of its executive appointments in the "People on the Move" column. Again, a photograph isn't guaranteed, but if one is supplied, there's a better chance the *Reporter* will use it for all ranks of employee regardless of whether the story is exclusive or not.

■ **Trade Features.** The trades are useful for dozens of other breaks, including the previously mentioned column items, travel movements, production chart information, personal data—births, marriages, deaths—and features. The latter is more a *Reporter* trait than *Variety*, possibly due to a space factor. On most days, the *Reporter* is much larger than *Variety* and thus has more room for feature stories. This is particularly true on days when the *Reporter* is publishing a special issue.

Feature stories are common in special issues because of the larger number of featured advertisements. It's a common rule that the bigger the ad buy, the more available feature space. The fact that your story is related to the "special issue" subject will help get you in the paper. If your company is announcing a major independent film, chances are that the "independent feature" issue will give you good play. If you have a top special effects person working on your film, his story will work well on a special effects issue. Placement in a special issue may unfortunately depend on whether your company is a major ad purchaser. But check with your beat writer and find out about special issue criteria. It will often depend on space availability and again, the relative importance of your story idea.

A note on the weekly edition of *Variety*. This is the edition of *Variety* that is published on the East Coast and services that part of the country (although it's also available in LA). I've always had the impression that *Weekly Variety* is designed for the executives who haven't read their *Daily Variety* all week. *Weekly* generally reprints *Daily's* coverage with a few kickers. But their format is changing: original feature reporting is now becoming more common. The international arena featured in the Tuesday *Reporter*, is comparably featured in the *Weekly Variety*.

Weekly Variety is also known for its expanded coverage of the national exhibition front. Theatrical box office gross is calculated for the major cities in specific regional reports which document revenue on a theater by theater basis. *Weekly Variety* is thus a popular trade for exhibitors.

The Critics.

They have the idiosyncrasies of the ages and the power to match. They hold the box office fate of a movie in their typewriter ribbons and if they want they can squash it like a bug. If you enrage a non-critic, a problem may arise, but it won't have a fiscal impact on your production. However, if you cross the line with a film critic, look out! His or her wrath could take that paycheck out of your pocket.

I'm not trying to inflate the importance of the nation's critics. I'm simply reminding you that of all the media people you will be dealing with, this relationship is the most critical. It's not so much that you have to develop a buddy buddy relationship with every reviewer. You simply have to make sure that they see your movie under the most favorable conditions. A critic that is unhappy with the viewing experience can go out and immediately write a negative review.

Very few publicists actually work directly with critics. This is a relationship that develops with the studio, agency or independent publicist who is working on the release campaign for the picture. This relationship has nothing to do with pitching stories, setting up interviews or set visits. This is the Final Hour, D-Day, the 6th of June. Your movie is about to hit the beach. Make the viewing experience a positive one.

■ **Walking on Eggs with Reviewers.** When I mention the "viewing experience," I don't mean the quality of the movie they are seeing. You have no control over that. You have to screen the stinkers with the classics. What I'm talking about is getting the invitation there on time, making sure a screening room with the proper number of seats is rented, having press kits available, greeting the critics and if possible, escorting them to their seats. This is the night your hosting powers must come across.

All of the above may have no effect on the quality of the review. However, to your bosses, you can be assured that you have done your job completely and professionally. However, if any of those elements are blown, the reverberations can strike home quickly. If your boss or the filmmakers are present at any of the screenings, a critic's negative comments on the quality of that screening can come back to haunt you.

An upcoming chapter will discuss the step by step method of setting up a critic's screening. For now, just note that it's very difficult to get a critic to come to a screening in the first place. You have all sorts of competition. Other films, the critic's taste, their personal and professional responsibilities that take them away from the screenings (critics are always traveling to film festivals, etc) even the reputation of your film company. The bigger the critic, the greater the challenge to get his feet planted in a screening room.

The advent of the television review program a la Siskel and Ebert has made the top critics in the country more accessible. When they have to churn out a weekly show, these critics are always on the hunt for new movies. And these shows are the most vital of all the critical outlets. Not only are the critics major media stars on their own, but their show goes national. A great "thumbs up" review can be on 200 television stations this weekend. A terrible "thumbs down" review can hit the same track.

Of course, some of the top critics are the most discriminating in their review choices. Bruce Williamson of *Playboy* isn't going to sit down and see the 19th "Freddie the Slasher" movie. The critics for *Time Magazine* and *Newsweek* are also difficult to pin down. Magazine reviewers as a whole can select the movies they wish to review, newspaper reviewers generally don't have that luxury. They have a public responsibility to review every new film that's advertised in their papers. Daily newspaper reviewers probably see more movies than even the most ardent fan. They're also the most demanding. When you visit any environment as much as they do, you're going to develop a pattern for enjoyment. If something prohibits that enjoyment, you're going to make a fuss. And they do.

- **Critical Etiquette.** Unless he's a personal friend or has given you permission to in the past, after a screening never ask a reviewer what he thought of the movie. It's very unprofessional. However, if he sidles up to you after the screening and gushes, you don't have to shut him up. All of this information will prove valuable to your superiors who are waiting nervously for positive reaction.

In the pre-release period, you're also going to approach some of the reviewers to gather advance positive quotes. Again some reviewers will cooperate, and others will not.

There's a funny audio bit at the beginning of the Albert Brooks comedy *Lost in America* in which Rex Reed while being interviewed by Larry King on the radio discusses how he prefers to see a movie before he reviews it. This bit is actually the most succinct description of a film reviewer's idiosyncrasies I have ever heard. Rent the movie and take notes at the beginning. Start memorizing these idiosyncrasies. This is the kind of knowledge that eventually pays dividends. For, one of the most frequently asked questions of publicists is "how well do you know that critic?"

Know them well.

Talk Shows.   In a typical movie campaign, talk show appearances take place closer to release time. Unit publicists rarely get involved in talk shows, although it is possible for actors to appear on local shows at a distant location. If you're shooting in Laramie, Wyoming, the local program may plead for an appearance by someone from the movie. However, appearances under those circumstances are affected by time constraints and the on-set responsibilities of cast and crew.

In terms of timing, talk show appearances can strike at odd times. An actor arrives on the set of the motion picture you are publicizing. A film he finished nearly a year ago is now about to be released. *Good Morning America* wants to interview him on your location. He's amenable, you're cooperative. Often, in the publicity game, you find yourself helping promote someone else's product so that, maybe, if you're lucky, the actor will remember to plug his current film project. Maybe.

■ **Plugging.** It's a key word when it comes to talk show appearances. It used to be a word associated with shooting someone. Remember? James Cagney sends two goons to "plug" Edward G. Robinson. However, the only person who gets shot these days is the publicist whose actor forgets to mention the movie. You certainly can't rely on the talk show host to mention your movie. They're interested in a good interview. They're not sitting there with a little warning bell that says "oh, Tom, you haven't mentioned the movie yet."

Hip 1960s novelist Jacqueline Suzanne was an expert on talk show appearances. As the story goes, every time she was asked a question, regardless of the subject, she would start her answer with the name of her latest book. Johnny Carson: "How was your vacation, Jackie?" Suzanne: "Writing my book, *Valley of the Dolls* was so tough on me, Johnny, that I needed that vacation." Johnny: What's your next project?" Suzanne: "After I finish this tour for *Valley of the Dolls*, I start *Once is Not Enough*."

Fortunately, most talk show appearances today are geared to a specific film project. If Eddie Murphy goes on *The Today Show*, the studio publicist is going to provide the show with a funny clip from his latest comedy. With the home audience more familiar these days with the filmmaking process, talk show interviewers no longer hesitate to ask technical questions about the experience. On *The Today Show*, for example, film critic Gene Shalit often does the movie celebrity interviews. He's not only going to ask technical questions about the new movie, but he's going to billboard the segment by announcing that—"Our next guest is the star of 'Rocky X,' Sylvester Stallone." It's nice when the host does his own kind of plugging.

■ **Booking.** The key to booking movie actors on talk shows is developing a relationship with the talent coordinators or bookers. Again, standard publicity procedures are involved. You must write a pitch letter, describing the new movie and the actor's part, and you generally provide some production notes.

Talent coordinators are paid to book stars. Competition is fierce on the morning national talk shows—especially between *The Today Show* and *Good Morning America*. Everyone wants an exclusive with Eddie Murphy or Kevin Costner. Sometimes with a superstar, appearances on both shows are possible.

When you have wonderful unknowns in your picture who have delivered incredible debut performances, the talk show circuit becomes a difficult gateway to crack. Until a movie becomes a hit and the actor's performance is acknowledged, unknowns do not increase ratings points. But don't give up on your pitch.

Once a letter is in the hands of the talent coordinator, you must follow up quickly with a phone call to get a simple "yes" or a simple "no." If a talent coordinator says "no," you can't go to the Supreme Court for a reversal. Go on to the next show.

Film publicists are usually in a better position after the talent coordinator has been invited to a screening of the new film, especially if you're not dealing with big stars. The coordinator may like the movie so much that you can arrange a booking the next day. He might even walk over to you after the screening and set up the appearance right there. And you wondered why publicist's stand in the lobby after a screening lets out?

Give the talent coordinator enough lead time. If your movie is opening on Friday, don't call on Monday to get a booking that week. Talent coordinators work at least a month in advance on some shows and even longer on the big ones like Carson, Letterman, Oprah and Donahue. The morning shows have shorter deadlines and sometimes they need people very quickly because of a cancellation.

Rules are made to be broken. I called my *Good Morning America* (*GMA* for those in the know) contact on a Friday for a Tuesday appearance the following week. It just so happened that she had a last minute cancellation and needed someone desperately. How fortunate that I should call. It was 5:00 p.m. on a Friday afternoon.

Morning show talent coordinators are usually long gone by then, but she was calling the world looking for a guest. I spent the next 45 minutes calling back and forth between my actor and the coordinator, finally wrapping everything up neatly at 5:45 p.m. I patted myself on the back, picked up my brief case, and walked out of my office only to hear the phone ringing behind me. I put down my case and picked up the phone. It was the actor, he wanted to cancel the whole thing. I sank into my chair. Thoughts of an early dinner evaporated. I spent the next 45 minutes trying to convince him to go on the show. He had all the proper excuses. He was exhausted from his last movie; his doctor told him to rest; his wife just had a baby; he doesn't like live shows; he gets nervous; he won't sleep; it's a holiday weekend, he wants to relax; he hates the advance reviews on the movie; he thinks the interviewer will put him on the spot. I didn't stand a chance.

The Radio Entertainment Reporter.

When I was 17 I bought my first car, a 1969 Mustang fastback. It had a Philco AM radio and when I turned it on that first day in May 1969, Tommy James and the Shondells were playing a 60s favorite, *Crystal Blue Persuasion*. For me, radio was music, usually in the car, and usually a total escape from reality.

As a film publicist, I no longer think like that teenager back in 1969. Radio is another informational outlet and a prime arena for promotions. Disc jockeys, morning comedy shows, all news programs, public affairs specials, entertainment spotlights, news breaks, even soundtrack records help spread the word on new movies.

Honestly, I don't work with the radio media as much as I'd like to. Preferably, I would like to invite every disc jockey and every news reporter to a new film screening. I would like to develop an ongoing relationship with these jocks similar to my involvement with columnists. Why? Because jocks talk all day and they talk about everything under the sun. If they see a movie they like, they're simply going to talk about it. And if they talk about it during the prime listening hours (known as "morning and afternoon drive"), you're going to be spreading some serious awareness.

- **Promotional Possibilities.** The studios in Hollywood understand how radio reaches the masses, especially the key filmgoing audience, ages 12-24. And if you listen, you'll see that the major studios will usually set up a promotion on the key stations in your market—trading a screening, T-shirts or a soundtrack album for the time it takes a jock to mention the contest, which over a 10 day period could be 50 promotional commercials. If you add to this an advertising buy of perhaps another 50 commercials, you'll saturate the station's listening audience. Stations will sometimes state that a promotion can happen without an ad buy, but my experience shows that the most effective promos don't work without one.

- **Radio Columnists.** In addition to local disc jockeys and news personnel who feature entertainment reports, there are also syndicated radio columnists, reporters and critics, some based in LA, others in NYC, who cover the film business. They're usually associated with a radio network—ABC, NBC, AP, UPI, Westwood One and their national reporting is invaluable to your film awareness campaign.

- **Radio Press Kits.** Just as video press kit companies are gathering materials to distribute to television stations on a national basis, there are companies in Los Angeles who produce featurettes and interview packages for the nation's radio stations. Sometimes they even use the same satellite delivery systems.

If you have money in your budget, radio press kits can be a useful tool. However, I can't forget what one of my superiors once said about film programming on the radio. He was a frequent radio listener and in all his days of listening, he had never heard a film interview on the airwaves. Despite the claims of the radio press kit producers, you have to wonder whether their packages are hitting the airwaves during prime listening hours. Entertainment industry programming is seldom given prime "drive time" slots. Consequently your publicity breaks may come in off-hours or on weekends when the number of listeners is down. So, if you hire a radio press kit specialist, pin them down on the exact nature of their air times.

Speciality Outlets.

In the fall of 1981, I was assigned to a film entitled *Endangered Species* which starred Robert Urich and Jobeth Williams. It was a contemporary mystery shooting in Wyoming about a plague of cattle mutilations that baffled local ranchers—based on actual events!

This was my first feature unit publicity assignment and I had been hired primarily for my writing skills to interpret the film in much the same way *The China Syndrome* had been interpreted—as reality drama.

What was challenging about *Endangered Species* were the number of speciality approaches to the film. The reality drama element appealed to upscale publications that were interested in political intrigue, environmental danger and the unsolved mystery. The fact that the story eventually involves new technology—the mutilators turn out to be government backed mercenaries testing germ warfare strains—made it intriguing to science fiction fans.

The latter group became particularly significant when we discovered that there were several theories about the mutilations, one presenting evidence that the attacks were being orchestrated by interplanetary farmers. The fact that we had Jobeth Williams fresh from *Poltergeist* helped my cause when I went to the science fiction film magazines.

The subject matter of your film often points you in a certain media direction which opens up non-traditional media markets. If possible, investigate story breaks that take the film off the entertainment pages to an even larger readership. On *Endangered Species* I contacted news publications (*Time, Newsweek, U.S. News and World Report*), science fiction fan magazines (*Cinefantastique, Starlog*), alternative press journalists (*LA Weekly, LA Reader, Chicago Reader,* etc.), even cattle industry trade publications like *Beef*.

Don't laugh at *Beef*. Although you can't base a marketing campaign on a specialty group, it never hurts to contact them. If you can guarantee awareness amongst any special interest group, the chances of creating positive word-of-mouth are increased. Hopefully your group has some significant filmgoers in its ranks.

Remember it's not your responsibility to determine if special interest groups go to movies. However, if you can build awareness for any sizable group that has a special affection for your film's subject matter, go ahead. They may be the first people in line on opening day.

7

PRE-PRODUCTION–
GETTING THE BALL ROLLING

Now that you've received a basic education in publicity, it's time to apply that knowledge to the work at hand. A movie is about to go into production and you've been hired to publicize it. What do you do? How? When? What for? Why? and with Who? This middle section of the book will focus specifically on the motion picture publicity campaign while the film is being made—known as "in production."

For the first time, you'll be exposed to all the publicity needs of the film, from pre-production, through release. I'm going to spread the information out on the table and let you see how campaigns are run.

All of the following information is based on my personal experience in all the various publicity capacities—agency publicist, unit publicist, advance publicist, studio publicist, independent publicist and consultant. This is no theorizing. My methods have been tested on the battlefield and I can now show you the results. I think you're going to be particularly interested in some of the psychological aspects of working on film with the various personalities—actors, directors, producers, crew, agents, publicists, studio representatives and, of course, the media.

There's a lot of information to distill here. Some of it is going to make absolutely no sense to you at this point. Other points will sound logical, but will have no immediate meaning. However, everything should come into focus by the end. As you read, whether you're a future publicist, a current producer or a film enthusiast, keep in mind that there is only one goal in publicity—to build awareness for a motion picture in the minds of the people who will ultimately have to decide, "should I buy a ticket or not?"

One thing I must point out. As a publicist, I take full responsibility for my publicity campaign. There are many other publicity entities which you could call on to do some of your work. If I can get support from an agency or personal publicist, that's fine. But I don't count on it. My experience shows that the only way to guarantee the kind of professional job I will be proud of is to do it myself. If I fail, I fail because I tried, not because I let someone else fail for me.

■ **Pre-Production Publicity.** Pre-production is the period prior to the start of shooting. It can be as little as two months or as long as two years. In the publicity departments of the major studios campaigns begin as soon as the decision is made to do a new project. This is especially true of films with major stars and directors.

Warner Bros. began making headlines with the *Batman* movie years before it was released. *Dick Tracy* with Warren Beatty, *The Two Jakes* with Jack Nicholson, a sequel to *Gone With The Wind*, *Ghostbusters II*, and any news regarding another *Rocky*—these are the type of ongoing stories about films that always make good copy in the entertainment press.

■ **Casting News.** In Hollywood, casting news is important news, especially if the stars are well known. You don't have to have Warren Beatty, Dustin Hoffman and Jack Nicholson to get breaks. If Jerry Mathers (*Leave It To Beaver*) is going to appear in *Halloween Part 62*, it's legitimate news. Get a release and photo out immediately.

And breaking a casting story isn't just feeding Army Archerd at *Daily Variety* or Robert Osborne at *The Hollywood Reporter*. If your casting is set in stone, get a photograph of the actor, hopefully in his new role. Getting a photograph of the actor in costume, especially if it's a unique one, immediately capsulizes your movie. Imagine the value of that first shot of Clark Gable as Rhett Butler.

Every entertainment journalist in town is hungry for new material—and casting announcements on new films are the best of all initial breaks. They whet the appetite of the media. If you can supply them with a good background release and colorful photo material (even colorful black and white photo material), you're off to a good start with the campaign.

Mailings of casting announcements are time consuming and expensive, but they pay off by launching the picture in the public's eye. You create awareness by getting the general public to say, "Did you hear about Madonna's new picture?"

Providing initial specs on new films also primes the media for the upcoming production publicity campaign. Having whetted their appetite, they're not about to say "What film, did you say?" when you call with your initial production pitches.

Pre-production publicity and post-production publicity are arenas of awareness that are generally under utilized by most film companies. Why? Primarily because publicists are usually not available at such times. Most film companies hire publicists during production (unit publicists) and prior to release (release campaign publicists).

Unit publicists are normally hired a week or two before production begins. If you're an independent company, you've had very little exposure prior to that time. Oh, you might see an item in the trades, but a pre-production publicity campaign isn't just a trade break. By the time the unit publicist comes to the film, casting is finished, the behind the scenes production team is in place and locations have been chosen—all good press releases ripe for mass mailings.

■ **Continuity.** My biggest complaint these days is the lack of continuity in a publicity campaign. It's like trying to get good exercise on a tennis court. You get the heart pumping and you stop. You get it pumping again, and you stop. And so on. You run around a lot, but you don't really get the kind of exercise which does your heart any good. Publicity, like exercise, needs to be done consistently for an extended period of time to be really effective.

There's a lot of excitement as production begins, which hopefully lasts through production if the unit publicist is good. And then once production stops, everything generally stops, until someone wakes up a couple of months before release and says "Hey, let's get some awareness going, quick." Suddenly, the excitement begins again. Trouble is, this time new publicity entities are often involved and they probably have no relationship with the people involved during production.

We need more continuity—whether it's a project director or a long term contract with a P.R. agency, or simply more publicists on payroll at the studios. As producers become more aware of these needs, hopefully more attention will be paid to the pre-production and post-production publicity periods. Otherwise, we will be stuck with the same kind of publicity campaigns we have today—which are often too-little, too-late, and not as effective as they could be.

8

THE UNIT PUBLICIST—
WHAT TO DO WHEN YOU GET THE JOB

When a film goes into production, the key publicity person is the Unit Publicist. No film can be adequately publicized without a Unit working the shoot. Unfortunately, many producers, especially those who work lower budget projects, believe that production publicity doesn't require a full-time unit publicist. In their opinions, all the publicity which needs to happen during production can happen in a couple days by a freelancer; just produce an adequate press kit, some serviceable still photos and send a few releases to the trades. Harry Brand and Howard Strickling, the great publicists of the past, would disagree—and so do I. The following sixteen chapters describe in detail all the work which needs to be done during production.

Knowing Your Material.

Let's say you got lucky. You've got the job as a full-fledged unit publicist. You're attached to the production. A producer has given you the nod. Go and make a name for yourself. What do you do now?

First, you must get to know your material. Read the script carefully. As the unit publicist, you must know exactly what the film is about because 2,357 people are going to ask you that same question. Not only must you give them a proper answer, but you must do it with all the enthusiasm of the previously mentioned 12 year old baseball fan. No hesitation, no lack of energy. Full amounts of oxygen in the lungs. No one wants to listen to a low key monotone mumbling the story line. Stand on a soapbox and belt it out like a carnival barker.

■ **Initial Positioning.** Here are some sample descriptions of famous movies:

"Ghostbusters" is a comedy about three wacky paranormal investigators played by Dan Akroyd, Bill Murray and Harold Ramis, who start their own extermination business for ghosts. In the process, they have to protect the city of New York from an end-of-the-world crisis.

"The Longest Day" is an historical epic about the Normandy Invasion of World War II, focusing on the average soldiers of all ranks who had to fight on that day. Every major American film star is in the cast including John Wayne, Robert Mitchum, Jeffrey Hunter, Eddie Albert, Robert Ryan, Rod Steiger, Henry Fonda and on and on...

"Terms of Endearment" is a contemporary drama about an ever-changing mother/daughter relationship with Shirley MacLaine and Deborah Winger in the leads and Jack Nicholson, Jeff Daniels and John Lithgow in the supporting roles.

"Aliens," the nightmarish sequel to the 1979 science fiction hit "Alien," once again focuses on Warrant Officer Ripley (SIGOURNEY WEAVER), who, this time joined by a squad of tough Marines, must return to the planet and the monsters that destroyed her original crew.

These are pretty compact paragraphs that can be repeated quickly and forcefully. They trip off the tongue into the ears of the nation's journalists, supplied by the unit publicist who has read the script carefully and has talked to his superiors—producer, writer, director about the movie.

One of the unit publicist's first jobs is to come up with this kind of "positioning paragraph" which adequately describes both the content and the style of the motion picture at hand. After reading the script carefully, the publicist needs to talk with the producer, the director and the writer so as to have a complete and accurate picture. Once approved by the producers, the position paragraph (or the gist of it) will be the key element of all of your pitches, both oral and written. It also eventually becomes the first paragraph of your press kit.

You develop this positioning paragraph by getting to know your material carefully. While reading and re-reading the script, get to know the characters in the story. You must know their character names and the actors who are playing them. They must become names in a batting order to be memorized. Whether you're dealing with Marlon Brando or Marlon Nobody, their names are vital. Marlon Nobody could be the Marlon Somebody of tomorrow. You never know.

■ **Set Pieces.** As you read the script, become aware of the film's large set pieces—in other words, the big scenes. Since you may be inviting journalists to the set or even your own video press kit film crew, it will be a good idea to immediately chart the scenes that will be the most interesting.

On some films those scenes are obvious. I'm sure the producers of the 1959 *Ben Hur* considered the chariot race the biggest scene in the picture and thus invited a large number of journalists to cover that sequence. Likewise the burning of Atlanta in *Gone With the Wind*, the exploding of the bridge in *The Bridge on the River Kwai* and the great desert battles of *Raiders of the Lost Ark* and *Lawrence of Arabia*.

Not every film has a "burning of Atlanta," but every film does have a sequence that could be visually exciting to a non-partial viewer. Go through the script and mark these, then consult the producer or production manager and find out when these sequences are going to be shot. The shooting schedule could provide an immediate answer. Get a copy from the production office and pore over it immediately. It's your blueprint for the film shoot. Only keep in mind that shooting schedules do change—often daily.

■ **Locations.** In addition to the big set pieces, note any interesting or unusual locations. Combining a big set piece like a battle, earthquake or chase with a location like downtown Singapore or the Grand Canyon or the top of the Empire State Building makes a very interesting set visit, press kit story or release. It doesn't even have to be a city or national monument. An unusual building, garden, street or set can also be exciting. I was on the set at Columbia Pictures when they built the top of the skyscraper, turned Sumerian temple for *Ghostbusters*. It was fabulous and it was in the heart of Burbank. Log those locations.

■ **Themes.** In addition to knowing the story, be aware of its theme or sub-theme. Journalists like to know where the story is going. All Vietnam pictures sound the same until you emphasize an unusual theme or approach to the material. "Why is this movie being made?" will often be a journalist's unspoken question. Answer those unspoken questions by talking about how the director, writer or producer sees the film.

Some examples: "It's the ultimate test of motherhood" (*Aliens*); "It's the first eyewitness portrait of the Vietnam War" (*Platoon*); "It's how one average American family might confront the end of the world" (*Testament*); "It's a movie about the ultimate comeback (any one of the *ROCKY* movies); "It's a wacky commentary on the differences between Americans and Brits" (*A Fish Called Wanda*); "It's a poignant look at the kid in all of us" (*Big*).

A theme isn't something you can immediately fathom from a read through the script. Talk the story over with the producer, writer, director—they'll have a pretty good definition of the theme(s) before shooting begins.

Know the Backgrounds of the Actors and Key Production Personnel.

Story isn't your only concern. You must also record in your bank of knowledge the biographies of all key actors and behind the scenes personnel. Like Sgt. Friday of the old *Dragnet* series, the media today is interested in "just the facts."

■ **The Academy Library—The Ultimate Source.** There are two ways to assemble a biography (bio). You can interview the actor from scratch and get all the information you need or you can pay a visit to the library of the Academy of Motion Pictures in Beverly Hills where previous bios can be simply and quickly updated.

Interviewing the actor at the start of production is often impossible and actually inadvisable. Actors, especially stars, have more important things on their minds than discussing the details of their lives. Consequently, the Academy library is a logical starting point for the assembly of biographical material.

At the Academy, there are production files of information on every major actor and film. These materials are never let out of the building but you can sit right there and collect the information you need. The Academy is stingy with photocopying, but you can get a few copies made, especially if you find the appropriate biography in a previous press kit.

Don't hesitate to utilize the information in a previous bio, especially if it is from a major studio motion picture. Not all biographies are correct, but major studio bios are less apt to be filled with errors. In any case, once you find a bio, run it by the actor to make sure it's correct. Actors generally appreciate seeing previous bios and they'll usually be happy to correct any errors. Correcting a previous bio saves them the time they'll have to spend supplying you with new information. So it behooves them to be cooperative. But they're actors, so be prepared for delays.

In my scheme of events, I like to have an advance press kit ready in the first week of shooting. Featuring initial production information, a presentation statement and short bios, this information is supplied to journalists as part of my initial pitch. Thus, I will need that bio information very quickly. So don't let the actors slow you up.

If the actor is an unknown or is just starting out in this business (a feature debut, no less), you will have to corner them quickly and try to get as much biographical information as possible for your advance kit. Newcomers, unless they're complete space cases, are much easier to work with because they haven't developed the techniques to be uncooperative. (Am I sounding very anti-actor? I'm really not, but they do the unexpected every time.) Also it will take far less time to complete a newcomer's bio simply because they haven't made any films yet.

Your bio responsibilities also extend to the key production personnel—specifically director, producer(s), writer(s) and any other person deemed indispensable to the project. Sometimes there can be half a dozen producers involved in a project. For the advance press kit, keep the producer bios down to a minimum. You can tell the other producers that you will include them in the final kit. Remember as soon as you announce to anyone that you are compiling bios, others will want to get in on the act.

Behind the scenes personnel can be researched at the Academy as well. Production files exist on many top directors, writers and producers. There are also many reference books which can give you credits.

- **Tracking Down Biographical Information.** If you have trouble getting information from the Academy, utilize the actor or director's contact—meaning his agent or publicist. Usually, if you're dealing with a newcomer, a resume will exist. That will at least give you a list of credits. You can then take that list to the Academy and get a few details on the film projects by cross-referencing. Resumes are particularly important when dealing with newcomers. They usually list academic achievements, plays, community theater, everything that is important to the actor, director, writer or producer. You could build an advance press kit bio on these facts alone.

- **The Actor's Publicist.** Contacting an actor's publicist for an up to date bio is a good way to break the ice with that publicist. It's the standard first phone call. This is also a good time to set up a lunch or other encounter with the publicist. Your reason: to discuss P.R. strategies for the actor during the course of production. Also, remember that the actor's publicist will know more about the actor's temperament and attitude toward publicity than you. Your job is to tap into the publicist's mind and secure that vital information. If the actor has certain media outlets that are sore points, this will also come out in initial discussions with his or her publicist.

However, agency publicists can also be very difficult. If you have trouble getting a bio quickly, it might presage difficulty down the line. However petty it sounds, the unit publicist is invading the agency publicist's turf. For the course of the production, you will be coordinating many of the actor's public relations responsibilities. Egos can be immediately jostled. Unfortunately, the phrase "we're all working on the same team" doesn't always apply or work.

Develop a very cooperative nature when dealing with agency publicists. If you appear the least bit threatening in terms of "taking over the campaign" and putting that publicist out to pasture, you're going to get into trouble. Remember that the agency publicist has that actor's ear. If he's feeling pressure and discomfort, he could communicate that to the actor who can and will develop the same symptoms.

I'm initially very nice to everyone and I give them time to cooperate. But I've learned that I can't wait for water to pour from a rock. If the outside publicist isn't providing you with a current bio—go to the Academy library and get one. If the outside publicist won't tell you if there are any problem media areas, speak to the actor and get the information directly. Be diplomatic but direct. The movie is your responsibility, the media is waiting and you need this information now.

Most of the time, your relationship with the agency publicist will be fine and cooperation is the key. Just be aware that this is one area of contact where your diplomatic skills may be needed. Also remember that there is a good chance that you will be working with this publicist again, so you want to maintain the best possible working relationship.

Your First Meetings— Superiors, Key Players, Photo Editor.

One of the first lessons I learned as a publicist was that everyone assumes you know exactly what you need to do. Millions of dollars are being spent on this motion picture and the producers are meeting daily with location managers, costume designers, set decorators, and every other craft person to determine the course of the film. However, when it comes to publicity, the producer may suddenly become quite speechless. His phraseology becomes less precise, less knowing, less aware of the big picture.

This attitude often extends to upper level publicity executives—not that they aren't qualified—it's just that they don't have the time to devote to coming up with precise strategies and checklists. Get used to being on your own. It is an element of the publicist's makeup that always appealed to me.

Personally, as I became better acquainted with the job responsibilities, I enjoyed the freedom of movement. I equated the unit publicist's job with a war correspondent, wedged into the thick of battle, sending back insightful reports, knowing as much as possible.

If you're fortunate enough to get into initial meetings with your producers or publicity superiors, ask as many questions as possible. Get a rough plan of action going in your head. The more intelligent questions you ask, the more impressive you'll come across to your superiors, and the more they'll leave you alone to do a job. But there are questions that must be answered immediately, such as:

■ **Does anyone have any objections to reporters visiting the set?** It must be established immediately whether the set is "open" or "closed." If you work on a Steven Spielberg film, you're not going to have a lot of visiting reporters. First, his films are usually produced under a complete cloud of secrecy, and secondly, Spielberg simply doesn't do a lot of initial interviews.

Spielberg isn't the only one who closes his set to publicity. When I worked on the sequel to *Porky's*, we had a closed set. The studio was sensitive about the film's sub-plot dealing with the Ku Klux Klan and they wanted to film quietly. It was frustrating for me because during that very summer of 1982, the first *Porky's* had just passed the $100 million mark at the box office, the most popular comedy of its time. Since I was already working on the sequel, I had a hot story and could have opened the set to a lot of additional coverage. Instead, I kept a pretty low profile.

Most producers want as much publicity as possible within limits. If you're shooting on a distant location, only the major studios are going to recommend or afford set visits from journalists and you're going to have to cull them down to a very select few.

What I generally like to find out is whether we can afford to bring in a select group of movie journalists. If the producer and publicity executive says yes, then I have my marching orders. That answer will keep me busy over the next few weeks determining who is interested, who can come, and how we can get them there.

If I discover that the set is closed to journalist's visits, then I know that I will concentrate my efforts in another place. Journalist visits are good but not crucial to any film. I like them because it gives me an opportunity to develop publicity coverage on a more personal viewpoint and if the writer will hold his story, and he often will, I know that coverage of the movie based on that set visit will break closer to release time (I may get more than one story as well). It's also nice, from a purely political viewpoint, to bring journalists onto the set.

When you're acting as "tour guide," setting up interviews and generally playing host, everyone sees you working. Everyone suddenly realizes why you've been hanging around for the last couple of months. It's a very positive feeling. Remember, as a unit publicist, you don't have to get up before dawn and shower in the dark. You don't have to crawl around the desert floor laying dolly track or make-up the stars at five in the morning. And since you spend most of your time in the production office on the telephone to journalists, very few people see you doing your job. Set visits are thus very good for your own image.

- **Do you foresee any publicity problems during the course of the shoot?** It's always good to problem solve before shooting begins. If you're dealing with an actor who doesn't like publicity, you should know up front how to handle things. I like to know the chain of command in the production because you never know when a stone wall might crop up. And you need to know how to get around, over or through any stone wall.

It's also important to know who is going to talk to the press and who shouldn't. If you have a whole cook's pot of producers, find out up front who is going to be speaking to the press. Egos can become heavily bruised on the set if the Time Magazine correspondent is speaking to one producer and not the others. Establish up front who is boss.

If you're meeting with the producers, find out who they feel are the key interviews on the production. I worked on an important studio film and assumed that the line producer was going to take a high profile. I started setting up interviews for him and discovered that the executive producer wanted the coverage divided between himself and the director. No interviews for the line producer. That bit of information put me in a difficult position because it was the type of rule that went unspoken. I couldn't tell the line producer what I had learned. And yet that same line producer was going to ask me at certain times why he wasn't being interviewed. Welcome to the typical publicist's tightrope walk.

Find out who's going to come to your aid during crisis situations. A typical question, "If the actor refuses to do an interview, who will help me convince her that it is important?" It will happen and it's vital to know who your friends are. Producers, directors and studio executives can exert certain pressure. This is a last resort measure. You, above all, have the responsibility of communicating to actors the importance of interviews. But have a backup ready.

■ **Are there any particular aspects of the production you would like emphasized during the publicity campaign?** This question helps you determine how you're going to initially position the film to the press. It can also apply specifically to large set pieces that will be good video or photo opportunities. I've already mentioned the chariot race for *Ben Hur* as a typical large set piece that is perfect for publicity coverage. After reading your script, you're going to know the film's large set pieces (if they exist). Find out now whether you can begin to arrange special coverage.

If your movie has a sensitive theme, background, location, or political viewpoint, find out now how you will present the material to the press. If your movie is about Vietnam, how much do you emphasize that in your coverage?

On *Desert Bloom*, a wonderful film about a troubled family living in Nevada during the first nuclear tests in the 1950s, we had to establish up front how much we were going to emphasize the background of the story. *Desert Bloom* wasn't about the nuclear age or the tests. It was about the family—an alcoholic father who was still having World War II nightmares (JON VOIGHT); a gambling obsessed wife (JOBETH WILLIAMS); a sexy philandering divorcee (ELLEN BARKIN); and an abused child (ANNABETH GISH).

Desert Bloom was a family drama, but family dramas are a dime a dozen on television and they're not particularly interesting to journalists unless you have a "hook." My hook was the background of the story. Through meetings with the producers we determined that we would utilize that hook as much as possible to introduce the story to the journalists—to intrigue them.

During these initial meetings, you will also discover where you will be going to work, whether you will have a desk in the production office, access to a typewriter and xerox machine and an automobile. You will also be provided with materials such as an updated script, shooting schedule, roster of cast and crew and travel arrangements.

Meetings with your publicity superiors are important and usually brief. You will most likely go over the same questions you've asked the producers. More importantly, you will learn the chain of command, who you will be reporting to, who you will be copying memos to, who will be your liaison with the production.

Publicity executives are sympathetic to your position but they're often too busy to pay attention to advance strategy. That responsibility is on your shoulders. If you appear reasonably competent—and after reading the script and meeting with the producers you should be—they're going to let you act on your own. Usually they'll simply say, "Keep us informed." And that's all you'll do.

Publicity executives—whether at the studio, independent company or agency—like to hear what's going on and they like to have the opportunity to approve set visits, or various publicity breaks, but they generally let you do your job unencumbered. Just make sure they receive their memos. Also, their involvement in your day to day activities is going to depend on the type of film and where it is shooting. *Batman 3* will be a major priority to a studio executive if it's shooting on the lot. An unknown family drama lensing in Sri Lanka will be less of a priority.

■ **The Photo Department.** One of the key chains of command you must initially isolate is how to deal with still photographs. At the major studios, it's pretty simple—you deal directly with the photo editor. Your still photographer will ship unprocessed black and white and color transparency (slide) film to the studio photo department and you will get slides and black and white proof sheets in return—at a regular clip.

Studio photo editors are in a class by themselves. They carefully organize the materials your photographer sends back from the field and when it comes time to prepare the film's press kit, they will have already gone through and selected the key representative shots. They also prepare color slide mailings to magazine editors.

The photo editor is one of your most important studio contacts. As a unit publicist, you are going to need photos almost immediately. Whether it's a representative black and white shot for national distribution, some color transparencies that must immediately be sent to *Entertainment Tonight* or simply some shots of the director in action, your photo editor will handle the delivery.

An excellent relationship with the photo editor is a must because I may need photo materials in a hurry. Also, remember that the photo editor interacts with everyone back at the studio and if you're having a productive relationship, people are going to hear about it. The appearance of exciting photographic materials back at the studio is a sure sign that the publicity team is working.

The arrival of black and white proof sheets on the set is always a welcome sight. Even though it involves work—captioning, securing approvals from stars—the arrival of the photos is another way of showing the crew how you're working. Nothing documents a production better than good still photographs.

Bringing proof sheets and slides to their attention is also another way of developing a productive relationship with your actors. Many actors are nervous and insecure on a movie shoot. Even though there's no guarantee, in my experience the appearance of good looking still shots can and will restore some confidence in their work on the set. As comedian Billy Crystal's "Fernando" character used to say, "It is better to look good, than feel good."

Good still photos are interesting to everyone. Near the end of production, every important department head is going to be asking you for permission to flip through the book of proof sheets to select "souvenir" or "portfolio" shots.

■ **No Photo Editor?** What do you do if you don't have a photo editor? This is a common problem for independent film companies who work outside the studio environment. It's a step by step procedure. First, make sure your still photographer has set up a relationship with a responsible film laboratory.

Still photographers can either have material developed on location (if a reputable lab is available), or material can be sent back to one of the many Los Angeles-based labs that specialize in processing motion picture still and slide film.

The LA labs are great to work with and they can easily send material back to location. They can also print the name of the film and the photographer on each slide and proof sheet. They're usually organized and professional so working directly with them will not be a problem. It's a good idea to contact the lab directly and get on a first name basis with their order personnel. Again they may be needed in a pinch.

Whereas the studio photo editor will be the repository for all photographic materials, on an independent shoot that responsibility falls on your shoulders. You will be collecting all of the proof sheets and slides and storing them in your office (or hotel room) until you arrive back home. And whereas the studio photo editor will order materials for you, now you will have to deal directly with the lab. Again, not a problem if you've developed the proper relationships.

For various reasons, the still photographer may also order material. That's fine as long as it's done through you. You don't want to confuse the lab with too many people calling in still orders.

Once an independent shoot is finished, those photo materials will be turned in to an executive with the company. They then become the company's responsibility. Sometimes the company has hired an independent public relations agency to handle P.R. In that case, photos can be deposited with the agency publicist. Whatever you do, sever your tie with the production by delivering the photo materials in an organized fashion. Those materials are as good as gold and the last thing you want is a phone call a month down the line asking whatever happened to the still photographs.

One last point. In terms of proof sheets for your black and white photos, you must determine up front how many you will need.

Usually, you will need one, the studio or agency will need one, and in some cases the producer will need one. Try not to order more than three or four. One set of color transparencies is plenty.

Meeting Cast and Crew on the Set.

You've made your home base contacts—publicity executives, photo editors, support personnel, agency publicists—and you know the key production personnel—producers, director, writer—now it's time to move to the actual set and introduce yourself to key members of the cast and crew.

From the publicist's point of view, everyone on a movie set is important, from Mr. Superstar to the lowliest go-fer. Their assistance, their backgrounds, their awareness of what is going on around them (it's great to have extra pairs of eyes) makes your job more interesting and effective. And because you have the time and freedom of movement, you can spend the course of the shoot getting to know as many people as you want.

I have known of publicists who remain entirely aloof from the crew, spending the bulk of their time on the phone and then coming out to the set for brief periods, hanging out with the actors and heading home. I think that attitude is common and partially responsible for the fact that no one knows what we do. If you don't introduce yourself to key personnel on the film set, I really feel you're not doing your job.

There are stories all over the film set, and the only way to learn what's happening is to make friends with personnel in the various departments. Movie sets are like summer camp. You develop a number of friendships over a two or three month period and then it is over and time to move on to another job. You will, however, never forget these people.

Certainly, the actors are my principal responsibility. My first job is to introduce myself to each actor and make sure they know who I am, what I am going to do, and where I can be found.

Be aware of the actor's attitude toward publicity by asking him directly. Don't be afraid to be honest and forthright. This is your job.

Initially, a simple introduction is all you need from the actor. You can get into publicity strategy later when the actor gets comfortable on the set. Aside from asking them to review an old biography, I try to leave my actors alone for the first week to 10 days. It takes a while for them to get used to their new surroundings as well. And remember there's always a great deal of pressure on the actor at the start of a production. They're learning a new character, learning to relate to the director, learning to deal with the demands of the film. You don't want to add to that pressure. Say hello and skedaddle for now.

There are other important people to introduce yourself to on the set, including:

■ **The Production Manager.** This is the producer's right arm, the person who makes things run smoothly on the set. Every detail, every piece of equipment, every transportation order runs through the production manager's office. An army master sergeant has less responsibility than the production manager.

The production manager will be one of the first people you'll meet, because he'll usually assign you to a desk, a typewriter, and a car and a hotel room. If you need any piece of equipment, access to any form of transportation, or if there is ever a specific problem on the set, go to the production manager. Here is a vital problem solver.

■ **The Location Manager.** If you're working on location, away from the studio, the location manager is your key to understanding how to get to specific location filming sites. He will be supplying the company with proper maps and specific directions. From the publicist's point of view, the location manager can also be a good source of information on the background or history of a specific location—information that comes in handy when compiling production notes.

■ **The First Assistant Director.** The director's right arm. How do you spot the first assistant director? He's usually the one who quiets the set and initiates the rolling of the cameras before the director shouts action. First assistants are generally the most imposing people on the set. They're whip crackers who keep the film moving. They also have to know exactly what is happening at all times from all department heads. When the director asks a question, the first assistant has to have an answer ready immediately.

The first assistant should always be pre-briefed if you're going to have a journalist or film crew on the set. If he knows you're coming, he can brief his own crew on the fact that "visitors" will be on the set. First assistants are also good sources of information. You don't want to bother the producer, director, production manager if you don't have to. Their minds are always filled with a thousand questions and priorities. Not that the first assistant isn't extremely busy too, but he's generally more accessible. Befriend the first assistant and get to know his team—the second and third assistant directors and the production assistants. They all should know who you are.

■ **The Costume Designer.** There could be a story in the costumes, especially if they're of an unusual nature.

■ **The Special Effects Director.** A perfect subject for coverage in the effects magazines. If journalists are coming to the set from more mainstream publications, they should always be introduced to the head of special effects because stories about their work—especially in a film which is heavily laden with special effects—could prove fascinating to general audiences.

■ **The Stunt Men and Women.** Again, a very active and unusual profession on the set, of likely interest to journalists, depending on the film.

■ **The Sound Mixer.** Another good pair of eyes for you and usually a talkative source. Since the sound mixers are working directly with the actors, placing their hidden microphones, making sure that sound clarity is excellent on every take, they also know the temperament of the actors. If you haven't been to the set all day for one reason or another, you can hang out with the sound team and get a feeling for what's going on.

- **Make-up Artists and Hair Stylists.** Always important people to know because they are forever tied to your actors. When journalists are on the set, and you're coordinating interview time or photo time, you'll always be interacting with make-up and hair simply because that's where actors can usually be found when they're not on the set or in their dressing room.

  Make-up artists and hair stylists are usually the most interesting people on the set—a real throw-back to the glamour of old Hollywood. They have great stories, they take great pride in their work and they usually have the coziest relationships with the actors. I try to hang out with these specialists because they add a certain dimension to the atmosphere of the set and their stories could lead to more fodder for my press kit especially if the make-up and hair is of an unusual type. They're also a good source of information when it comes to determining the temperament of your actors on any given day.

- **Casting Director.** Another good source of information on the background of actors—particularly the unknown ones.

- **Production Secretaries.** They can be your lifeblood in terms of how smoothly your office work flows. The fact that they take messages for you is alone an important reason for befriending them and keeping them on your side. Your line of communications is a vital link between you and the outside world. A single message could have an important impact on what is happening on the set. Keep the production secretaries happy. Message taking is the one area I allow to be handled by someone else. In terms of office work—typing, copying, filing—my experience is that you shouldn't bother the production secretaries with it. They're usually busy with the details of the movie so don't depend too much on office personnel to do your job. Having a hands-on knowledge of the company copy machine is definitely one of your priorities on a movie set.

9

GETTING SET UP ON LOCATION

I remember well my first motion picture unit publicity assignment. It was on *Endangered Species*. I arrived at the airport in Los Angeles for a trip to Sheridan, Wyoming where I would be spending approximately 10 weeks. As the plane boarded, an assistant director with a clipboard and a sign saying ENDANGERED SPECIES was checking off our names. I felt like a paratrooper about to land in World War II. What's the Army's main slogan—"It's not a job, it's an adventure." Well, welcome to the movie business.

Once you get to location, you have to spend some time setting up your office. You're meeting a lot of people, shaking a lot of hands, smiling, nervously greeting major actors, identifying the key players, tasting the new climate, hearing stories about the food and accommodations from the location manager who has already been on location for over a month.

First off, locate your desk or your assigned area. Amazing as it might seem, the unit publicist isn't always in the forefront of everyone's mind. So your appearance on location could be a surprise to the production manager. Don't be shocked if you don't have a desk, phone, typewriter or supplies. But be assured that this can be remedied quickly.

The production secretary has immediate access to furniture and equipment rental people and things can move quickly. Your most important tools are your telephone, your typewriter and your rental car.

You must have your own phone instrument. You will probably make more long distance calls than anyone on the set (unless the teen actress has a boyfriend back in LA), and you must have a phone in the production office where someone can take messages.

Sometimes there isn't any room for you in the production office. Production offices can be pretty tiny. On a three month shoot in

Calgary, Alberta, I set up shop in my hotel room. I rented a typewriter, had access to a phone and handled things. But I didn't like it. I try to spend as much time as possible in the production office.

Being strategically placed in the production office is important. You'll find yourself close to the main artery of the production. You get to know people faster, you strengthen relationships—things get done faster. When the assistant directors come racing back after a day of shooting, they come to the production office and if you haven't been to the set that day you can find out how things went. You get a call sheet which explains the extent of the shoot for tomorrow and you're immediately up on what's happening on the movie. When you're somewhere else, isolation can set in.

When it comes to a rental car, I won't take no for an answer. You can't perform your job by relying on company transportation. Your schedule is too informal to rely on a teamster's production vehicle and you certainly don't go to the set every morning on the crew bus. A rental car keeps you mobile and allows you to develop your own schedule and priorities.

Unlike the cast and crew, which is confined to the set every day, you have other duties and places to be. These include:

✔ Mail runs to the local post office

✔ Visits to the local newspaper, radio and TV station

✔ Trips to the airport to pick up visiting journalists and usher them out to the set.

✔ Visits to local officials to set up press conferences, interviews, lectures, personal appearances (you may be addressing the local Kiwanis or Lions Club)

✔ Quick visits to and from the set. You may need to ask a quick question, get a picture signed, gets stills okayed, alert an actor to an upcoming interview. And then you have to return to the production office.

✔ Trips to and from the hotel.

Depending on the film, the distance of the locations and the location of the hotel and production office, you may have other off the set responsibilities. Access to a car is thus vital. If you're on a film with a limited budget, you may have an argument with the production manager. But don't let an argument start. Go to your producer and explain your situation.

Even the teamsters, one of Hollywood's most powerful unions, understand that publicist's needn't rely on company transportation. In fact, the teamster captain usually becomes one of your most staunch allies. Not having to drive you around allows him to free up a man for more important, regimented duties. Get that car!

Some other quick rules about setting up shop.

✔ Again, do your own typing and copying. It is not the responsibility of the production secretary.

✔ Utilize the production office mailing system. If there is a postal meter, get to know it yourself. Production office personnel can be enlisted for large mailings if you need help.

✔ In terms of message taking, alert the secretaries or receptionists as to the importance of those messages. There are major national journalists whom you need to speak with.

✔ Once you have your space, take over. Put up a sign on or over your desk identifying that space as the Publicity Department. Once identified, you're less in danger of being invaded by stray production personnel who are in need of a desk. You're also publicizing yourself. The crew will know that "the publicist is on duty."

✔ Learn as much about the town and the surrounding area as possible. Routes to set, local restaurants (for taking the press to lunch), etc. Your location manager is a good source for maps.

Working With the Still Photographer.

The publicist on the movie set has a strong ally in the still photographer. Together, you will be responsible for documenting what happens during the course of the shoot. Between your sparkling production notes and daily calls to the nation's media, the public will begin to know that your film exists. The still photographer will illustrate your campaign.

In the heyday of the old studio system, the still photographers were treated like the great artists of history. Hollywood's approach in those days—the whole fantasy world of glamour, mystique and sex appeal—was spurred on by the amazing attention to detail it paid to its stars and the careful planning of their everyday lives. Still photography was very much a part of all that. Just look at portraits of Clark Gable, Jean Harlow, Barbara Stanwyck and Vivian Leigh and every other major star of the 1930s and 1940s. Their look was very carefully conceived. The bigger than life status they enjoyed was very much due to how they were presented to the public—glamour photography of the era was quite an art form.

Glamour today? Where? Still photographers are still with us but like many of Hollywood's most important crafts, the exacting standards practiced in the golden age, have fallen. There are excellent still photographers today, but they are a small elite group. Hollywood's superstars are photographed for magazine covers with a certain degree of style, but often the magazines provide their own photographers and settings. And for every film that spends a few careful hours with Mel Gibson and Sigourney Weaver, there are 20 that take no care whatsoever in preparing the photographic coverage on the film.

As a publicity director working on independent films, I'm often shocked at the quality of stills I see—mostly from films that shoot without a publicist supervising the location. Like publicity, still photography is seldom understood by the producer or, for that matter, anyone else on the crew. Astonishingly, actors often avoid photo coverage just like they avoid interviews. I've seen photographers abused by both actors and crew.

The still photographer on a motion picture has one of the most difficult jobs. He or she is on the set all day long. They get up at the crack of dawn and ride to location on the same bus that carries the assistant directors, propsmen and grips. During the course of the film they will shoot thousands and thousands of black and white stills and color slides.

Those thousands of pictures will eventually be culled down to a handful of representative shots which will go in the press kit and be supplied to national magazines. If the still photography is excellent, and there are stars working on the film, the chances improve for national magazine coverage. If there are no usable stills or nothing beyond pure normal coverage, major opportunities could be missed.

See *Premiere* magazine with Mel Gibson on the cover or Sigourney Weaver on the cover of *Life* or Sean Connery on the cover of *Rolling Stone*—those shots and many like them were taken either on the set of their respective motion pictures, or in carefully prepared "special" sessions. With stars of that caliber, a very specific photography plan must be engineered during production. Once filming is completed, those stars will travel on to their next project and there is a good chance the photographic opportunities will not be present again.

Getting Good Stills. During that first meeting with your still photographer, take some time to strategize the shoot. Still requirements can be broken down into several key areas.

■ **Portraits.** Mel Gibson's shot on the cover of *Premiere* is a "portrait"—usually taken under specially engineered conditions away from the film set. Photographers can set up portrait sessions almost anywhere provided they have the right equipment, access to a studio, and the cooperation of the actor and the publicist. The major studio publicity departments often have the luxury of planning special portrait sessions after the film is finished shooting. They have the muscle to get Mel or Sigourney or Goldie or Sean into their studios where their very high-priced portrait photographers, hired for the occasion, will shoot the portraits that will appear on the national magazine covers.

As a publicist on the set, I can't be thinking about what the studio might be able to do down the line. I can't afford to assume there will be a "down the line." The still photographer and I are responsible for coverage now. And every portrait completed on the set is one less portrait that will be needed many months later when publicity directors are trying desperately to present the film to the media in the best possible light.

A note on "special photographers." Given a budget for "special photography," the film company may hire a special photographer to cover a certain aspect of the shoot which also may include portraits. Amazing as it may seem, there are still superstar photographers like Annie Liebowitz and Steve Schapiro, who, if available and interested, will come to the set like visiting media, and shoot the stars.

Special photographers often have easier access to the national magazines and provided you have the star power, you have a reasonable chance of getting coverage in the magazines if you invite the "special" to the set. They're a luxury item, though, and if you have a competent still photographer on the set, you can accomplish the same tasks without spending the extra money.

Sometimes all the special work in the world accomplished in post production can't duplicate what you can do on the set. One of my favorite accomplishments occurred on the John Hughes film, *Pretty in Pink*. In that film, we had three very youthful photogenic stars— Molly Ringwald, Andrew McCarthy and Jon Cryer.

I knew a three-shot of the group would be useful but it was difficult to get all three actors together because they had separate schedules. Molly had scenes with Jon, and scenes with Andrew, but Andrew and Jon never had scenes together. I finally found a day where Molly and Andrew were working together and Jon had the day off. Thankfully, Jon was cooperative enough to come in on his day off, get into costume, and be available for the three-shot.

As it turned out, I had approximately ten minutes to work with my still photographer, Laurel Moore, to set up the shot. We grabbed the actors and went behind a building in Santa Monica where we were shooting. Director Howard Deutsch joined us and we carefully utilized those ten minutes.

Little did I know that those wonderful three shots would become the poster art for the entire film.

■ **Scene Stills**. The majority of the stills and slides taken by the still photographer will be scene shots—pictures of the actors performing in the film's various scenes. Still photographers spend hours on the set clicking away with their cameras enclosed in a "blimp" housing which masks the sound of the shutter. Over the course of a sixty day shoot, they're going to take 6-10,000 pictures of the movie.

Scene stills showing the actors in dramatic or action oriented poses are the most important element of the shoot. They literally tell the story of the movie in pictures. However, because still photography is not a priority on the set—the will of the director and the need of the movie comes first—there are times when the actors are not in positions conducive to being photographed.

It is the responsibility of the still photographer, with the help of the publicist, to wait until a scene is finished and then pose the actors for a dramatic still shot. If Robert Mitchum is squaring off against John

Wayne in a small room and the only place the still photographer can shoot from is behind John Wayne's back, it's not going to make for a great photograph.

The photographer must get up after the scene is finished and reposition the actors so that a still shot can be taken. We call them "photographic opportunities" and they cannot be missed.

Recently I was looking at a black and white still book from a movie in which the two lead actors appear together in only a few scenes. Not once did the still photographer take a decent photo of them together.

I'm always looking for "photographic opportunities." It's part of my job. Whether you find them often depends on the location, the temperament of the actors, the mood on the set and whether there's enough time to accomplish the job.

Usually, photographic opportunities pay off. They become poster art, book covers, magazine covers, album covers, etc.

■ **Behind the Scenes Shots**. When a film goes into production, it's a story and to help illustrate that story you should build a good set of behind the scene shots or crew action shots. This is certainly logical when the director is a major name like Coppola, Spielberg, Lucas or DePalma. But it also applies to unknowns. Those unknowns could be the Spielbergs of tomorrow.

The film magazines such as *Premiere*, *American Cinematographer*, *American Film* and *Film Comment*, also like these kinds of shots because they show another side of film making—the inside.

Behind the scenes shots are also useful during a particularly large set piece action sequence. If you've ever seen the photo shoot on some of the great historical epic films of the past, some of the most interesting and unusual shots are those that show the crew relaxing. Kirk Douglas in full *Spartacus* regalia, chumming with director Stanley Kubrick in standard 1960s civilian clothes. An exhausted Audie Murphy in World War II battle dress posing for still photographers on the set of *To Hell and Back*. Michael Rennie surrounded by crew members preparing the set of *The Day The Earth Stood Still*.

Those shots became historical treasures.

■ **Special Photographic Requests**. On the set you get a lot of strange requests. Your job is to make sure everything moves smoothly, so fulfilling even the strangest of requests becomes your duty. The production manager may request that an actor pose in front of a store that has been extra helpful to the production. The studio may request that you shoot certain products that are being used in the context of the movie—shots that can then be sent to the company headquarters to pave the way for promotions closer to release time.

An actor's family may suddenly appear on the set and he might ask you to shoot a few pics. Or the mayor might appear, or the sheriff, or the president of the chamber of commerce. It's all basic public relations. Alert your photographer and accomplish these shots professionally.

Make a habit of checking in with your photographer on a daily basis. You are a team and don't forget that.

■ **Photographic Approvals.** Stars have a lot of power on the film set and they have the right to approve still photos and slides before they are sent back to the studio for distribution to the press. It's written into their contract.

If a star has such approval, get them materials as soon as they are developed. If you've waited the whole shoot to start approving stills, you're in trouble. Not only are you not supplying any approved photos to important media, but you're about to lose your actor. And you certainly don't want that actor to take the shots back home with him. So get busy.

The actor should be provided with a grease pencil to mark an "x" across black and white shots that appear on the proof shoot; a "lupe" magnifier which will allow him to see the shots clearly; and the developed proof sheets and slides.

In my experience, actors will simply keep the rejected slides and dispose of them. That's okay, provided that enough shots are approved. Usually a contract says that an actor must approve 50% of all photos. Make sure that's enforced. Some studios or independent companies have different rules for dealing with rejected transparencies, so before you allow your actor to keep his "kills," discuss it with your photo editor.

You should be sending proof sheets and slides over to the actor on a regular basis. Don't let them pile up. The sooner photos are approved, the sooner you can caption them and ship them off to the studio or lab.

Once a black and white photo is rejected by the actor with a slash across the frame on the proof sheet, keep a record of it. You can type the rejected numbers on a piece of paper and then send them off to the studio or lab. In that way, your support folks back home can keep a running tab on what's been approved and what's been rejected.

Color slides are already numbered. Since the actor is usually disposing of the slides himself, you don't have to keep a running log of color slide rejects.

I do like to cull through and collect a group of good usable color slides as my "production key set." I can then send these back to the lab and have multiple copies made. If any magazine has an art request, I can supply them with approved shots from the key set.

What can be confusing about approvals is if more than one actor has the same right in their contract. Simply put, if three actors have 50% approval, you could possibly lose most of your shots.

Obviously, actors cannot hold onto the rejected slides if other actors must see them. Have the actor make a small colored mark in a corner of the slide if they wish it rejected. In terms of the black and white proof sheet, continue to have them mark an "x" with a grease pencil. You're just going to have to hope that you end up with enough usable shots for a key set. Instead of sending the book with actor A's kills to Actor B, get Actor B his own set of b/w proofs. Generally, you don't want actors seeing each other's b/w kills.

■ **Captioning**. Since you are on the film set and you are the first marketing specialist to meet cast and crew, it is your responsibility to caption the photos.

Here is another difficult chore. The major studios usually require that you caption every single black and white frame—which can number 10,000 photos during the course of a shoot. It's a long, tedious process that is simply part of your job.

In terms of the color, you're normally asked to caption only your key list of shots. Otherwise, you'd be duplicating the black and white captions (since photographers usually shoot the same scene with both black and white and color).

Captioning is extremely useful when you're dealing with unknown actors or crew members who pop up in final press kit or key set photos. Someone should always have a record somewhere of who is in those photos.

10

Locking-in Your Written Materials and Sending Them Out

Before you begin your phone campaign to the national media, you must lock-in and distribute your written materials. Anyone can call up the media and request coverage. The intelligent publicist carefully prepares the media for a call by first sending in the advance production notes and a first class pitch letter.

The Advance Production Notes Package.

A well-prepared set of materials is essential if you're going to get the kind of coverage you want from the national media. There are no formulas, but the following checklist will help you make sure to include all the essential elements.

✔ The whole package should be 10-15 pages, no more. One page for your presentation statement; two pages of information on the film's story line and locations; and 7-10 pages of biographies, depending on the number of stars and key production personnel you have. Note that behind the scenes material, a key element of the final press kit, will be added later when the shoot is finished.

✔ All materials should look crisp and clean. Hire a professional typist if your typing skills are less than professional. Don't accept anything less than perfect copies either. Photocopies that are crooked or smudged give the appearance that you don't care about your work. I supervise my own copying and I carefully arrange, collate and staple the finished product. Since the distribution of advance press kit information will take place on location, there is the temptation to give this somewhat tedious task to one of the production assistants. Forget it. Handle it yourself. Presentation counts!

✔ All materials should be double spaced.

✔ A title page should feature the name of the film centered in the middle of the page and the words "production information" centered underneath the title. The name of the production company and your address and phone should be typed in the bottom right corner.

✔ Plain copier paper is fine for this set of materials. I don't use any form of bond paper, erasable paper or stationery. Your pitch letter can be typed on the latter.

✔ The materials should be mailed, along with the pitch letter, in a 9" x 12" envelope (I prefer white over "natural.")

✔ Always use first class mail.

✔ Never release anything for copying and distribution unless it has been carefully proof-read by someone other than yourself. You may be an outstanding writer and scrupulously careful about mistakes but don't trust your own eyes to be the only proof-readers. Always have someone whose intelligence you admire proof-read everything you write.

✔ Make sure all advance production notes are approved by the Producer, Studio Publicity Chief, or Agency Publicist. In rare instances, it may be necessary to send your advance materials out to an important journalist before you have received final approval. What I do is type "NOT APPROVED / NOT FOR DISTRIBUTION / FOR BACKGROUND ONLY" on the front page. Then I make sure to follow up with an approved set just as soon as it is available.

The Pitch Letter.

When you pitch the media you are competing with hundreds of publicists who are pitching simultaneously, each trying to appear more interesting and appealing than the next. Your job is to a) perfectly present your project in the best possible light; b) be direct and specific about what you have to offer and what you would like the media to do; and c) give your pitch a personal touch so that the media person feels as if he's dealing with a person and not a computer print-out.

Even if you're pitching 200 media people at once, don't send out form letter pitches, addressed "Dear Media Person." I personally address and direct all my pitches, carefully typing in the salutation and making sure the letter goes to a specific person. Think about it, we get hundreds of pieces of mail each year that are mere form letters (even if Ed McMahon's picture appears on it). How often do we get a specific letter, directed to us, and signed by someone. In this day of automation and computer generated mailings, a personal letter is still to be prized.

I would very much recommend that you become familiar with "word processing" on a computer. In the past, I would make 200 copies of the body of my letter and then carefully type in the name, address and salutation at the top of the letterhead. I was careful to make sure that the address information and salutation was even with the body copy, but I hated having to be so careful and having to re-type things when I made mistakes. Thanks to computers and their attached printers, now each letter can be individually "typed" and all you have to do is change a few words on the screen for each one and tell the computer PRINT.

Personal touches get noticed. Don't hesitate to send letters to those media people you do know with a personal salutation—"Dear Jack." On the other hand, pretending to be on a first name basis with someone is bad form. I always sign every letter, even if I'm sending out 500 copies. There's nothing more impersonal than an unsigned letter.

Media Lists.

Acquiring an effective list of important motion picture journalists is an on-going task. Publicists are normally hesitant to help other publicists by passing on their list of contacts. Fortunately, there are some good reference sources available.

Start with the "Domestic Press Directory" of the Motion Picture Association of America. This lists all media people in the LA area who are accredited by the major studios (they attend industry screenings and receive all press releases). Probably 75% of the movie journalism community in Los Angeles is on this list. Contact the MPAA (they're on Ventura Blvd. in Sherman Oaks). The book sells for about $35.00 and you receive periodic updates on new journalists.

Unfortunately, while the book is heavy on its writers, it does not include many magazine and newspaper editors, television and radio reporters, and any New York based, or national contacts.

Initially you should send your advance production notes to:

✔ Key LA press—newspaper, magazine, television and radio.

✔ Key NYC press—newspaper, magazine, television and radio.

✔ National newspaper journalists—top 25 markets.

✔ Any press person with national reach, wherever they live.

✔ A list of key studio and independent executives. In addition to providing your superiors with a copy of the advance notes, it doesn't hurt to pass them on to key executives at the branch offices (if you're working with a major), or advertising agencies who regularly service your studio or independent company. Contact your head of distribution and find out if any key exhibitors should be serviced. There are exhibitor marketing people who would appreciate hearing early details about a new movie.

Also remember, if your advance kit is well written, use it as a calling card. It's showing everyone in the universe that you can write and that you are doing your job properly. No one can sit and monitor your phone calls to see if you are good at what you do, but people will always read your notes to see if they are good. Make sure they are.

To acquire a good New York press list, purchase the New York Media Outlets directory. It runs a little over $100 and is a generic media directory not specifically tuned to movie journalists, but at least, it lists all the outlets. You then have to go through it and check off the important ones and find the contact you need. The same company that puts out the NYC directory also publishes a national TV outlets directory which lists every television station in the country and every talk show produced; a California Metro media directory which is a west coast counterpart to the New York Media Outlet directory; and a national Family Pages directory which covers all the papers who feature "lifestyle" type sections which include movie coverage.

Personally, I would acquire all of these directories for your library. And don't fret, you will be updating and changing your media list constantly. It's a chore. Another way of acquiring names, especially magazine editors, is to simply buy the key publications and read the masthead.

There are two ways to do mailing labels once you have gathered your list of names. The old fashioned way is to type the names on a form which can be photocopied onto pressure sensitive mailing labels. The modern way is to use a computer. There are lots of programs which can help you maintain your names and addresses, and print them out on labels with very little effort.

A word of caution about dispersing production notes. While it is standard procedure to precede publicity pitches with written materials, be sure to discuss this matter with your superiors before you send out *anything*. Some studio P.R. departments frown on initial mass mailings, especially when the set is closed. Also, there are instances, especially on films with major stars where you can start your phone calls to the media without mailing advance production notes. This happens on the big pictures, but most of the time a mailing of notes followed by a phone call is good practice.

11

YOUR FIRST CALLS TO THE MEDIA

You've completed your dispersal of advance production materials. You're safely ensconced in your production office cubicle. The movie is in production. It's time to hit the phones.

Actually, your first responsibility it to get stories placed that announce the actual start of production. The fact that cameras are about to roll on your movie could guarantee you some instant coverage. These outlets include:

■ *Entertainment Tonight*. If they get a color slide early enough, you could get an announcement and a photo on the air. Consider start of production stories for the other television entertainment news shows as well. These include: Group W's *Entertainment Report*; cable's 24 hour E! Entertainment Channel; the Showtime and Movie Channel entertainment news segments; MTV's *The Big Picture* (especially if the movie has strong music elements); USA Network's *Hollywood Insider* and any other program you can research that deals with immediate news in Hollywood.

■ *Los Angeles Times*. If the story is big enough, it might get into their "Morning Report" news column in "Daily Calendar"; or if there is an unusual angle, it could become a Sunday "Outtakes" piece. Other columns to be considered for start of production stories are: Larry Van Gelder's Friday movie column in the *New York Times*; Bob Thomas' entertainment column distributed by the *Associated Press*; and others.

■ **Gossip Columnists.** By all means, supply materials to every gossip columnist, but for the major outlets, come up with a different angle for each. Remember, wherever they are, whenever they publish, all gossip columnists consider themselves in competition with one another. Customize pitches to Army Archerd at *Daily Variety*; Robert Osborne at *The Hollywood Reporter*; Marilyn Beck; Liz Smith; Larry King at *USA Today*; "Page 6" in the *New York Post*; the "INC."

column in the *Chicago Tribune*; and the "Hollywood Freeway" column in the *Los Angeles Daily News*.

- **National Newspaper Entertainment Reporters.** I have a list of newspapers in the top 30 markets and their journalists who cover the movie scene. Chances are that they will not be coming to your set, so it's important that you keep them supplied with a continual stream of written materials. Start of production information should be definitely sent to them because they feature weekly movie coverage in their columns.

- **National Magazines.** I consider these outlets extremely important and they fall into three categories:

✔ Mass Market Consumer Magazines with short lead times, including *Time*, *Newsweek*, *U.S. News and World Report*, *People Magazine* and *US*. These important national outlets operate on short deadlines, as little as a week, so they can get material into their pages quickly. Get into the habit of sending them something on a regular basis. Good quality color photos will be appreciated throughout the shoot. But before you send photos, discuss the pitch with your publicity superior.

✔ Mass Market Consumer Magazines with long lead times, including *Cosmopolitan*, *Esquire*, *Premiere*, *Vanity Fair* and *Mademoiselle*. It is not uncommon for magazines of this ilk to have 4-5 month lead times.

If you're working on a film that is shooting September 1st, *Vogue* magazine may already be working on its February issue. If your movie is tentatively scheduled for a summer release, then you had better hurry and get something going with that publication. You could blink twice and miss their pre-release issue(s).

Your objective is to at least get a picture and some production information into any column that features movies in these publications. It's important to make a prioritized call list and be sure to get materials to publications that are going to press well before their deadlines. It's tough to break into national magazines, especially when many of the "women's magazines" use very little material from new movies. They will do major celebrity interviews on a regular basis, but you may be working on a movie without major stars.

✔ Special Interest Publications. Depending on the subject matter of the movie, you will be contacting special interest publications also known as "genre publications." Almost all genre publications need plenty of lead time so be sure to contact this group early.

If you're working on a science fiction, fantasy or horror film, then you must immediately contact such publications as *Starlog*, *Cinefex* and *Cinefantastique*. These magazines specialize in movie coverage and if treated properly, will give you excellent coverage. Their writers love to visit the set where they get into incredibly detailed conversations with writers, directors, actors and especially make-up and special effects people.

You can research special interest publications at any well-stocked newsstand or at a large public library. A film with a scientific angle might be of interest to publications like *Omni*, or *Scientific American* or *Popular Science*. War movies fit into the scope of *Soldier of Fortune* or *Vietnam* or *Seapower*.

In contacting these outlets, approach the situation from two directions. By all means, send production notes to the magazine editors, but also consider supplying information to freelancers.

Editors determine the types of articles for each issue and they must be approached first and foremost. Freelance writers can also generate new story ideas on their own. If you can get a freelancer interested, they can start pitching the story too, thereby giving your film double attention.

The *Domestic Press Directory* of the Motion Picture Association of America contains an excellent list of freelance writers.

Responses— Is the Campaign Working?

Publicity efforts during production, as we have seen, involve mainly making sure all the outlets know about your movie. After you've sent out your press materials and made your calls, you've done about all you can.

You don't have to break in every paper, magazine and TV show now. Remember, you are laying important groundwork for the post-production and pre-release publicity and promotion campaign as well. Unless you come across as an unprofessional idiot, you are going to get your share of breaks—a column item here, a photograph there, some wire stories and trade stories. Every break is important because it is something you can immediately show to your bosses—the producer and the studio P.R. department. You always want to keep them happy.

Despite any pressure they put on you to perform, remember that you have absolutely no control over what the press prints or says about your project. You could mount the most fabulous production publicity campaign, and get very few breaks. But because of your effort, the publicists who work on the film later will be dealing with an informed and interested press.

You must document everything you do. The publicity response memos that you compose will be of immeasurable value during the post-production and pre-release period. In this regard, you become an intelligence gatherer. Your comments on the relative interest in your movie shown by the various publications and television shows will become a blueprint for future publicity activities, so be concise.

Let's talk about the types of responses you will get from your pitches:

- **Immediate Interest**. Journalists will actually call you at location and ask about interview possibilities. If you're working on the latest Dustin Hoffman, Tom Cruise, Sylvester Stallone or Steven Spielberg project, you're going to feel like a traffic cop, trying to let a few top journalists through the crowd onto the set (if the filmmakers will allow it).

  There's no way to judge journalist interest in a project, but any film may generate calls for a variety of reasons. Deal quickly and efficiently with each request. If the journalist wants to come to set, determine his or her importance and get the proper approval.

  Never invite anyone to set without getting approval from your superior. Set visits, especially if you're on a distant location, should be reserved for a select few VIP journalists like Jim Brown of *The Today Show*, or an *Entertainment Tonight* crew or a top freelance interviewer with major magazine contacts. Too many journalist visits might cause logistical problems and also be upsetting to the cast and crew.

  Now there's always the possibility that your film is so big that the publicity department back home decides to have an entire press junket to location. In that case, you might be accommodating 25 journalists on the set. But that is rare.

  My experience is that actors working on a film are not very interested or excited about speaking with the press—in fact most of the time you can count on them to be downright uncooperative. After all, they have the pressure of making the movie on their minds. So, if you overload them with press interviews, you're going to run into problems.

  If journalists come to set, schedule their visit toward the end of production when actors are more comfortable with the film experience. At that time, *they will also have more to say*. Unless an emergency develops, never schedule any press visits in the first three weeks of shooting. You're just beginning to develop a rapport with cast and crew, don't rush it.

  Again, don't judge the success of your campaign by the number of set visits you organize. While some may call for actual visiting privileges, others will ask for written materials, photographs and telephone interviews with cast and crew. These requests will turn into column items, photographs, production stories, and more in-depth coverage "down the line."

- **Interest "Down the Line."** The entertainment journalist is a finicky bird. Sometimes, they'll move heaven and earth to come to the set. Other times, they couldn't care less about your movie.

  Journalists do have their own priorities. A negative response to your pitch could simply mean that: a) they're too busy with other stories to give yours much attention; b) they're not sure if the movie is the type they like to cover; or c) they're in a lousy mood and nothing looks good right now.

I mention "mood" because it's a factor in publicist/journalist conversations. Haven't you ever answered the phone when one of those telephone sales pitchers is trying to stick you with a year's subscription to a magazine you would never even look at, and, because you were in a good mood, you let them talk for a full five minutes before you said no?

If the journalist is quick and to the point with you, go into your down the line approach. Down the Line is one of my pet phrases during a pitching campaign. With this approach, every pitch is a win-win situation. First, no journalist is going to categorically say no if you offer to send additional materials and call back at a later date. "Perhaps we can come up with an appropriate angle down the line" then becomes a typical summation.

For example, you pitch one of the gossip columns in *People Magazine*. The editor likes the idea, but really can't make a decision without looking at some interesting photographs. You offer to send the photos when they become available, and the editor agrees.

Or, the *Los Angeles Times* "Calendar" section is interested in the fact that a certain composer is involved with your film's music. Although, the editor is not interested in a set visit, he thinks the music department might be intrigued by a piece on the composer, perhaps during the scoring phase of the movie. Keep in touch and provide ongoing materials.

All of these responses come into play. You'll place photos and column items, some on a national basis as well as a few set visit stories, but much of your work on the film's production publicity campaign will involve the preparation of "leads" to follow-up in the post production and pre-release period.

One of the realities of publicity coverage is that many journalists, particularly those who write for magazines, will not make up their mind about a story idea until they get a chance to attend an actual screening of the film. That is why so much is accomplished in the pre-release period (1-3 months prior to release). Making an editorial decision however, at that point, eliminates many of the long-lead magazine outlets which should be your priority during production.

TV, Radio and newspaper journalists have shorter deadlines and can get something going prior to the film's release. Still, I like to pitch everyone immediately because you go for your best positive scenario— multiple coverage in each outlet. Three breaks in the *NY Times* are better than one.

- **No Interest.** There are no guarantees when you pitch journalists. Some are going to give you a "no" outright. And there's nothing you can do about it. Don't embarrass yourself by pleading. This isn't your Uncle Harry. Generally you don't have that kind of relationship with the media. There will be times when you call in a favor or two, but if a journalist says no, I never question the call.

First, you have too many calls to make and too much ground to cover to waste time with one journalist who is intransigent. And, as I said above, even a negative response now could become positive if the journalist receives additional material down the line.

If the producers of the movie or your P.R. superiors question you on why certain outlets haven't covered the film, you simply tell them the truth. Remember, there are no guarantees in P.R.

12

WORKING WITH THE LOCAL MEDIA

If only the national media outlets had the enthusiasm and tenacity of the local journalist. Life for the publicist could be very easy. No matter what others may say or feel, the local journalist is not a pest. I don't care if she represents a paper with one subscriber, she deserves as much cooperation as possible.

The local media? We're referring to outlets that service the community where the film is shooting. It might be the Armed Forces radio station in Manila, or the Lions Club newsletter in Moab, Utah, or the Buffalo News.

In the scheme of the marketing master plan, none of these outlets are going to have a dramatic effect, but if they feel that they are not getting serious attention or cooperation, they can cause trouble that will have a definite effect on your job.

It just takes one spark to light a fire. Joan, the journalist, never gets her calls returned. When she shows up at the office, you refuse to see her—you're just too busy. She tells her editor, Frank, who is attending the Rotarian dinner that night. Frank tells Rotarian president Pete that the production is being uncooperative with the press. Pete was going to lobby for the production to get access to an old Victorian house on Windover St., which has been denied by the historical society.

But now he doesn't want to bother. Why should he? His own paper won't even get a story. Gabe, the hardware store owner, hears about Pete's problems and wonders whether he should order a custom wheel that the key grip is trying to find to repair the camera dolly. Why bother? Kelly, the pharmacist, was going to spend some time on the set as a medical tech during key stunt sequences—as a backup to the regular medic. Why bother?

Once you arrive on location, the local journalist is going to be your first challenge. *Time Magazine* isn't going to be sitting on your doorstep. The *Picayune Times* writer will be. What generally happens is that local media will start covering a film as soon as location managers and construction personnel arrive to start the film. Depending on the scope of the production, this could be anywhere from 3 months to 6 weeks before the start of principal photography.

Location managers and construction bosses are usually cooperative with journalists and they allow photographs to be taken and basic information on the film to be given out. If there is a film commission in the area, information can also be filtered down to local journalists through that office. However, invariably, once a publicist is assigned and on the way, everyone says "wait until our publicist gets here."

I well remember my first unit publicity assignment. I arrived in Sheridan, Wyoming—population 6,000—and my first six phone messages which were waiting for me on the receptionist's desk, were from the local journalists. Roll-up-the-sleeve time.

Be friendly.

Local journalists can detect a highbrow attitude a mile away. Here are some quick guidelines for dealing with local journalists:

■ Stall them as long as possible. Notice I didn't say ignore them. Rules for setting up interviews with national press also apply to local journalists. Your actors should not be bothered with any interviews until the third or fourth week of shooting. Only then will you be able to gauge their comfort on the set and their willingness to cooperate. In the meantime, supply the local media with your all-important advance production notes and let them know that for the time being you will be their primary source of information.

■ Never promise anything. Let the locals know that you will do everything you can to provide them with the interviews they seek. But if you promise them Mr. Superstar and he doesn't want to talk, who are they going to be mad at,. Mr. Superstar?

■ Local newspaper reporters are very eager to get photos of the film shooting. This shouldn't be a problem. Alert your key crew members—director, actors, assistant directors—that a photographer will be on set. This is very important. Strange photographers can be spotted quickly and their presence can be upsetting to the uninformed. Alerting your crew in advance avoids those "how come I wasn't informed about this?" responses.

Give the local photographer a time frame. He shouldn't just be told to show up and shoot as much as he wants. An hour is plenty of time to get a few rolls of good behind the scenes shots. Also, don't forget to give him some rules for set etiquette. Since his camera will not have a "blimp" housing to mask the shutter sound, he must be told to shoot only between takes. The last thing you want to hear is your director screaming at a local photog for ruining a take. If you have a touchy actor, don't hesitate to alert the photographer. Be candid. It's okay to say, "Don't stray too close to Mr. Superstar." Everyone will appreciate such guidelines. Oh, and don't forget to let your actors know that a local still photographer will be on the set.

Lastly, it's a good idea to stay on the set when your local photographers are shooting. An hour is not much time to spend making sure everything goes smoothly.

Avoid posing your actors for local photographers. Actors are generally uncomfortable doing posed shots and you've already tried their patience enough getting posed pics for your own still photographer. However, if the Mayor arrives for lunch on the set and your producer wants to take a picture with him and some of the actors are nearby, I would probably ask them to come over for a quick pic. The producer will be happy, the local officials will love you, and since after lunch is usually a good time for any photos, the actors probably won't mind.

■ If you have one local newspaper reporter, delaying key interviews until the end of production is not going to be that big a deal. However, if there are 8-10 local journalists requesting interviews—newspaper, TV, radio and speciality publications press—it might be a good idea to set up a press junket on the set where you can get all of the interviews completed at one time.

The best time is during lunch. You should allow your actors a minimum of 20 minutes to eat, but you can play this one by ear. Some actors will grab an apple and be ready for interviews seconds after "Lunch" is called. Others will need to be pried away from lunch table chatter. You have a limited time for this junket, so inform your actors well in advance, and move forcefully to get your interviews done before the lunch period ends.

A junket to the set is similar to the one you conduct prior to the release of the film. Set up a table for each key actor and the director. Place a journalist with each personality and give them ten minutes of interview time. When the ten minutes are up, move your journalists around. Do this until everyone has had their ten minutes. It's an efficient way of conducting lots of interviews and you can generally do everything in less than an hour.

The above scenario works best if you have six personalities and six journalists. Everything is even. However, if you have two personalities and ten journalists, you're not going to be able to utilize your time efficiently and still give ten journalists their own personal ten minutes of one on one interview time. In this case, you're going to have to seat the journalists together with the personality. If you have an hour for interviews, then each table will get thirty minutes with the personality. At the end of the thirty minutes, simply switch tables. And don't hesitate to enforce these rules. You are in charge.

13

GETTING COMFORTABLE ON THE SET

Although every movie set is different, your responsibilities will always be the same. Over the course of the shoot, you must gather enough written materials to fill a press kit. You must supervise the still photographer so that you get a sizable number of good quality photographs. You must keep the press informed on any unusual occurrences that could make excellent column items. And by all means keep the home studio or production company or P.R. agency informed on the shoot's progress.

Getting comfortable on the set simply means organizing your time so that you can accomplish as much as possible. Each day is different, but you can come up with a basic regimen fairly easily. Here are some tips:

■ **Try to spend time on the set each day.** This is especially important during the first few weeks of shooting when you are establishing relationships that will make your job easier. Actors are notoriously shy around strangers, and only after a few weeks on the job will you be able to break the ice. It is important that you develop a good relationship with cast and crew and you won't accomplish that by barricading yourself in the production office on the telephone.

■ **Don't forget your office responsibilities.** If you spend all of your time on the set, you will fall behind in your campaign to alert the media. Once you send out your advance production notes, and start your phone calls, you will have a continuous workload—as many as 100 or more important calls to make. That, combined with keeping in touch with the studio, P.R. agencies, photo departments, product placement people and other elements, will keep you busy throughout the course of the shoot.

But you can't accomplish everything in one day or one week. You may spend weeks getting a single editor from *Rolling Stone* on the telephone. You may have to send two additional copies of your advance notes to the *Los Angeles Times* because they "never received" the first ones. You may spend a couple of weeks getting a specific photo together for *People Magazine* or you will start organizing an *Entertainment Tonight* visit that has logistical problems that have to be worked out. All of these tasks can be ongoing.

- **Develop a good balance.** I usually start my day in the production office making my calls. I then try to make it out to the set before lunch. Publicists can be the butt of jokes so don't take them personally. On my first unit assignment, the sound mixing crew knew that I was a fledgling unit publicist. When I showed up on the set before lunch, the mixer would always say, "Here comes the publicist, it must be lunch time." (In a later chapter I will outline methods of improving your own public relations on the set.)

- **Arrive on the set before lunch.** I like to see some shooting before the cast and crew breaks for lunch. Lunch time is probably the most important period of the day for the publicist in terms of getting any work done on the set. Everyone suddenly relaxes and eats. It's a daily occurrence on the set that has far more significance than you think.

Movie making, especially location movie making, is incredibly stressful for all concerned. When scenes are not working right, when the director is falling behind, when weather cancels a particular scene or equipment breaks down, a ripple effect occurs that casts a pall over the whole shoot. Sometimes, you can walk on the set and cut the stress with a knife. During times like these, the rule is *publicist beware.*

In the actor or director's mind, the movie comes first. Publicity is not a priority on the set. That is why I try to accomplish all of my publicity business at lunchtime when the director or the performers are not locked into their roles. Everyone relaxes at lunch, even the most difficult to approach actors. If you are trying to set up an interview with an actor, now is the time to arrange the details. Still approvals, biographical material, personal appearances, publicity strategy, messages from the LA-based publicist—anything business-wise can be conducted at lunch.

Try to let the actor eat first, and then knock on the trailer door. Don't be intimidated by the stature of the actor or the apparent sanctity of his motor home. You have a job to do on the set and you're not going to accomplish it cowering in the shadow of his door determining whether or not it is the time to bring up an interview request from *Bop* magazine.

- **Remember that actors are unpredictable.** One day they can be chatting with you like your long lost cousin from Dubuque. The next day they can be stand-offish, rude, even belligerent. It often depends on how well the film is going. And here's another reason why you develop good relationships with production managers, assistant directors and crew people. They become your spies—they can give you good intelligence on how things are going on the set.

On *Desert Bloom*, the still photographer, gave me daily reports on how tense and difficult it was in the "Chismore House" (the home of the characters depicted by Jon Voight, Jobeth Williams, Ellen Barkin and Annabeth Gish). Unusually, the film took place almost entirely in this single-story 1950s frame house constructed on an empty lot in downtown Tucson, Arizona.

Not only was the film's geography restricted, but director Gene Corr was a first-time director. Seasoned actors can get very nervous and testy around a new director. And *Desert Bloom* was hardly a lighthearted story to begin with. It was a delicately balanced family drama about an abusing alcoholic husband, his wife the chronic gambler, their daughter, the inhibited emerging teenager and the divorcee sister all living in Las Vegas prior to the first nuclear tests.

Everybody was uptight on that movie. Still, because of the unique subject matter and background, I was given complete authorization to generate media breaks during production. I could set up telephone interviews, brings journalists to the Arizona location, organize special photos.

The actors kept us waiting at times, but they were never rude to visiting journalists. Even Voight, who is an extremely focused presence on the movie set, would arrive at interviews and give his best. I was patient with him. One day, we had our own video unit on the set gathering materials for the "electronic press kit" and we literally had to wait six hours to do the interview. Unfortunately, the schedule had shifted and Voight was forced to shoot an extremely intense, enormously emotional sequence prior to our interview. So you can imagine my hesitancy to disturb him.

■ **Your visiting journalists must be patient**. Remember also that interviews aren't the only materials a journalist collects while set visiting. Catching the ambience of the location, seeing the crew at work, interviewing the producer, writer, cinematographer, editor— these are other events that can keep the journalist busy while he is waiting for Charlton Heston to step down from Sinai.

If the journalist gets impatient, you just have to stall. It's part of your work to "entertain" visiting media. You are the host on the set, be creative, come up with ideas. In many ways you are the Universal Tour guide, keeping the public happy with events every few minutes.

■ **Be aware of reporter etiquette**. My experience is that journalists usually don't need minute to minute hand-holding —in fact they can resent it. However, make sure the journalist understands that all actor interviews are scheduled by you, the publicist. *A journalist should never walk up to an actor and set up his own interview.*

You can let the journalist wander around and observe, but don't ever leave that journalist on the set alone, unless it's an emergency. And even then, try to get one of the assistant directors or production assistants to stand in for you and keep an eye out. Journalists should never be allowed to poke their head in where it's not wanted.

I had an interesting problem once with a local journalist. He had come to the set to specifically talk to a local electrician who was working on a movie for the first time. It was another one of those local color pieces—the type of article we've seen a million times. So I brought the journalist out to the set and he did his interviews and took the requisite photos.

Following the interview, he hung around and watched a sequence with a young actress who was also making her film debut. He was so enchanted by her performance and demeanor, he quietly asked if he could have a few moments with her too. I didn't think there would be a problem. She was so new to the business that I thought a little local media attention might break the ice.

The next day the article broke with the writer mentioning the electrician and the actress in so many cross references that anyone could easily infer that they were romantically linked. What a disaster! The young actress was in tears. Her family was upset because (unknown to me) there had been some prior personal problems with this particular electrician. And compounding the whole mess was the fact that the girl was 13 and he was 40.

I had my hands filled trying to make up for this one. Eventually, I convinced everyone that it was an awful coincidence. (One of the other more experienced actresses interceded on my behalf.) But I had learned an important lesson: spontaneity can backfire on the set. If a journalist comes to the set for a specific purpose, don't allow yourself to be sidetracked. Journalists should be "pre-interviewed" to determine their exact needs. In this way, you can first contact the star or actor and find out if they'll cooperate. In the young actress' case, she had no experience with the press and could not come to an intelligent decision on whether to say yes or no to the interview.

The unit publicist comes in extremely handy during times like this. You become a master of protocol, observing conventions and guidelines of which crew members are totally unaware. Your key understanding of these procedures can preserve the delicate relationship between the actor and the press.

■ **Your actors come first**. Try to keep everybody happy but when push comes to shove defend your actor's rights. If a journalist asks a controversial question or the photographer requests an unusual picture and the actor refuses, don't try to convince the actor to change his mind in front of the journalist. That journalist is going to be on the set, at the most, for a couple of days. You will be living with the actor for as much as four months. Don't let your zeal for a good story get in the way of your responsibilities as a set publicist.

On location, actors are defenseless. They can't lock the doors to their homes, they can't disappear from the set, they can't immediately contact their own publicist, lawyer, manager or agent. Only you can defend the actor's rights.

If the actor for a minute feels that you are being unfair and siding with someone else against him, he will retreat into a defensive posture that could last the entire shoot.

■ **Don't hesitate to play policeman on the set.** You don't have to hover over an interview with a stop watch, but you do have to stay in control. If the actor is due back on the set get him moving. Don't allow the journalist to monopolize the actor's time or prevent the actor from performing. Actors can give you very important signals on whether they're enjoying the interview process. Pay attention to them. If Mr. Superstar is laughing and cajoling with a journalist, you can infer that everything is fine and that it's an enjoyable encounter. But if he summons you over to ask "what's happening on the set," he's telling you he wants out as diplomatically as possible.

Set visiting journalists carry a bit more weight than other interviewers because they have traveled a certain distance to get the interview. So you must make sure that they don't come away empty handed. If the actor is being evasive or even downright surly, you must maintain your own patience level and somehow get the interview arranged.

There are extenuating circumstances for cancelling an interview. The actor isn't feeling well. The day has been too stressful and the actor wants to unwind on his own. It's just not the right time.

You and the visiting journalist must understand the idiosyncrasies of the actor. However, there comes a time when you must put your foot down and give your "he's come all the way from LA, let's get this done" speech. And you must be genuinely persuasive. Any element of phoniness is going to be picked up in a minute.

14

THE LOGISTICS OF SET VISITS

The journalist is interested. The actor is cooperative. How do you bring them together?

In the olden, golden days of the movies, it was common practice for the studios to junket writers and editors to the set at the studio's expense. For days upon end, the fourth estate was pampered with lavish dinners, entertainment, little gifts—oh, and interviews and set visits. In return, the writers and editors were supposed to write glowing pieces about upcoming movies.

Well, this practice continues today—but to a lesser extent and with some important differences. Today, most junkets occur, not during production, but close to release time when the writers can actually see the finished product and judge for themselves. Having seen the film, they can then walk into an interview the next day with some sense of perspective and hopefully some intelligent questions.

If set visits do occur during shooting today, they are usually not junket-sized. They involve only a small number of writers, or TV crews, and because of logistical complications, they don't come all at once.

Journalists today have more power than ever. If you invite them to set, or to a junket, it doesn't mean they'll write nice things about your movie. You have no control over what they write or how they perceive a film. You only hope that if you give them sizable access to your talent, you'll get as much coverage as possible. Writers can trash a film with negative reviews, but there's always the chance that they'll also write some neutral feature stories based on the interviews they completed on the junket.

■ **Paying for the Trip**. Every journalist has his or her own criteria for paying travel costs. The *Los Angeles Times* will not fly anywhere on someone else's ticket. But if they're interested they'll pay to fly their journalists to a film location at the edge of the world. Some papers, shows, or columnists feel strongly about not "sacrificing their independence" to the studio. Is paying travel expenses a form of bribery? I don't think so, but some journalists avoid even the appearance of impropriety.

Once the journalist becomes interested in a possible story and set visit, simply ask the question, "Can I pay for your flight and accommodations?" You will get a very quick answer, I assure you.

Once that question is out of the way, you must determine the appropriate time for the set visit which, of course, should work within the writer's schedule. That's when you put on your organizer's cap and open the calendar book. You also must be familiar with the shooting schedule.

■ **Selecting the Best Visiting Time.** Journalists, like amusement park patrons, are partial to action, adventure and excitement on the set whenever possible.

Leaf through your script and shooting schedule and find an interesting, or unusual attraction for the visiting press. Avoid interiors whenever possible because they're the most claustrophobic of all locations. You have limited access and your journalists may not even be invited inside. The last thing you want is the writer outside while the action is going on inside.

I prefer daytime exteriors with some action involved. Every movie set becomes tedious after a while, even for the most curious journalist. Outdoor sets have more going on and offer more distractions—and if there are photographers along, "photo ops."

■ **Length of Stay.** Keep set visits relatively short—two days max. One day of interviews, one day of observation. That's plenty of time to cover the location. Some journalists may fly out on a Friday night, observe and interview all day Saturday and fly home on Sunday. Perfect.

The less time they stay, the fewer meals you must plan, the fewer logistical hurdles, the quicker you can get back to your campaign to track down the editor of *Rolling Stone* or planning the visit of the next journalist.

■ **Stay Close to Your Visitors.** During a set visit, you're basically a baby sitter. You must make the visit go smoothly, and sometimes that means keeping the journalist out of trouble. I made the mistake once of scheduling two set visits at the same time. One was the in-house video crew, and the other was a TV crew from the local *PM Magazine* affiliate.

I left the *PM* crew filming the main action inside a huge factory while I took the in-house crew to film another location. Mistake! Our director was having a lousy day. At one point he turned around to give a direction and found himself nose to nose with the cameraman from *PM*. Suddenly, the walkie talkie was crackling with "Get Rubin up here, right away!"

Publicists are never called on the walkie talkie. If you suddenly hear your name called, it means that there's trouble and it has your name on it!

■ **A checklist for set visits**:

✔ Get all set visits approved by the producer and your publicity superior. Never invite a journalist or TV crew to set without proper approval.

✔ Supply visiting journalists with all the material you have on the film, including advance production notes, any representative stills and a shooting schedule. If production will allow it, also give them a script.

✔ Accommodate if possible any of their special requests, such as photo opportunities. If the actor is jovial and cooperative, it's always nice to have his picture taken with the visiting journalist. An 8" x 10" enlargement of that picture is the perfect gift to send back to the journalist.

✔ Once the set visit is concluded, find out as much information as possible about where and when the article or story will appear. This information is important for your memos and for possible follow-up in the pre-release period.

✔ Plan on acting as the journalist's chauffeur during the course of the visit. This is one of your strongest reasons for having your own car. Always pick up the journalist at the airport and take him back there. Personal door to door service is expected protocol.

✔ If you're working on a particularly exotic location with interesting sightseeing opportunities, don't hesitate to entertain the journalist by paying a visit to the points of interest. Set visits aren't always work. They can be fun too and if you show your visitors a good time, it will always reflect well on you and the film.

✔ During the course of the stay, make sure the journalist meets all of the right executives on the set, especially the producer. Remember, on the set, the producer is your boss. When journalists come to visit, it's an opportunity for your boss to see you working which is always a good idea.

✔ If you recommend an interview to the visitor and he declines, be diplomatic. Don't ever force an interviewer to talk to a subject. On the other hand, don't hesitate to ask the journalist if he would like to speak to someone. If Actor C wishes an interview after Actor A has been interviewed and the writer doesn't want to speak to him, at least you've asked. You can then tell Actor C that the journalist declined at this time because he has limited time or any other appropriate excuse. But always ask.

✔ When you take a journalist to lunch or dinner off the set, pay with your own money, you will then be reimbursed by the production out of petty cash. Always type up your expense reports on a clean sheet of paper and enclose receipts. The entertaining of visiting or local journalists is a legitimate business expense.

✔ Three or four visits from top media outlets is plenty of set visit coverage for a location shoot. Try to include one national TV outlet (an *Entertainment Tonight*, E! Entertainment Channel or *Good Morning America* type program); one national columnist (*Associated Press*, *USA Today*); one major city paper (*NY Times*, *LA Times*) and perhaps a couple of freelancers with national outlets. If you're on a major film with plenty of set visit requests, you're going to have to prioritize. Don't hesitate to contact your studio or independent P.R. agency for advice. And get your producer involved. He may have his own ideas on who he wants visiting his set. Always seek set visit approval from your producer.

✔ Follow up your set visits with a "thank you, it was nice meeting you" letter. At this time you can enclose any special photographs, etc. It puts a nice capper on the visit.

✔ Regarding set visits "in town" (LA, NY): Local visits can easily be one day visits. The same rules apply, but you will have less time to accomplish your tasks. The luxury in town, though, is that journalists can come back to set if work is not completed on a specific day. If the journalist is spending the day at the studio, always plan on taking them to lunch. Even though you're not in West Zambezi, you still have to play the perfect host. Also, regarding TV crews, check with your studio and make sure their labor relations department is aware of all visits. This is a union matter on most film sets and you need their approval, although it generally isn't a problem.

15

THE VIDEO PRESS KIT

Video press kits are a useful part of the publicity portfolio. Basically, they consist of one-on-one interviews with the principal actors and behind the scenes personnel (writer, director, producer, etc.) and "B-roll" (behind the scenes footage).

Behind the scenes documentaries aren't new. They used to be quite common, but they were enormously expensive, shot in 16mm, usually fairly long (up to 20 minutes) and included pricey film clips from other movies.

Video press kits were invented because they were cheaper and they were easier to produce. The popularity of *Entertainment Tonight* and its national reach opened up a whole door of interest in the behind-the-scenes world of Hollywood. More and more, film coverage was featured on a national basis. Local television reviewers began requesting clips and anything available on hit films so they could tinker together their own mini-documentaries for the local folk.

The emergence of cable television (with big programming holes to fill) and new entertainment news programs further increased the demand for video press kit materials.

Video press kits are usually produced by independent companies which specialize in them. The studio P.R. Department or the producer takes care of hiring the video production company, although sometimes you will have some input. The main reason studios hire outside companies to produce video press kits, other than the fact that as specialists, they have demonstrated their ability to deliver a quality product, is that an outside company will be able to get interviews and B-roll during production, *and* they will also be around closer to the film's release when film clips will be available and need to be added to the press kit. A unit publicist is not going to be around for that long. So, even though you may be qualified to assemble video press kit materials yourself, it's best to let an outside production company handle it.

In the rare instance that an independent company isn't brought in to produce the video press kit, then the responsibility will fall into your lap. The following guidelines will thus be very useful.

Costs of a Video Press Kit.

A video press kit now can be engineered for about $25,000. The principle costs include:

$ A per-day creative shooting fee. Between $1000-2000, depending on the location.

$ Any equipment rental above and beyond the creative fee.

$ Travel and accommodation expenses to location.

$ Cost of raw tape.

$ Post-production costs to complete the documentary.

Post production (which is the lion share of your budget) includes:

$ First cut (the "off-line" version), used to get approval from the production and the publicity department. You can have as many as 10 off-line versions of a single video press kit. This is cut on ¾" tape.

$ Narrator's creative fee and the cost of putting his voice on tape.

$ Any audio sweetening fees for improving the quality of your soundtrack.

$ Final cut (or the "on-line" version) which is cut on 1" tape is extremely expensive. Make sure your first cuts are thoroughly approved before scheduling on-line time at a local post-production outlet. The last thing you want to do is on-line your kit and find out you have to go back and change it. That could send your budget into the stratosphere.

$ Cost of duplicating the off-line and on-line versions. This is an area that is always under-budgeted. Once the kit is finished, everyone wants to see a copy, and if you budget for only two copies, you're going to go over-budget quickly. Copies are made on 1" (usually for storage although there are outlets like HBO who will request a 1" copy for their use (fortunately, this will come under the publicity department budget and not your own); ¾" which is the universal style for broadcast usage; and ½", a style for convenience, used to play your materials at the producer's home or studio when a standard ¾" machine is unavailable.

Elements of a Video Press Kit.

In the beginning, the studios made video kits like they made the long-form documentary. Today, based on a decade's worth of experience, and due to the demands of the marketplace, the materials and their various lengths have changed. Generally speaking, you need:

✔ A featurette program, or mini-documentary 4-5 minutes in length, combining interviews with B-roll and scene footage.

✔ One or two personality profiles (1-2 minutes in length) concentrating on a particular member of the cast and crew (usually a superstar actor or director).

✔ Some open-ended interview footage (where the question is asked on audio and an edited video response from the actor is featured (4-5 questions is normal).

✔ Raw, unedited B-roll.

✔ Film clips or review clips (4-5), usually selected by the studio or production company and sent to you.

I feel that video press kits or EPKs (electronic press kits) are valuable as long as they're done cost-effectively. At $25,000, they're reasonable. Any more than that, and I feel they become frills. Any good marketing director will tell you that frills are not part of his budget.

Not all films need video press kits. If you're working on a film with no name stars, no special effects sequences, no unusual art direction or stunt work, or a very small dramatic story line, an EPK would be a waste because nobody would play it anyway.

Gathering All The Materials For Your Video Press Kit.

Since video press kit materials are usually gathered during the production phase of a film, responsibility for a production shoot goes to the unit publicist. How you deal with an in-house video crew covering the set is no different than how you deal with *Entertainment Tonight*. The same criteria applies, only the in-house crew because of its nature can spend more time on the set and can be closer to the action.

It's not unusual to put a microphone on the director and follow the course of the filming from his perspective. An in-house video press kit shoot can be fun and should be treated as such. Since you have complete control over what footage you use (something you never get from normal media coverage), your cast and crew can be more at their leisure. If Actor A cracks an off-color joke on camera, he knows that it's not going to appear in the final featurette. (It better not!)

When a video crew is coming to set, briefing your cast and crew becomes even more important than usual. Because there is always the possibility that no national television outlets will be visiting the set, your video crew may be the only source of behind the scenes footage. Thus, every second they are visiting is precious time.

Sometimes, you never know what you're going to get. On the original *Ghostbusters*, we had a crew on the set with the likes of Bill Murray and Dan Aykroyd and they could be quite outrageous. In fact, while they were shooting on the cavernous apartment building set on the Burbank Studios lot, they were visited by Chevy Chase and Robin

Williams. Although most of the footage ended up on the cutting room floor, behind the scenes filming was quite exciting.

Unlike a typical TV interview, when you interview cast and crew for a video press kit, you can act like a director. If the actor says something that doesn't come out quite right, you can say "cut" and start the question again. One of the most important guidelines during video interviews is to make sure the actor says complete sentences and that he starts his sentence with a complete thought. His response to the question, "What was it like filming that chase sequence?" should not start, "It was great." A complete-thought answer would be something like, "Filming the chase sequence in *The Great Escape* was amazing..." The person asking the questions can be one of the members of the video crew—they do it all the time and generally are pretty good. However, since I have some experience, I try to conduct the interview myself. If you have the video people do the interview, make sure you supply them with some production notes and guidelines for questions.

Determining when to bring the video press kit crew is similar to all media visits. You're looking for colorful, outdoorsy, action, adventure or any form of movement. However, you don't get a Ben Hur chariot race everyday. Work closely with the crew and determine the most colorful time to visit. Also check your shooting schedule and make sure your principal actors are going to still be there. It's all fine and good to schedule a video press kit shoot for the last great action piece of the film, but it's a disaster if you find that your principal actors won't be there.

How much time on set? Set aside three days. Two days for behind the scenes coverage and a day for interviews. That's an average figure. If you're working a James Bond film or an Indiana Jones film, you might set aside 4-5 days, depending on the location and the action. Any longer than a three day stay, though, and your budget starts to escalate significantly.

Make sure your talent looks good on camera. If you catch your actors at the end of their lunch break, generally a good time to do interviews, make sure their make-up and hair looks fine. The smart, experienced actors, will usually take a trip to the make-up artist or hairstylist prior to the interview. Since the interview process is usually interesting, it's not surprising to find your make-up and hair people hanging out during the interview.

The video press kit also gives you the opportunity to interview those B and C actors who sometimes feel left out when the national television outlets come to set. You may not use the footage in the final cut, but you certainly score some points with these actors. Like the director of the film, you never know what you're going to use until you get into the editing room.

Don't hesitate to offer input to the video crew. No one knows the set better than you. Your insight is invaluable. During your travels, you might have discovered that the assistant set dresser worked on *Gone with the Wind* and used to put Clark Gable in the saddle. There might be a story there and putting it on video could be a wise move. Sets are filled with history. It only takes a curious, enterprising publicist to find those stories and preserve them on video.

16

EXPLOITING SPECIAL PUBLICITY ANGLES

Every motion picture has a hook—that all important "angle" which helps you pitch the film to the media. Some examples:

- On *Honey, I Blew Up The Baby* (Walt Disney, 1992), my hook was having the sequel to one of Hollywood's greatest sleeper hits, *Honey, I Shrunk The Kids*. The cast was back, the A team of FX engineers was on tap once again and a 112 ft. baby was ready to make his debut.

- On *Gladiator* (Columbia Pictures, 1992), I had a tough boxing story in the style of *Raging Bull* with a gritty script co-written by Nicholas Kazan (*Reversal of Fortune*) and a classy group of performers top-lined by James Marshall (*Twin Peaks* heart-throb), Brian Dennehy, Robert Loggia and Ossie Davis. Story and cast were the key.

- On *Spacehunter: Adventures in the Forbidden Zone* (Columbia Pictures, 1983), my hook was the concept of 3D and how the technology had changed since 3D had been introduced in the early 1950s.

- On *Endangered Species* (MGM, 1981), I researched and wrote a number of articles on a real twenty year old national mystery involving strange cattle mutilations.

- On *Rad* (Tri-Star Pictures, 1986), I introduced the fun of BMX bicycle racing to the mass market audience, keying in on the bicycle industry and their trade publications.

- On *Ghostbusters* (Columbia Pictures, 1984), the video featurette program I co-produced went behind the scenes with Richard Edlund's incredibly talented special effects team, introducing the wild FX elements that would contribute to the film's success.

■ On *Desert Bloom* (Columbia Pictures, 1986), I introduced journalists to Las Vegas circa 1951, the time of the first nuclear bomb tests and how they affected a troubled family group.

Pitching to Specialty Magazines.

On every motion picture you publicize and promote, it is your job to find the angle and make sure that you pitch it not only to the mainstream media outlets but to all appropriate speciality avenues as well.

It is true that a *Time Magazine* "People" item will reach a huge segment of the potential movie going audience. However, if you have a science fiction film, you'd better get a feature piece going in *Starlog* too—it's the *Time Magazine* of the science fiction crowd.

If your movie has a number of cute teen actors, don't ignore the teen/fan magazines. *Seventeen, Sixteen, Teen Beat, Teen Machine*—the list is almost endless. And they are extremely cooperative with new movie projects especially if they sense a possible hit.

Time Magazine is generally a long shot. If you can get a photo placed in their "People" column during production, then you're entitled to a promotion to Captain and the Publicist of the Week award. Unless your film is a big enterprise with major stars—like *Gorillas in the Mist, The Last Emperor* or *Platoon*, that "People" item will be your only *Time Magazine* break.

The speciality magazines can be a richer source of breaks for you. Take, for example, *Starlog*. I've known about this publication since my first days on the science fiction circuit promoting United Artists' *Invasion of the Body Snatchers*. It's the monthly bible for the country's science fiction fans.

If you contact *Starlog* during production you can start coverage in the publication with a set visit and production piece. *Starlog* writers love to do multiple interviews. They cover actors, the director, the special effects team, the make-up team, the art director, the costume designer, even stunt players if their work is breaking new ground.

Each of these interviews can possibly lead to an individual story in various editions of the magazine. If it's September and your movie is due out in June, you might have an introductory story on the film in the January issue; a follow-up interview with the make-up person in February; a production piece in March; and perhaps a cover story in June timed to the release of the film.

Not only have you utilized the speciality aspect of your film to the fullest with this publication, but you're reaching the targeted audience with the best possible coverage.

When dealing with a special effects laden picture, make sure your press kit materials are geared to the specialty elements like effects, art direction, makeup.

On *Nightflyers*, a New Century/Vista film based on a classic science fiction short story, we featured a piece on the author of the original story, George R.R. Martin. To the average citizen on the street, Martin was an unknown entity. But for the science fiction fan, he's a titan. Writers are generally a low key element in the press kit—unless they happen to be "hyphenated" like writer-director, writer-producer, or actor-writer.

However, writers on specialty projects are usually your first stop for feature story information and pitching ammunition. Having interviewed screenwriters for previous books and magazine articles, I also know that they have the best stories. Since they most often initiate a project, they can also tell about its background from the beginning.

Identify the Specialty Elements.

Identifying the specialty elements of any motion picture is an important and early task of the publicist. Time runs like a jack rabbit during production. You'll find that the film shoot is nearly over before you get a chance to write anything beyond your advance production notes.

If you have a film with strong speciality elements, sending out your advance production notes to mainstream media just isn't enough. You're not thinking creatively. Having specially composed written materials will impress the media and your superiors. It also allows you to become more familiar with the film's angle and helps you pitch its strongest points.

By all means, include your photographer in your specialty campaign. A good black and white still highlighting the special area is an excellent accompaniment to any press release. With the price of multiple copies of a b/w still quite reasonable these days, consider sending out approved photos to your speciality outlets.

If possible, I like to illustrate my releases with the unusual. If Nick Nolte and Kathleen Turner are filming on the world's largest merry-go-round, get a picture of them together having fun. Write up a release detailing the merry-go-round's place in history, add the pertinent facts about your movie and its stars and send the photo out in this case to mass market outlets. Consider a color slide for those publications which can use color—*Time, Newsweek, USA Today*.

Now a merry-go-round does not make an entire specialty campaign, but it's unusual enough to inspire a release and photo. Once these photographic opportunities happen, pounce on them like a journalist with a deadline. You never know when *Time Magazine* is having a slow week and is dying for a cute "People" section photo.

Let's say that Michael J. Fox and Molly Ringwald are working together on a film about deep sea diving in Truk Island Lagoon. Since this is a geographical spot with a rich history, you can construct a specialty campaign around it.

With superstar actors like Michael and Molly, there are photographic opportunities galore. Combining a movie with deep sea diving and an historical location gets you access to a whole parcel of speciality publications dealing with recreation and travel.

Your first step—research the history of Truk Lagoon. I happen to know that it has one of the largest collections of sunken World War II Japanese warships. It was a major Japanese naval base during the war that was bypassed by American forces, yet, it was bombed into oblivion. Because of the amount of tonnage sunk in its harbor, it has become an extremely popular diving spot for scuba enthusiasts from around the world.

These are relatively interesting historical facts that have been reported on in travel publications and newspaper travel sections for years. Old news, right? Right. However, add the faces of Fox and Ringwald and you instantly freshen up the material.

Photos and releases from this film should immediately be sent to your typical mass market outlets like *People Magazine*, *US*, *Time* and *Newsweek*, but jump into the speciality area. Send the same release and maybe a different photo of the two actors to *National Geographic*, *Travel and Leisure* and newspaper travel editors in the top 30 markets. Get a list of travel columnists and feed them the release. Get a list of skin diving publications and service them as well. After your research is completed, you may have discovered 50 new outlets for the film and each one valuable to spreading the word on a new movie to an important speciality audience.

Here's a list of popular films and some of the specialty outlet areas that were utilized:

MOVIE	SPECIALTY OUTLETS
The Right Stuff	Space, history, science, astronomy, aviation and military publications.
Gorillas in the Mist	Science, anthropology, nature, environmental, animal rights publications.
Wall Street	Business editors, finance, investment and stock publications
Baby Boom	Family, lifestyle, women's, maternity publications
Imagine: the John Lennon Documentary	Music publications and newspaper music editors.
Platoon	Military, political, veteran's, historical publications; newspaper opinion sections.
Star Wars	Science fiction, fantasy publications, special effects magazines

17

DEALING WITH PRODUCT PLACEMENT OPPORTUNITIES

Long before the film begins shooting, the producer and later the production manager and prop master, begin to make deals with various companies who are seeking "product placement" in the film. "Product placement" is a fancy marketing term for a practice that has been commonplace since the earliest days of the motion picture business. Major corporations, from automobile manufacturers to apparel giants, spend serious time courting the movie producer for screen time.

If ET eats Reese's Pieces, will it affect sales of that candy? Yes, and dramatically so. If James Bond eludes his pursuers by driving a trick-filled Aston Martin sports car, will auto sales skyrocket? Yes, of course. Creating an association between a famous "personality" and a product, whether it's in a TV commercial or on the big screen can be a major part of the marketing plan. It is thus important for the publicist to understand that these relationships do exist and that they begin on the movie set.

I worked on a science fiction film that was shot in Calgary, Alberta. Our product placement person (a third party hired by the producer) made arrangements with a top motorcycle company to get three free cycles for the production. It was a logical idea—the hero of the film was a young cowboy who rode a cycle instead of a horse. In fact, he had bull horns mounted on the handle bars, saddle bags draped over the back of the bike, and mud splattered everywhere.

I had nothing to do with this motorcycle placement. However, after shooting was finished, I started to get requests from the cycle company for photographs of their bike in action. They wanted to see photos and film clips so they could decide if they wanted to do a national promotional tie-in with the film during its release.

I pored through the still photographer's book looking for shots of the bike. But my search was fruitless. Since no one had bothered to inform me about the product placement opportunity, I never instructed the still photographer to pay any special attention to the motorcycle. Thus, we had very few usable shots and virtually none with the manufacturer's name plate visible. Since the bike was always mud splattered, no one ever thought of cleaning the name plate so that we could at least see that this was a specific manufacturer's bike.

From that company's point of view, their product placement was useless. The public wasn't going to make any association between the loveable hero of the movie and the brand of bike he rode.

What could the unit publicist have done in this situation? Plenty. If the publicist is informed that there is a product placement in the works, he knows that by the end of the shoot, he must have a set of usable slides and stills of the bike. A creative publicist may even take the lead actor out to a special setting and do some special photos with the bike. And, if the manufacturer's name plate is mud splattered, he will take out a handkerchief and wipe it clean. It's as simple as that.

Defining Your Product Placement Opportunities.

Product placement is desirable to a production in three ways. First, the production might get some free props (cars, clothes, etc.). Second, a company might pay a fee to the producer for the privilege of having its product prominently featured in the film. Third, the most important reason for trying to make product placement deals is the possibility of free publicity generated by promotional tie-ins close to the release date of the film. A major effort to place a prominent beer company's product in a film is a wasted exercise unless that same beer company does some advertising for the film with, for instance, thousands of point-of-purchase displays in beverage stores and supermarkets. Whether the company actually gives dollars up front, or guarantees a certain amount of advertising during the release of the film, the success of the product placement/promotional effort depends on keen cooperation between the movie and the company. Documenting the product placement opportunity with great still photos is part of that process which falls under the aegis of the unit publicist.

The producer will generally determine, in consultation with a product placement or promotional company, which products or companies will be showcased on a motion picture. Opportunities fall into several categories:

■ **The movie company is paid to showcase the product.** On a recent motion picture, a prominent convenience store franchise paid a producer $70,000 to sponsor a racetrack featured strongly in the film. Under those terms, the company's logo was plastered all over the track.

■ **Products with tie-in potential are given to the production.** In this case—with no back-end promotional commitments—it is going to be the producer's job to convince the company that their placement is strong enough to elicit a possible back-end promotion (back-end, meaning during the release period of the picture).

In reality, very few placements guarantee promotional opportunities. After the film is finished, the producer must still show the footage to the company to determine how interested they are in promotional opportunities. Even the most carefully planned promotions can be forfeited if the product presence is unsatisfactory. However, if the product placement is good (with excellent still photos documenting that fact), the chances for a promotion are considerably more viable.

■ **Products are placed with guaranteed promotional backing.** If your movie is important enough—if it's a top picture with big stars and great hit potential—companies are going to be competing to showcase their products on the screen. It is under these circumstances that some promotional guarantees develop.

■ **Products used solely as props with no plan for promotion or release period activity.** The prop master's job is to supply the film with hundreds, sometimes thousands of prop items. Some of these items have great promotional potential. In a baseball film, the actors are going to have to wear gloves—why not Spauldings. Another film might feature a grandfather and grandson fishing—they both could be using a well-known brand of pole. In a film like *Wall Street* or *Working Girl* important scenes happen on the telephone—what if all the phones in the movie were made by A T & T? In situations like these, the prop people will generally try to get these items donated by the manufacturers.

However, it is also a good idea for someone on the production to keep track of the items and how they are used in the film. Still photos, in color and b/w can accomplish that. You never know when a perfunctory product placement turns into a major promotional opportunity. And one of the first questions the producer will ask is whether there are any good photos of that placement.

Dealing with Liaison Organizations.

Today a whole infrastructure of product placement liaison companies has grown up around the studios and independent film companies. The major corporations and manufacturers pay these liaison companies a fee to place their products in movies and television shows. On the other hand, the liaison companies save the movie producer a great deal of time by offering quick and direct access to the marketing people at major companies.

If you've ever thought of contacting major companies on your own, forget it. You can get caught in endless amounts of red tape. I'm not saying it can't be done, but product placement liaison firms get paid to do this kind of thing, so why bother?

As a publicist, your job is to document important tie-ins, and although this area does not interest your publicity department back at the studio or the P.R. agency, it is a job that is vital to your film's well-being. Taking an interest in this area will also endear you to your producer—someone who may also be in a position to hire you for your next job.

Don't wait for the product placement liaison company to help you document placement opportunities. During production, their influence doesn't extend very far and sometimes communications can be lost. Occasionally, one of their executives may come to the set for a visit. Instructions may even be given to the prop master to get some pictures, but my experience shows that this area is not sufficiently covered.

Photo Opportunities.

Don't hesitate to be creative in photographing products and signage. Provided the actor is agreeable, both personally and legally, don't hesitate to snap a picture with the product or sign in the background or foreground. Star presence in photos is a great selling tool.

Work closely with your still photographer to get these photos. If film action takes place around the prop, get a series of action shots. If the film features unique sets or backgrounds, don't hesitate to get some of that feel into the photos. Provided his company was still afloat, I'm sure John DeLoreon's marketing department would have loved some photographs of Michael J. Fox's "Deloreon Time Machine" sitting on a 1950s street in *Back to the Future*.

Once the photos are taken, make sure they are delivered to the right people. Copies should go to the producer and the product placement company, the latter delivering them to the company.

Press Release Opportunities.

The use of a certain product in the film may even demand a press release and photo. When James Bond donned a Bell jet pack to go flying around France in *Thunderball*, United Artist publicists serviced a photo of the strange flying machine to the nation's press. It became an unusual news story. The automobile trade magazines are also very fond of the Bond movies and their unusual trick cars.

Always be aware of new products that are making their debut in your motion picture. The publicity opportunities are tremendous.

18

THE PUBLICIST AS PSYCHOLOGIST

When you work in a stressful people-oriented profession there are bound to be problems—not just missed publicity opportunities and deadline pressure, but personality problems that can cripple a publicist faster than a downed phone line.

It's great to have a "gung ho," "I want to do the best possible job" attitude on the set. Your enthusiasm and excitement can't help but be a plus. However, don't expect that spirit in everyone. You'll find some people on every set who have the exact opposite attitude toward the picture. They want to make life difficult for everyone around them—especially the publicist.

As I mentioned earlier, the problem with publicity on the set is that you find yourself continually having to ask people to do things—things they often don't understand or, worse, find unimportant and distracting.

You have a job to do. You can't let personality problems drag you into the dumps of despair. I find that there are enough positive personalities on a set to always overcome the sour apples. Even the sour apples often have a sweet core (if you can find it).

Because of all these potential problem areas, it is important to be prepared with a little "damage control" psychology on the set. I am not a psychologist but I do listen to people and I have been through enough crises on the set to be able to offer some advice.

The Problem Actor.   I've mentioned this character before. He or she becomes a roadblock each time you try to do your job. You'd think you were bringing bubonic plague to the set every time you bring up a media request.

In fairness to all actors, they have their own priorities: learning their lines, giving the best possible performance, getting along with the director, keeping the energy up. These are their job requirements. Sometimes, anything else is just a chore.

I don't like being a "chore." I think of publicity as one of the necessary activities on the set. During the "Golden Age," actors were required to discuss films with key press contacts and appear downright jovial about it. But the old studios are gone and today actors call their own shots like never before—especially the stars, with their enormous salaries and their batteries of lawyers, agents, managers, personal publicists and psychiatrists.

Ironically, there are more media outlets than ever before. Unfortunately, the bigger a star becomes, the less he or she wants to give their time to publicity. I get on a set and the young actors, the fledglings, the novices, the neophytes, the fresh off the boat thespians, flock to my banner. They love to talk about publicity and its importance to their career. Unfortunately, when these actors become "stars," their enthusiasm quickly disappears. In my cynical mood, I think that actors can't wait for that first time when they can say, "No. I think I'll pass on that."

Never get into an argument with an actor. In fact, try to avoid arguments with anyone on the set. You can't win. You don't have the authority or muscle to kick things into gear by getting hot under the collar.

Persuasion is your only tool with problem actors. Persuasion and timing. I'm like a restless panther when it comes to problem actors. I'm always observing them, looking for the right time to ask a question or carry on a conversation.

Once you get over that sense of awe at being in the presence of Mr. Superstar (do you ever really get over that?), you find that they're just people with every day problems. If Mr. Superstar is upset with his performance, he may take it out on his wife, his children, the make-up artist, and you. Don't take it personally.

If Mr. Superstar doesn't feel like talking to *Entertainment Tonight* today, it's not the end of your career. Tomorrow, he might surprise you as he walks by your office, casually saying, "Let's do that *ET* thing today." Again, never force a situation. Even if you're on the slopes of Mount Everest and the *ET* crew has traveled 12,000 miles to do the interview, don't get into an argument with the actor.

Find our the source of the problem and then seek a solution by getting support personnel involved if needed. If I can work out a problem with an actor, I'm not going to go to the producer, the director or the actor's publicist. You should go to them only in a last resort situation.

Developing the Actor/Publicist Relationship.

Even the most difficult actors have a light side. A sense of humor can be helpful. Try to get into conversations with your actors whenever possible. You're trying to develop a relationship, so give them a chance to get to know you.

Some days, actors feel pressure from all sides. The wake-up call, the make-up artist, the hair stylist, the dialogue coach, the stuntman, the assistant director, the director, the producer, the writer, the cameraman, the agent, the wife, the mistress, the kids, the dog, the food, the lack of privacy, the autograph seekers, the business manager, the driver, the backed-up toilet, the weather... Of course, on that day, you have scheduled interviews with three important outlets and you can't understand why he isn't "feeling comfortable" about them.

I tend to my actors everyday. If possible, I cheer them up with good photos to approve, news that I've heard, people that have been saying nice things about them, hellos from back home, anything positive. I treat them special and more often than not it pays off.

It doesn't matter if you're dealing with superstars or first picture neophytes, they all deserve the kid glove approach. A neophyte can also say no to *ET*.

If problems persist with any one actor, don't force the situation. Before calling in the "fire department," take the "stay away and let it die down" approach. Maybe the actor is just going through a bad situation and needs time. An average movie shoot lasts 6-8 weeks. There is always time to rearrange press visits, phone interviews and photo shoots.

Dealing with Ego.

Everyone has an ego—from the executive producer and super star to the lowliest production assistant. Because ego plays such an important part in the games that are played on the movie set, publicists should at all times be aware of the various levels of power that exist, and pay strict attention to etiquette.

I follow strict rules in dealing with people on the set:

■ Treat everyone with equal respect. Never let your emotions or mood affect how you deal with people. One slip, one insult, one aside, can quickly spread out of control. People on a movie set develop instant attachments and strong camaraderies. The production assistant you give a hard time today may be sleeping with the actor, or even the producer, who gives you a hard time tomorrow.

"But what about my ego?" you might ask. "I don't want people to walk all over me." True, you want to be treated like a professional. I resented it whenever the sound guys called out "the publicist is here, it must be lunch time." But that was also my first unit assignment. It took time for me to learn how to "talk back" to them. For the moment, I had to just put a lid on my ego.

■ Maintain positive working relationships with everyone. If you want to work in show business, you can't afford to burn any bridges behind you. Spend your valuable time developing good relationships and protecting them. Don't waste your time protecting you ego, worrying about your self-worth or inflicting your importance on others. You'll get into trouble.

- Debate but never argue with your superiors or the actors. Everyone is entitled to their opinion on the film set, even the publicist. However, when opinion leads to an argumentative stance, break it off. If you want *Good Morning America* to interview Bette Midler and she doesn't, don't argue with her. Try discussing the media break with your superiors—the producer or the director. Let them know her position and let them take it up with her.

- Always keep discussions private. Don't debate anyone in a crowd of people. If you have information to give to someone on the set try to take them aside, or see them in their motor home or dressing room. It's good etiquette.

- Know when to leave actors alone. Actors who are trying to focus on a dramatic scene are continually being distracted by electricians, grips, production assistants, shouting assistant directors and someone who is chewing loudly. Don't compound that distraction by suddenly asking a media question under those circumstances.

- Be prepared to answer questions and give progress reports. Having information to give to a producer or actor shows them you are doing your job and that you can contribute something to the creative process of making movies.

- Before you enter into any serious discussions, know what you are talking about. You always have to do your homework. An actor will need some information (some actors more than others) before they make a decision. Typical questions actors ask include:

  ✔ Who will be doing the interview?

  ✔ When will the interview or story appear?

  ✔ Who else will be interviewed?

  ✔ Where will we do the interview?

  ✔ When will we do the interview?

  ✔ How much does the journalist know about the movie?

  ✔ Have they been given a press kit?

  ✔ How long will the interview take?

  ✔ Am I allowed by the producer to give interviews?

  ✔ Can I choose the location?

  ✔ Can it be postponed?

  Armed with the answers to these questions you can participate intelligently in a discussion and contribute sound information and opinion. My most embarrassing moments occur when I have to keep coming back with additional information before anyone can make a decision.

- Be aware of how fragile the film artist's ego can be. I say film artist because "ego" knows no boundaries on the film set. You might have an art director who simply loves publicity. You're escorting the freelance writer from *American Film* around the set and the art director suddenly announces that he has all the time in the world to speak to the press.

What are you going to do? You can't just say, "We don't want to speak to you." You have to have a battery of answers ready for people who suddenly declare their interest in being interviewed, even though they're not on the interviewer's schedule.

You can stall—that's one form of answer. "We don't know how much time we have to do interviews, but we'll try to squeeze you in." Never tell someone that their interview would be a waste of time for the reporter. On a film set, everyone has an important job to do and you just bruise their ego by suggesting the press isn't interested in their story.

If someone expresses enthusiasm about doing interviews, even if you can't accommodate them on the set, I always include that information in my wrap-up report which goes to the publicity people who will be involved in the release campaign—the studio or the agency. Since so many people are suddenly uncooperative during the release campaign, new interview subjects are always welcome.

Stroking. Wasn't it Hitchcock who referred to all actors as scared rabbits? Probably because he was scaring the hell out of them with his outrageous movies. However, one must accept the fact that the acting profession is by design a frightening/demoralizing business. 58 rejections in a row can affect the most self confident person.

Because of its nature, acting breeds insecurity. Needy, quirky, unfocused, in the clouds, snappy, moody, irresponsible, obnoxious, pompous, rude—all these qualities describe many of the actors I've worked with. In this discussion I'm not paying attention to actors' good qualities. You don't have to memorize them—just like you don't have to memorize the spots in a mine field where there aren't mines.

How to stroke? Get to know your actors. Memorize the following bits of information: spouse's name, children's names, home town, favorite sports team, hobbies, parents' names, favorite food, any noticeable ailments (insomnia, arthritis, allergies), sense of humor. I pay attention to these "real world" tidbits. Actors appreciate being reminded that despite the pressures of the movie set, they're not so different from "real people."

It pays to think of things to bring the actor to cheer them up. Snack foods, good reviews, copies of the trades, flattering photographs, feature stories, notes from admirers. On *Porky's II*, I was dealing with six very different men in their mid-20s. They were a cliquish group, and presented a challenge as far as establishing an effective publicist/actor relationship. But they were also voracious card players.

Virtually every night, between scenes, they would meet in one trailer or another and break out the match sticks and play poker. One day I bought a poker caddy with plenty of plastic chips and brought it over to their game. They looked up at me with wonder in their eyes. It was the perfect gift —akin to Burt Lancaster bringing the football to the sandlot game at the end of *Jim Thorpe All American*.

Not only were they thankful but they let me sit in on their game. (I think they saw me as the perfect pigeon.). For three summer months in Miami, I played poker with the boys of *Porky's*. I listened to their stories and found out what made each of them tick—information that I could never have learned as an outsider.

Attending to their poker needs was a form of stroking. It was my admission ticket. Toward the end of the shoot, I showed them my appreciation for their trust by arranging for a Las Vegas chip manufacturer to design a case of professional poker chips with *Porky's* emblazoned on them. The guys went nuts.

My biographies, feature stories, still sessions, special photography— all of my duties on *Porky's* were enhanced by my intimate knowledge of the cast. In fact, I received a commendation letter from a top P.R. executive at 20th Century Fox, for all of my writing on the film. He said it was some of the best he'd ever seen.

Stay Away From the Tough Scenes.

Everything is going well for you. The actors are cooperating, media breaks are occurring with regularity, you're getting complimentary notes and comments from the studio and your producer. Beware! A carefully developed publicist/actor relationship can disintegrate in an instant if you intrude during the wrong scene.

What is a tough scene? Any scene in which the actor has to draw upon strong emotions. When an actor has been crying his eyes out on camera for 4 hours, you don't walk up to him and ask how he feels about doing the Johnny Carson Show. He'll bite your head off.

On particularly emotional days, I keep it simple. You have to learn how to diplomatically handle actors. There are times when it's comfortable to ask questions or field media requests, and you'll learn that there are times when you simply tip your cap and walk away.

Some actors can turn off their character like a light switch. "Frankly, my dear, I don't give a damn! Cut. Oh hi, Steve, what did Hedda Hopper say?"

They're rare. On a movie set, concentration is hard to maintain because of the start and stop nature of filmmaking and because there are always so many people milling about. Some actors will go off into a corner to find a moment of peace. Let them find it. Make it one of your top priorities when you get on the set to learn your actors' habits—when they're approachable and when they're not.

Of course there will always be the actors who are *never* in a good mood to see you. In cases like that, you simply take a deep breath and ask your questions. You are a professional, being paid to do a job, just like they are. Do it.

The Last Week of Shooting.

As the film draws to a close, the pressure to complete the film can diminish. People can see an end in sight. It's akin to the last few yards of a marathon race. A certain euphoria will set in, driving the muscles on to greater heights. Some of cinema's brightest moments were created in the final few days of a film. It's natural. Actors by this time have become comfortable in their roles and the director, especially the veteran, knows them like a book. (Conversely, the first week of shooting is usually the toughest as everyone tests the water.)

A publicist can accomplish a lot in the final week of shooting. Actors will be more cooperative after having survived the shoot: they will have plenty to talk about; they can look upon the film as an experience; their fellow actors are comrades in an adventure; the director is an old friend. Even reluctant actors can usually be persuaded with the argument that this is their last chance.

Now is the time to finish your press kit interviews, complete your still approvals, perhaps set up a few phone interviews with national columnists and bring in the in-house video crew.

Dealing With A Difficult Publicist.

Get used to the fact that you are not going to be the only publicist working on this movie. Actually, I once thought that the more hands that stirred the publicity cauldron the better—the buddy system. Forget it. It's dog eat dog out there. Agency publicists are fighting to keep their clients and justify their monthly retainers. Studio publicists are fighting to keep their jobs amid constant administrative changeovers. Freelance consultants, acting like pompous "know-it-alls," are trying to impress the producer so that another job may be forthcoming. When it comes to publicity cooperation between various entities, dogfighting is the rule.

Personal publicists can be especially difficult to get along with when you're the unit publicist. Their job is to protect the image of their client—the star. Your job is to get that star to make himself or herself available to the press to help promote the film. It can be an oil and water situation. Because that star is the key to your campaign, the personal publicist is actually determining how effectively you can work.

You can't blame the personal publicist who is trying to do his job. However, there are publicists who misuse their responsibility. I schedule a *Newsweek* photo, the personal publicist says no. I invite *Entertainment Tonight* to the set, the personal publicist says let's do it closer to release time. I set up a special photo shoot for *Gentleman's Quarterly*, the personal publicist prefers another magazine.

Get the picture? The responsibility for your job is taken out of your hands and given to someone who is promoting his client's interests.

What to do? Unfortunately, you must become a negotiator, and like all negotiators, you must know what you're negotiating. When you come to the table with a potential media break, be prepared to explain how important it is to the campaign. You're going to need that ammunition.

To take the personal publicist's side for a moment, the lack of good unit publicists has furthered their careers. Sometimes, a unit will not promote a certain actor because the publicity campaign focuses on some other aspect of the movie. Or if I have a film with 6 leads and 3 supporting performers, I may not get around to pitching supporting performer number 3 to every magazine in New York. In such cases I can understand actors hiring personal publicists to supplement what the main unit is accomplishing for the film itself.

Today, a single unit publicist can't do everything. Personal publicists can accomplish a lot for their clients. But I despise the fact that certain personal publicists can and will develop an adversary relationship with units. Cooperation can and does exist. But be prepared for the worst.

Dealing with a Demanding Producer.

Producers don't have time to get involved in every facet of movie marketing, especially during the stressful period of production. They're responsible for a multi-million dollar project that could collapse at any given moment. They just don't have time to ponder whether Michael J. Fox should be interviewed by *Seventeen* instead of *Young Miss*.

However, just because they're consumed by the making of the film, don't assume that your efforts are unnoticed. I have never met a producer who wasn't excited when I showed him a media break about his project—whether it was a two paragraph blurb in *Daily Variety* or a cover story in *Premiere*. The smart producer knows the value of publicity.

Producers, by definition, are demanding and they can easily misunderstand why certain things are not being accomplished. "Screaming" producers, like screaming office managers and screaming truck drivers, are common.

Mr. Superstar may say something in an interview that is entirely inaccurate, but before you have a chance to explain, the screaming producer is yelling you out of the room: "How can you be so stupid?" "How the hell did this happen?" "Where were you?" "Don't you ever brief your actors before they open their mouths?" "Why did I hire you in the first place?" "Do you know that you're sabotaging our film single-handedly?" "Get the hell out of here!"

You try to interrupt, "But, but, but..." but it's no use. Don't take it personally, this producer has probably just berated the first assistant director, the costume designer and the chief electrician before you. So you're in good company.

To develop a good working relationship with all producers, even the screamers, follow four basic guidelines.

■ **Set Your Goals Up Front**. Beyond the initial, 'hello, you're hired' meeting at the beginning of production, be sure to have a meeting early on to discuss production publicity strategy. Get the producer involved. After you do your homework by reading the script and generating angles and creative ideas, ask for and get the producer's opinion. State up-front that the producer's opinion is important. Sometimes, even the best publicists can start off on the wrong foot by assuming that everything will be okay. 'I'll just go off on my own and do a good job.' Bad idea. Never make any major decision without consulting the producer.

Producers like to have reference data, something up-front to know if you are going to do a good job. With actors, there are contracts; with directors, there are shooting schedules; with costume designers, there are sketches; with publicists, there are production publicity proposals and outlines.

Get your ideas and plan of action down on paper *before the movie starts shooting*. If the producer then wants to gauge how the P.R. campaign is going, he can always refer to your outline. Producers also like to get memos. They may not read them, but if you don't keep the producer informed with a steady stream of memos, when something goes wrong you won't have a life-line to keep you from drowning.

■ **Be an Expert**. A movie crew consists of a team of experts in their field, people who can answer all possible questions. The producer relies heavily on the team member's expertise. The publicist is one of those experts.

A producer doesn't have the background, or the time, to evaluate the cover possibilities of *Seventeen* or *Young Miss*, but you do. If you don't know an answer to a producer's question, promise to find out *right away* and then do what ever it takes to get the answer.

Be an expert in all publicity matters and the producer will treat you like one of his team.

■ Remind the producer about the reality of P.R. breaks. A demanding producer will sometimes ask for a public relations miracle: the cover of *Time Magazine*, or a major feature in *Rolling Stone*. Let it be known that miracles do happen, however if they happened all the time, then they wouldn't be miracles.

Producers can't be expected to understand the specific idiosyncrasies of the media. Thus, they will often make unreasonable requests. For instance, you're shooting on location, say in Mobile, Alabama, and the producer naturally wants a *Los Angeles Times* set visit piece. When you call to set it up, the *Time's* response is "not this time. We've already had two reporters out this month and we're fairly satiated on set visit stories." Such a reaction is commonplace. You could have the most interesting film in production, and the media may simply be too busy to cover it. Another reason might be that Mobile, Alabama is a bit off the beaten track—thus a more expensive trip for the *LA Times*, which always pays its own way.

Don't be afraid to tell a producer he can't get a certain media break. Realities can be annoying, but they are the facts of the business. You are not a miracle worker.

■ **Cover Yourself**. Always make an effort. Don't ever let your producer catch you forgetting to contact a certain media outlet. In his eyes, you are suddenly a forgetful sort. And forgetful sorts are not hired back.

No publicist is perfect. There have been times when a producer has asked me about the reaction to the film from a certain outlet, and I haven't a clue. Why? Because I forgot to contact them.

My response? (A bit of a fib here.) "Uh, they haven't called me back yet, but I should hear this week." It's a cheat, but it gives you time to race back to your office and correct your mistake. It's okay to forget just as long as you still have time to get the job done.

There are some mistakes which you won't be able to fix. You don't have much of a fall back position if it's the last week of production and you've forgotten to call *Premiere* magazine about a possible set visit. Cover yourself by following your original media blueprint. If you give your producer a checklist of what you're going to do, use it to check off the outlets as you call them. With such a blueprint, it's impossible to forget a key outlet.

In the publicity business, especially during production, all efforts are rewarded. If *Premiere* passes on the set visit, they may come around during release period with a feature story. All is not lost if they pass now. But if you forget to contact them at all, and the producer inevitably finds out, more than the publicity opportunity will be lost. Cover yourself, always.

19

MEMO WRITING

When you're the unit publicist you're on your own. You're away from the authority of superiors back home—studio executives, independent company executives, agency owners. Such freedom can be a double-edged sword. Some people need constant direction in their job. They have a million questions and they like the comfort of having superiors available with plenty of answers. Others enjoy the "hands-off" situation—the freedom to move and work at one's own pace and schedule.

No matter how you work and how you handle the isolation, you have a responsibility to not only perform, but to report on your own performance. In the absence of your teacher, you will be filling out your own report card and sending it home. The excellent publicist will document everything and send bi-weekly memos back to the appropriate executives. Like the immortal radio operator in the bombed out shell crater on some god forsaken Pacific island, you are the communications link to the outside world. And in terms of your performance and how it is evaluated, you can live and die by your memos.

Your memos are also useful to the marketing and promotion people who come after you. If you do a good job documenting your activities during production—including making suggestions for following up on certain leads—your memos can provide a blueprint for the pre-release campaign.

As a unit publicist you are the first marketing element on a film project, you're the first to start selling the film to the media and the public. Your memos establish you as a leader, as a source of information, and as a valuable forward element on the marketing team.

What follows are some notes about how I write memos:

The Production Publicity Outline.

At the start of the production, you should file a "production publicity outline" memo detailing your approach to your job. Such a memo would include:

✔ Positioning paragraph—how you intend to describe the film.

✔ Publicity positives—what you see as the marketable angles (e.g. a superstar actor).

✔ Publicity negatives—angles you want to stay away from or potential pitfalls to a successful campaign (e.g. Mr. Superstar won't do interviews).

✔ Target audience—description of the film's demographics.

✔ Potential media outlets—a list of the outlets you intend to pitch.

✔ Notes on cast—along with angles, this will point out any specific characteristics that might prove useful to other executives working on the marketing campaign.

✔ An initial outline of upcoming locations and events that might also be of use to executives back home.

✔ If it is available, always enclose a shooting schedule with your publicity outline memo.

In a perfect world, your publicity outline would be appreciated by your publicity liaisons in Los Angeles and New York, or at the various agencies who represent actors on the project. New York liaisons could immediately contact long-lead time magazines and determine their interest in your project. Agency publicists could approach their own contacts and declare that their actor client is in a newsworthy project. LA based P.R. executives can offer guidelines on which outlets are most apt to appear receptive to your upcoming pitches.

Generally, none of this happens. But a steady stream of memos from you will remind everyone that they're all on the same team.

Whether my effectiveness on a project is a threat to the agency publicist's job or not, I still like to copy them on all major memos. My ideas can spark them to make their own contacts on behalf of their clients. A media break is a media break no matter who initiates it. And the more information an agency publicist receives, the better. A supply of progress memos keeps them on the team. However, if you're working for a studio, get approval from your boss before you copy agency publicists.

In terms of studio or independent liaison personnel in LA or NY, the memo is also very useful—more in terms of establishing your effectiveness on the job and your chances for rehiring, than for initiating a major production publicity campaign.

The reality of the motion picture business is that studio and independent publicists may not concentrate their efforts on the marketing of films in production. They are concerned about the films that are opening next week and two months down the road. That is why being a self-starter is so important to your task as a unit publicist. You have to take the initiative even when your superiors are consumed elsewhere. The studio or independent company will always vary from film to film, depending on the subject, the stars and where you're shooting. Still, an effective memo will put your film in the back of their minds. It doesn't hurt for them to know about the progress of your film especially when they're talking to media people every day—some of whom will ask about current projects.

Bi-Weekly Progress Reports.

Plan on filing a publicity progress report every two weeks. On a ten-week shoot, these five memos will be the most important communications you will have with your superiors. Your memos literally document everything you do.

Two weeks between progress report gives you enough time to compile a record of the outlets you've pitched and their responses without putting you under the gun. You will also have plenty of opportunities to observe the set and discover new angles and the effectiveness of old ones. And don't worry if you miss your bi-weekly deadline by a few days, no one is clocking you with a stopwatch.

If you're doing your job, it shouldn't be difficult to compose your memo every two weeks. Information is literally everywhere, including:

✔ Progress of the production, including exciting highlights.

✔ Actor's idiosyncrasies. Their attitude toward media requests.

✔ Newly discovered story angles.

✔ Stories that are breaking.

✔ Stories that are about to break.

✔ Pitches.

✔ Media interest.

✔ No interest.

✔ Leads for future interest.

Wrap-up Memos.

A wrap-up memo is due at the end of production. It should sum up the information listed in the previous memos and project future ideas on the project. Don't hesitate to be specific. If a certain actor is causing problems with his refusal to do publicity, then document it. The P.R. entities that will follow you onto the campaign will appreciate the advance warning. On the other hand, if another actor appears to cooperate, it will alert future publicists to the opportunity to pitch that actor for coverage.

Speaking of availability, document any information you might gather on the future plans of your actors. If Mr. Superstar is headed for three months in Italy, that information will be immediately useful to your superiors back home. If Miss Superstar plans on being incommunicado for the next six months because she's having a baby, that is also essential information.

Succinctness.
Getting your memos written on time is one thing, getting your message across clearly is another. People generally don't like to read memos so keep them factual and to-the-point.

Here are a few dos and don'ts of memo writing. Let's say you've had a couple of conversations with the film editor at *Rolling Stone*. She likes your pitch and is going to bring it up at the next editorial meeting. With Kevin Costner playing Paul McCartney, it might even be a cover story. One publicist might report this as follows:

I contacted Joan Smith at *Rolling Stone* (who recently replaced Gary Farr as senior film editor) who did not return my phone call for three days. I finally reached her and she found my story pitch interesting. They've done Kevin before, but the idea of a movie about Paul McCartney is intriguing to her. She will bring up the idea of a feature story at their next editorial meeting. I will be contacting her next Friday. A cover story in *Rolling Stone* is a possibility.

This tells the story, but it's not a very good memo:

✔ You don't have to pinpoint your exact movements. You don't have to say "I contacted" or "I'm going to call back on Thursday" or "She didn't return my phone call for three days." If you're doing your job properly, your boss will assume that you will follow-up and confirm any break.

✔ No one is going to be interested in the fact that Gary Farr was replaced by Joan Smith at *Rolling Stone*. Keep your information pertinent to your superiors' interests.

✔ Underline and CAPITALIZE the name of any outlet you mention— <u>ROLLING STONE</u>.

✔ If you're trying to communicate that *Rolling Stone* is considering a feature story, don't undercut yourself by prefacing with "they've done Kevin before." Concentrate on the fact that Costner is playing a role which should appeal to *Rolling Stone*'s readers. If they eventually decide to pass on the story, your memo can simply report it was because "they've done Kevin before." At that point, the reasons are useful.

✔ Don't mention cover stories until they happen. Producers will get very excited when they hear the word "cover" and they will drive you crazy with "what's happening with our cover story?" questions. When *Rolling Stone* comes back to you and agrees on a cover and actually schedules a photo shoot with Costner, then you can spread the word.

✔ Include a contact phone number for possible follow-up. You can then use your progress memo as a phone sheet, without having to look up numbers all the time. There is also the outside chance that someone on your contact sheet is personal friends with Joan Smith and will be delighted to know that they are considering a feature story. A call to the contact from a friend (and only a friend) is not a bad public relations move. It also makes you look like you're doing your job—spreading useful information to the powers that be.

Here is the best way to present the previous information in memo form:

ROLLING STONE Film Editor Joan Smith (212) 555-1212) likes Costner and the McCartney character and is presenting a feature idea at next week's editorial meeting.

Short and sweet. As additional information comes in, you can add it to your follow-up memos.

Possessing the ability to not only create media interest in your project, but to expertly document that information, is a valuable skill. Film publicity is not just phone work, or press kit writing, or rapport with the actors. It's operating as the first link in the marketing chain. Every bit of information you collect on a location, whether it's phoning in a column item to *Daily Variety*, or discovering that your actor will not do interviews will prove valuable during the road toward release.

20

Working With A Film Crew

Film publicity during production involves more than developing a relationship between you and your media contacts. You must also develop a positive working relationship with the entire crew.

Your personality plays a factor here. Some publicists are lone wolfs. They spend most of their time with phone work and when they do come to the set they offer a perfunctory hello to the producer, director, or star and ignore everyone else. It's a snobbish approach that I avoid. If I don't know the name of 90% of the crew at the end of a shoot, then I haven't done my job. My feeling has always been that good public relations begins at home. If I make an effort to get to know all crew members—from caterers to camera assistants—they will make my job easier.

When a movie is in production, you're in the business of "bothering" people. In the eyes of a crew, laboring 10-12 hour days on the set, your visiting media are fleas. Actors or producers may not say it to your face, but interviews are a distracting burden whenever they take place. And if there is any opportunity to avoid them, they will.

It Pays To Have Good Relationships With Everyone.

Developing healthy, friendly, cooperative relationships with crew members is very important. You begin to develop an identity on the set, you become a part of the action, you are no longer a stranger. As an example, if Miss Superstar sees you having fun telling a story to the grips, she may come over and want to get in on the fun, perhaps relating her own story. Loosening up the actors in this manner is vital.

There are other advantages:

- **Sources of Information.** The demands of the job prevent the publicist from spending 12 hours on the set every day. Yet you need to know everything that happens which might make an interesting story. If Fred Savage breaks the window in the director's trailer while taking batting practice, you need a friend on the set who will call you with the scoop. It would make a smashing column item.

■ **Help During Media Visits**. You'd be surprised how needy you become when you have media visiting the set. The TV crew wants to interview the lead actor at the end of the lunch break. Not only must the assistant directors know so that the actor can be escorted to the interview, but the lighting crew may have to standby and provide a key light on the set for the TV crew. Make-up and hair must be available to touch up the actor prior to his interview and you may need wardrobe to provide a key garment. Can you imagine Indiana Jones doing an interview without his leather jacket? Additionally, props may even be able to provide a couple of director's chairs for the interview. And transportation has to standby to provide a ride back to the hotel for the visiting crew. A media visit is a collaborative effort and you're going to need lots of help. It's much easier to ask a friend for help than someone who doesn't even know your name.

■ **Intermediaries in Disputes**. If by chance you develop a stormy relationship with someone on the set, it helps to have friends to intercede on your part. In my experience, film crews have generally been a delight to work with. Their creative backgrounds, their easy-going demeanor and their fanatic love of the business make the publicity work exciting. Occasionally, however, there can be someone quite willing to throw a wrench into your carefully laid plans.

Despite the circus-like atmosphere of the set, film crews have a strict chain of command: the grip reports to the key grip who reports to the director of photography who reports to the director who reports to the producer, etc. If you have a problem with one crew member, try chatting with the person above him. It's almost never necessary to have a direct confrontation. Unlike the publicist/actor relationship where you must try to work out any problems one-to-one, when dealing with a crew problem, don't hesitate to seek advice from someone higher on the chain of command.

In most cases, problems won't occur. As the publicist, you are a very benign influence on the day's workload. You're not going to be escorting media on the set everyday. Most of the time, you're going to be in the office on the phone. Some publicists are rarely on the set. So your presence is never in the forefront of the crew's mind. But when you do appear, you want to make a strong positive impression.

Crew Newsletter.

"Good publicity begins at home"—a phrase that will be repeated throughout this book—is perfectly embodied in the concept of the crew newsletter. In fact, it should be emblazoned on the newsletter mast head like the *New York Times* motto, "All the news that's fit to print."

My first experience with crew newsletters came in 1981 when I was attached to the *Endangered Species* crew shooting in Sheridan and Buffalo, Wyoming. It was my first unit assignment and I was bumping my head left and right trying to figure out what to do to get the job done (I didn't have this book at my fingertips).

During a particularly hectic day, one of the production assistants handed me a crew newsletter. There was an article about a particular crew member's background, a funny column *à la* Army Archerd, mentioning quite a few crew names, a cartoon, even a tongue-in-cheek title contest to come up with the best alternative to *Endangered Species* which to this day sounds like a National Geographic Special (the winner turned out to be "Altered Steaks").

Crew newsletters can be a chore to turn out, but they are worth their weight in gold. Here's why:

■ To the crew, you, as the editor of the newsletter, develop an immediate identity. Remember, most of the work you do during production is off the set. You can remain a mystery person on the set, a P.R. ghost. The newsletter gives you a chance to mingle and start conversations. Crew members will even come to you with article ideas, bits of information, and gossip. As editor of the crew newsletter, you're a part of the team. The ice is broken. Your job is easier.

■ Newsletters can be a rich source of information, useful for your final press kit. On a film set, everyone has a speciality and a wealth of experience. There's always a grip or an electrician who worked with Clark Gable on *Gone With the Wind*. The stories they tell are not only interesting, but they may lead to angles for press kit stories. On *Endangered Species*, a newsletter profile on one of the cattle wranglers, inspired me to approach *American Film* magazine about a piece on the lost art of wrangling. They bought it.

■ Newsletters allow you to trumpet your set visits. When you have press coming to the set, you can announce their arrival in the newsletter, just as if the Queen of England was arriving in town and you were the local newspaper editor. Such announcements make you look good ("the *LA Times* is coming? Hey, Rubin is doing a good job!"), they prepare the cast and crew for the interview process, and the press often gets a kick out of seeing their own name in print (they're also very appreciative that the stars have been primed for their visit).

■ Newsletters are a repository for all sorts of information, including announcements, welcomes and farewells, crew extracurricular activities (softball games, etc.), thank-yous, football pools, even want ads.

■ **Here are some tips on putting together a good newsletter:**

✔ Newsletters work best on location because the crew is isolated from the outside world and their own daily regimens back home. On an LA, NY or any big city shoot, crew members go home after work. On location, they are more sociable, more inclined to intermingle, and more interested in a tabloid about themselves.

✔ A newsletter should have a regular publishing schedule. For the ambitious, publish weekly, however, a bi-weekly newsletter is fine.

✔ Try to give your newsletter an interesting look. Type up the stories in columns. Pepper your issues with interesting graphics, headlines, cartoons, and photos. For graphics, I mine local and national newspapers and magazines. If I see something interesting, I simply clip and paste. Crew newsletters turn you into a collage artist.

✔ Order some photos taken by the still photographer and use them as illustrations. Since crew members will almost never see any of the photography until release time, this gives them their first opportunity to see the film in pictures. If the pictures are arresting, it also makes the still photographer look good. Don't hesitate to use Polaroids as well, or take advantage of the burgeoning one-hour photo shops to get some quick and easy color snapshots. Candids really add spice to your newsletter.

✔ Invite submissions. You don't have to write the whole newsletter yourself. Be the editor, collect material from all sources. If spontaneous writing isn't your strong suit, nose around and find out who wants to report and write. The caterer's assistant might be an aspiring novelist. I find that production assistants, usually right out of college, are all up and coming screenwriters. Get them to submit a piece.

✔ Play "columnist" on the set. Compose a gossip column. It's usually an attention-getter and a source for plenty of humor. But keep it clean. If you spotted a certain crew member sneaking out of someone's room in the middle of the night, don't print it in the newsletter. You want to survive the shoot in one piece. Gossip pieces can be cute, but they must be tasteful.

✔ Come up with a cute name for the paper, playing off words in the film's title or characters. Ironically, on *Rad*, the lead character's name was Cru. So it was logical to call the paper the *Cru News*. On *Desert Bloom*, each actor had their own newsletter issue named after their character. Recently, I worked on *The Taking of Beverly Hills* which was shot entirely in Mexico City. Appropriately, our crew newspaper was called *The KAOSPECTATOR*. Matt ("Max Headroom") Frewer helped me come up with the name. The newsletter on *Honey, I Blew Up The Baby* was appropriately called "Baby Talk."

✔ A three-page newsletter is a good size. Any more than that becomes a bit unwieldy. (You also might take some heat for using so much xerox time.) Make sure you print enough copies for every cast and crew member, and keep some extra copies to send back to the studio or the independent production company.

✔ Always ask permission from the producer to write a weekly newsletter. I forgot to once and discovered, to my chagrin, that the producer had wanted to publish his own newsletter!

✔ By all means, enjoy the experience. With all the other things you're doing, the newsletter might appear to be frivolous, but it will be worth the effort.

Crew Photo Needs.

Everyone on the crew is going to be interested in your still photos and even though the still photographer will sometimes take the initiative to provide free samples to certain individuals, the responsibility of dealing with still photo requests from the crew will usually land in your lap.

The art department needs a specific shot of Harrison Ford holding his leather jacket a certain way. The producer likes a particular shot of himself on the set, looking authoritative. He wants multiple copies right away. Your leading actor wants a nice shot of himself to send to his mother in upstate New York. The stand-in for Ms. Superstar wants a shot of the two of them together on the set.

All of these requests are time-consuming, taking you away from your pitching duties. Nonetheless, fulfill those requests. Making allies and keeping the peace is important and nothing does that better than a good photo.

Unit publicists have a great deal of power when it comes to ordering photos. You are the first marketing executive on the set, you are in charge of selecting good initial stills and no one is going to question your authority. If you deem it important to service certain photographic elements to the crew, then you have the power to do so.

Whether you're working through a studio photography department or ordering directly from the lab, all requests for crew are legitimately part of the production publicity campaign. However, before everyone on the set goes "hog wild" picking out their favorite shots, set up some rules and be firm about enforcing them:

■ I usually grant the producer, director and top actors carte blanche in picking shots. If they like certain shots, fine, I order the prints.

In the actor's case, if he's picking shots out of the proof sheet book, he's actually helping do your job. Because in addition to killing shots (as part of the still approval clause in their contract), nothing says an actor can't also suggest his favorites as well. Your publicity superiors at your home base are going to appreciate receiving still suggestions that have been personally endorsed by the lead actor. And whereas they'll sometimes question your own taste in still photos and transparencies, they generally will take into strong consideration any suggestions the key actors make.

■ Avoid bringing stills and slides directly to the set. If you start showing photos to one crew member in public, there will soon be a crowd around you. Everyone will want a look, and the actors who haven't had a chance to see the photography will suddenly say, "How come the grips are seeing my pictures and not me?"

- If you must come to the set with photography, keep the shots in an envelope and take them personally to the actor or director's trailer and try to accomplish your business at the end of the lunch break.

- If an actor or crew member must borrow the book of black and white proof sheets, let them keep it for a specific time. Usually 48 hours max. That book is a constant reference source for you and if it's stuck in someone's hotel room it's not doing you much good.

- Try to avoid giving anyone access to color materials. Unless an actor has still approval, there's really no reason to bring out color materials en masse. Binders filled with color slides are unwieldy and slides can fall out of their sleeves and be trampled upon. The black and white proof sheet book is designed for mobility and no one can really harm it. It should be your primary photo contact point between yourself and cast/crew.

- Keep a loupe (magnifier) with you at all times when showing photography. An extra loupe should be left with the actor when you drop off the proof sheet book. Proof sheets cannot be analyzed without a loupe.

- Aside from the top actors and key executives, keep crew still requests down to one or two shots each. Unless the art department suddenly requests 24 key shots for an important reason, there's no reason to go overboard when servicing crew still requests.

- If the Production Manager requests a certain shot to service a local store or organization which provided services to the film, I fill those requests immediately. A still photograph of the film crew at work on their premises will score a number of public relations points.

- At one point, the still photographer will take the crew photo—a ritual that occurs toward the end of production. Usually, the photographer or the production office will take care of servicing the shot to all crew members. If possible, stay out of this one. A good still photographer will take the shot, have it copied, and deliver it to the production office for dispersal to the crew.

- When you're thumbing through the proof sheets and you see a particularly good shot of a specific crew member, get a copy made and give it to that crew member. This becomes particularly effective when dealing with the assistant directors who can be very helpful to you when you have set visits. One photo can provide a lot of P.R. advantage. I have yet to meet a crew member who wasn't delighted to get a good photo.

- All photo requests are generally serviced free of charge. The last thing you want to get into is determining the price of a photo. However, if the assistant cameraman suddenly feels that he needs 34 shots of the crew in action, explain to him the cost of an 8" x 10" enlargement, and work out a deal. Thirty-four shots is quite a bit above the two shot minimum.

- Unless a specific size photo is requested, all orders should be for 8" x 10" glossy black and whites. They're the rule.

- Don't hesitate to pick a couple of shots of yourself working on the set. If anyone asks you what you did for three months in the jungles of Singapore, you've got proof in your own scrapbook.

Extra-Curricular Activities: The Publicist as Recreation Director.

Your freedom of movement during production because you are not tied to the set 12-14 hours a day, can get you into unusual situations. Generally, I maintain a "can do" attitude during production. If I am asked to help out with some activity, I lend my support. The nature of publicity is to be an on-going problem solver anyway. This is just one more job that needs to be done by someone who has access to the entire crew.

Your freedom makes you the ideal candidate. A grip hangs out with grips. Camera assistants spend time with camera assistants. Makeup and hairdressing are confined to the set. The publicist can be everyone's buddy. So who is the logical person to organize the crew softball game on Sundays in the park?

You'll need to secure a field, find the proper opposing team, gather equipment, and keep everyone informed. Depending on your location, opponents are generally numerous even in the small towns and byways of America.

Local radio or TV stations often field their own softball teams. On *Porky's II*, our company team played a doubleheader with the local radio station and the local fire department. The radio station promoted the contest on the air and we donated some money to a nearby hospital. Everyone had a great time.

If the actors want to play in a sporting contest, make sure the game is scheduled at the end of production. The production cannot afford to lose an actor to a sporting injury. My producer on *Desert Bloom* reminded me of the incident involving actress Meg Tilly on *Amadeus*. She had been signed to play the wife of Mozart. However, prior to the start of shooting, she broke her ankle in a volleyball game and was prevented from being in the movie (Elizabeth Berridge replaced her).

If your location is in a particularly scenic spot, you will also be called upon to help arrange weekend tours and cultural activities. On *Porky's II*, I organized a bus trip to Cape Canaveral to watch a shuttle launch. It was a rare and delightful opportunity.

The P.R. value of doing things in the local communities can often be great. For instance, you might be shooting on the island of Tahiti and the local chamber of commerce invites your production's VIPs on a weekend cruise around the island. This is a pure P.R. assignment. As the company spokesperson, you will be assigned the task of determining the extent of the tour, arrivals and departures, dress, and the number of guests. Photo opportunities with local bigshots may also be organized.

Screen these invitations as you would screen media requests. Remember actors are more inclined to kick back and relax on their holidays. They don't like to be bothered with local dignitaries and photo opportunities. They'd rather finish that off on the set during lunchtime anyway. However, if a particularly scenic trip or tour is on the line, they might be very receptive.

Sometimes crew activities have direct correlations to your publicity campaign. If a contingent of actors make a trip to the local race track and you go along, the track officials may want to take a photo and publish it in their local newsletter. If the same group goes out to Yankee Stadium, you may want to contact the team public relations person who might see an even larger photo opportunity. Movie stars and sports stars make good photo opportunities. Breaking onto the sports page of any newspaper during production would be a coup.

Photo opportunities with local stars or dignitaries are not confined to sporting activities. They extend to rock concerts, nightclubs, comedy clubs, any type of activity. Always be aware of these opportunities, especially if you're accompanying the cast or crew.

Developing an excellent relationship with your crew should always be a priority. Not only will good crew relationships help you do your job, but it will make the experience of working on a movie an extremely positive one.

21

PRODUCTION JUNKETS

Can you imagine being the publicist on the set of *Gone With the Wind* in 1938. Prior to the start of shooting, David O. Selznick would have probably turned to you and said, "When we shoot the burning of Atlanta, feel free to bring a good press contingent to the set, we want national coverage."

You would have walked back to your office at MGM in Culver City, opened your media directory and started to check off the most important outlets. And they would have come, all of them, because *Gone With the Wind* was one of the most eagerly awaited films of all time.

When to Hold a Junket.

Whether you're working on *Gone With the Wind* or *Police Academy 71*, there will come a time when you decide whether to junket the press to set. Junketing simply means bringing a group to location, usually out of town press. A contingent may come from Los Angeles, or New York or from various cities. Some of the major studios have been known to invite as many as 50 national journalists to the set of their major films. However, these days, the really large junkets are reserved for the pre-release period when the journalist can arrive in Los Angeles, see the finished movie and interview the principal stars. More on pre-release junkets later in the book.

Production junkets are important when you have:

■ A spectacular or highly unusual sequence that should be documented by the press. The moguls of the past, showmen in the true sense, were publicity hounds and I would not have been surprised to see a large press contingent at the chariot race in *Ben Hur* or at the beach landings in *The Longest Day*.

Large set pieces like these are also logistically good sequences for junkets, because you have plenty of room to maneuver in. The last thing you want to do is bring a large press contingent to an interior. It would be a disaster. Did you ever try to keep two journalists quiet during an interior sequence, let alone twenty?

Some scenes, no matter how grandiose, are not appropriate to show to the press. I would be surprised if there were press people on the set when they shot the spaceship landing in *Close Encounters of the Third Kind* or when Harrison Ford and Karen Allen saw the opening of the Ark of the Covenant in *Raiders of the Lost Ark*. Some key sequences should be surprises to filmgoers.

■ Major stunt sequences. You don't have to have 3,000 extras crossing the Red Sea to justify a press junket. Sometimes, an unusual stunt can have the same impact. If you're shooting in Los Angeles, there's a good possibility that at least one of the local news shows will feature your stunt on the nightly news. And if it's a slow day, you might get a number of crews to come out, depending on the film and the available stars.

For distant locations, the stunt sequence had better be unusual. If journalists are going to travel long distances, they're going to need to see something special. I would have brought a junket to watch Steve McQueen's motorcycle chase in *The Great Escape* (however, I would have kept them away from the ending when his motorcycle crashes— let's keep the audiences guessing).

■ Unusual locations that have not been featured in films before. Do they exist? By now I would think Hollywood film makers have covered every inch of the globe. However, you never know when your producer decides to film in the closest Eskimo outpost to the North Pole, or on an uncharted island in the Pacific. Usually, the real distant locations preclude a major press junket, simply because air fare alone would be enormous. On these occasions, one major TV crew from *Good Morning America*, *The Today Show* or your in-house video crew would be sufficient.

Locations in North America are more accessible and less expensive for junkets. If you were attached to a new production depicting "Custer's Last Stand," and you were filming on the Little Big Horn in Montana, then it would be appropriate to bring in a major press junket.

■ Unusual casting or star power. Oh, the value of today's stars, and oh, the problems they can present. A producer announces that he has the casting coup of the decade—Dustin Hoffman, Al Pacino and Robert DeNiro portray the Marx Brothers in a remake of *A Day at the Races*. Fabulous! Unbelievable!

Unprecedented! A banner headline in *Daily Variety*. No sooner is the production announced than the publicity department learns that the set will be closed—no publicity during production.

Often, the theory is that the bigger the star the less he or she will do on the set. This is when the star starts dictating to the studio what their publicity strategy will be on the picture. It's a sad fact of life and certainly an operational plan that the original studio moguls would have found distasteful.

Someday soon I plan to teach a class to young actors on their future publicity responsibilities, a concept that was probably second nature to Shirley Temple before she was ten years old.

If your production boasts major stars or an unusual group of stars, and your set isn't closed, recommend a junket to set for a number of journalists—writers who are always looking for star attraction.

Organizing a Successful Junket.

Interviewing actors on the set of a movie is a great idea. The actors are there, they're working, the journalist gets an opportunity to observe the creative process, the actors are a captive audience, there are other people available for interviews, there's the ambience of the set, there's an immediacy to the proceedings and a sense of personal involvement on the journalist's part. It's a veritable Disneyland attraction for the press and you're the tour guide. If you can organize a production junket and get it to work, you're a champion.

Here are some tips on organizing junkets to the set:

- Don't invite the world. Unless Paramount is going to send half their field force to help out, you don't want to turn your set into a United Nations tour. Your actors will also rebel if there are too many journalists around.

  How many is too many? On a major production, I would junket a maximum of twelve journalists. On a smaller film, half that many. Remember, journalists don't just appear like magic and then disappear from whence they came. Each will demand precise travel and accommodation arrangements, appropriate meals, and, of course, interaction with the production and the actors. Even on the best of days, a journalist can be a handful on the set. Multiply their numbers too much, and you're asking for trouble.

- Pick and choose your visiting journalists carefully. Inviting a journalist to set could cost thousands of dollars. Your producer may ask a simple question, "Where does this journalist break his stories?" You better be ready to justify all expenses.

  The best journalist to junket is a freelancer who breaks in a number of publications. It's also nice when the freelancer has a definite assignment with a national publication. When freelancers are unavailable, the national magazines may send a staff writer to cover your picture.

  Your major national magazines should be considered first—*Time, Newsweek, Premiere, Rolling Stone, People Magazine, Life.* A writer or freelancer from any of these publications is worth a round trip ticket to most sets. If they are not attached to the above magazines, you still might want to junket some freelancers who break in multiple magazines and newspapers.

I once invited a freelancer to set who had a cover story assignment from *Playgirl*, plus additional assignments for two daily newspapers, a music trade publication and *USA Today*. He was definitely a plum for the production.

Key newspaper journalists are junket candidates but you will find that they're a tougher pitch because their publications usually demand that the journalist pay his own way. This applies to such key publications as the *Los Angeles Times*, *New York Times* and the *Chicago Tribune*. If these journalists have firm assignments for production stories, by all means, invite them.

In terms of electronic outlets, most of them like to pay their own way—*Good Morning America*, *The Today Show*, *Entertainment Tonight*, *20/20*. Again, if they want to come, and you have clearance to bring them to set, then invite them. There are other excellent electronic outlets like E! Entertainment Channel, VH1's *Flix*, Group W's *Entertainment Report*, MTV's *The Big Picture*, the show business segments on HBO, Showtime, and The Movie Channel and USA Cable's *Hollywood Insider*. However, sometimes it is better to hire your own video crew and shoot interview and B-roll footage for those outlets. You'll probably get more coverage if you invite the shows to set, but your budget may also be limited.

I cannot over-estimate the value of an in-house video documentary unit. During a production with star power, the footage you collect on the set can be of immediate value to electronic outlets thirsting for production stories.

- Take charge of visiting journalists, you are their lifeline. From the time the journalists get off the plane to the time they re-board, they are completely and utterly under your guidance and care. Whether you're introducing them to Bo Derek or buying them aspirin at four in the morning, you are responsible for their well-being.

Junkets turn publicists into experts in protocol. On the one hand, you're the battle hardened sergeant constantly explaining the situation to a group of green war correspondents. Simultaneously, you're the gracious, happy-go-lucky bon vivant glad handing the press, stunning them with your intimate knowledge of the production while introducing them to the stars with a smile, a touch of reverence and a little bit of the cheerleader.

You're also the proverbial worry wart, watching everyone with a wary eye lest cardinal rules of etiquette be broken.

- Don't hesitate to say "no" if necessary. As much as you want to create the best possible impression on the visiting media, remember who you are working for. If Miss Superstar doesn't want to do interviews, nothing the press is going to say will change her mind. In a case like that, your hands are tied. You must side with your actress. Unless a producer or director or fellow actor can intercede, you will have to lay down the law for the press.

I made the mistake once of siding with a Newsweek photographer who wanted to take a particular shot of an actress with her boyfriend. It was a reasonable request, but the actress stormed away from the set and sulked in her trailer for an hour before I could apologize. Always take a step back from confrontations and weigh the stakes. That journalist is going to be on the set for two days. That actress is going to be with you for fifty-eight days.

■ Keep the cast and crew well-informed. It's a simple procedure, but you would be surprised at how many times publicists forget to alert cast and crew about an impending junket. Never surprise an actor with an interview. It's embarrassing and it makes everyone look like an idiot.

After your producer has approved the set visit, you've alerted the assistant directors and the actors have agreed to do the appropriate interviews, don't hesitate to remind them of the visit. Utilize the call sheet as a reminder to the crew that press visits are imminent.

■ Keep press away from trouble spots. If there is trouble brewing, you want to keep the press as far away as possible.

A good publicist has his eyes and ears always open. If Actress A is in a foul mood today, maybe Actor A should be giving the interviews. If the director is suffering from a cold and is snapping at everyone, maybe you shouldn't put the *Entertainment Tonight* crew two inches behind his left shoulder. He could turn around and blow them back to Hollywood.

If Actor A, who normally doesn't like to give interviews, wants to conduct the interview with Actress B at his side, try not to overrule him. The journalist might squawk about not getting the "one on one," but you might lose the whole interview if you'd don't give him his way. Bear in mind that some actors are a little gun-shy around microphones. Sometimes they seek out company to diminish the stage fright.

Always lead, never follow. Journalists should never approach actors on their own for interviews. On the set, you are the principle liaison. You introduce the journalist to the star, and set up the interview, you direct them to a place, and you leave them to their business (unless you are invited to join the party).

When you're junketing, sometimes you have too many bodies to watch. While you have journalists A, B and C interviewing actors A, B, and C, journalist D suddenly sees the director and goes for it. Most of the time, the director, if he's available will be a sport and sit down and do the interview on the spot. However, there will be times when the director will resent the direct method and will later say that you should be providing a screening service for such encounters.

■ Press conferences sometimes work best. Logistically speaking, it's always going to be difficult for an actor to do more than one or two interviews during his lunch break. If you have six to 12 journalist visiting the set for a short period of time, and you are unable to schedule enough time for "one on ones," then the press conference is your best choice.

A press conference allows you to fit all of the journalists into the actor's schedule at once. You might even bring additional actors to the table to field questions. Under the proper circumstances, press conferences can be quite practical. If the journalists still insist on one on one interviews, try to accommodate them as best as you can.

■   Round-robin interviews are another solution. Round-robin interviewing, a process very common in pre-release junkets, is also effective on the set. In a sense, you're setting up a series of press conferences with different actors. At a given time, usually about fifteen minutes on the set, you switch the actors from table to table, giving the journalists equal time to speak to all available talent (including the director).

It's amazing what you can do during an hour lunch break, given enough lead time and actor cooperation. Again, one on one interviews are preferred, but under time constraints, the round-robin interview may be the only solution available. Even the most determined journalist is going to be happier with a round-robin or press conference interview, than no interview at all. More on the logistics of round-robin interviews later.

■   Keep television coverage to a minimum. Because TV crews are the most obtrusive of set visitors, it is advisable to keep their number to a minimum. Try to avoid having more than one crew on the set at a time, especially during interior sequences. TV crew sizes vary. Usually there is a camera person, a sound person and a producer. However, I recently invited a crew to set and they came with five additional bodies.

During junkets to major production sequences, you will probably have to prepare for multiple camera coverage. If you're about to blow up "The Bridge on the River Kwai," *ET* is going to have to be content to film alongside *GMA* and MTV.

■   Keep your junket visitors informed at all times. When a journalist leaves the location, he should be as much of an expert on the film as possible. And you will have supplied that expertise. Your advance production notes will be helpful. Also, get permission from the producer for the journalist to see the script. If he says okay, the script becomes an additional source of information for the journalist.

Most of all, you are the answer person. During the course of an average junket, you will be asked hundreds of questions about the production. Impress your media contacts with your knowledge and your ability to get answers quickly and efficiently.

22

Dealing Calmly And Efficiently With Emergency Situations

In addition to your many hats during production—diplomat, journalist-at-large, tour guide, psychiatrist, spy and marketing genius —during emergency situations you may be asked to don the fedora of the trouble shooter.

Emergencies can and do happen on any movie set, anywhere. Imagine if you had been the publicist on the night of the *Twilight Zone* helicopter accident or on the science fiction film during which actress Natalie Wood drowned off Catalina Island. These are horrifying tragedies and they can cause immediate public relations nightmares.

The Publicist's Role in an Emergency.

Responding to crisis situations requires a cool, calm approach that P.R. professionals in all fields understand. Emergencies vary in their intensity. Whether you're dealing with a senseless accident on the set or a personnel problem that results in firings or mass layoffs, you must develop a specific crisis posture that will help you deal with your producers, the studio, the performers, the crew and, most importantly, the media.

Most of the time movie making is about as far as you can get from dealing with the real world. While the whimsical phrase "why grow up when you can make movies" is applicable to most movie sets, the crisis situation changes everything. Attitude-problems, irritating personalities, immature people and complainers, sober up quickly. It's adult time in the asylum.

Here are some guidelines for dealing with crisis situations:

■ Identify the crisis and get informed immediately. If you're sitting in the production office reading the *Hollywood Reporter* and the telephone brings you news of a plane crash involving crew members, you get moving immediately. If the production manager is running for his vehicle, you run with him. If his car is filled, get another. If the scene is accessible, get in there and find out what happened.

Like any good reporter, you've got to uncover the facts and try to piece together a situation report. A well-informed publicist will be of much more value to the crew than one who is in the dark. Don't try to be an investigator on your own, but be on top of the situation. You don't want to be in the production office when the head of the studio calls and you have nothing to report.

Also, remember that disasters have a tendency to draw media like moths to a light bulb. If at all possible, get to the site of the emergency before they do and be prepared to start answering some tough questions.

■ Stay close to your authority figures. Don't be a maverick. Disaster planning involves close communication with your superiors. You will be developing a strategy by consulting with them frequently in the next few hours. In disaster situations, you're suddenly thrust into the position of playing presidential press secretary. The Pearl Harbor attack has been launched and every media person in the country wants to know what the President is going to do about it. Call no one, communicate nothing without speaking with your superiors.

■ Determine a course of action with the media. If the producer wants the press kept away, keep the press away. Don't second guess the producer. He will have plenty of time to develop a rational approach to interviewers. Right now, there is a situation to be evaluated. You've seen a thousand movies with press swarming around a disaster situation. TV cameras everywhere, photographers running around, microphones thrust into people's faces. The last thing your production team needs is to deal with reporters. That's why you are there.

Don't hesitate to seek some help. You cannot physically keep five camera crews away from a crash site or an explosion. Ask the production team for some muscle. Be authoritative, speak up and out, and don't back down. You are going to cooperate with the press but on your terms not theirs. Today's news teams get their story regardless of how much you to try to protect the sensitivity of the situation, but you must try to maintain order.

How to deal with the press? Your first question is going to be to your producer, "What would you like me to do?" He will usually say, "keep them off my back until we figure out what's going on here." And you will do just that.

The chief production executive at the disaster site will generally be on the telephone to his superiors to make a report. During this time, an approach to the media will be discussed. If fatalities are involved, families must be notified prior to any media approach. Producers will usually make the phone call, or local medical personnel, or members of the clergy, but don't be surprised if you are suddenly thrust into that situation.

- Be an effective spokesperson. During crisis situations, aside from drafting a press release after discussions with your superiors, there is a chance that you will be the spokesperson for any press interviews. Be as cooperative as possible, but don't forget your responsibilities to the production. If as part of the decided approach, you must keep facts from the press, then follow orders. Don't start blurting out information that has not been authorized by your superiors. Be the diplomat and deal directly with the press without sounding like an idiot.

"I don't know, but I will try to get that information for you" is a correct response. A response like "I can't give you that information at this time" is a red flag and it's only going to prompt further interrogation on the part of the media.

Don't hesitate to contact your own P.R. superiors at your home base, especially if you need advice during emergency situations. Wake them up if you have to. They're going to appreciate it in the long run, because if the production is on location, local press in LA or NYC (depending on the site of your headquarters) are probably going to be contacting them immediately.

- If you're isolated from the media, resist the temptation to just keep quiet. Encourage your superiors to report the disaster to the media. Failing to send out a press release is not the same as a cover up, but it can look like one. The news is going to be discovered by the press sooner or later. You can do more to protect the privacy and the reputations of your fellow crew members by being in control of the situation. It's up to you to make sure a truthful, carefully worded statement is sent out emphasizing that everyone is doing everything they can to help the situation. But if your superiors decide against that approach, there is nothing you can do.

- Releases should be sent to a few select outlets. Don't prepare unusually large mailings during crisis situations. If you're on a distant location, phone, fax or air express a release to *Entertainment Tonight*, the *Los Angeles Times* and perhaps an *Associated Press* entertainment reporter. Those outlets will cover the bases initially, everyone else in the entertainment media community will start to piece together a story from their initial coverage.

In crisis situations, don't worry about exclusives. This is a crisis, not a media opportunity. If *The Today Show* is upset that *ET* got the exclusive, don't worry about it now. You have other priorities.

In non-emergency crisis situations, I try to keep a very low profile, especially when it comes to firings. Even though the firing of your director can bring an entire production to a halt, it's not a situation the public needs to know about.

When lives are not at stake, I feel no strong urgency to go shouting to the media that we've lost our director. Reporting the news can often be done in subtle ways. On one film, I called *Daily Variety* and the *Hollywood Reporter* and told their production chart coordinator to simply change a name in our production listing. The fact that I was changing the name of the *director* was no big deal as far as I was concerned. Of course, on their end, that reporter could have whistled over to the City Desk and a reporter could have jumped on the hot tip and been onto a juicy story before the hour was out. Fortunately, nothing happened.

With personnel changes as with emergencies, you may be called upon to act as company spokesperson. Usually, you will be asked to simply repeat the common excuse, "creative differences." Keep to the party line: don't suddenly develop a desire to be candid about the conditions on the set.

23

DEALING WITH INTERNATIONAL PRESS REQUESTS

There was a time when the international box office arena was the poor second cousin to our domestic theatrical scene. To producers, journalists and domestic publicists, the bottom line was what the film was generating in the U.S., not the gross revenue in Spain or Argentina. If you wanted to know the international gross for any given picture, you'd have to search for it in the back pages of *Weekly Variety* or consult one of the international trade publications like *Screen International* or *Movie and TV Marketing*.

Changes came slowly and dramatically. The *Hollywood Reporter* started to include international grosses in its Tuesday edition—a section that has grown in importance. The dramatic changes in the international political arena—particularly in Eastern Europe— have opened new territories to the American motion picture. And while ancillary markets such as home video have had vast implications domestically, their impact on foreign shores has been no less spectacular. As the world has shrunk, so has the potential impact of Hollywood. Today, you can't ignore the fact that international revenue is inching up every year, even as U.S. domestic box office levels off.

I mention these facts because during the course of a movie publicity and promotion campaign, you, the publicist, will most likely have some contact with the international press community. If you're working at a major studio, international marketing executives may inquire into the possibility of junketing some journalists to the set. A request may come down for special photographic materials that could be used offshore. Or a freelance journalist who writes for several international movie magazines may simply call requesting interviews. On independently produced features, the same requests may be filtered your way.

When it comes to dealing with international media requests, the major studios have an advantage because the distribution patterns of their films internationally are often established before filming begins. They know they have rights in certain territories, they know who is going to handle those films in those territories and there is a place for publicity materials to be funnelled. The independents often have no idea how the international distribution arena will be organized. It is very possible that a film will shoot without an international deal in place, so even though you'll receive media requests from international press outlets, there is no plan in place to deal with the needs of the journalists after the film has finished production. Most likely, a P.R. agency will be available to coordinate requests of this nature. But be prepared to act independently.

You have no control over the deal structure—domestic or international. Your job is to generate awareness and the needs of the international journalists can no longer be ignored. Here are some guidelines for dealing with international requests:

- **Treat international journalists like you treat any journalist, with respect.** Just because they write for a publication you've never heard of doesn't mean they have any less impact in their territory than your *New York Times* freelance writer or *Entertainment Tonight* in the U.S.

- **If you're working with a studio, never deal directly with international journalists without first consulting with the international marketing executive assigned to your film.** Even though you may have little contact with them, the international marketing departments at the major studios are beehives of activity. In Hollywood, these departments are usually the point units for offices throughout the world—all of which generate daily requests for information on new films. These LA-based units are interested in your film. Undoubtedly, they will be looking into the possibility of set visits, phone interviews and tours—the type of activity once reserved exclusively for domestic press.

- **Don't wait for the international marketing executive to call you.** Make their office one of your first stops during your orientation in Los Angeles. A short "hello" will be warmly appreciated and you will be able to put the face with the voice once international requests start coming through. It doesn't hurt for a top executive with the company to see you being conscientious. Positive word of mouth on your sense of mission can be passed through the ranks. Remember, international marketing does interact with domestic. So word of your effectiveness as a publicist can travel to the people who will eventually consider you for future jobs.

- **Unlike domestic set visit requests that trickle in one at a time, international requests usually come in the form of groups.** Studio international departments usually like to bring foreign press junkets to set in groups of 3-6 people. Because of the numbers, it will be necessary to conduct set interviews in round-robin fashion, just like you do on any domestic press junket.

If you have the opportunity to conduct one-on-one interviews, do so. The international journalist will be just as appreciative as your *People Magazine* writer or the TV crew from *The Today Show*.

For junket interviews, don't let the number of journalists daunt you. Provided the set isn't completely crazy on their visiting day, round-robin interviews with a group can be as easy to organize as a single one-on-one. You do have to draw the line, though. Be aware of the logistics of the set. Plan junkets on days where large set pieces are involved—battle sequences, exterior action sequences, etc. Don't invite junkets to intimate interior sequences where everyone is on top of each other. It's going to be nearly impossible for a group to get access to the set, let alone stay out of the way of the cast and crew.

Try to schedule international junkets just like any domestic press visit—find days in which there's plenty of room to maneuver and keep groups down to six or less. On any given motion picture, two groups of that size are plenty. If you're working on an epic like "Batman Returns" or *Lawrence of Arabia*, be prepared for larger groups. But don't forget your responsibilities to the production. You can't overload your actors with interviews during particularly stressful periods in the filmmaking process. Space out your visits and don't give the actors the feeling that they're on a media assembly line. They'll have plenty of chances later during the pre-release period.

- **When to schedule foreign press interviews?** I usually like to follow the same guidelines I use for domestic—bring them during the last third of the filming schedule. By then, the actors have had a chance to work with one another, they've established some opinions on the experience and they have their anecdotes. But there are rules. A recent film that featured a German director invited foreign press to visit the set during the first few weeks of production. With a German director in charge, the story had that much more immediacy to certain international outlets.

- **Use the same strategic guidelines for international as you use for domestic.** If the set is closed to journalists, that means all journalists. As urgent as an international request might be, you must still follow orders. If you're being pressured, refer the calls to your producer. He can be the ultimate judge.

- **If you're junketing international journalists to a distant set, ask for a member of the international department at the studio or the independent agency to accompany the junket.** Although you're completely capable of playing tour guide to six journalists, the demands of the set may take you away from that responsibility. Remember, you are generally not the one who pitched these reporters in the first place, so it's most likely that you don't know them, you haven't been responsible for making their travel and accommodation arrangements and you aren't familiar with their needs or idiosyncrasies. It thus makes complete sense for an international marketing executive to accompany the tour. Past experience has shown that if I request someone to accompany the group, they will come. But you have to make that request. Major studios as well as agencies are inclined to pair down their costs and expenses if they can and they'll be perfectly happy leaving the entire group on your doorstep. So don't hesitate to say something. You will still have to play host, but you will also have a compatriot in international who will help you on all fronts.

■ **After filming is completed, the international department will take over responsibility for gathering their materials—press skits, photos, videos, etc.** But whether you're on staff at a major or working freelance for independents, or simply involved in the release campaign, you will still have contact with the international press community.

International outlets may request color art before anyone in domestic. Foreign publications use a lot more color than those published in the U.S. Be prepared for heavy color requests so keep a good supply of key color art on hand. Increasingly, in the independent sector, international P.R. agencies are handling media requests following the end of production. Follow the same guidelines you have for dealing with the major studio international marketing executives when you deal with the agencies. It is not your responsibility to determine international publicity strategy. Simply identify the correct international chain of command and help supply them with materials.

Screenings.

Although international executives at studios or independent agencies are usually in charge of setting up foreign press screenings, there may come a time when you will have to personally invite these journalists. There are a couple of guidelines:

Accredited foreign press are listed in the Motion Picture Association of America (MPAA) International Press Directory. These are the key journalists that are based in Los Angeles and who would normally attend foreign press screenings.

International journalists based in their own countries often see films through screenings arranged overseas by local marketing entities. Some of the major studios have full service publicity, promotion and advertising organizations in foreign countries and they are fully responsible for all media activity that occurs within that territory.

Because of the high profile taken by their annual Golden Globes Awards show, the Hollywood Foreign Press Association is well-known in Hollywood. When dealing with this organization, a different criteria applies. Although, it's uncommon for domestic publicity executives to have interaction with international journalists during the domestic release period, the very fact that these journalists determine the nominees for Golden Globe Awards each year puts them in a category of interest for the domestic publicity department (studio or agency). And because the Golden Globes are determined by Hollywood-based journalists and the Awards are given in Hollywood, the whole show becomes a source for domestic publicity opportunities at a key time prior to the annual Awards derby.

So, even as a domestic publicist, you may be asked to set up a screening and press conference for the Hollywood Foreign Press Association. Again, this usually happens if you're involved on independent films. At the majors, the international department will have this responsibility. In order for a film to become eligible for a Golden Globe, it must be screened in Hollywood for the Hollywood Foreign Press. A press conference must also be organized exclusively for members. No screening, no press conference, no potential nominations.

24

WRAPPING UP THE PRODUCTION PUBLICITY CAMPAIGN

Location work can go by quickly. Before you know it there's a week left of shooting, your photographer hasn't taken any portraits of the cast, or you haven't interviewed your leading actor for the press kit, or *Entertainment Tonight* never did an on-set interview.

If you've been hired simply to work during production—a typical unit publicist will be released two weeks after production ends—then you'd better get moving. The studio or independent production company is going to need things wrapped up in a tidy bow and you don't have much time left.

On the other hand, if you're on staff with an independent production company or you've been hired to work on the film project through the release period (as a publicity project director), there's a little bit more time available and you can prioritize you needs. But publicity project directors are the exception, not the norm.

Final Weeks of Production.

With that production clock ticking, here are some last minute duties that you should concentrate on:

■ **Finalize all interviews**. Even before the last shot is completed, your lead actors will have made their travel plans for all points of the compass and you may never see them again. If the actor is a major star, the odds are that during the release period, he or she may be working on another movie and be virtually inaccessible to the media. So now is the time to finish every possible interview.

Don't forget your own needs for the final press kit, either. By the end of the production, you should have completed an interview with all of the lead actors. If you've received authorization to hire a video press kit crew, that interview will be on tape. Generally, I send all completed video interviews to a post-production house where I have them make audio cassettes duplicates. From these audio cassettes, I can then transcribe the tapes, providing me with valuable information for the press kit production information and biographies.

■ **Finish your press kit.** If you will not be staying with the film, which is the case with most freelance unit publicity assignments, you have two weeks after wrap to complete your press kit. Make sure to have all the information you need to do the final press release and final report to your superiors before you leave the location. I usually postpone writing the final press kit until I arrive back at the studio or independent production company. With my completed interviews in front of me, the positioning approach from my advance production notes and my memory, I can then write the final kit with a clear head and no distractions.

Make the kit a quick page turner. Your three page positioning statement should bounce off the page. It should not be the same statement you made in the advance production notes. Remember you wrote the latter prior to the start of the film and now, after all of your own experiences and those of your cast and crew, you should have a more complete picture of the film and its intent.

Your 5-10 pages of production notes and behind the scenes information should be colorful, interesting, informative and unique to your production. Biographies should be no more than three pages. Include bios on all of your lead actors, in addition to the director, producer, writers and any especially interesting crew members whose work is intrinsic to the film. For instance, if the movie is a dance picture, a bio of the choreographer is appropriate.

■ **Take care of local press requests.** Although I try to keep the local press happy by supplying them with production notes, photos and as much information as I can, I generally hold off on interviews until the very end of the production. I'm cooperative, but firm. I must give priority to national media contacts and set visitors. I can't afford to bother my actors with local press requests until the end of production. When actors begin to see the end in sight, their attitude toward press interviews begins to loosen up. They've worked on the film, they've been that character for months, they've developed close personal ties to other cast members and crew, and they usually have something to talk about.

Don't solicit interviews with local press—now is not the time to go after local journalists. But if they've come to you with an interview request during the course of production, fine. Bring the local press people onto the set individually or set up the previously discussed press conference or round-robin interview session. Be a gracious host. You've spent two to three months in a foreign town or city. You've enjoyed local hospitality. Here's a little payback opportunity. A short interview with your lead actor or director will be warmly appreciated by local press.

■ **Finalize all photographic opportunities.** If you've procrastinated, or if you've been too swamped to get everything done, it's OK. Some things can get accomplished after you leave the set: editorial press kits can be pieced together, or interviews can be scheduled by phone, but after you wrap, you are out of luck if you don't have all the photos you need. Pay particular attention to group shots of the actors, and individual portraits. These photos are vital to the post-production and pre-release publicity efforts. If you look at any magazine that features film coverage, you will discover that a majority of the shots feature actors in single portraits or groups, usually on the set and in wardrobe. These are the types of photos that you just can't duplicate after wrap.

Also remember a movie shoot is not like a tour bus to Ireland. You don't end up with the same number of passengers you start with. Most of the time, actors finish their work at different times. If you've waited until the end of production to get a group shot, you may discover that half your group is gone. That's why it's a good idea to pay attention to shooting schedules and breakdown charts which actually show when actors are going to be wrapped.

- **Get your photo approvals from your actors**. Those actors who have still approval must complete their selections before the end of shooting. If you've been smart, you've been giving the actor photos on a regular basis. Otherwise, you're now going to have to walk over to his trailer with a huge stack of proof sheets and transparencies—not a very nice thing to do.

Even if you're getting still approvals at the last minute, never allow actors to take materials home with them—proof sheets and transparencies must never leave the location. Make sure you get the black and white proof sheets marked with their approvals (actors, according to most contracts are required to approve at least 50% of all photos) and a stack of approved transparencies. Usually, they will destroy their transparency kills, which is fine. The smart actor is not going to hand back to you slides that he's killed. However, if more than one actor has still approval, you will have to explain to the actors that all slides will have to be circulated among other actors and that they will not be able to destroy their kills. Imagine the situation if you have four actors with 50% still approval. If everyone kept their kills, you could end up with zero coverage. After every actor with still approval has gone through the material, you may have to go back to one or two of the actors and try to get a reversal on a kill. It's a difficult assignment, but it could be crucial to your photo campaign. Some studios will not allow slides to be destroyed under any circumstances. Make sure you discuss this policy with your photo editor or P.R. superior.

- **Finish your photo captions**. It's a painstaking job, but you're the only qualified person to do it. Fortunately, according to most studio standards, you are only required to caption black and white photos. If you haven't been doing them a little as a time, set aside a full day to just sit at the typewriter or computer screen and do the captions. It's going to take 12-14 hours to caption the typical collection of proof sheets.

■ **Finalize your media report.** Your final publicity progress report is not only a listing of all current breaks, but a blueprint for publicity executives who will eventually follow-up on your campaign. Since the wrap-up report is the last memo you will compose, it will also be the most important one your executives read, so make it complete.

I generally start off with an overview on how well the shoot has gone and whether all key elements are working. I try not to be a critic, but I will report on certain positive elements in the film because they will eventually become good pitching angles for the media. If the stunts are particularly spectacular there could be a story on them. If the art department really came up with some incredible sets and designs, that too could make a story idea down the road. The same for other facets, including costumes, makeup, choreography, props, locations, plus the personalities of the director and the actors.

Document the interview potential of the key actors. If Actor A is slow, indecisive and boring, let your superiors know. It would be a waste of their time and money to send him on a 20 city promo tour. Conversely, if you think one of the actors is particularly interesting or easy to interview, let everyone know about it.

In addition to editorial comments on an actor's effectiveness as a promoter, I also provide as much contact information as possible: home address and phone numbers, names and phone numbers of his agent, publicist, manager, etc. Sometimes it's important to pass along notes about an actor's future plans, especially if he or she is scheduled to begin shooting a new film on location in a foreign country. When Phil Donahue's producer calls six months from now and wants to put your actor on his show it will be nice to know how, or if, he can be reached.

Don't hesitate to provide contact information about yourself as well. When an important question comes up down the road, your superiors will appreciate being able to reach you easily. Who knows, their appreciation might also help them consider you for future assignments.

■ **Write an "End of Production" story.** A one-page press release will suffice. This will be sent to *Daily Variety* and the *Hollywood Reporter*. You simply state that *Rambo 21* has completed principal photography outside Cleveland, Ohio. Repeat your positioning paragraph on the film, mention the key cast and crew members, and if you have a release date, call it to their attention. It is not necessary to send this story to anyone other than the trade reporters. This is more of a formality than a news announcement that would be of interest to the other entertainment outlets.

In addition to submitting an end of production story, another formality is sending a list of production personnel to *Daily Variety*.

This list includes all crew members, other than the producer, director, screenwriter and actors. Try to do this before production wraps. *Daily Variety* generally will not publish the list if the film is finished. The convention for this list is to type the names of the crew members in ALL CAPS, followed by their title in Title Case (capitalize the first letter of each word, i.e. First Assistant Director.) You, the Unit Publicist, are always listed last.

■ **Consider gifts for production personnel and publicity liaisons.** Gift giving is always a nice touch at the end of production. Remember the people who have helped you do your job for the last couple months: the production secretaries, messengers, and assistants.

If you've worked closely with the publicity team back home, then consider gifts for them as well. Some momento from the production or location is always nice. It's not bribery but it doesn't hurt to show your appreciation for their cooperation, especially when they have the power to hire you for your next job.

Take time to make your farewells. Like summer camp, a movie shoot involves a number of farewells. I usually try to personally thank as many people as possible for their cooperation, especially the actors. Take a moment to chat with your producer and indicate that you're always available if he has any questions about the production publicity campaign. Of course, if you're staying on the project to supervise the publicity campaign prior to release, then you don't have to say goodbye at all. You'll be seeing a lot of that producer in the next few months.

Also take time to chat with your publicity chief back home—whether it's at the studio, independent company or P.R. agency. Let them know that you are available for questions and thank them for the opportunity to work on the project.

I usually have a special relationship with the photo department, so I extend them a special farewell. Photo people can be the publicist's best friend in emergency situations. A gift to them is well spent.

25

AS THE POST-PRODUCTION PERIOD BEGINS

Your involvement in a post-production publicity campaign can begin on many different levels. In a perfect world, you're the project publicity director, so you have already completed the unit publicity and you're ready to make the transition to post-production publicity pitching. At a studio, you might be a staff publicist, ready to take over the job from the unit publicist who has already left to find another unit assignment. Or, if you're at an independent film company or a public relations agency, you're also taking over from a unit publicist, if one was assigned to the film.

By the way, whenever I mention the post-production publicity period, I simply mean the time between the end of principle photography and the beginning of the pre-release period. I refer to the pre-release period as about two or three months out from actual theatrical release. During the pre-release period, awareness is beginning to be generated by theatrical trailers, early television and magazine advertising and other marketing elements.

Wherever you're coming from at the beginning of the post-production period, you must first inventory your materials.

Press Kit Materials.
If the unit publicist has followed the advice in this book you will have most of the information you need to finalize your press kit: interviews, bios, production notes, positioning statement, etc. But in some cases, you will have absolutely no press kit materials. This situation calls for your immediate attention, whether your movie is due for release in two weeks or ten months.

Before the movie is screened for the press, you're going to need top quality press notes which will include a good amount of behind-the-scenes information, consummate biographies with quotes from the actors and a presentation statement that reflects the marketing approach. It's wise to hold off finalizing the press kit until the marketing approach of the film is determined in post-production marketing meetings. Why? Because you want your background notes to support the overall marketing approach.

Let's say you're promoting a romantic film that takes place in the Soviet Union and out of a publicist's natural instinct you want to provide a great deal of information about the Soviet Union, local color and customs and how it applies to the film. But then you discover that the marketing approach is to stay clear of overt references to the background of the story. Perhaps because of some audience test screenings or other market research, it was decided that the Russian background of the film was not the film's most marketable element. If you went ahead with your own press kit ideas, they would immediately conflict with the marketing strategy.

There is something to be said for uniform strategy and approach on all levels of marketing, including publicity. Remember if you write about the Soviet influence in the press kit, the journalist will probably write about the Soviet influence in his or her articles and the public will hear about the Soviet influence in the papers and magazines and the word-of-mouth will begin that Paramount is releasing a love story about Russians. Get the point?

Photography.

Make sure you have the book of black and white proof sheets and that all negatives are safely stored with a local photo lab. Do not keep negatives in your office. They can be lost or mutilated by errant handling. When you need 8" x 10" glossies you simply call the lab and the photos will be delivered. Make sure you get to know the order personnel at the lab. You depend on their ability to get you photos quickly and efficiently.

Color transparencies should be stored in plastic sleeves and kept in three-ring binders. During the course of the next few months you will be continually going through those binders to select slides for a hundred different reasons. If your slides are organized, you can make your selections and have them duplicated easily. You will probably want to store the originals of the slides you need duplicated often at the lab. (Have a dupe set made for your own reference.) Sending originals back and forth to the lab can blow a full day of processing time.

For black and white, I like to have a key b/w set available at my office for anyone who needs to see photos on a moment's notice. If a publication suddenly needs a shot, I can order it from the lab, or in an emergency I can give them one of the office shots (which can be replenished later). There should be a minimum of 20 key b/w shots.

What if you don't have enough good stills from production? In a pinch I've had to pull frames from the actual film to make photographic materials for publicity purposes. Because these have to be transformed from color to black and white, the quality of the images is generally not very good, but what choice do you have?

How many good photos do you need? In terms of the press kit, from 6-10 black and white stills are normal. I also select one or two good shots from time to time for special mailings.

Magazines prefer color material. I ship photos to magazines in the form of slide "sets." A good color slide set consists of 6-10 of your best shots, including portraits, action shots and behind-the-scenes photos. You can have several different sets, tailored to the different kinds of outlets: women's magazines (emphasize good shots of your lead actors); film magazines (make sure you have some good shots of your director in action.), etc.

I like to have about 20 color sets in my office at all times to send out as needed. Color slides, if they're of excellent quality, are one of your best selling tools. Although their primary use is in magazine articles, you may also be providing these transparencies to:

✔ your own advertising department who will use them for the basis of preliminary ads;

✔ licensing and product placement executives who will be sending them to companies that have tie-ins with the picture;

✔ foreign sales and marketing executives who will be pitching the film around the world;

✔ allied P.R. entities, including actor's publicists who will be using them in their own pitching campaigns;

✔ television programs that will utilize the art as graphics in the stories they televise on your film;

✔ dozens of other outlets that need impressive color materials.

Remember, don't give anyone original slides. Always send first generation duplicates (or "dupes"). A good lab will provide you with slides that are perfectly reproducible.

Occasionally, a top magazine outlet will need a shot so quickly that you will not have time to duplicate the photo to make their deadlines. Depending on the outlet, this is the only time you part with your originals. If you forewarn the outlet that you need the shot back, and if you remind them ever so gently, there is a chance that you will get it back, but I don't recommend this practice. With the volume of transparencies running through top magazine outlets like *Time* and *Newsweek*, there is always the possibility that even the most conscientious photo editor will misplace a shot of yours, and when it's gone, it's gone.

Video Materials. If video materials were shot during production they will be used during the post-production publicity campaign, so it is important to be organized and ready to make them available.

Are all of your video interviews complete: principal actors, director, producer, special effects chief? Remember, once the film is finished, cast and crew members are free to travel anywhere and if they do return to your home base, they may not stay around very long. On *Eddie and the Cruisers II*, I interviewed star Michael Pare during the last day of shooting. It was fortunate, because the day after filming was completed, he took off for an extended vacation in the Greek Islands. When he came back to Los Angeles it was for only a brief time before he started another film in Italy.

In Michael's case, that *Eddie and the Cruisers* interview paid off immediately. Several entertainment media outlets expressed interest in producing an early story on the film, and because they could not get access to the actor, they were happy to use my own interview footage.

Having a working knowledge of how to put together a good EPK (electronic press kit) is getting to be an essential skill for the good publicist. True, you can hire outside video companies to produce finished pieces for you, but in this age of cutting your marketing costs, less and less money is available for these independent video producers.

In my own case, I have hands-on experience in video press kit production. One year, I took time out from handling unit publicity assignments to actually work in a video company that produced the kits for several studios. It was a valuable experience.

I learned how to hire a camera crew and get them to location, I worked on my video interviewer skills, and I learned the post-production process where the video materials are cut into finished pieces.

If you can get some solid hands-on video knowledge, it will be of tremendous value to you. Some of the major studios have their own video production departments which will supply you with whatever video materials you need. Otherwise, you're on your own and the more you know the better.

One quick technical note: if you have anything to say about it, have your interview and behind the scenes materials shot with a Betacam, which is a professional ½" video camera. For about a decade, the Betacam has been the state of the art video camera for professional broadcast use. The quality is fantastic and perfect for your video press materials.

I can remember not too long ago shooting press kits on 16mm film, which was an outrageously expensive process. Video filming and editing is much simpler and less expensive.

What do you do with the raw footage? Take the stack of Betacam cassettes to an editing facility and have them make "window dubs." These are duplicate cassettes which have a little window added to the bottom of screen showing the "visible time code." This allows you to precisely identify every split second on the tape. Say you're looking for the best scene showing Burt Reynolds conversing with director Blake Edwards. When you come across an interesting shot, pause the tape and look at the little window. It might say 01:27:33:09. That corresponds to one hour, twenty-seven minutes, thirty three and nine-tenths of a second into your tape. Record this number in your footage log with an identifying phrase: "good Reynolds/Edwards interplay" and you'll be able to come back to it easily.

These window dubs are vital to your own inventory process. Which format should you get? ¾" or ½" VHS? It depends on what type of player you have at the office. If you have a ¾" player with a remote that allows you to pause the tape, then get ¾" window dubs. If you only have a VHS player, again with a remote, then the ½" VHS dubs are the way to go. The remote is crucial. You can't keep getting up to stop the player manually. It will take you days to log your tapes.

Make a footage log of all your video interviews. Watch them carefully and choose the moments in which the actor is lucid and animated. Avoid moments of hesitation where the actor is trying to spit out the phrase, but it won't come. The media outlets will never utilize these segments. Avoid any comments which are in any way critical of the film and especially avoid any off-color remarks or coarse language.

A note on film clips: In addition to interview and behind the scenes footage, your media outlets are going to request clips from the actual film to run with their stories. Trouble is, the film isn't finished yet. Editors, directors and producers are spending long hours piecing together little bits of film, but it's almost impossible at this point to get them to authorize anything you can send out as a "clip." In most cases you have to wait for an "answer print" to be finished before producers are even going to consider requests for clips.

Sometimes a little creativity on you part can get you what you need. Once, soon after completing production on a film, I discovered that the editors were working feverishly to put together a product reel for the Cannes Film Festival—about 35 minutes of cut footage. Although, the footage was not the finalized footage from the finished film, I was able to get access to a key scene for my media contacts. The producers were comfortable enough with the footage in this form to let it go, and it became part of a wonderful break on a national show.

How many initial clips will you need to feed your media outlets during this early post-production phase? One good clip that showcases your top stars in an interesting sequence will work. Stick to that clip: the media will request others, but hold them off for now.

Initial clips, even though they can be difficult to get, are very helpful and can be used in many ways. It's becoming more common to use a ½" VHS cassette as a teaser for the media. It seems everyone has a VHS recorder in their homes and offices and a short tape featuring clips from your film is a real attention-getter when you send out information to the press. Initial clips can also be used for product tie-ins, and for foreign and video sales.

Some directors object to reducing scenes from their wonderful 70mm film with Dolby Surround Sound to little ½" video cassettes. It's understandable, but when it comes to generating awareness and interest in their film, video beats still photos hands down. You will find that any video materials you develop—featurettes, mini-profiles, open-ended interviews, generic B-roll (behind the scenes footage), clip reels—will be extremely valuable to the marketing process.

You don't have to develop all of these materials yourself. There are a number of companies in the marketplace who specialize in the preparation of video press kit materials. If you're not familiar with them, seek out advice from other industry professionals. Everyone has a favorite company they can refer you to.

Interview these companies and have them screen some of their recent work. Here are some key questions:

What films have they worked on in the past? (Have you heard of them?)

Do they appear enthusiastic about your film and are they suggesting ideas, even in the initial meeting?

Personality-wise, do you think you can work with these people? Remember, you are going to be spending a lot of time with them, and you have to be critical to get what you want. A personality conflict could torpedo the whole creative process.

How about price? Check with industry professionals about the criteria here. In 1992 dollars, I wouldn't pay more than $25,000 for a full video press kit, including a featurette and two personality profiles. Don't be intimidated about asking price and getting the price down. I have yet to meet a company that will not negotiate their price.

Can they distribute the video material they produce to TV outlets across the nation? Companies with distribution capabilities often have a better understanding of what the TV media outlets are looking for.

Consult with fellow executives on making video deals. Don't feel that you have to make a decision without advice. The video business is continually changing and new companies emerge all the time. Price structures and criteria are also changing along with the technology.

Leads Needing Follow-up.

Follow up on publicity opportunities developed during production. While you're preparing an inventory of your publicity materials—words, photographs and video footage—prepare to carry on with any publicity activity that was previously initiated.

In many cases, you may be starting from scratch. Aside from an announcement in the trades, many films shoot without any production publicity plan at all. No one contacted the LA Times about a set visit. No one gave *Entertainment Tonight* an exclusive interview with the star. There were no mailings to national press to announce the movie and provide an advance still photo or two. No one banked any video interviews. There may or may not even be a serviceable press kit.

The Plotting Board.   Whether you're starting from scratch or carrying on a publicity campaign, organize your campaign by utilizing what I call a "plotting board." It can be on a blackboard, a whiteboard, a bulletin board or you can use 3 x 5 cards tacked to a wall. It's simply a method of displaying your campaign so that you and everyone else who walks into your office can see what is happening. And believe me, your boss, your producers, anyone will walk in there and ask you what's happening. The board can tell them.

I usually divide my plotting board into sections. One topic heading is listed as "Breaks." Here you list all the publicity breaks that have taken place thus far, whether you coordinated them or not. Your second column can be titled, "Stories in the Bank." These are publicity breaks that have not yet hit the papers or the airwaves. A third column should be identified as "Pitching." This allows you to keep track of the journalists you are contacting.

I used to construct my entire campaign on a deck of 3 x 5 cards. As breaks occurred I would put the 3 x 5 card up on the wall while pitches would remain in the deck. Today, my computer is a more efficient way to keep track of all my activities. I start off with an alphabetized list of media outlets and as I make pitches and as breaks occur, I simply insert notes in the list. This computer list is particularly useful when I prepare my progress reports.

I highly recommend learning how to use computers, if you're not already "computer literate." I use mine for organizing information about publicity breaks, keeping track of my phone calls—the ones that come in as well as notes about the ones I make—and I do all my writing on the computer. Whenever possible, I make sure the computer my secretary uses and mine are compatible so we can share information without having to re-type anything.

In my very first publicity job, I remember noticing that one of the top executives always had a list of phone calls to make each day. Names would be added and subtracted throughout the day as he waged his publicity campaign. I adopted this phone list idea, but managing the hundreds of calls I needed to make was a chore. I often spent hours fine-tuning my list, adding as many calls as I could and writing little notes next to the phone numbers to remind me to pitch my film in a certain way. It got to a point where I was spending more time on the list than on the calls. Enter the computer.

Now I type my phone list in the computer where it is much easier to add, delete and change my notes. Whenever possible, I also have my secretary put all the incoming calls into the computer too, thereby getting rid of those pesky little phone message slips which always clutter up your desk.

26

WHAT TYPE OF FILM ARE WE SELLING?

Just what are you selling? The word "marketing," applies to all efforts employed in selling the movie to the public—publicity, promotion, creative advertising, research and media buying. Initial marketing meetings, involving executives who represent all these areas, are sometimes held long before the movie goes into production, but generally the marketing ball doesn't get rolling until the film is in the can.

If you have been involved during production as a unit publicist you're in a great position to offer advice about various marketing strategies: you know first-hand what the movie is all about, you know the idiosyncrasies of the actors, you know about the best available photography, and you have begun to have some feed-back from the media about which selling points or pitches work best. However, my advice is to keep a low profile at the beginning. The egos involved in advertising and marketing are generally much larger than the minds that go with them. If you make enemies at this early stage, your life is going to be miserable and your effectiveness as a key member of the team will be reduced. Wait for the right time to express your opinions, keep your observations sharp and incisive and wear your diplomat hat at all times.

Early Marketing Meetings. Let's talk about what goes on in those early marketing meetings. A film, just like a new type of toothpaste, must have a specific identity which sets it apart from all the other films. The public has to be convinced that it "needs" your product. The agenda in these marketing meetings is to figure out the positive and negative selling points of the film, to isolate the target audience, and to decide which type of marketing—publicity, advertising or promotion—will be emphasized.

- **Positive and negative selling points**. If you were to make a list of the positive selling points of the 1988 hit *Big*, Tom Hanks would be at the top of the list. As one of America's premiere comic actors, he has a great reputation and several top hits behind him. He's a known factor with a built in audience identification.

  Next, on the list would be the fact that the film is a comedy. In the last decade, comedy films have dominated the box office charts.

  A negative selling point might be the subject matter of the film. Normally, this story idea would be a positive: Tom Hanks portraying a youngster in the body of an adult would appear to be the perfect comedy vehicle for his talents. Unfortunately, when *Big* was released, the marketplace had already been saturated with a number of comedies involving switched bodies and personalities. Dudley Moore had starred in a movie called *Like Father, Like Son*, Shelly Long and Corbin Bernsen had frolicked in *Hello Again*, George Burns had made *18 Again*, Timothy Hutton and Kelly McGillis had starred in *Made in Heaven*, and Steve Martin and Lily Tomlin had inhabited each other's bodies in *All of Me*. At that late date, emphasizing the body-switching story line of *Big* wouldn't be such a good idea.

  Aside from the freshness of the story line, given the saturation of the marketplace, there really aren't any negatives about the film which would have to be de-emphasized—a fact which I'm sure caused a ripple of excitement in the marketing meeting.

  Sometimes the real positive and negative selling points for a film aren't obvious until you have a chance to screen the completed film. *Big* on paper must have been charming. But the biggest selling point of the film jumped off the screen the minute you saw Hanks' tour de force performance. On the other hand, a great story with a fresh approach can be sitting on the positive side of your column until you see the film and discover that the execution was dreadful. What started out as a classic comedy may have wandered into stupidity land.

  Once you have your list of positive and negative selling points, they will affect every aspect of the upcoming marketing campaign, especially in publicity and promotion. If you have a movie about a family living near a nuclear test site and you've determined that the nuclear element is a strong negative, you know that you're not going to approach *Time Magazine* about a tie-in story dealing with the history of nuclear tests. You'll concentrate on the positive aspects, perhaps the story of how the family survived its ordeal through love and understanding or how the stars interpreted the lead characters.

- **The targeted audience**. If you're publicizing an amazing new seedless watermelon, your audience is limitless—virtually everyone on the planet will enjoy a seedless watermelon. However, if the product is a new heavy metal rock album, your audience is going to be limited to young rock and roll fans, mostly boys.

As a publicist, you must make sure your message reaches the right audience, concentrating your energies where they will do the most good. Don't waste your time pitching your heavy metal group to women's magazines, it's the editors of rock and roll magazines, some of which specialize in heavy metal, who will be able to help you deliver your message to the target audience. Not only will they be receptive to your stories, they may go out of their way to give you more than one break, and possibly contests and promotions.

One of the first questions asked at the very first marketing meeting is, "Who is the intended audience for this picture?" Sometimes the answer is obvious: if your movie is *Indiana Jones* or a James Bond film, then your prime audience is everyone from 8 to 80. But even a wide spectrum film needs to define a core audience.

Movies are often made for a certain audience. Research has shown that young people between 12 and 24 go to lots of movies. Movies are a relatively cheap and easy form of entertainment for this socially active group. During the age of *Animal House* and *Porky's*, it seemed that every other film made was a "teen comedy." Thankfully, Hollywood has returned to more adult fare now that the "baby boomers" have grown up.

Marketing campaigns generally identify a specialized target audience, while at the same time not ruling out a wider audience. The Shirley MacLaine/Anne Bancroft ballet film, *The Turning Point* became a big hit with wide appeal for 20th Century Fox in 1977, but it was targeted first and foremost to the female audience, 18-49.

Women's magazines were a key media outlet as were morning talk shows and features in the cultural sections of major newspapers. Although the film would eventually appeal to men as well, the women were targeted first with the hope that they would spread the word.

Conversely, *Die Hard*, the Bruce Willis thriller about a terrorist assault on a Century City office building, was targeted to males 18-49. It was a big action movie with plenty of combat violence, comic book dialogue and macho posturing. Story ideas would be sent to *Esquire* and *Playboy*, not *Woman's Day*.

Developing a target audience can sometimes be tricky. Case in point: a recent musical had the perfect elements for a young teen audience—music, dancing, young romance, and a bit of adventure—however, because of some scenes which included drug related violence, the movie was given an "R" rating, limiting the audience to 18 and above—the wrong audience.

■ **Decide what kind of marketing to emphasize.** Every film offers a different marketing challenge. Some films are publicity-intensive, some films are advertising-intensive, some films are promotion-intensive.

A film like "Halloween 7" is not going to do well with a publicity-intensive marketing campaign. You probably don't have any stars to promote. Your producers are probably not going to let you screen the movie before it is released (the critics will probably be unfavorable). And even if you were able to develop some publicity breaks, your main audience—the kids—are not going to be reading stories—unless you get a few going in the monster effects magazines.

Most lower budget films that go for the simplest audience reaction—either shock value, in the case of "Halloween 7," titillation in the case of a *Porky's* or blood and guts in a Charles Bronson *Death Wish* type film—are advertising-intensive. Though I would hesitate to say that Freddy Krueger isn't a star, (he's a huge one for the kids), the *Nightmare on Elm Street* series was always advertised as an exploitation exercise. Krueger has turned into a pop cultural icon and the publicity and promotional departments of New Line Cinema are to be congratulated for taking him out of the sewer of exploitation monsters and elevating him to such status. Still, the advertising campaign sold those movies. Everything else was gravy.

What's an example of a publicity-intensive film? *Platoon*, the 1986 Academy Award winner for Best Picture was a film that on the surface could have been dismissed as another Vietnam movie. There were no great stars that leapt to mind. Charlie Sheen, Tom Berenger and Willem Defoe were good actors but hardly media icons. The story was grim and realistic. And yet, because of the efforts of the publicity executives at Orion, that film became the biggest Vietnam war film of all time, a true box office champion.

The marketing campaign for *Platoon* created a special aura around the film. It took advantage of the fact that writer/director Oliver Stone was a veteran who served in Vietnam. It emphasized that this was the first true soldier's account of the war. The publicity people were able to pre-screen the film for important critics and magazines allowed them to start generating important review quotes prior to release.

Although there was a healthy advertising budget, the review quotes and the way in which the film was positioned helped *Platoon* off to a great start. Opening in a few theaters and building the excitement also helped generate the all important word-of-mouth. The fact that *Platoon* was a great film certainly helped, but the publicity department was responsible for building the film's reputation before it was released.

Promotion-intensive marketing campaigns are driven by the possibilities of tie-ins with other products. A big film like *Batman* or *Hook* is automatically promotion-intensive because it is such a hot property. Most often promotion tie-ins are best suited to the comic book genre of films and those with sound-tracks by popular music groups.

Promotions involving toy products are common and they help get the word out to the key buying audience—the young people. But a film doesn't have to be *Roger Rabbit* to take advantage of these kinds of promotions. You might find yourself working on a small film which is the first to explore the life of a radar controlled robot disc jockey rock star. That robot could become a media star in your specialized campaign—a promoter's field day. Music films, or ones with soundtracks by popular recording artists, give you the opportunity to approach radio stations, MTV and other music outlets for tie-ins. Having the soundtrack played on the radio, so that listeners start talking about the music before the film comes out is a major plus for any film's chances at the box office.

I remember one film that was too one-dimensional in its promotional approach. It was a terrible film called *Million Dollar Mystery*. The whole campaign seemed to be based on the fact that if you entered the contest and solved the mystery, you could win a million dollars. The promotional campaign assumed such an importance that the average consumer forgot there was a movie involved. You could have the greatest promotional event in the world, but you still have to convince the public that the movie's good. I think that the company that released *Million Dollar Mystery* got out of the motion picture business and into the lottery business. The fact that the film grossed less than the amount that went to the winning contestant was their just reward.

Any good campaign will involve all three types of marketing— advertising, publicity and promotion. Which one becomes "intensive" will decide what role you, as the publicist, will have to play.

27

BEGINNING THE PRE-RELEASE PHASE

As you begin the all-important pre-release phase of publicity and promotion, the circle of people you are involved with on a regular basis will grow in size and importance. During the production and post-production phase you were pretty much a one person show. Although you should have been keeping your superiors informed of all your activities in your publicity progress reports, their minds may have not been focused on what you were telling them. Now that the film is within three months from release, many people will suddenly take a keen interest in what type of campaign you are planning.

Who are these people and how do they relate to you in the pre-release period?

You and Your Office Staff.
It's important to set yourself up as the center, the nucleus, of the publicity campaign. If you don't, you may find others who want to take charge themselves—producers, agency heads, personal publicists, the director's new girlfriend, etc. Publicity and promotion prior to release can be volatile. There can be petty jealousies, intense arguments with co-workers and superiors, ego battles, and back-stabbing. Welcome to Hollywood.

In the heat of the publicity battle, don't forget that you are the wheel around which everything turns. If you've worked on the film since production, then you can adopt the leadership role easily because you already have intimate knowledge about the production, the actors, and various campaign strategies. If you're taking over from the unit publicist, having been placed in charge of the pre-release campaign, then you have the rank—so pull it, lead the campaign and make it work.

Don't play second banana to anyone. Don't allow another publicist, in any other liaison capacity to usurp your authority. One of the major problems that develops in any publicity campaign is that everyone does their own thing with little communication or cooperation.

Some of the other players on your publicity team include:

- **Fellow Staff Publicists**. Although it's getting to be the exception and not the rule, there may be publicists other than yourself who are responsible for specific areas. For instance, there may be a publicist working with you whose job is planting stories in newspaper and magazine columns or one who is particularly good at getting coverage on television. In general, at the major studios publicity responsibilities are shared while at the independents solo operations are the norm.

- **Publicity Assistants**. Anyone assigned to you as support personnel—could be a full or part-time secretary.

- **Marketing Head or Publicity Head**. The executive who takes your progress reports and evaluates your performance—usually your immediate superior.

- **Creative Advertising Head**. The person who plans and creates the key advertising art and trailers.

- **Media Buyer and Researcher**. This person, or group of people at an agency, identifies the film's demographics through research and develops a plan to buy advertising in newspapers, magazines, billboards, radio, television and any other media form.

- **Promotions Director**. The person specifically assigned to handle national promotions for your film. He or she supervises everything from the design and manufacture of T-shirts and gimmicks (glow in the dark yo-yos with your film's title printed on them) to the activities of the field promotional force.

- **Distribution or Sales Personnel**. The people in the company directly responsible for putting the film in theaters. As you get closer to release time, you will become more aware of how this department functions. Your publicity responsibilities may extend to the theaters themselves.

Outside Publicity Entities.

In an earlier chapter, we discussed various outside publicity organizations—agencies, consultants, independents, etc.—who are involved with the production phase of a motion picture. Now that the film is headed into release, some of these entities return to help you, often with bigger roles to play.

Hopefully, your relationship with agency publicists has been a good one and you can now consider them a productive part of your "exploitation" team. And you should. I copy agency publicists on all my media memos, from production through release.

These people are going to the media well every day, with a lot more clients and angles than you have. If you've developed a good working relationship, there's a good possibility that the agency publicist will start "talking up" your picture (if it's in the interest of their own client, of course). Agency publicists often come to me with publicity opportunities that are above and beyond what I have planned.

It pays for all publicity people to try to involve each other. Back scratching goes a long way when your job is generating interest and enthusiasm. And yet there are cases in which the studio never bothered to find out whether some of its stars had their own publicists. And there are agency publicists who never bother to share with the studio what they are doing on their own. Frankly, that's crazy.

I welcome support from any quadrant. I do not personally know every media contact. Nor do I know what excites them and what is the best possible story idea for them. Agency publicists who deal in a volume of personalities and angles are more apt to know what's going on in the media frontlines.

Once I received a call from a New York publicist who represented an actor who was starring in the picture I was publicizing. She informed me that an editor from *US Magazine* had called her regarding their upcoming Summer issue on "Hollywood Hunks" and that they had requested our star to be one of the photo features. Knowing this bit of information created a terrific opportunity for me to publicize my film, in conjunction with this *US Magazine* story.

One of the most difficult bits of information to ascertain is what the journalist is planning for an upcoming issue or show. You might be selling a movie on race horses and not realize, until it is too late, that *Life Magazine* is devoting their September issue to famous horse racing movies. Agency publicists who deal with the magazines on a more frequent basis may have access to this information. And, if your relationship is good, they may decide to share that fact with you.

On the other hand, if that personality publicist has been left out in the cold, if they're treated as a second class citizen, they may say "what the hell" and keep the information to themselves. Their attitude might be "why should I help the film company, if they don't appreciate my point of view?" It's regrettably an understandable point.

Producers, Actors, and Other Production People.

In the post-production and pre-release phase, the number of people actively working on the film dwindles to a handful of editors, the director (on and off), the producers and of course the marketing people like yourself. Because film making is a freelance business, all the actors and crew people are off doing other things. But you still need their help to generate interest in the film. After all, the public goes to movies to see stars. Get used to the fact that once a film is made, they disappear into other projects.

Getting members of the cast and crew to help you out may be a real challenge. If you find that none of your key interview subjects are at home waiting for you to set up interviews, don't despair. Find out where they are and how they can be reached. Phone interviews can be coordinated on location, and if necessary, TV cameras can be brought to the new movie for lunchtime interviews. The fact that Jobeth Williams was working on a new movie, *Desert Bloom*, when she received a request to promote her last picture, *American Dreamer*, didn't prevent her from saying yes to appearing on *Good Morning America*. She agreed to have me pick her up at five in the morning so we could be at the local Tucson ABC television affiliate to be interviewed in one of those "live remote" broadcasts.

Good Morning America was an important break and I wasn't about to pass up the opportunity to get a *Desert Bloom* mention on national television at the tail end of the interview. The fact that Jobeth was happy to help promote her last picture even though she was quite busy with a new project was a great credit to her.

Some actors aren't so helpful, especially if they have decided the film is going to be a "real turkey." In the past, during the days of the studio system, an actor was given his publicity orders and told to march regardless of the quality of the final movie. Today there are no such restraints. When the smoke clears after a turkey is ready for release, you may find yourself completely alone on the battlefield of exploitation. Nobody wants to take responsibility for the project, and of course, nobody wants to go on national television and promote a project that is going to be rejected at the box office.

However, no one can predict box office success and I believe actors and creators have a responsibility to at least present their work to the public. I can understand an actor avoiding publicity after the film has bombed at the box office, but prior to its release there should be a responsibility to pre-sell the project to an expectant public.

Producers also deal with publicity in different ways. Some producers are veritable publicity hounds. They will be constantly asking you about publicity activity—the "what are you doing for my picture" attitude. These are usually experienced producers who understand how important the P.R. process is to their production's box office fate. Don't be intimidated by them—they're probably haranguing the advertising director as well, and the media buyer, and the trailer maker, and the studio executive who is shepherding the film toward release.

My experience shows, though, that many producers today are not as sophisticated about the marketing of their films as they should be. They rely on your advice and expertise. They can tell you what should be emphasized and, perhaps, who should be getting the lion's share of interviews. But when it comes to selecting specific publications or shows that relate to their film, they will generally leave the details up to you. Today's producer is too busy to follow the format of various entertainment shows or read all the latest entertainment features in movie magazines. He's out there making deals. He's going to be happy with any type of coverage regardless of where it appears.

Of course, that doesn't mean you should slack off on your own campaign. I always want to have an answer on any media question thrown at me by the producer. If your previously unsophisticated executive producer suddenly calls up and wonders why the film is not featured in this month's *Rolling Stone* "Random Notes" column, you should know the answer.

If you're looking for interview subjects from the ranks of the producers, the Executive Producer, the executive who usually puts the film deal together and shepherds the project through its various phases, is generally your best bet. He or she is considered a "creative producer" as opposed to what is increasingly referred to as a "line producer"—a technically proficient producer who is involved in production details only.

The director should also be counted on to help you sell the movie, especially if he or she has a reputation. Imagine working on the publicity for an Alfred Hitchcock movie. You would probably turn around one afternoon and find him sitting on your typewriter ready for his marching orders. Hitchcock was your classic promoter and no director has equalled his success as a media star.

In addition to the producer and actors, other creative personnel will join your publicity team during the course of the release campaign, depending on what aspect of the film is being emphasized.

Being a writer myself, I always think the writers on a movie project have lots of interesting things to say about their film. But you'd be surprised how seldom a journalist asks to speak to the writer. Only when a writer becomes a hyphenate—either as a writer/director or a writer/producer—does his image change. Lawrence Kasdan, John Milius, George Lucas, Paul Schrader, Walter Hill and James Brooks are good examples of low-profile writers who have become media celebrities because of their hyphenate status.

You might get Lawrence Kasdan on the cover of *American Film* or *Film Comment*, but probably not *Premiere* or *Time*. The magazines, the newspaper feature writers, the television entertainment shows all want the stars. *Entertainment Tonight* might have opened the door to interviewing people behind the cameras, but they still truly concentrate on the lifeblood of the movie business—the stars.

People go to the movies not because of a certain director (Steven Spielberg may be the exception), but because they want to see a certain story or a certain cast. A feature story on the director in any publication is a good break, but if you don't get it, it's not the end of the world. That's why I concentrate on getting my stars the lion's share of the attention.

If the movie you're publicizing is a special effects feast, then your publicity team extends to the crew that created those magical effects. Just as you would supply materials on teen stars to the many teen and fan magazines, the science fiction, fantasy and horror publications must also be dealt with. Don't hesitate to approach your effects team. They generally take great pride in their work and like all magicians, they're a little bit of the ham at heart. This group might extend to the production designer, the various art directors, the special makeup effects team, even the stunt coordinator. The daily newspaper film journalist may not have the space to cover every aspect of the effects film, but you'll find that genre magazine journalists (*Cinefantastique*, *Starlog*, etc.) want to cover the film as completely as possible.

As you determine what element of the film is to be emphasized in the publicity campaign, other performers will come into play, including the costume designers, cinematographers, makeup artists, animal wranglers (aka handlers) and technical advisors.

If the film is a music film, then you have the entire gamut of creators as possible subjects for interviews—singers, musicians, record producers, record company executives, choreographers, dancers, and engineers.

In the final analysis, as the publicist on the project, you can have a veritable army of interview subjects at your disposal. Don't hesitate to get them involved. The more subjects you turn into sales people, the better you can build awareness for your project. In this case, lots of cooks can only enrich the pot.

28

ORGANIZING YOUR FIELD FORCE

While publicity campaigns are initiated and supervised out of Los Angeles or New York, the army of support personnel in the local markets does much of the leg work helping spread the word throughout the country. Regional distribution offices, advertising agencies, P.R. agencies and local consultants are loosely referred to in marketing parlance as "the field." Their work is crucial to the success of any campaign.

Local Agencies Are Vital.

To publicize and promote a film that is opening nationally, it is virtually impossible to do everything out of LA or NY. Local agencies, many of which are contracted by your film's advertising department to buy space in the local media, can also help your publicity efforts by servicing your press kits, passing along story ideas to the local press and helping implement any promotional ideas you've developed.

These local agency people and consultants work in their markets every day. They know the journalists who cover the movie beat. They know the local night clubs and retailers that are receptive to movie tie-ins. They know where to screen the film for critics. They have lists of contacts who can help spread the word on new pictures. In other words, they know their turf.

Local publicity plays an important role in a national publicity campaign. Not only does it produce awareness of your film at the local level, which of course sell tickets, but favorable reviews from regional critics often spawn some additional feature story coverage, photos, "think" pieces, and, eventually increased awareness (and box office attendance) outside their local area.

I can sit in an office in Los Angeles and contact local radio stations myself. I can also service local journalists with press kits and story ideas and I can arrange for film prints to be shipped to certain theaters or screening rooms so that the critics can see the film in advance. Technically, I can do all of this. But, unless I know many of these people personally, which I don't, I am simply another voice on the telephone promoting one of hundreds of films that come into the local market every year.

A field force can personalize the campaign and increase its local effectiveness. The major studios realize this and each year they go to the trouble and expense of flying field personnel to Los Angeles or New York to view the new product before it is released. During these "field junkets," strategy is discussed, publicity and promotional materials are distributed, and a plan is developed. Because of this special treatment, it is guaranteed that the major films are going to remain firmly in the minds of these field people when they return home.

The major studios, however, do not have a lock on local publicity and promotion. Local agencies of course know that the big studios are bread and butter accounts. But smaller, independent film companies can also hire them and the smart agencies will treat them with equal respect. You never know when a one-picture-a-year independent will become a ten-pictures-a-year independent.

Developing a good relationship with local and regional entities is crucial to the success of your campaign. I first became aware of the field when I was planning the national promotional tour for Columbia Pictures' *Spacehunter: Adventures in the Forbidden Zone* in 1983. This was a $13 million 3D science fiction extravaganza that was executive produced by Ivan "Ghostbusters" Reitman. Columbia would eventually pump $9 million into the marketing campaign. As part of that campaign, I had sold Reitman and the studio on the idea of touring, via truck convoy, the full-sized science fiction props and costumes from the movie to shopping malls, college campuses and fairs in 15 major cities prior to the film's Spring release.

To help me coordinate promotional events and media coverage in each city, the head of the studio's field force gave me a list of Columbia Pictures' regional field offices. The studio maintained staffed offices in such cities as New York, Chicago, Toronto, and Atlanta. In the other cities I would visit, I was given a local contact which in this case was usually a college representative who represented Columbia Pictures' interests on campus.

The field offices were very helpful. Prior to our LA departure, they provided me with many different lists, including local college campuses, top shopping malls, hot night clubs and any events that would coincide with my arrival in town.

In Dallas, I remember, we were able to exhibit at a huge rock concert/carnival sponsored by the top rock radio station. This event which took place in the cavernous Dallas Convention Center, gave us the opportunity to show off one of the "space trucks" (which was being transported on a 60-foot tractor trailer) for three days to over 300,000 people.

In Washington D.C., a representative from the New York field office came down and arranged for us to exhibit on the downtown Mall. In Atlanta, field personnel accompanied us, in costume, to local shopping malls where we handed out 3D *Spacehunter* buttons. In Chicago, we would not have been able to get our exhibits onto the Northwestern college campus had it not been for a resourceful field representative who figured out a way for us to negotiate a route around several railroad bridges which were too low to provide clearance for our truck convoy.

Another vital service all the field offices provided me with on that trip was office space and access to a phone or typewriter so that I could report my progress to the studio back in California. My reports included the events we were involved with, an estimate of the size of the crowd who attended and any media coverage we received along the way. The field offices were also very cooperative in forwarding copies of any news stories which resulted from our efforts to me at my next destination. At the end of my journey I had a fat file of publicity breaks, including two national wire stories circulated by the Associated Press.

The field played an important role in another film I worked on in 1987. It was a horror film called *The Gate* released by the independent film company, New Century/Vista. In that movie, three teenagers discover the gate to hell in their own suburban backyard. Our enterprising promotional director had discovered that there is an actual town called Hell, located about forty miles west of Detroit and we quickly concocted a promotional event which centered around the idea of "the first live broadcast from hell."

Our field contact in the area was the advertising agency which represented us in Detroit. Their account executive helped us with some preliminary research on the town of Hell, sending us photographs and geographical information and became our primary liaison during our ten days in "hell." He was especially helpful in providing answers to our barrage of questions: Where was the nearest movie theater (for a possible premiere)? Could a local television station provide satellite gear for a national broadcast? Could a set be built duplicating the gate to hell? Would local television and print journalists be interested in covering the event? How would we set up a party in hell?

Making The Initial Contact.

If you're working at a studio, there's the possibility that coordination of the field P.R. campaign will be handled by someone else. If you're involved with an independent project, you could have direct contact with the field, so you should know how to deal with them. Whether you're releasing a film nationally or just in one market, take inventory of your regional P.R. support. Contact your own advertising department and find out which agencies they are using to buy media ads. Remember that the advertising department is not going to coordinate your publicity campaign. They will, however, give you a list of advertising agencies who will be buying for them in the markets where the film will be released.

Most advertising agencies around the country which do business with the film industry are two-tiered operations providing both advertising and publicity support. New York is an exception, where because of the size and complexity of that market, you'll need to hire a separate P.R. agency.

Your contact at the ad agency will most often be an executive whose responsibility is handling local P.R. and promotions. In some tiny companies, executives handle both advertising and P.R. but often you won't be working directly with the account exec who buys advertising. After you get a list of ad agencies from your advertising department, you'll need to put together a contact list of these P.R. people. A word of caution: The advertising department may not decide which agencies they will actually be using until the last minute so be sure you get permission before you make direct contact with any agency on your list. Start making contact with as many agencies as you can and the ones which aren't decided yet you'll have to put on your "we'll handle that later" list.

Call each local agency and identify yourself. Start selling the movie from your first second on the phone. Because they are P.R. people, they should be easy to talk to. But unless you've worked with them before, don't expect them to be too chummy at first. Remember, they're probably working on 20 other films besides yours.

I like field agency P.R. people. First, they are usually very knowledgeable about what can and can't be done in their local markets. They also know all of the right media people in town and how they can be reached most effectively. Most of all, they can and often will generate great promotional ideas.

Once you've identified yourself and you start to sell the movie, make sure they know the release date of the film. If your own advertising department has done its job, the local agency will already know the release date and a memo about the film will have been circulated around the agency. But don't take anything for granted—even to the point of repeating yourself. You have to create a mind-set here. If you start talking up the movie and its date, I guarantee you the title will start floating around the regional agency office and it will be placed on all the right calendars. An informed agency is an agency ready for action. The campaign can then begin.

Publicity Materials.   Once you've established contact with the local agency or P.R. contact, begin the process of supplying them with materials. These will include:

■ **Strategy Letter or Report**. You may be able to explain to the agency exactly what you need in the local market, but it is probably better expressed in a strategy letter, detailing every aspect of the campaign. In the letter, present any information you have on the film that will be valuable—including results from your advertising research that pinpoints audience demographics. It will be very helpful for your agencies to know which target audience they are trying to reach. Also include any publicity reports you've prepared detailing upcoming national breaks that may be seen in the local markets. Why? Because when the local agency is trying to pitch a promotion to a radio station, it might be helpful for them to see a major story on *Entertainment Tonight* or in the *New York Times*—material that may impress them or their contacts with the importance of your film.

■ **Press Kits**. First, send them a sample so that they can read up on the movie and find out what they are selling to the public. Then, find out how many kits they will need to service their territory. Sometimes you will be asked if you just want to hit the top critics and writers, or whether you want to blanket all media. Your answer depends on the film. If you're releasing a low-budget horror/exploitation film in St. Louis, the top critics and writers will be enough. Unless its the umpteenth version of *Friday the 13th* or *Nightmare on Elm Street*, low-budget horror films as a rule have a short life span in the theatrical market and little interest amongst the various media. If, however, you're opening *Ghandi* in St. Louis, every journalist with a pen or a microphone needs to know about it, so if the local agency wants 71 kits, supply them.

■ **Color Photos**. The b/w's will always be included in the press kit. But don't overlook color photos. Some regional newspapers use color photos, just like *USA Today*. Local television programs may want to use a color slide as background for their review or story. When you ask the local agency about how many press kits they will need, be sure to mention that you have color transparencies (slides) and find out how many sets of these they will need.

■ **Video Materials**. If you have produced a video press kit on the film, let the local agency know about it. Even though you might have hired a video distributor to send out the cassettes, it doesn't hurt to check with the local agencies about who will need video press kits in their area. The distributor might have overlooked some. You can also put the video distributor in touch with the local agencies so they can compare lists. If you don't have a video distributor, make sure you are prepared to supply this important material yourself. If the movie has a music video, also let them know about it. There may be a music video show—with a regional MTV format—where the video can be played.

- **Video Clips**. In order for the local television reviewers to present a film review on the air, they will need a selection of film clips from the film (usually referred to as "review clips"). Go ahead and select 3-4 clips with a duration of not more than one minute. Review clips should not meander—they need to perfectly sell the picture with good pictorial elements and hard-hitting dialogue. Cutting them to a minute or less will not be easy, but the duration is important. Most film review shows will show only about 30 seconds of clip footage so it makes absolutely no sense to give them a two minute clip. If you do not have a video press kit which of course includes these review clips, they should be duplicated onto their own cassette and shipped in the appropriate quantity to the field.

- **Promotional Items**. Local agencies pride themselves on their ability to create local awareness through promotions on the radio, at night clubs, and various other events that might help the film. In order for them to generate excitement, they need some promotional items. On *Witchboard*, a horror film about a murderous Ouija board, we created two thousand Ouija boards, dubbed them "witchboards" and sent them into the field. Field agencies particularly like T-shirts, because they are the perfect giveaway items on radio—and even though they've been used for years, they're still very popular. In any case, if there is a budget, make up enough promotional items to blanket your releasing territory—whether it's national or regional. The local agency will give you the numbers it needs. Generally, each radio station will ask for between 25-100 shirts (for its promotion). The agency will probably need another 100 shirts for local promotions at night clubs or events.

- **Contests and Games**. In addition to T-shirts, Ouija boards and other promotional materials, you might have a specific contest or stunt in mind to use as a promotion. Although the local agencies like to come up with their own promo ideas, don't hesitate to get them excited about the contests and games you've created at the home office.

Creativity From The Field.

Local agencies and consultants usually work on dozens of movies each year. They have experience with every type of film genre and promotional concept and they're used to thinking on the run. Tap into that. Although it's important to communicate your philosophy to them—give them the basic plan—don't restrict the local agency too much.

I've found that agencies work harder on the promotions they've conceived in-house. It's a natural reaction, even if all they're doing is customizing your idea to fit their market.

If the promotion calls for a parade of antique cars down the main boulevard on the Saturday before release, the agency in Cleveland may decide to add a local antique fire truck to the procession; or the agency in Denver may want the mayor to lead the parade in a futuristic Buick; or the Chicago agency may want to add a marching band.

Consider these additions and encourage local creativity. As long as your events stay within their budgets, any additional excitement is welcome.

After you've approached the agency about the assignment, request that they respond with a promotional proposal on what they think they can do locally. Once you get 30 promotional proposals back, you can then set up a meeting with your superiors to determine which is the correct approach. You'll be surprised at the number and variety of ideas that come back from the field.

Budget Guidelines.   When you're coming up with your budget for field publicity and promotions, keep the following items in mind:

$ **Creative fee.** This varies, market by market. Local advertising agencies who are already buying your newspaper space will often charge only expenses for servicing local media. Their publicity department provides a service that comes under the overall fee they receive for their full-marketing effort. Sometimes, I will see a minor service bill of $500 on top of their expenses, which include mailing, printing, and some travel. If the agency is buying advertising, I would never pay a creative fee of more than $1000 per market.

Although we'll talk more about a New York publicity liaison in a later chapter, keep in mind that publicity help in the Big Apple is going to cost quite a bit more than what you are spending in other regions. What kind of fee are we talking about? First of all, it's doubtful that you'll get a free ride from the ad agency which is making media buys for your advertising department. They generally are specialists and don't have the kind of in-house publicity liaison you'll find elsewhere. You can expect to pay at least $7500 for a full campaign on a major film with some of the top publicity agencies asking for $15,000 or more for their services. More on New York later.

$ **Theater rental.** Promotional screenings, which are planned in conjunction with a local radio station, usually take place on the night before the film officially opens in theaters. Since you're renting the theatre (called buying out the performance) on a weeknight, generally a slow box office period, the cost of the theater rental should be reasonable—around $500 in most cities outside New York and Los Angeles. For my promotional screening budget, I usually budget at the high end, going to $1000 per screening, which will cover the added costs in the big cities, and give me a contingency elsewhere. Generally budget promotional screenings in no more than the top 25 markets.

$ **Press screenings.** Unless the local advertising agency has their own screening room, you will also have to pay a fee to screen the film for local press. Again, your costs will be considerably lower outside New

York and Los Angeles. Daytime screenings for film press are common and the theaters or screening room usually charges considerably less than they would for an evening performance. Budget on the high end at $500 per market. This will give you another contingency that may come in handy if you have to book more than one screening. For New York, I often will budget for up to 10 screenings because New York critics and writers are finicky. Seldom will they all come to the same screening. For New York alone, that screening fee will be between $2500 and $5000 ($500 per screening). In Los Angeles, I usually plan one major screening for the majority of my critics costing between $1000 and $2000—and leave the door open for additional, smaller screenings if the need arises.

$ **Shipping**. Although the cost of creating press kits and promotional items have already been figured into your marketing budget, you must add an additional fee for shipping them all over the country. I budget $200 per market for shipping costs which allows most material to go out UPS 2nd Day Air, with an occasional emergency overnight delivery.

$ **Printing**. Printing costs for ticket shells, local flyers or any signage are usually figured into the overall promotional budget but I put a small contingency printing amount of around $100 into my pre-release budget. Hopefully I won't have to spend this money, but it's a good budget item to have.

$ **Travel**. The major studios spend enormous amounts of money to fly their field agencies into Los Angeles for strategy conferences. However, field people usually do not travel. They are responsible for their own territories, and they accomplish their work on the telephone or by driving around their own city by car. I generally do not receive bills for auto mileage, unless a trip to a neighboring city is involved. If the Dallas office is planning a promotional event in Fort Worth, you can expect to receive some gasoline and mileage receipts. The same may be true if a Chicago P.R. media person has to journey up to Milwaukee to service press kits. Budget $100 per market for travel.

If you are planning a publicity junket to one of these cities, your junket is budgeted separately from your local agency costs.

$ **Miscellaneous expenses**. This could be literally anything, including telephone, xerox, postage. Budget another $100 per market for this item.

Follow-up Continuously.

Keep in touch with your agencies. They are as much a part of your team as your own staff. Remember, if you don't contact them regularly they'll turn their attention to their other ninety-four clients who do keep in touch.

Once you've made your initial contact, you've given them a publicity plan and they've received materials, keep sending them what I call "publicity motivators." If the *New York Times* breaks a major story on your film, copy it and send it to the field. If *Entertainment Tonight* is running a piece tonight, get on the fax machine and alert them. In most cases, unless you keep them posted on what great events are occurring in your overall publicity campaign, it will be difficult for you to motivate the local agencies to do any more than what they normally do—and that isn't enough.

To me, "normal" means "average" and "average" means "boring." You don't want this campaign to be like the last sixty-five. The local agency has to be genuinely excited about the project so that they can genuinely excite the local media. Of course, with four or five hundred movies to report on and review each year, it's going to be challenging to make every one an event for the local journalist. In my mind, however, every project I work on is exciting and it's my job to communicate that to the local agency. Pick up your cheerleader pom-poms once again, get out your megaphone, motivate, motivate, motivate.

Even if you don't have a specific break to announce, keep supplying information to the field that will at least keep them close to the flow of the campaign. Everyone has an ego, and when the field receives a memo that has their name on the "cc" list at the bottom with all of the other marketing executives involved in the campaign, it will help them realize that they are part of the team.

Reviews Just After Release.

Once the movie is released, the first thing you're going to need—and thank the lucky stars for fax machines—is a copy of all local reviews. These reviews need to be immediately dissected and quotable quotes pulled—the type of positive review quotes you always see in motion picture advertisements. Positive reviews from the field are important. You never know when a single word used by a Dallas critic could be the headline in the film's upcoming ad.

In addition to any reviews, remind the agency to send you virtually everything they see on the film in their local papers—stories, photographs, advance mentions, capsule reviews and comments, anything. If the review appears on TV or radio, get them to send you a transcript or a tape.

Transcripts from the field are more vital than the actual tapes. Although it's always nice to see exactly how the review or story was presented, it can also be a logistically difficult procedure to get tapes and sometimes its very expensive.

In Los Angeles for instance, if I have a break on *Entertainment Tonight*, I can call a company the next day that will provide me with either a full tape or a transcript. The tape might cost $65.00. The transcript is $20. Since I trust that the transcript is complete, it will do for my publicity report. Of course, if I know that *ET* is running in LA, I usually set my own VCR at home to tape the break—a procedure that some of the local agency executives follow. But transcripts are useful and they can be faxed along with reviews to your office.

If the local agency is planning a radio-supported promotional screening, you should receive a concise report on attendance to the screening and reaction. In this case, the agency becomes your ears and eyes at the event. Attendance and reaction will be useful to your superiors in determining any advance word on the film's box office potential. If the screenings are packed and the crowd is applauding like crazy at the end, then it's vital that the agency get that information to you as soon as possible.

Even before the reviews are published, it's also useful for the local agencies to provide you with any advance word from the critics or writers. Some critics, if they really treasure a film, will be free with a loose comment or two. These words can also be useful to your superiors in tracking the potential of the film. Of course, if the film is not enjoyable, you can get the same comments—of a negative variety and they should be reported as well. Many critics are very close-mouthed about their reaction and you'll just have to wait for the printed or televised review.

When the campaign is completed, the agency should provide you with a concise report of everything they've done for you. The report should document the press and promotional screenings, and any special event that took place in the market, including nightclub promotions, shopping mall displays, parades, contests, etc. If photographs have been taken of any of these activities, encourage the agency executive to send them on.

Although you've already received fax copies of all the reviews and stories, the agency should follow with "hard copies" of the original papers, which you can copy yourself for dispersal amongst your CC list. (Copies of faxes can be illegible.)

Thank-yous.

I expect the field agencies to do a good job and after I receive their report I always reciprocate with a personal thank you letter. Never send a form thank you letter to the field agency—it's a very big insult. You've worked closely with these people, they've helped you engineer a national campaign for a hopefully successful picture—you owe them, at least, a personal thank you. And don't base your thank you on the success of the film. Even if the film bombs in the marketplace, you still owe them a vote of thanks for the work they do. Another movie may be coming down the pike shortly and you'll once again be teamed with the field.

29

LONG-LEAD-TIME MEDIA PITCHES AND BREAKS

Sowing the seeds of audience awareness from the very beginning of production is vital. With cooperative actors, and an interesting angle you will be able to exploit many P.R. opportunities. However, much of the work continues after production is completed and it will carry on until the release of the film.

Whether it's the first day of shooting or the first day after wrap, your primary concern is to reach as many "long-lead-time" outlets as possible. Contacting *Playboy Magazine* a week before the film comes out may be a spontaneous thought on your part, but it's not going to result in any publicity. Even if they liked your fabulous idea and wanted to go with it, the editor is going to ask you, "Why didn't you contact me three months ago?"

Magazines work two, three, four and five months in advance on their issues. They're usually the first outlets you approach, hopefully while the film is still in production. If you have a film with some top female stars, it is especially important to plan an early campaign, for, the many women's magazines are definitely long-range planners.

Magazines aren't your only long-lead-time media outlets. Freelance writers, syndicated writers, some television entertainment shows, even your regional writers require your information as early as possible.

Early contacts sometimes don't pay off until just before the film opens. You might contact a journalist with a local newspaper way in advance and find out that although he will consider the story now he'd prefer to be contacted closer to release time. The standard reply being, "Your film is opening in July? Okay, why don't you contact me in late May or early June," or "I can't write the story until I see the film. Call me when you have a screening."

Magazine editors are shrewd enough to realize the importance of "star power" and its correlation to their circulation. That's the advantage of star power. If you're working on a Mel Gibson, Sean Connery, or Dustin Hoffman film and you're offering the publication an interview with the actor, they're usually not going to stipulate that they must see the film first. Of course, if you have a great film with no names, it's going to be tougher to arrange advance coverage. When it comes to media pitching, everyone's from Missouri, the "Show-Me State."

Be Organized.

List your magazine contacts in order of importance and stay organized! Time flies when you're in the heat of a national campaign. Don't be caught staring at a calendar one day realizing that you've missed some key magazine deadlines.

Even the best publicists miss deadlines, but it happens most often to those who keep their files on little pieces of paper scattered on a cluttered desk. During a national publicity campaign, mail seems to come in by the truckload. Little pieces of paper quickly get buried in the mess.

Keep your long-lead-time outlets in an organized list, either in a file on your computer, or neatly typed on a sheet of paper. Alphabetize them and make sure each has a contact name and telephone number.

As I mentioned in a previous chapter, you might also create a "progress board"—a black or white board with all your outlets written on it. It's always nice to be able to sit on the telephone and stare over at a chart which keeps you organized. I will usually keep my running calls on the computer and then, as breaks are established, I put them on the progress board.

The key is to get rid of those little pieces of paper, any notes you make after phone calls and the innumerable phone messages that come in. You must keep your desk relatively clean and cleared for action.

Publicity Materials Must Be Ready.

Once you have your list in place, make sure you have publicity materials to send to these outlets when they express interest. Hopefully you will have been on payroll during production and already have an "advance" press kit which summarizes the film and provides relatively short biographies.

Use the advance kit until the final kit is ready. Don't worry if the material is not finalized. Long-lead press need only a taste of the project at this time. Since you're going to be dealing with magazine outlets, remember you'll need a good supply of color transparencies.

Some publicists are pretty stingy about giving out color. I find that if you order enough color in advance, the per-unit cost is actually less than black and white enlargements which are also needed during a long-lead time campaign. Pick a "key set" of color—say, 7 shots which are definitely your best. Type out a caption sheet which identifies those shots, then order in mass quantity. For long-lead press, I would order 50 sets to start.

Remember that you are pitching with these photos. They're giving the magazine editors a visual feel for the film. When definite interest in your project is established, the magazine may use some of these materials, or they may plan their own photo shoot, or request additional exclusive shots. The advantage of shooting thousands of transparencies comes into play here. You can provide exclusives to many outlets.

You'll need some black and white stills too—between 10 and 20 shots in your key set. Make about ten sets to start. The long-lead-time press doesn't need b/w sets at this time so don't bother with ordering 3000 copies of your b/w set until you're sure your press kit is finalized.

Your key color set should always include a few behind the scenes shots. Some magazines, mostly the film trade publications, will request photographs with this type of film crew presence.

Your special portrait or gallery art will also be valuable at this time. When long-lead magazine outlets are considering giving you coverage, they'll be particularly interested if you can show them really good photographs of your stars. If you're going for the cover of a magazine you have to hope that your special portraits are exceptional. The major studios spend huge sums on special photographs of their stars. Check out the magazine covers that appear on a new film by the majors and you're going to see a lot of special art.

Sometimes, if the magazine is really interested in your star, they will also schedule their own portrait shoot. For *Eddie and the Cruisers II: Eddie Lives*, I received a call from *Playgirl Magazine* during production and they were very interested in a cover shot of Michael Pare and they were willing to set up the shoot in New York when production finished. Photo shoots tailored to a specific outlet are great because the magazine will foot the bill. Your logistical challenge is to make sure the actor is available. And don't forget to attend the special shoot wherever it is. You never know when the actor will be asked to do something that is uncomfortable for him. You need to be there to supervise. Don't be too obtrusive, but be aware of how you would like the actor portrayed in the shot. You have the right, in consultation with your actor, to refuse to cooperate with a shot you find disagreeable—even when the magazine is paying for the photo session.

For your electronic outlets, I always like to have some advance materials. These days, more and more outlets are forecasting the upcoming film picture with "collage" pieces on new product. If your movie is coming out in December and *Entertainment Tonight* is doing a piece on Christmas movies in October, it pays for you to send them some advance materials.

These materials include an advance film clip, some behind the scenes material from your video press kit, perhaps some interview material from the same. As a teaser, you may want to throw in a trailer if you have it.

Advance electronic materials can be sent to many outlets. These days, with the omnipresence of VHS recorders, you might even send some of these materials to your key print press outlets. It doesn't hurt for you to show them some film. Even to seasoned editors, a picture can be worth a thousand words.

Pitching To Long-lead Media Outlets.

Before you pitch a single outlet, memorize your film's *theme*, its *relation to the marketplace* and its *strongest selling elements*. For instance, on the film *Russkies*, I was pitching the film as the "first motion picture of the *Glasnost* period." With Premier Gorbachev lowering traditional barriers of communication and cooperation with the West, we were about to release a film about a Soviet sailor who washes up on the shore of Key West, Florida.

Thematically, it was the other side of the typical cold war film. In this film, the sailor is found by three Army brats who through their political conditioning, view him as the enemy. However, as the film develops, the two very different sides eventually find trust and understanding, and the boys vow to get kindly "Mischa" back to Russia.

Theme: Trust and understanding among "enemies";
Relation to the marketplace: The first American film that relates to Gorbachev's *Glasnost*;
Strongest selling elements: ...
This is where we ran into some problems. Even though the film presented a novel approach to the cold war, the producers had cast the film with mostly unknown actors. On *Russkies*, my two biggest names were teen actors, Peter Billingsley and Leaf Phoenix.

Without any female stars, I had no hope with the women's magazines. Without any adult stars, I had no shot with the major national magazines. Even though they were sympathetic to the theme of the film, they were interested in star power. The only real outlet then for *Russkies* was the teen and fan magazines. Fine on their own, but not the basis for a strong national campaign.

Let's take another film. On *Pretty in Pink*, writer/producer John Hughes had fashioned another of his delightfully insightful looks at teenage life in contemporary America. I had teen stars Molly Ringwald and Andrew McCarthy in the leading roles, and a basically fun story about how a girl from the other side of the tracks meets a rich boy who asks her to the high school prom and then, because of peer pressure, has to "un-ask" her. Not only is the boy ostracized by his "richie" friends, but the girl loses the respect of her best friend and her unusual click of "zoids."

Theme: A modern Cinderella story with touches of "The Ugly Duckling";

Relationship to the marketplace: Another insightful look at teenagers from the filmmaker who brought you *Sixteen Candles* and *The Breakfast Club*;

Strongest selling points: Two of America's top teen stars, Molly Ringwald and Andrew McCarthy. With Molly, there was immediate interest from virtually every woman's magazine. McCarthy was also popular. National magazines were intrigued by the next step in Hughes' theatrical examination of the American teen.

All around, it was a very easy film to be pitching. This time the producer had shrewdly combined a very sellable theme and presentation with some actors who could spark media interest.

Know what you're selling. If you don't have the star power, emphasize the uniqueness of your theme and keep your fingers crossed. However, if you have some stars, you don't have to worry as much about the theme or storyline. The magazine editors will be interested in whether you have good photographs of the stars and when they are available for interviews. Once you get their attention, find out about their deadlines so you can be sure to get into the issue closest to your film's release.

- **Two breaks in one magazine?** It's a possibility. Depending on how many actors you are pitching. These days, many magazines, like many newspapers, are putting together collage stories on upcoming movies. If you know their publishing schedule in advance, you can probably get a photograph and some editorial information into that collage piece. Hopefully, an interview piece will follow in an issue closer to release time. Although it's difficult, it's not impossible to get two interview pieces going if you have the star power. If you're doing a film with both Mel Gibson and Glenn Close, Vanity Fair may want Mel for July and Glenn for August. That would be a nice coup.

With stars of that caliber you should also go after cover presence. The magazine cover is the ultimate media break. More people may see a *Today Show* interview or a segment on *Entertainment Tonight* but there is something very unique about a magazine cover. After all, for a monthly magazine, only twelve cover subjects are chosen each year, whereas a *Today Show* may have a thousand guests during the same period.

- **The Cover?** If you have the star power, go after the cover. It takes a great deal of negotiating and a lot of cooperation from your star. First, the magazine has to express interest in the story and a writer must be assigned to interview the star. It is at this point that the publicist tries to anchor a cover story to the interview. Depending on the star, you may have some leverage.

In most cases, the star's publicist is also involved and may even take the lead in negotiations. Some magazine covers will be easier to crack than others, again depending on the star. *Time* and *Newsweek* will never guarantee a cover. An important world event could happen suddenly and guess what story would get the cover? Many a show business cover story has bitten the dust in favor of "hard" news.

You'll have a better chance of anchoring your cover story with the monthly magazines. Sometimes, they'll even surprise you by suggesting a cover. Whatever you do, plan your cover strategy as carefully as possible. It makes absolutely no sense to go blindly after 24 magazine covers, without consulting with the actor or her publicist. Remember, in most cases, the magazine will ask for its own private photo session, and very few actresses will sit still for 24 sessions.

Work with the actor and determine at an early date which magazines are the most logical for cover stories. You will still be affected by the actor's schedule and availability, but with a short list of important magazines, you may get your photo sessions completed.

Sometimes a cover comes after hard months of pitching with no guarantees. You send slides and advance production materials from the set. You invite a freelance journalist to the location for an interview with the star. The journalist raves to the publication about a great interview. After wrap, you send more color materials to the magazine. You start talking about the release date to the editor. Gradually, you begin to ask about the potential for a cover story.

In my experience, cover potential is usually pretty black and white. Either the magazine is impressed enough with the star and the project to give you positive feedback, or you don't stand a chance.

Competition could hurt you. If you're releasing a film in the summer, a number of film companies will be going after the same *Premiere* magazine cover. It's often a great deal of luck to nab the cover at the right time. Luck and negotiation.

Don't forget to ask, though. Never assume that you have no chance at the cover. Failing to ascertain cover availability is a major sin.

If you're working on a film with a teen idol, there are a number of teen magazine covers to shoot for. Some young actors and actresses are cover regulars in these magazines. Note that teen covers are usually busy with an average of 6-7 actors featured each month. You have a much better shot with these publications because there is no exclusivity.

Your cover might also be tailored to the subject matter of the film, rather than a particular star. If your movie is a prestigious one, on a unique topic, with a star director, you have a definite shot at a film magazine cover—especially the more intellectual ones like *American Film, Film Comment* and *Films in Review*.

A music film might also appeal to a number of music publications while a top science fiction project might make the cover of *Cinefantastique, Starlog* or *Cinefex*.

When a cover is planned, the magazine will most often pay for its own photo shoot. You will be responsible for getting the talent to the shoot and remaining there as a creative liaison. Photo shoots are usually exhausting for the actor. We're not talking about a roll of Ektachrome and out the door. It's more like three to four hours and several changes of clothes. Magazine editors can be fickle about their cover designs and they usually like plenty of shots from which to choose. Your presence is necessary to keep the actor from pulling his hair out. It's times like this that your effortless charm really comes into play.

There are times when the publication will choose to go with your own special art for their cover. No wonder the major studios go to huge expense to prepare their own gallery sessions with top talent. You never know when an editor will call and ask for special cover art. As I mentioned in an earlier chapter, gallery sessions during production are crucial especially when you don't know if the actor will be available for photography after the film is finished.

If you have top stars involved, try not to give out the same art to every publication. Magazine editors like to know that they have something different than the competition. Hopefully, the success of your own gallery shoot will give you plenty of selections.

If a cover doesn't work out with a particular magazine, there are still options open to you, including a major feature story in that publication. If you've interested the magazine in the film or star and a writer has completed his interviews on the location during filming, then you've done your job.

Once the film is finished shooting, don't assume that magazine coverage is finished. If the star actor is available, you might still be able to schedule some interviews during the post-production/pre-release period, especially if a celebrity is involved. The length of your magazine campaign is usually determined by the amount of time available between the end of principal photography and the release of the film. The shorter the span, the shorter the duration of your magazine pitching campaign.

On *Eddie and the Cruisers II: Eddie Lives*, we finished the film in May and scheduled it for release in August. By the time I returned to Los Angeles from the Montreal location, we were already bumping up against most magazine deadlines. Every freelance magazine interview I completed on the set was thus extremely valuable because they could be fed directly into the publications with August street dates.

On major releases like the *James Bond*, *Indiana Jones* and *Batman* series, with long post-production schedules, it is much easier to plan extended magazine coverage. Unfortunately, on shorter turn-arounds, due to those long-lead deadlines and actor availability, once production is completed so is the bulk of your magazine campaign.

30

DEVELOPING AN EFFECTIVE SCREENING PROGRAM

Screenings of your film are an effective way to generate interest among the press and the public, provided of course you have a genuinely good movie. However, if you're working on the 17th chapter of the *Friday the 13th* series, you may want to avoid showing the film to critics who may be less than favorable about another blood feast for the nation's impressionable youth.

If the movie is terrible and you know the critics are going to hate it it's probably better to not show it to anyone before it opens. Even the worst picture could get some opening week business if it's kept away from the reviewers. A great advertising campaign and your skillful publicity and promotion should be able to attract crowds of expectant moviegoers. Word-of-mouth will sink it eventually, but coin could be made for a few days.

If your film is not a turkey, you'll need to do some soul-searching to decide whether a screening will be useful or not. Your goal is to get some quotable reviews, but a big, blaring headline slamming your film is worse than no reviews at all. I try to never pre-judge what the critics will say. I've screened films with absolutely no redeeming value that have been adored by some reviewers. (Sometimes, I look to see if there has been a typographical error and they've given my film the wrong review). Conversely, I've seen marginal, even harmless little films crucified by critics.

Some films seem to be review-proof and should be screened for the sake of any possible publicity value. Youth-oriented films fall into this category, so do films with lots of violence (such as the Chuck Norris and Charles Bronson vehicles). Usually, it is safe to say that the fans who flock to these films do not read reviews. If the marketing campaign creates some sizzle, the attendant negative reviews will not hurt the film. That's the theory.

Another argument in favor of going ahead with screenings is that many people do not necessarily agree with what critics say. They might like the concept of the movie and the cast and decide to go anyway. This applies particularly to comedy films.

Another theory suggests that if you don't offer a screening before the film is released, the press will think you're trying to hide something. This could stunt any publicity you're hoping to get. In addition, when reviewers do see the movie, "on their own," they might be negatively pre-disposed. This theory may be valid, but if you're not screening in the first place, you're not going to benefit much from last minute publicity anyway. If the critics are negative after the film opens, it's not going to matter, because the film has already made its opening coin. It's run its course and the public has already made up their mind by reacting to your advertising campaign.

But what happens if you have a marginal film that could benefit from some good critical response. If you don't pre-screen, you lose the possibility of quoting from any good reviews—quotes that could appear in your opening day advertisements. These quotes are important, especially for adult-oriented films, which are going to be seen by filmgoers who do read reviews.

Filmgoers aren't the only ones who you want to affect with a good review. Today there are so many media outlets for publicizing movies, that a good review quote could create interest and excitement among other reviewers. It doesn't happen every time, but if Reviewer A gives the film a rave, it may influence Reviewer B to at least take a look at the film and judge for himself. Remember that reviewers can't possibly see every film that comes out. Initial positive reviews can wake up the media to a potential hit or, at the very least, a film that should not be dismissed.

The Iron Triangle, a Vietnam War drama that starred Beau Bridges and Haing S. Ngor (from *The Killing Fields*), was the first film told from the Viet Cong's point of view. It was released two years after *Platoon* and interest in the Vietnam War was waning, but as marketeers, we thought the unique angle of this film would intrigue reviewers. We also had a very good newcomer (Vietnamese Liem Whatley) playing the leading role of a Viet Cong soldier.

We took a gamble and screened the film early. The reviews were wonderful and we were able to build our entire advertising campaign around quotes from these good reviews. Some reviewers also provided additional coverage—feature stories, and the like—which is the bonus publicity that can result from positive responses to screenings.

Although the film did little theatrical box office, it became a very big video hit, selling over 80,000 cassettes. The video company made good use of our positive review quotes and they were delighted with our marketing approach.

Screenings don't always turn out so well. As I said before, it's tricky. At New Century/Vista, we had a modern fairy tale/comedy called *Maid to Order* which starred Ally Sheedy as a spoiled rich girl who takes a job as the maid in the home of an obnoxious talent agent. The film had what we thought was a wonderful charm. I even cried at the end.

I also cried when I saw our reviews. We were killed by the critics. Fully 80% of our reviews were negative and it hurt the film tremendously. Because New Century/Vista couldn't afford to roll the film out in 1500 theaters, we weren't able to take advantage of at least a week of pre-review business. We had to release in a series of waves—450 prints the first week, 200 more the second week, 100 the third and so on. Unfortunately, because of the negative reviews, many of which came out nationally, we could never establish any momentum in the new markets.

In the old days when reviewers were regionally based, you could move from one market to another and start fresh with the filmgoers. Today there are many national critics, including the most famous, Siskel and Ebert in Chicago. Their reviews are televised nationally and everyone hears about them. If they both give their "thumbs down" to your picture, you can be dead in the water before you even begin your release campaign.

Other national outlets include USA Today newspaper and the New York Times which is now laser printed in a national edition. The critics from these newspapers have a tremendous readership, and a great deal of influence when it comes to spreading the word on new movies.

Screening Guidelines.

If you decide to mount a screening campaign, there are rules to follow. Screening a movie is a delicate process. It's your first opportunity to show the project to the people who can pave the way to its financial success. Here are some screening guidelines:

- **Plan your screenings months in advance**. Never assume that if you get the movie on Monday, you can show it to the press on Wednesday. Even if you can get the invitations out, and the press is all available, what happens if all the screening rooms are booked? You can't show the film on a sheet in the lobby of your office building. One of the best theaters in the country to screen at is the Samuel Goldwyn Theater of the Academy of Motion Pictures Arts and Sciences in Beverly Hills. It has 1100 seats, a huge screen and a fantastic sound system. It's also booked months in advance.

Once you're given a release date, and you know you have a movie that everyone must see, book the Goldwyn. Part of organizing screenings is making sure the situation is conducive to a favorable reaction. There's just something magical about 1100 people attending an 8:00 p.m. screening at the Goldwyn.

LA has other excellent facilities—the Director's Guild has a large screening room which is booked almost as much as the Goldwyn and all the big studios have screening rooms which they rent when they're not using them. Screenings can also be held in commercial theatres like the AMC 14 in Century City, one of LA's multiplex theaters. There's something nice about having the opportunity to buy popcorn and drinks while attending a film screening. Does it help generate a more positive review? I don't know, but it's probably worth a study to find out.

Of course, if you're not given a release date until the last possible moment, you're going to have to scramble for screening facilities. Fortunately, if you can do without the big presentation, there are enough smaller rooms—50 to 100 seats—to accommodate most of your press.

Interestingly, in New York City, big screenings are not as common. Whereas I can pretty much guarantee that 80-90% of my LA critics will attend one screening at the Goldwyn or Director's Guild, in New York the critics like to have multiple opportunities to see the film in smaller screening rooms. You may have to hold 5-8 small screenings to get to all of your critics.

■ **Schedule your screening so that it doesn't conflict with other big screenings.** The major studios have worked out an arrangement to facilitate all-media screenings in LA. In order to minimize conflicts, the Motion Picture Association of America (MPAA) keeps a schedule of screenings planned by their members. Since you don't want to organize a screening that nobody comes to because they're all attending one by a major studio, it's crucial to contact the MPAA to get clearance for your screening.

This is the way the MPAA system works. Each year all the major studios are given a specific day of the week on which they will hold most of their screenings. For instance, Paramount might screen on Wednesdays, Fox on Thursdays, Tri-Star and MGM on Tuesdays, etc. By spreading major screenings out this way, potential log jams where five major screenings are trying to squeeze onto one night are avoided.

You don't have to be a MPAA member to take advantage of their schedule. (Most independent film producers aren't members of MPAA.) You can call the MPAA office and they'll tell you if the night you want to book is clear, then if it is you can get on the schedule. All parties, MPAA member or not must book six weeks in advance.

There is no rule that says you have to call the MPAA to clear a screening. You're free to screen whenever you want. But you won't want to face your superiors the day after no one shows up for your screening because it conflicted with one by a major. So make the call, get clearance and then let your superiors know in advance that the MPAA has cleared your screening night.

- **How early to screen?** Let's assume you have a good movie and you expect good reviews. The bulk of your critics—newspaper, television and radio—won't want to see the film until a week or two before it opens, just enough time to get their review to the public. However, there's another important group of critics—reviewers for *Playboy*, *Cosmo*, *Vogue*, *Penthouse* and other magazines. But remember, magazines work on long lead times and unfortunately, it's rare that a finished print is ready for screenings three to six months before the release date.

  An early print can reach other audiences besides critics. If you have a film with potential, you may want to hold a word-of-mouth or opinion maker's screening. Although press are invited to such a screening, it may also include industry VIPs, civic leaders, non-entertainment press, anyone who has a constituency that might benefit from positive word on a new film. You wonder how good word-of-mouth begins—it starts in screenings like this.

- **Special individual screenings for VIP critics.** You learn early on that in New York, Los Angeles and sometimes Chicago, all of your key critics do not attend the same screening. In order for everyone to see the picture, you will have to schedule individual screenings for certain critics.

  The idiosyncrasies of some critics is hilariously illustrated in a scene from Albert Brooks' comedy *Lost In America*. If you aren't familiar with it, rent the movie. The scene is in an opening sequence at Brooks' suburban home—the radio is on and critic Rex Reed is telling late-night talk show host Larry King about his own screening preferences.

  Reed is one of those critics who likes to see a film by himself—no crowded theaters, no talking during the film—no audience reaction around him. He's just alone with his thoughts. He claims that the collective experience of watching a movie with an animated crowd has no bearing on his review. If he finds a comedy funny, he'll laugh. He doesn't need people around him to validate the comedy.

  In addition to preference, some critics will need to have an individual screening simply out of logistics. To meet a deadline on their review show in Chicago, Gene Siskel and Roger Ebert may have to see your movie at 11:00 a.m. on Monday. Otherwise, they will not be able to review. After going through your key reviewers list, you'll find that there are a number of special screening appointments you will have to make. Because these are VIP critics, most with national audiences, it's important to accommodate them, especially if you're optimistic about your film and you think there might be a chance to get a positive review quote.

- **Daytime versus evening screenings.** Screening times vary around the country. In Los Angeles, weekday evening screenings are common, preferably Tuesday thru Thursday. You generally don't want to screen on Monday, the theory being that reviewers may have less energy after a long weekend. Friday is also a taboo because it's the weekend and reviewers do not like to work on a weekend if they can avoid it.

New York reviewers like a mixture of weekday daytime and evening screenings. You provide them with about six chances to see a new film, three night, two morning, one early afternoon. For some reason, New York reviewers are more apt to attend a daytime screening than LA reviewers. At the end of the day, many New York journalists hop a train or car to the suburbs. They don't like to stay in the city if they don't have to.

Outside of New York, LA and Chicago, screenings are usually scheduled in the morning—around 10 a.m. The main reason for this is not the personal preference of the critics, but money—it costs much less to rent a theatre during the day. It's hard to justify $500 or more to rent a commercial theatre at night when daytime rental costs (at the time of this writing) are only $100-200 in the smaller cities.

■ **"Opinion makers"—people to invite to your screenings, other than the media**. When it comes right down to it, there are a very limited number of film critics in the country and they alone cannot fill screening rooms to capacity. In order to "pack" the house and create the optimum atmosphere for an effective screening, it is often necessary to invite additional people to the theater. Hopefully, these guests will enjoy the experience and create an atmosphere of excitement in the theatre. It's also hoped that they will help you generate the all important word-of-mouth.

Opinion makers to include in your screenings may include:

✔ Your Own Company VIPs, employees and friends. Every company you work for will have its own family of employees from the chief executive officer to the messenger. Each of these people will want to see the finished film and you should count on them as part of your initial audience. Remember, without making it too obvious, it is always a good idea to have some friendly faces in the audience.

✔ The Filmmakers. Although a separate "cast and crew" screening can also be scheduled, many times these people will attend your press or opinion maker screenings. Inviting actors to a press screening is fine as long as it's a large screening (400 seats or more). Never seat an actor in a small screening room with film critics. It's not a good mixture. Both sides could get very uncomfortable.

When you invite cast and crew members to their first screening, remember that they often applaud during the credits (we're talking serious camaraderie). Thus, right from the start, you're going to be creating some positive vibrations in the theater. Film critics in LA and NYC are used to this initial boisterousness, so it's not a potential negative.

You can get into trouble, though, if you pack the house with boisterous young people. In order to generate some audience excitement, many studio publicity departments have made the mistake of filling press screenings with youngsters, especially if the film is of the exploitation variety. Although it's a good idea to get an enthusiastic audience primed for the film experience, I find that critics resent the noise. I will invite young people to press screenings, but not in significant numbers. I try to avoid giving the press the impression that I need youngsters there to make the film look good.

✔ Industry VIPs. I always maintain a good list of industry VIPs for large screenings. If you have a good film, it's important to show it off to the film industry. If they enjoy the experience, VIPs can help spread the word faster than any group. This is important, especially in Los Angeles, where favorable word-of-mouth usually originates.

Agents speak to producers who speak to actors who speak to agents, etc. My VIP list consists of hundreds of top actors, producers, directors, agents, and studio executives. Usually, you invite them to your largest screenings. Remember even if the President of Universal Pictures doesn't show, his executive secretary may take the ticket and initiate the positive word-of-mouth.

✔ Screening Organizations. Sometimes you won't have enough press, family and VIPs to fill your theatre. What do you do? You contact one of the screening organizations.

Screening organizations, simply put, are groups of people who like to attend new film screenings. In Los Angeles, there are two large ones—the Los Angeles Film Teachers and the Academy of Science Fiction, Fantasy and Horror. Both groups can invite up to 500 people to help fill your theater.

Although they're capable of inviting people at the very last minute, it's a good idea to give them at least 3-4 days notice. The more time you give them, the better your chances of a good turn-out. Most of these organizations have telephone hotlines on which they announce screening opportunities which means you don't even have to print up invitations for them.

Depending on the film, you should alert the screening organizations about the demographics you need. I remember inviting the Film Teachers to a screening of a new youth adventure film and about 300 members in their 50s and 60s showed up—definitely the wrong audience. It was particularly embarrassing because my boss was standing there watching these seniors enter the screening room. The Film Teachers are very capable of inviting younger members to screenings as long as they are forewarned.

The Academy of Science Fiction, Fantasy and Horror is perfectly suited to films in their genre. President Dr. Donald Reed has assembled a huge organization of the ultimate fans who love the thrill of seeing new films. Science fiction, fantasy and horror fans are great spreaders of word-of-mouth. Just ask George Lucas and Steven

Spielberg. However, if the film is a dog, this group will be your most severe critics.

What is particularly effective about these groups is that their people show up. If you invite 500 Academy of Science Fiction members to a major screening, you can be confident of filling 500 seats.

✔ Create Your Own Screening Organization. Collecting names of people who are opinion makers in your community can be a simple process. If I can ever find the time, I would love to assemble a list of every barber and beauty parlor stylist in Los Angeles. I think I would have the ultimate word-of-mouth group. This type of list could be the core of a screening organization in any city.

You can also recruit members by going to a movie theater and collecting names of frequent filmgoers. I started a "Movie Club" when I was working at New Century/Vista by going to a test screening of a film and passing out registration forms. Although this audience had been invited by an independent research organization, I was able to get their names for my own Movie Club. Using this tactic, you could eventually have a pool of 500-1000 people from which to draw an audience for your word-of-mouth screenings.

These people could also be available for recruited test screenings when your production and marketing executives are determining the effectiveness of the film itself.

✔ Special Interest Screenings. Occasionally you will be screening a film with a special interest tie-in. For instance, on *The Iron Triangle*, I organized a screening for Vietnam veterans. They were particularly interested in the subject matter, the film being the first look at the Viet Cong and the way they fought, and our technical consultant had a good list of vets from which to send out invitations.

Special interest screenings are similar to "opinion maker" and word-of-mouth screenings. You simply assembly a group of people whom you hope will love the film and help spread the word.

If I was about to screen *The Towering Inferno*, I might consider a special interest screening for firemen around the country and their families. For *The Sands of Iwo Jima*, I would consider a special interest screening for the U.S. Marines. If someone really likes the film, you might be able to generate an informal endorsement as well. It doesn't hurt for the Commandant of the Marine Corps to say he thinks the film is great. At the very least, you'll get a great national column item out of it.

■ **Sending out your invitations and setting up an RSVP hot-line.** The quality of your invitations depends, of course, on the size of your screenings and the amount of time you have to prepare them. If you're planning a major press, word-of-mouth and opinion maker's screening at the Samuel Goldwyn Theater or any large screening facility in LA or NY, go to the trouble of creating printed invitations.

Screening invitations are normally printed on a simple 9" x 4" glossy card that can fit into a standard 9½" x 4" (#10) envelope. If possible, print your advertising art on one side. It's generally not necessary to reproduce this art in four colors—black and white or one color is fine.

On the back of the card you will print your screening information. Let's look at typical invitation copy:

You and a guest are cordially
invited to attend an advance screening of

Rocky XII

Starring Sylvester Stallone Jr.

at 7:30 p.m. Friday August 12, 2007
at the Samuel Goldwyn Theater
8949 Wilshire Blvd. in Beverly Hills.
(see attached map for parking instructions)

Please RSVP to Stephanie at (213) 555-1212.

Rocky XII opens nationally on August 26th.

Review Date is Opening Day

Adding a "review date" is a message to your film critics stating that you prefer all reviews to appear no earlier than the opening day of your film—the last thing you want is a negative review breaking before the film opens. It's bad for box office. Critics will do what they want anyway, but you have to say it. In Los Angeles, the key newspapers and trade press will almost always observe this rule, but it's very difficult to get the same cooperation from the TV critics. Because of the limited amount of time they can devote to film reviews (one a night is all they can accommodate) and the sheer amount of film releases scheduled for each weekend, they have to spread their reviews over the course of the week. And there's little you can do about it.

Adding a review date to your invitation is also a way of covering yourself in case a review does break early. If you're also screening in New York, make sure they get the word as well. If a *Variety* reviewer sees the film in NYC, he may not know about the LA review date and his review could definitely break early.

Unless you want to completely tie-up your phone system, you will want to create an RSVP hotline. This is a separate phone line with an answering machine attached. The message on the machine should include all the appropriate information about the screening. The people invited to the screening call in their RSVP by leaving their name, affiliation and the number of people in their party.on the machine. Sometimes, a request will come in to invite some extra people. Provided they leave a phone number to return the call, you can then call back and authorize them to bring the extra guests.

The RSVP line is such a useful tool it's a wonder more companies don't have them. It's a waste of time for your assistant, or the receptionist to answer the phone 500 to 1000 times just to take down someone's name. One argument against the RSVP line is that phone machines can't answer questions. But if guests, especially the press, have questions, they can call your regular number. Be sure to mention it on the taped message.

As the RSVPs come in, transcribe the tape onto an alphabetized list daily. You need to have easy access to who is coming, and more importantly how many will be attending your screening. I often keep the RSVP lists on 26 pages of a legal pad, one page for each letter of the alphabet. It's easy to add names to a set of lists like this, and it's much easier to type up your final guest checklist for the night of your screening if the names are already roughly alphabetized. Of course if you or your secretary have a computer on your desk, use it because it's great at updating and alphabetizing lists.

Never attend a screening without a neat, double-spaced, alphabetized list of the press people on your RSVP list. If you have a number of assistants available, each of them should be given a copy of the list, so that the line into the theater can move smoothly without bottlenecks. It's vital that you know which press representatives have attended your screenings. Two important reasons for this are that you want to know if any important critics have missed your film, and when your boss asks you if so and so has seen a screening, you have to know the answer.

When you print your invitations, always create an overage. If you have 1100 seats to fill at the Samuel Goldwyn Theater, print 3000 tickets. If you have 500 seats at the AMC 14, print 2000. It's better to overbook than underbook. Normally, twenty percent of the people who RSVP to a film screening do not show. Overbooking is thus a common procedure. You want the house packed and ready. Between your press list, your VIP list, your friends, family, cast and crew, plus special interest groups and screening organizations you should be able to fill your screening.

Screening Night.

A press screening can be like a huge party with you playing host. You greet the guests at the door, you engage in typical "hi, how are you, glad you could make it" chit chat, and you make sure that everything runs smoothly. What happens at a screening? Lets take a look.

■ **Before anyone arrives**. For large screenings, get to the theater at least one hour before screening time. You have some chores to perform. Take a look around and make sure everything is clean. Fortunately, thanks to the people who run screening facilities in LA and NYC, I have never seen a dirty theater (probably because no one is allowed to eat or drink inside).

If you're screening in a public theater, the manager will already have organized his clean-up crew to make sure the house is free from piles of garbage on the floor. If you get there early and the house is still dirty, don't hesitate to contact the management. They are working for you on screening night.

Establish a plan for dealing with your company executives, key VIPs or celebrities. You should rope off some seats for a VIP section. Never refer to it, though, as the VIP section. The last thing you want a press person to hear is that you've seated your Uncle Gus in the "VIP Section." The journalist or even another less-connected VIP will begin wondering why he isn't in the VIP Section and a negative-feeling toward you and the movie will develop. Why take a chance?

Recently for a huge screening at the 1100 seat Samuel Goldwyn Theater in Beverly Hills, I determined early on that I would have a large contingent of general VIPs, and a smaller contingent of press and company VIPs. To make sure that all the press and our company people received the best seats, I roped off 300 seats in a prime area of the theater. The press must be your first priority. They should have the best seats, along with your company VIPs. Everyone else, unfortunately, is going to have to fend for themselves. I would rather keep the *LA Times* critic happy than the agent of the actor who happens to be friends with an actor whose brother's in your movie (VIP screening passes, even though they often say "non-transferrable," get passed around a lot and there's nothing you can do about it.) If you have a roped-off section, station one of your assistants or another company employee in that area to help seat people. You can't do it all yourself.

How do you let your ushers know who should be seated in the roped-off section? Recently, I have been using a colored-card system. When the media or company VIP checks in at the front table, I hand them a colored-card which they can then hand to an attendant (or "usher") in the auditorium.

■ **Journalists arrive**. Make sure you've established a "position" inside the front door. You should have a counter top, a podium or any kind of table so that you or your assistant can greet the media. You should even have a pre-printed sign which says, "Press Register Here." With your alphabetized press list, you can then check off their names and hand them a press kit. No one ever refuses a press kit. Put on your most cordial face. Appear jovial (even if the film's a dog). Remember, if you're grim-faced, it's going to get the evening off to the wrong start. Treat the screening like a party, keep everybody happy, at least going into the theater. How they feel when they leave is beyond your control.

■ **VIPs arrive**. In the past, for large screenings, I have prepared an alphabetical list of VIP guests. I now find that unnecessary. If they have an invitation, simply let them in. If you start to check off VIP names, you're going to create a huge bottleneck at the front door.

- **Checking out the house.** While your assistant covers the front door and checks off the media, go into the theater and check out the house. Make sure everyone is finding a seat. Determine how the house is filling up. Smile.

- **Establish communication with your manager/projectionist.** They should know that the screening can only begin after you give the signal. You're going to find that very few screenings begin on time. There are always late arrivals. I usually start my screenings about five minutes late. If you've checked out the house and everyone appears to have found their seat, and only a trickle of people are still entering the theater, then it's okay to give the signal.

- **If announcements are to be made, you will probably make them.** The larger the screening, the less-likely you have to make any announcements. But be prepared. If for some reason there is a delay due to technical reasons, then you will have to explain that to the audience. When one of my films went out of synchronization one night, I had to keep an audience entertained for 40 minutes. Remember, each member of that audience is your personal guest. It's your party.

- **Take care of any special requests.** If a media person needs color slides or a video press kit, or any information you don't have with you, take their business card or give them yours and arrange communications for the following day. Be helpful.

- **Try to watch the movie, even if it's your 75th screening.** An important executive in your company who does not attend the screening may ask you about it. Part of your job is to be the "key observer." You do not want to be eating at Joe's across the street when 35 people walk out of the movie. This screening is very much a part of your job description. You are working tonight. You should make mental notes (written ones if you can) about audience reaction. If the film is a comedy, are the people laughing? If the film is a drama, is their attention rapt, or are there unintentional laughs? If the film is a horror film, are people jumping out of their seats?

- **After the show, be available to your guests.** Before the end titles, leave your seat and position yourself outside the auditorium so that people can walk up to you afterwards and say how much they loved the film (or hated it). Sometimes, no one will come up to you (then, you know you're in trouble). At other times, even the toughest, most non-committal critic in town will walk over and ask if the lead actor is available for interviews (then, you know you've got a winner). Work the after-screening crowd. Get reactions, gauge your reviewers, keep smiling. Usually, if the audience likes the movie, they'll hang around and talk about it in the lobby afterwards. Conversely, if they don't like it, they usually walk straight out without uttering a word.

- **Thank-yous and clean-up.** After everyone leaves, make sure you thank your projectionist or the manager (if he's still there), collect the remaining press kits and lists, dispose of the invitations that you've received and exit. Your job is finished, until the next screening.

31

TEST SCREENINGS

Market research is a term used to describe the process of gathering information about what your customers want before you try to sell it to them. Pepsi Cola conducts taste tests, Procter and Gamble holds focus groups, and movie companies have test screenings for recruited audiences. Although the publicist's job, strictly speaking, is in the public relations arena, there can be times, especially if you're working for an independent film producer, when you are called upon to help the advertising department conduct its market research by organizing a screening.

Normally, the advertising department will hire a company like NRG (National Research Group) to gather market research data. For a substantial fee, these companies will recruit an appropriate audience, screen the film, distribute survey cards, and conduct "focus groups" with selected audience members.

Depending on whom you speak to, research is everything or nothing. Some executives swear by their figures, while others don't have any use for them and consider the results of market research to be unrepresentative of the public at large.

Whatever their value, survey questions, known as "the cards," can reveal some very interesting reactions from the audience. One of the most celebrated research findings of recent memory concerned the Paramount Pictures super hit, *Fatal Attraction*. At an early test screening, the cards revealed that the recruited audiences did not like the original ending of the film in which the Glenn Close character committed suicide and Michael Douglas was arrested for her murder. Changing the ending by putting a gun in Anne Archer's hand (she blows Glenn Close away) helped turn a potential disaster into one of the year's biggest hits.

If you're working for a major studio, you won't have to organize any test screenings—the advertising department will handle that function. However, in the smaller companies, you may suddenly become the screening expert and the test will fall into your lap. It is thus important to understand the process.

- **Who is your target audience?** Before you hire a research company or organize the screening yourself, you should determine the demographics of the screening. The key question: who is the target audience? If you're screening a heavy metal rock and roll picture, you're going to appeal to a young audience. You should thus recruit young people, say 12-24. If you have a general audience film like a *Fatal Attraction* or a *Ghandi*, you want more of a cross-section of the populace, so you expand your demographics, perhaps targeting 18-49.

  I am not an advertising expert, but I do know that older people do not attend movies on a frequent basis. Older people? How old? You can expect a significant drop off after age 30. That's why the core demographic for moviegoers today is in the 12-24 range. Why? Because they love to go to movies and they go frequently (it's the perfect date for the dating set, right?) Thus, when you're testing a general audience picture, make sure you always have a significant number of people in the core demographic. You can invite older people, but their opinion will not be as valid as the core's.

- **Where are you going to find your target audience?** To get any results at all, you will need to show the film to a minimum of 100 people, and probably between 200-300. Unless, you're rushed to put together a screening tomorrow at noon (where you literally have to grab people off the street), you will have time to either hire a company to recruit the audience or do it yourself. How? These days two ways are most popular: one, called "mall intercept" has recruiters with clipboards and screening passes simply walk up to people with the correct demographic profile in shopping malls and offer them seats; the other way is to canvas lines outside theatres to hand out passes.

  Some research companies have lists of people they draw upon for test screenings. Be careful when you use groups like these—some have been used so much that they're too "movie oriented," critical and a little jaded. These people can have a tendency to think of themselves as overly important in the movie decision-making process. Be particularly careful in Los Angeles where test screenings are common. You want a very fresh opinion.

  If you don't hire a research group, put together your own team and go out and recruit. Remember, you have to overbook your test screening. To fill 300 seats, you'll have to recruit at least 1200 people (a four to one ratio). Why? Because people are not compelled to show up and if given any opportunity, they won't. This ratio applies to all types of screenings—test, press, radio promoted, word-of-mouth, etc.

- **Where to screen?** There was a time when studio executives didn't trust an audience in Los Angeles to test the general public's reaction to their films. They would drive up to Santa Barbara or down to San

Diego for recruited screenings. You hear the tales of Jack Warner pacing the lobby while his films were being screened for preview audiences.

Those were also in the pre-*Entertainment Tonight* days when there was such a thing as an "unsophisticated market." Today, thanks to shows like *ET* and expanded movie coverage in all media, everyone understands the filmmaking process. Audiences in Los Angeles are not that much different than audiences in Albuquerque or St. Paul. Consequently, most test screenings these days happen in Los Angeles. Why spend a fortune on recruiting an out-of-state audience when you can get a pretty fair reaction in your own backyard?

■ **Prepare a "recruiting paragraph" on your film.** In order to intrigue a potential attendee, you need to capsulize the film's plot in a simple sentence or two. You may want to include the names of a star or two, if you have them, but don't embellish. You're just telling the story, not selling. The audience should be interested enough to attend the screening, without being over-hyped.

Some producers prefer the screening experience to be a total surprise for the test audience. In this case, the recruiting paragraph will not include the title of the movie or the stars. Your recruiters are simply going to tell a basic plot outline. Will the public come? Yes. There's always enough interest in new films to guarantee an audience will show up. You'll get a decent sampling as long as you overbook. For a surprise test, I would overbook even beyond the four to one ration previously mentioned.

■ **Prepare your cards.** If you hire a research company, they will prepare the cards to your specifications. If you're doing it on your own, there are some standard procedures. Size of the card varies. It's usually about half the size of a normal 8½" x 11" sheet of typing paper (5" x 6" is fine). It's called a card, because it's printed on lightweight card stock. Have your questions typeset—sometimes printers offer this service although if you have access to a computer and a laser printer, it is much cheaper to "desktop typeset" your questions. Take your "camera-ready" questions to any quick printer and have them run off as many copies as there are seats in the theatre, plus a few extras. Purchase some tiny pencils (the same kind that golfers use) and tape them along with the cards to the back of every seat in the theater.

The questions you ask on your cards will depend on what kind of information your producers need. Be sure to allow enough time to write, re-write and get final approval for them. There are some standard questions featured on almost every card. The two key questions are "How would you rate this movie?" and "Would you recommend this movie to a friend?" If the scores are high for these two questions—say 80% or more marking the highest or next highest choice—there will be a sense of elation amongst your filmmakers. What that means in terms of the film's eventual success is anyone's guess. Let me tell you that there are many movies that have tested high, extremely high, and have gone on to flop at the box office. But yours is not to reason why. Right? Some standard questions include:

A. *How would you rate this movie?*

Excellent ❑

Very good ❑

Good ❑

Fair ❑

Poor ❑

B. *Would you recommend this movie to a friend?*

Definitely ❑

Probably ❑

Not sure ❑

Probably not ❑

Definitely not ❑

(To determine demographics of your results.)

C. *What is your age?*

16-18 ❑

19-21 ❑

22-23 ❑

24-25 ❑

Over 25 ❑

(To expand upon your demographics.)

D. *What is your sex?*

Male ❑

Female ❑

(These questions, using *Fatal Attraction* as an example, focus on reactions to the film's salient elements.)

E. *How would you rate the following element?:*

	Excellent	Very Good	Good	Fair	Poor
The plot	❑	❑	❑	❑	❑
The suspense	❑	❑	❑	❑	❑
Glenn Close	❑	❑	❑	❑	❑
Michael Douglas	❑	❑	❑	❑	❑
Anne Archer	❑	❑	❑	❑	❑

F. *How would you describe this film to a friend?*

(If you have a comedy,
and a good percentage of
your audience would
describe it as a drama,
then you're in big trouble.)

Horror film ❑

Mystery ❑

Drama ❑

Suspense film ❑

Comedy ❑

Adventure ❑

G. *Do you have any additional comments on the film?*

(Allows the audience
to expand on their
opinion.)

_____

_____

_____

H. *How often do you go to the movies?*

(Optional: to determine
if your core audience
consists of frequent
moviegoers.)

Once a week or more ❑

Twice a month ❑

Once a month ❑

Less than once a month ❑

Additional questions may focus on a specific element of the film. If you're testing *Star Wars*, you might want to get the public's reaction to the special effects. If you're testing *Dirty Dancing*, you want to know their reaction to the music and dancing, etc.

■ **Screening night**. Get to the screening facility early. Tape your cards to the back of every seat. Rope off enough seats for your executives and VIPs. When the audience is seated, make an announcement. Welcome them to the screening and let them know that after the film is finished they will be asked to fill out the cards in front of them. Thank them for their trouble and get the screening started.

After the screening ends, and while everyone is filling out their cards, station your team at the exits so that they can collect the cards. Make sure they have a little box for the pencils (they'll come in handy in the future).

■ **The focus group**. In addition to the general audience reaction, you may decide to get a more specific reaction by selecting, say, a dozen audience members for a "focus group." These people are always chosen prior to the screening. They're supposed to represent a cross-section of your demographic and they should appear talkative and possibly a good barometer for the film. Of course, animated people may suddenly become shy in a question and answer period after the film, but you do your best to get a lively group.

The whole point of the focus group is to "focus in" on the movie and the crowd's reaction. How each person reacts will be recorded on tape.

Here, an intelligent examiner can begin to gauge the public's reaction to the film and why they reacted in a certain way. If the film has problems, the members of the focus group can explain why they didn't like certain elements of the film. A professional researcher can gain a great deal of information in a short session.

During this focus group, which is usually held in the theater after the screening, your executives and VIPs will probably be seated nearby, listening intently to the reaction.

The professional researcher, who should be hired to run the focus group, will then prepare a document based on the focus group results. These results, combined with the reactions that appear on the "cards," represent the sum total of the test screening.

Some researchers will even get the phone numbers of some of the focus group members so they can be called the next day to get additional information. On the day after, people sometimes come up with additional reactions which can be helpful when evaluating the whole test screening.

The advantage of hiring a research company is that they have the ability to quickly break down all of the information into its salient elements, percentages and results. They can also interpret the scores for you. If you have a certain percentage, they can tell you if that falls within the average range, etc.

This is what they do for a living. If you have the budget, and your producers want to know more than a general reaction to the test screening, hire a research company. Contact several and shop around for the best deal. If you don't have the budget, I've given you enough information here to get started on your own.

32

DEVELOPING AN EFFECTIVE MOVIE PROMOTION CAMPAIGN

Publicity and promotion are two very different disciplines. A crackerjack publicist may not necessarily be an equally proficient promoter, while a top promoter may not be disciplined enough to perform the duties of a publicist. Many of the smaller companies hire one person to handle both jobs but in the midst of a full-scale movie campaign, it will be a very difficult task. There are simply too many bases to cover.

First, let's re-define promotion. Promotion is a trade-off between the film and the "promotional partner" which may, or may not be the media. Promotions come in two basic formats: **third party promotions** involve you with another company like McDonalds or Burger King who become intimately involved in the release campaigns; **promotional stunts** are created in-house and often do not involve a third party. In third party situations, the film provides an element—T-shirts, soundtrack cassettes, an actor's image, a trip to Nova Scotia—the promotional partner provides TV air-time, advertising pages, point of purchase displays, radio spots.

Unlike publicity, promoters do not deal with journalists. If the media is involved, the contact is a promotional director, advertising executive or merchandising specialist. Sometimes publicists and promoters pass each other like strangers. They're dealing with the same outlets, but on totally different wavelengths.

For instance, I might contact the movie editor of *LA Weekly*, a local paper, about a possible story on Tom Hanks' new comedy. I'll send in my pitch letter, follow it up with a phone call, and if the editor is interested, arrange an interview between the reporter and Hanks. The resultant story will appear opening week. Bingo.

The promotions department, which probably is not even aware that I've contacted *LA Weekly*, will have simultaneously worked out a deal with the advertising director of the paper for a free full-page advertisement which promotes some kind of tie-in with a local record retailer. If a patron goes into the record retailer which is also featured in the advertisement, they can pick up two free tickets to a screening of your new film. This "freebie ad" is probably contingent on the film company buying at least one full page ad, but the promotions game is all about making deals. In this case, everyone's happy. The film gets two ads for the price of one, the record retailer gets some exposure and, hopefully, some foot traffic, and the paper gets closer to its advertising quota, while also associating itself with a new movie.

Although obviously tied to an ad budget, promotional opportunities like the one described above, have to be carefully researched and orchestrated. At one time, no one had ever approached *LA Weekly* about a "two-fer" opportunity. It took an imaginative promoter to contact the paper and determine their interest. It also takes a conscientious promoter to gather all the proper materials and make sure the promotion works efficiently.

Promoters have to be the most conscientious of marketing specialists. A publicist might get away with pitching a journalist without a press kit or a screening. Promoters have to be much more careful and deliberate as they put together promotional deals. Incredibly detailed letters have to be written. Weeks are spent on the telephone to even reach the right person and get an answer. You always seem to be waiting on the production to provide you with the proper pitching materials—press kits, color slides, video featurettes, trailers, advertising art, the film itself. And once a promotional deal is made, there are still a thousand opportunities for it to fall apart. Promotional partners may back out at the last minute or the size of their promotion may dwindle to a pittance of what was proposed.

Unless you're "ET 2" or "Star Wars 4," it's never easy. It's always an uphill struggle to get the promotional ball rolling. A top radio station which has eleven movies to consider for its "movie of the month" promotion has to be wooed, tantalized and cajoled into choosing your project. And, whereas most publications and electronic outlets will get around to cover the movie, from a publicity point of view, they have no such compulsion when it comes to promotions.

There are some incredibly exciting elements of promotional work, though. First, it's the most imaginative of all the marketing arenas. Provided it doesn't cost the moon, you can conceive of virtually any kind of event, happening, or tie-in.

Promotion is a very old-fashioned kind of business. In the early days of the movies, promotional stunts were all they had. When premier promoter/P.R. man Russell Birdwell was preparing his *Gone With the Wind* campaign in 1939, there was no network television buy, or 24 hour E! Entertainment Channel, or satellite press conferences. Promoters in those days used to think on their feet. With 20-30 movies to sell every year, these studio professionals were always running from one event to another. They were P.T. Barnums in their own way. And they knew what they were selling. If you had to sell, weren't movies the best sales item in the universe? After all, who didn't want to hear about the latest movie? And who didn't want to be associated with it?

I often mention P.T. Barnum because I believe that he perfected the technique of modern promotion. Like the movies, the circus was what dreams were made of. And he took the public's fascination with their dreams and fed it huge doses of information and wonder. Information got them to the circus on time, wonder made sure they came in the first place.

In the 1990s, movie promotion is going to become an even more important element of the marketing plan. As the cost of advertising campaigns skyrocket, everyone will be looking for a cheaper way to sell the sizzle of new movies. The right promotion is always a bargain.

Promotional geniuses who can put together clever, successful events are not easy to find. Whereas you can recruit public relations executives from agencies, or trainees directly from the college P.R. programs, promoters are a different story.

It's an unusual discipline. There are few college courses in promotion. Many top advertising agencies have promotional departments, but few of these well-trained executives find their way into the film business. P.T. Barnum types like the late Marty Weiser of Warner Bros., or Birdwell of MGM were unique individuals who revelled in their tasks. Their skills have not been passed on.

Like the best film publicists, movie promoters have to love their product. They have to be capable of maintaining their enthusiasm throughout months of preparation for the proper promotion. They have to sell with a smile, even when they know their product is dreck.

I knew *Born American*, a Cold War adventure, starring Chuck Norris' son Mike, was not going to win any awards when it was released in the Summer of '86. It was a creaky piece of propaganda about three kids who, while on vacation in Finland, happen to sneak across the Soviet border where they're captured and thrown into a concentration camp.

There were no stars, no real publicity hooks—aside from the fact that the film was banned in Finland (and while I'm sure that being banned in Finland was once a great promotional plus, today, it doesn't matter).

So what "hook" did I come up with? I decided that we could grab some attention from the media by staging a Russian invasion of Hollywood. In the spirit of *Red Dawn*, *Amerika* and *Invasion USA*, fully uniformed Russian Troops with armored support would march down Hollywood Blvd. and the tanks would park in front of the theater on opening day. With this kind of spotlight, the media wouldn't be able to miss *Born American*.

Gaining full support from the marketing department, I put together a modest budget of about $4,000, and contacted a movie vehicle rental service in the Santa Clarita Valley (north of Los Angeles) which provided military hardware for motion pictures and television shows. Within my budget, I could rent a Russian armored car and a soft-skinned military truck for parade duty.

I then hired six stout young men and took them to Western Costume in Hollywood where they were outfitted in regulation Soviet Army gear. From a weapons rental firm in Burbank, I was supplied with realistic rubber AK-47 assault rifles.

I knew that getting permission from the Hollywood police to hold a parade on opening day would be impossible. Unless you're Disney or Fox, and you have a commitment from Mickey Mouse and Donald Duck, the red tape stretches for miles. So I had to get creative.

I knew that it was legal to park my military vehicles in front of the theater for promotional purposes. However, for the media to come out in force, I had to give them something more interesting than a couple of Russian army vehicles parked out in front of Hollywood's Vogue Theater. I had to think dramatically.

The stunt I came up with had some risks, but I was pretty sure it would work. I contacted the parking enforcement department of the city of Los Angeles and explained to them that I was *off-loading* some vehicles for a film promotion in Hollywood. Would they give us a hand and make sure we had no trouble getting the vehicles in position in front of the theater.

I was shrewd enough, though, not to tell parking enforcement that I was going to off-load the vehicles *a half-mile from the theater*. My secret plan was to stage an impromptu parade down Hollywood Boulevard, with my six uniformed marching Russians preceding the slow-moving army vehicles. Young Norris and the other actors from the movie and director Renny Harlin, would stand in the back of the truck waving to their fans.

I set up the media coverage like a military strategist. Since, in addition to my promotional responsibilities, I was also the film's release publicity coordinator, I sent out press releases to every news crew and photographer in town, alerting them that "Hollywood would be invaded by Russian troops on Friday at 3:00 p.m." I further noted that the troops would be fully-uniformed regulars equipped with submachine guns and that armored vehicles would be present.

At precisely 3:00 p.m. my vehicles were off-loaded on Gower St., my troops arrived in their woolen uniforms (unfortunately, it was one of the hottest days of the year, so they were a bit uncomfortable), and, true to their promise, the city sent a parking enforcement officer.

Putting the parking scooter in the front of the column, I organized the six soldiers into two parallel columns (one officer would lead them forth—he was carrying a pistol), and ordered them to march ahead as slowly as possible. The military vehicles, including the long-barreled armored car, would follow.

As this impressive ersatz military convoy proceeded down Hollywood Boulevard, the press arrived—three television news crews mounted on the back of pickup trucks, a dozen photographers, some local reporters, a radio news team—a whole slew of media, some of whom waited back at the theater to catch the drama of the approaching column.

There was only one glitch—my star, Mike Norris, was nowhere to be seen as the convoy pulled out. I kept searching as we slowly proceeded west toward the theatre. Halfway down the boulevard, a stretch limousine coming in the opposite direction, stopped in the middle of the street, and out popped Norris and his girlfriend. Traffic everywhere halted. Holding a glass of champagne and looking like he just came off the beach in Newport, he and his girlfriend were hoisted aboard the armored car, and the column pushed forward.

Arriving in front of the theater, the convoy parked and the Russian soldiers stood guard—actually they posed for photographs with cast and crew—and genuinely participated in a pre-*Glasnost* rapprochement with the media. That afternoon, we appeared on the local news—TV and radio, and the following day, an AP wire service photo broke throughout the West.

Born American went on to become another "one week and out" movie bomb, but the promotion was deemed a huge success, so much so that when Cinema Group released their next film—a horror thriller called *Witchboard*, they were waiting for my latest brainstorm. But more on the "giant Ouija board" on Hollywood boulevard later.

Let's talk about the various promotions that have become standard in the film business.

Radio Promoted Screenings and Contests.

In marketing circles there is considerable disagreement about the effectiveness of radio in promoting motion pictures. After all, movies are visual, radio is not. However, proponents argue that radio advertising is cheap compared with television and newspaper, and the core movie audience—the 12-24 year olds—listen to radio all the time. Opponents argue that it is difficult to get a movie message across on the audio air waves, that a large portion of the adult population doesn't listen much at all, and, that the radio universe is so diverse that it eventually does become expensive to get the penetration needed to build a good advertising campaign.

For promotional purposes, there are a number of different ways to develop a radio campaign:

■ **Determine the scope of the campaign and your target radio stations**. Are you opening your movie in one city or fifty? Start contacting your target stations a minimum of two months in advance. The stations with the best ratings do a lot of film promotions and their calendars fill up early. That's not to say that if you're given a film assignment a month before it opens that the job is impossible. It's just going to be difficult. The good stations go quickly.

In large markets, there are usually several good stations to pick from. Work closely with your advertising department as they may have preferences about which stations are best. If you're promoting a youth-oriented film like a *Pretty in Pink* or *The Breakfast Club*, it's best to go to the CHR stations (Contemporary Hits Radio, also known as Top 40) as they have the most teen listeners. If your movie is a horror film, especially if it has graphic violence and an "R" rating, some CHR stations may turn you away because of their own advertising policies. But most rock & roll stations will be happy to work with you.

If the film has an older or more mature appeal, say for "baby boomers" or the "yuppie" crowd, you'll want to approach the top AOR station in the city (Album Oriented Rock). Always start with the top rated station in each market. After rejections, move down the line, until you've covered each station in ratings order. If you've been rejected by each station in the AOR category, then you can approach CHR stations.

Stay away from speciality stations that play classical or "easy listening" music. The demographics are usually too old to appeal to any sizable filmgoing crowd. Occasionally, you'll be dealing with extremely specialized stations that are appropriate, but it's rare. If you're promoting a rock and roll film with a strong 1950s influence, you may want to approach a station that plays only classic rock. (There's one specialty station I know of that only plays Elvis, and another that plays only Christmas music—year round!) However, my experience is that these stations have an extremely limited audience and that they're not worth the time you'll put in to develop the promotion.

■ **The most popular radio promotion is the pre-opening screening.** You supply a print of the film and the theater and the station guarantees a number of promotional spots ("air time"). There was a time when they would even send their top disc jockeys down to the theater on screening night (for live remotes, etc). Today, they charge extra for that.

Screening promotions have several positive elements which benefit both the film company and the radio station. (Remember when you're approaching the stations that you're not asking them to "give you free advertising. You're providing them with an opportunity to get something they need—listener response. You supply the movie screening event, the station promotes it to the kids, the kids call up for their free pass. Everyone gets something: the station gets important listener interest, you get free advertising to build awareness among your core audience, and the kids get to be the first ones to see a new movie, for free.

What happens when you try to do a radio promotion without a screening? It's more difficult to get the station interested, but not impossible. If you have T-shirts, or other promotional items, it's often possible to get the same trade-off. Again, it depends on the movie. Like the publicist, the promoter has to convince the radio promotion's director that the film is hot and perfect for the station's audience.

Radio-promoted screenings on youth-oriented films are worth the cost of securing a theater and providing a print. If the station is top-rated, you're going to develop good awareness among your core audience.

■ **How do you establish contact with radio stations?** If you're working for a big studio, they'll probably have field agencies which handle media buys and coordinate promotions. In this situation, all you need to do is contact the local agency and give them the details of your radio promotion. They'll have up-to-date information about the top stations, and will be best suited to set up the promotion.

Although the agencies are handling the radio promotions, you should keep a running log of each city and the station targeted for promotional activity. Once the promotions are in place, you will be sending the fulfillment materials to the agencies and they will pass them on to the stations—screening passes with printed logos from the film, T-shirts, etc.

That's the easy way. If you don't have the luxury of having field agencies to do the work for you, you're going to have to do it all yourself. For a national release, making all the contacts to set up the promotions is a major undertaking. You may have 25-30 cities to cover and every promotions director I've ever tried to reach is a very busy person.

Every radio station has someone responsible for coordinating promotions—usually they're called Promotional Directors. Identify yourself, describe the movie, let them know your opening date and immediately find out if they have an opening for doing a promotion with you. Unlike dealing with media, sending a letter first is not a good idea in this case. Because of prior commitments, the station could be already booked and your letter becomes an exercise.

When you can get a promotional director on the phone—and they are elusive—they'll tell you immediately what the calendar looks like. There's no magic involved here. There is a possibility or there isn't. Promotional directors are always more interested if your movie has some star power, but don't be discouraged if you're promoting a Grade C horror flick. The station may want it to fill a hole in their calendar.

Movie promotions are generally fun for the station and they don't require much work. If the movie is hot, the station will be proud to bask in the glow of the film's success. If the movie is a bomb, the station will still be happy that it's been able to provide its listeners with a service—a free screening or giveaway items.

In exchange for the screening, ask for a two week promotion. You'll probably end up with a week or ten days of radio airtime, but go for as much exposure as possible.

You're responsible for setting up the screening, but ask the promo director if he or she has any special relationships with local theatres. If not, contact your distribution department and they'll help you arrange for a theater. The exhibitor will charge you a rental fee. In effect, you are buying out one of their weekday evening performances and they'll ask for as little as $100 up to $500.

Don't worry about inviting key radio personnel to the screening. The promotional director will take care of that. Encourage the station to overbook the screening by a minimum of four to one—if you have 500 seats to fill, have them give out 2000 passes. You want a packed house—it's embarrassing to have a skimpy turn out for your big "movie premiere."

I used to think that the radio promo time you received from the station was the key to the promotion—75 spots over 10 days is significant advertising exposure, especially if you're promoting on the top station in town. However, your bosses will also be curious about attendance on screening night. If the film is perceived as a hit and the theaters are packed, everyone feels good going into the release period. However, half-empty theaters are not a good harbinger for things to come.

■ **No screening?** Go for a giveaway promotion or anything else you can think of. If the station turns down a screening because they already have one in place, don't hang up. They may be interested in another promotional idea.

If you're responsible for setting up radio-promoted screenings in the top 30 markets, you will, of course, have to go down the line until you find a station that will accommodate a screening. However, if you fail on that attempt, consider these possibilities:

✔ Promotional item giveaway. Essentially, you're trading T-shirts for promo spots. Supply the station with 75 shirts, and secure a 10 day promotion. If you have speciality items, like Scuba watches, or Ouija boards, or baby Smurfs, they'll work just as well.

✔ Trivia contest or any other contest you can think of. In this case, you're also using the promotional giveaways, but you're tieing them into something more creative than "here's an item, come and get it." Radio stations like contests and if there's an opportunity to employ some unusual trivia material, go for it.

✔ Ticket giveaway—your last resort. Contact the local exhibitor that will be showing the film and arrange for 50-75 "run of performance" passes. These passes, good for two admissions, are usually valid Sunday through Thursday and are given away just like T-shirts. Once again, you're trading for promotional spots. Unfortunately, ticket giveaways are so common on local radio that it's hard to get excited about them. The station isn't excited about them, the public isn't excited about them, and they're not the most exciting promotional concept. However, they are a last resort if you've been turned down everywhere else.

Publicity Stunts and the Attendant Media Coverage.

Publicity stunts are an anachronism today. The imaginative promoter, with his off-the-cuff, wildly creative ideas is often considered an oddball by the more conservative members of most marketing teams.

Picture a dozen men and women in business suits discussing the advertising expenditures for the top ten ADIs. Buzz words like "maximum penetration" and "targeted audience" hum about the room. To them, your movie is just another product on the store shelf. It's paper towels, aspirin, bowl cleaner.

Just as the ad pros finish their discourse, the promotional executive looks up and says, "I think we should build a horse forty feet tall and tour it coast to coast. In fact, let's build two giant horses, and we'll work them on both coasts." There is a moment of silence. Giant horses? There's nothing in the book about them. What's their targeted audience? How will the public react? How will the media react? Will they laugh at us? The questions will continue until the wildly creative executive is voted down.

I'm not saying that this happens in all cases. But there are fewer and fewer publicity and promotions executives willing to risk a stunt these days. You get the standard cop-outs—"It's too complicated." "No one knows how to do it." "We can spend the money better elsewhere, on TV ads and newspapers." "It's a risk."

Obviously, I'm very much in favor of stunts. I think they set your film apart from the others in the marketplace. If you can pull it off and get the attendant media coverage, then you're a winner. Stunts are a great launching pad for a film. The energy created by a perfectly produced publicity stunt can add immeasurably to the effectiveness of the other marketing techniques.

There are some definite risks. But if you do your job correctly, they're worth taking. Let's look at the steps for creating an effective stunt.

■ **Some films are appropriate for promotional stunts, some are not.** A *Batman* or a *Texas Chainsaw Massacre* has stunt potential. But it's hard to imagine an effective stunt for a film like *Out of Africa* or *Ghandi*. In this case, the argument that promotional stunts cheapen the film's image is probably correct. On the other hand, stunts can figure perfectly into a *Batman* because the movie is an event in itself. *Batman* is a pop icon, it's fun, whiz-bang adventurous, colorful, tongue-in-cheek. It also appeals to the kids who are the more appropriate audience for stunts.

My "Russian troops marching down Hollywood Blvd." stunt for *Born American* was designed to appeal to the young at heart. Everyone loves a parade.

When you're designing your stunt you're thinking about the film's audience, but keep the media in mind. You have to be unique enough to appeal to their own theatrical sense. In one sense, they're your main audience. Even if you attract 3,000 excited moviegoers to your stunt, if the media doesn't show up, you've failed. The media, with their cameras, mics and recorders, will send that stunt to hundreds of thousands, perhaps millions of potential filmgoers and those are the numbers you need to make a stunt successful.

In my stunts, I always try to get a chuckle out of the media. If they start to giggle, then you have them.

■ **Be cost conscious.** Forget about a big budget when you're preparing your stunts. Because they're inherently risky, promo stunts aren't given serious consideration in most marketing budgets.

Occasionally you get a break though. In 1983, I worked for Ivan (Ghostbusters) Reitman on *Spacehunter: Adventures in the Forbidden Zone*. Budgeted at $13 million with a marketing price tag of $9 million, this was a major summer release for Columbia Pictures.

I convinced both Reitman and the studio to back a national tour which featured the weird space props, costumes and vehicles from the film. We mounted the film's big "spacetruck" on a flatbed tractor trailer and drove it 14,000 miles in 63 days. We promoted at shopping malls, fairs, college campuses—everywhere. The price tag: $80,000. A sizable sum, but the money bought a lot of awareness.

It takes a fast-talking, extremely determined promotional person to sell a big $80,000 stunt to the marketing department. In my case, I was able to show that the stunt was practical and it related directly to the film. It also helped that Reitman liked the idea and was on my side.

■ **Get the media involved as early as possible.** Publicity stunts cannot work without the media's cooperation. There are no guarantees, however, even if you have a great stunt. Many times, to the chagrin of the promoter, TV crews have been on their way to the stunt only to be diverted to a five-alarm fire or an auto accident. It's an occupational hazard.

You cannot be responsible for no-shows or the fickleness of the media but you can schedule your event so the press should be relatively free to attend. Don't make the mistake I made when I scheduled a stunt on the day the Hollywood Chamber of Commerce was giving out a star on Hollywood Blvd. Try to find out what is going on in the city on certain days. You can get a schedule from the Chamber of Commerce, you can also get schedules of major events from various publications that keep track of such things. Check with your local newspaper society editor to get the name and publisher of the local social calendar.

You need to know about these events, because the media is going to cover some of them, and you don't want your own coverage diluted by competition from the Ladies Temperance Society on the day they give George Bush a Life Achievement Award. Plane crashes and car wrecks you can't predict, rival media events you can. Do your homework.

Also, give the media plenty of lead time. They need a full press release and schedule at least a week in advance. Then, keep after them with faxed progress reports and information sheets. Remember you're competing with hundreds of other people who want coverage and you never know when a news director is going to pass on your forty foot horse in favor of the blind harmonica player from Pacoima.

Alert every television station within your territory, every radio station, every newspaper, and as many photographers as you can find. Photographers are divided into two groups: the news, wire service and agency photographers who are generally listed in the MPAA media directory; and the paparazzi, those freelance photographers who will cover anything with some star appeal. In some cases, you can reach all of these photographers by calling a phone number in your city and leaving the details of the event on the tape. Check with your local Mayor's Public Information Officer about such a service.

Follow up on all of your press releases, pitch the stunt like you'd pitch a feature story on a lead actor. Make personal contact with the editors. On the "Russian troops" stunt, I told everyone personally that "Hollywood was going to be invaded by Russia on Friday at 3:00 p.m." I spoke with a true sense of drama. "Tanks, armored cars and uniformed Soviet troops are going to be parading down the boulevard. You can't miss it."

Don't leave out any media outlet. These days, the number of television outlets has doubled. It's no longer just the seven local television stations and *ET*. You have E! Entertainment Channel, Group W's *Entertainment Report, Hollywood Insider, MTV News*, Showtime, HBO, The Movie Channel—all of which have TV crews for special programming. And that's not mentioning all the ethnic TV and radio outlets.

Everyone's hungry for a good stunt. If Warner Bros. had gone ahead and turned Westwood Village into a huge *Batman* set, as they had originally planned for opening night, the media coverage could have been even more spectacular than it was.

■ **Get your company involved.** Planning a stunt is like planning a party. You're going to need manpower to help make it work. Don't hesitate to draw on the company personnel pool. If the stunt is truly fun, then your people will want to participate anyway. If you have to dress up 25 people to look like "sponge people from the Planet Mongo," you're bound to get a few takers from your fellow office workers, and they'll probably recommend some of their friends as well.

If you have to hire people to be part of your stunt, it's going to eat up part of your already small budget. Plan on spending $50-75 per person, plus lunch. Although if you design your stunt with fun in mind, you shouldn't have any problem finding volunteers. I had more company employees than I could use once on a stunt I did for a film which featured the "California Raisins" of TV commercials fame. When word got around about the full-size dancing raisin costumes we were creating, I had a waiting list of volunteers who were willing to wiggle their behinds to "I Heard It Through the Grapevine" in front of the theatre for coverage on *Entertainment Tonight* and *AM Los Angeles*. I couldn't have afforded to pay dancers anyway, because the costumes were relatively expensive—$500 a piece. Fortunately, the California Raisin Advisory Board picked up half the cost, and they got the costumes after we were finished.

You should also look to company employees for help with crowd control. You'd be surprised how ridiculous it can be when you're the only one controlling the event. You really need help and it's best to draw on people you know.

■ **Bring in partners if you can**. The California Raisin Advisory Board is an example of a promotional partner who helped defray the cost of our stunt. Don't hesitate to get promotional partners involved who can trade services for the attendant media coverage.

Promotional partners can provide a space for the stunt, chairs and tables, public address equipment, even food. For the 1983 James Bond Trivia Marathon, an AMC theater provided us with an auditorium for three hours prior to the start of *Never Say Never Again*. They were delighted with the media coverage which included *The Tonight Show*, the *Herald Examiner*, several wire services and *USA Today*.

In 1987, for a horror movie entitled *Witchboard*, we planned a contest stunt which featured a giant Ouija Board. (The film was about a demonic Ouija board on the loose.) I hadn't found a good location until I happened to drive by the Hollywood Wax Museum on Hollywood Blvd. Here was the perfect spot. There were two advantages to this location: it was convenient to most of the Los Angeles TV stations and the museum was suitably eerie.

Inside, I discovered, to my delight, a sign stating that the wax museum was haunted—just the right situation for conjuring up some ghosts with our Ouija board. The stunt consisted of a game in which under each letter and number of the Ouija board was a prize, including several cash prizes. The owners of the Hollywood Wax Museum were happy to cooperate, providing us, free of charge, with the front of their building as our location. It was a fun stunt. The stars of the film worked the Ouija board as the contestants called out what they thought were the right letters and numbers. Television crews showed up to record the events. Even the ghost who haunts the museum had a good time, so we heard.

- **Document the event.** Always hire your own photographer to cover the event. You may need his or her photos if, for instance, an Associated Press or UPI photographer doesn't show. You can always send the film directly to the wire service editor where it will be considered as a legitimate story break. Those photographs may also be handy if your boss forgets to show up or is detained.

Make sure you get copies of all the appropriate newscasts after the event. You can buy copies from the various monitoring services, but their fees are pretty steep ($100 for a tape is common). Even the cost of a simple transcript is expensive these days ($25.00 or more).I usually set my own VCR and do it myself. Type up an after-action report, describing the stunt, the attendant media coverage and the general reaction. If your stunt is a success, you'll have photographs, stories, column items and transcripts to help illustrate your point.

Consider hiring your own video crew to document the stunt. The resultant footage, like your still photos, can be sent to media outlets that use "canned footage."

You might also consider hiring a satellite company to not only shoot the footage but beam it to national media outlets. For a large picture with a good promotional budget, this could be a viable alternative.

For *The Gate*, a horror film about three kids who discover the "gate to hell" in their backyard, we hired a satellite company to cover a stunt we hyped as "the first broadcast from hell" and beam it live to morning talk shows in the top twenty markets. We had found a town called Hell not too far from Detroit, Michigan and we shot an interview with the director and star in front of a hastily made set—the gate to hell.

We played up this unusual stunt to all the media and it worked well: we had national coverage, plus plenty of column item activity. When the film opened it was number two at the box office, only a few thousand dollars behind the number one film, *Ishtar*. With all their magazine covers, television coverage and assorted hoopla surrounding Dustin Hoffman and Warren Beatty, they barely beat us. I'd like to think that our promotion had something to do with it.

Contests: National and Local.

Just like stunts, contests apply only to certain films. The movie may have been a terrific bomb, but it was probably quite logical for *Million Dollar Mystery* to hold a "Million Dollar Sweepstakes." They had a corporate tie-in (a garbage bag company as I recall—although the concept of putting motion picture information on garbage bag packaging somehow doesn't register) and a story that related directly to the movie.

In retrospect (when it comes to predicting why films fail, everyone is a Monday morning quarterback), it was probably a mistake to place so much emphasis on the contest. After all, people go to the movies to escape and enjoy a story—nobody wants to watch a movie so precisely that they don't miss a clue—you'd turn into a fanatic. Instead of getting huge numbers of people to return many times to watch the mystery, they attracted only a few people who found the film a complete turn-off (it probably worked on video though, especially for those who can automatically pause the picture and scan it for clues).

The best film-related contests are simple affairs where you can fill out a slip of paper and participate in a drawing to win the Batmobile or the shirt off Michael J. Fox's back, or a year's supply of Jacqueline Smith cosmetics. Contests are primarily attention-getters.

Another aspect which can be exploited with contests is everyone's excitement at winning something. In my youth, I remember going to the Pickfair Theater in Los Angeles and during the intermission, the manager of the theater would come out in front of the audience with a giant bottle of beans. Three youngsters would be called up and asked to guess the number of beans. The one who guessed closest was given two free passes. I won one of those contests and boy, was I excited.

Movies have a special appeal. It's not necessary to have million dollar prizes to get people excited about a movie contest. When the manufacturers of "Tidy Bowl" bathroom cleaner have a sweepstakes their prize has to be something more exciting than a lifetime supply of their product. When MTV and Warner Bros. have a contest to promote "Batman 7," a simple offer to fly the winners to Mexico for the start of shooting will generate enormous excitement.

Contests can also get you additional magazine coverage. I once conducted a giveaway contest in twelve different teen magazines. I got a hold of the wardrobe from the film, received permission to use it as prizes, and then fashioned some fun contests in which the contestants could literally win the clothes off the actor's back. Combining the costumes with soundtracks, posters and some T-shirts, we received great coverage in the magazines—multiple coverage over the key three month period prior to release.

If you have a promotional partner, contests can take place on a very large scale. You've seen the Disney/McDonalds tie-ins. Not only are the contests and giveaways promoted in point of purchase displays at the theaters and restaurants, but they're also advertised on national television. That's called "clout" at its most impressive. Disney has, of course, a distinct advantage in that their animated films, for the most part, were completed about thirty years ago. They know what they have in product inventory and they can plan tie-in contests literally years in advance—a time frame perfectly suited to the major corporations in America like McDonalds who are slow to commit to any promotion until they see the finished film. In most cases, by the time the film is finished and ready for screening, it's much too late to put together a contest.

By all means, contact companies you feel are perfectly suited to a national sweepstakes (especially those that have products in your film), but for the most part consider simpler contests that can go right into magazines and newspapers. Here are some guidelines:

- **Try to relate the contest directly to the film.** Remember you're building awareness for your film. If you're promoting a fun in the sun frolic like *Beach Party*, don't offer to send your contestant winners on an Antarctic cruise. You want your contest to make people think about your movie.

Again, not every movie merits a contest. An African safari might seem to be a logical sweepstakes prize for *Out of Africa* but serious films don't seem well suited for contests. For *Abbott and Costello Go To Mars*, though, it might have been a good idea to send lucky winners to Cape Canaveral.

- **Be as unique as possible.** Don't assume that every possible contest has been done. There is always new ground to blaze. In 1981, nearly twenty years after the release of the first James Bond film, I conducted the first "James Bond Trivia Marathon." It had never been done before and I received great press response. Contestants flew to Los Angeles from as far away as Florida and New York.

If you can't think of a truly unique event, go back to your "tried and true" concepts—write-in sweepstakes, trivia games, "name the character" competitions, "what's wrong with this picture" mysteries.

- **Determine your media outlets for the contest.** You have the entire universe of media to consider—from a national television contest to one in your local shoppers guide. Try out your contest on all the media outlets you can think of. You never know where you're going to find a good fit. I read about a national cable television network that gave away over 30 Corvette sports cars to one lucky viewer who sent in an entry blank. According to their statistics, over two million people wrote in. That is a pretty big contest.

Don't hesitate to contact national television outlets for potential promotions and contests, although it's rare to get the networks, or even the local free stations involved. The cable networks, however, are becoming increasingly promotions conscious. The E! Entertainment Cable Network has a very aggressive promotional team and they are on the lookout for any possible tie-in between the network and a new movie. Strong promotional possibilities exist with MTV, VH-1, Nickelodeon, USA Cable, and many other cable networks.

Unlike dealing with the corporate sector—the fast food franchises, toy companies, automobile manufacturers which can literally take years to make up their mind about a promotion or a contest—the cable networks can put a contest to bed in a matter of months, which is a good timetable for a film. Three months out, you will be able to generate still photographs of the project, even pre-release footage to give the promotional partner an idea about the concept of the movie.

It's a process. Nothing is going to happen with a single phone call. You establish your initial goals and then you begin to feed your promotional partner with materials. This is particularly true of the cable television networks which need video footage for their promotion anyway.

What can you do with a cable or free television network if they're interested in a contest? Providing a trip is one possibility—especially if it relates to the film. The trip may incorporate other elements, such as dinner with the stars of the film, perhaps even a part in the film (although a contest involving a part giveaway is very difficult because it has to take place before the film starts shooting). Sometimes, a contest for one film is promoted during the release of another, although the idea really only works when you're dealing with an established series such as the James Bond films or the *Nightmare on Elm Street* series.

The bigger the media outlet (i.e. the networks), the more demanding they're going to be in terms of the contest. After all, in the last few years, MTV has given away entire islands in their contests. Playing "can you top this" with them could be very expensive on your part. If you have the film—such as *Batman* with Batmobiles and huge props available for contests—then you can play the high stakes game that some of the networks demand. Otherwise, stick to the smaller promotional items that are staples—T-shirts, posters, soundtracks, etc.

The other media forms are less demanding. I can set up a contest in a teen magazine with nothing more than the right movie (one that appeals to their age group) and some T-shirts. If you have a couple of hot teen stars and a youth-oriented concept, the teen magazines are going to want to cooperate with you. Keep in mind though, that because you're dealing with a magazine, publishing deadlines are going to require you to get things in place very early. Instead of three months out, it's advisable to start contacting the magazines as much as 6 months out.

Unlike many national magazines that work three and four months ahead, the teen and fan magazines have shorter lead times, sometimes two months or even less. However, if you want multiple coverage in those publications—an announcement about the contest in one issue, details in another, and the contest itself in the third— you have to get to the magazines very early. The nice thing about teen magazines contests is that they don't cost anything. Provided you get the promotional materials to the magazine in time, you can get good free exposure.

Another possible outlet for your contest is the local newspaper. This is the type of event you plan very close to the release of the film—

usually opening week. Like television, you're probably not going to attract the biggest outlets. Major newspapers like the *New York Times* and the *Los Angeles Times* are not viable promotional partners—they seldom do anything with even the biggest films. It's not an impossibility, in the future they may become players, but I find that your best promotional partners are the smaller papers—those that specialize in entertainment coverage. In Los Angeles, that could be an *LA Weekly*. In Chicago, the *Reader*. In New York, there are dozens of small entertainment papers which are friendly to contests.

Unlike magazines, however, newspaper contests will have a cost. Usually you will be asked to purchase one full page advertisement in return for a free page devoted to the contest. It's an opportunity, but, depending on your ad budget, your marketing people may balk at that cost.

Sometimes that cost can be waived if you provide a major prize to the contest. It makes a difference when you go to the paper with a five Cadillac giveaway contest. They know they're going to get a sizable response from their readers which will out-weigh their need for advertising dollar support. But how often are you going to be able to afford five Cadillacs? Most often you'll be lucky if you have a T-shirt budget.

Another possibility for a promotional tie-in which doesn't cost you advertising dollars is known as a media-directed contest. The local newspaper may offer as an incentive to close a big advertising contract with a nightclub, record store or other retail outlet an opportunity for them to participate in a promotion with a major movie. Again, everybody wins: you get free publicity, the paper gets a bigger ad contract and the store gets to be associated with something exciting like a movie.

This kind of tie-in where you don't have to commit any advertising dollars can work the other way too. Instead of the newspaper (or magazine) initiating the tie-in, you can find a promotional partner who will let you ride for free on advertising they've already committed to. Let's say you're promoting a movie that features a new automobile. The car company is probably already committed to a regular schedule of ads in several national magazines. They might be receptive to including your contest as part of one or more of their ads. It doesn't cost them any more than what they were already planning to spend, and it ties them in with a movie that relates directly to their product.

Creating promotional opportunities is up to you. Each time you have a motion picture product that relates directly to an advertised item—from turbo-charged sports cars to toothpaste—do yourself a favor, research the manufacturer's magazine buys and figure out a tie-in. The worst that can happen is that someone says, "No!" The best scenarios, with national magazine or TV coverage, could create significant audience awareness for your film.

Radio is also a good contest medium, but it's best served by the screening and giveaway type promotions we discussed earlier in this chapter. Although it's certainly important to consider national contest tie-ins with the big radio networks like Westwood One, the local giveaway contests are usually sufficient to start building the awareness you need. You will probably want to save your major giveaway prizes for either national cable or free television competitions or magazine promotions. Radio is best served on the local level where T-shirts, free-passes and premiere screenings can go a long way.

Giveaway Items.

Promotional items with some advertising logo printed on them—T-shirts, baseball caps, pens, mugs, etc.—are part of our culture. Practically every business uses giveaways.

In the movie business, giveaway items are most effectively used as prizes for contests. T-shirts—the most popular of all promotional items—can be used for any kind of contest—radio, magazines, national cable TV outlets, local newspapers and any other contest or publicity stunt you can create.

Here are some pointers to consider when planning your giveaways:

- **Emphasize tried and true items.** T-shirts, sweatshirts, jackets, soundtrack albums, posters, buttons are the staples of giveaways. These items, especially the T-shirts, have worked in the past and there's no reason to believe that they won't be appreciated in the future.

This doesn't mean you can't be creative. The companies that specialize in premium items will have many new ideas for you in their hefty catalogues. If you have a movie about dinosaurs, I'm sure you'll be able to find a company that sells inflatable Godzillas. If you're ordering 10,000 of them, you'll probably get a great price too. But I question whether anyone is going to be excited about a giant inflatable Godzilla when what they really want is a simple T-shirt with the film's title and some advertising art splashed across the front.

Sometimes, if you can get them inexpensively, speciality items related to a specific film can create a good impression and can even be used in tandem with T-shirts. On *Rad*, a BMX bicycle racing movie, I had an art-house design a series of stickers which featured 8 different bicycle acrobatic positions with their slang names. Since the bicyclists were known to collect stickers, I knew this would be a popular item, and it was. (They all included the *Rad* logo to give us some product identification as well).

For *Eddie and the Cruisers II: Eddie Lives*, I composed a phony newspaper headline that announced Eddie Wilson's return from the dead and had it printed on newsprint. It was very popular as a media giveaway item and it benefited the film's quite successful video release.

Sometimes it's best not to be too cute. Giving away cleaning supplies for a movie about a Beverly Hills maid may seem funny, but who is going to get excited about a free can of cleanser?

■ **Be budget conscious.** Promotional items appear as a line item on every marketing budget but this particular budget item is always scrutinized for waste, and the percentage of your overall promotion budget allocated to giveaways is usually tiny. Think about ordering promotional items—T-shirts, stickers, etc.—to be able to cover at most your top fifty markets. Figuring about 100 giveaways per market, a typical national T-shirt order would be 5,000. If the film does extremely well, you can always re-order.

There are two ways to buy T-shirts. You can order them directly from a shirt vendor and get a fair price, or, if you have a tie-in with a T-shirt manufacturer who is going to merchandise the shirts, you can go there and get a better discount. Merchandisers pick only a handful of films each year for T-shirt tie-ins, so the odds are that you're going to have to make your own deal. Still, don't hesitate to look into merchandising tie-ins, they could save you a lot of money.

Smaller items like buttons, key chains, stickers, mini-frisbees can be ordered for promotions but don't think that just because they're small and relatively cheap that you'll be able to saturate a market with them. Manufacturing 300,000 buttons may seem like you're getting a lot for your money, but in reality even that total isn't going to go very far. In 50 markets, that's only 6,000 per market. And they really can't be used by themselves as a contest prize so you'll have to spend money on prizes as well. Stick with the T-shirts.

■ **Hoard your items and take inventory.** Once your promotional items arrive at the office, everyone is going to want some for their friends and family. Be careful about this. It's okay to supply your key employees with T-shirts, but you'll quickly run out if everyone in the company has their hand out for five or six shirts.

When you place your order, plan on having enough extra items to give some away "in house." Each key media person can get one or two, sales department personnel (in your own office or in the field) will want some and theater owners and their staffs should all have one. It's wonderful to walk into a theater on opening night and see the ushers and candy counter employees wearing your shirts.

Parties. Provided they are done as inexpensively as possible, a movie-related party is always a good promotional idea. These "promo-parties" should not be confused with celebrity-attended opening night premiere parties which are usually a publicity department event and will be discussed in a later chapter.

Here are some guidelines:

■ **Promotional partners.** Whenever possible bring in a promotional partner. Recruit a local bar, restaurant or nightclub. The point is to bring in partners who can provide "something for nothing," in this case a free location. Sometimes you can bring in another partner who will help share costs and act as "ticket central" in exchange for the extra foot traffic. A video store is a good choice but you can be creative when looking for promo partners. For instance if your film includes a lot of golfing scenes, a local pro shop might be a good location for ticket central. Or for a movie like *Shampoo* seek out a well-known hair salon.

■ **You want your party to be nice, but watch your budget.** It's not uncommon to see movie companies rent out ballrooms, or cruise ships, or even bowling alleys for a special theme night, but these extravaganzas are usually part of a bigger promotional event and are the "prize fulfillment." The cost of such a party would be included in the prize budget of that bigger contest.

Big parties can get expensive very quickly: facility rental, catering, music, invitations and security for the party are expensive elements. That's why the major studios usually monopolize this promotional concept.

Sometimes, a fast food franchise or a soft drink company will help cover the catering costs. If a record company is involved in the film with a soundtrack artist, sometimes they will offer that artist to play at the party. The appearance of that artist, alone, may be reason enough to have the promotional party.

Stars and top recording artists usually show up at opening night premieres, but don't assume that they're not available for public events. Many celebrities and would-be celebs are publicity hungry and will be interested in increasing their own profile by tieing in with a movie. Remember, when you're offering a movie tie-in, you're operating in one of the highest classes of tradeoffs. A successful movie can be good for anyone's career. So don't hesitate to make that call.

■ **Pay strict attention to theme.** A party with no theme or no special venue or no special entertainment is just another party and will do nothing to benefit the film. However, if the party is unique, it can become an event, even for the media. And if the media arrive in force the marketing value of your party increases dramatically.

A unique party usually starts with developing some thematic aspect of the film. Avoid sterile hotel ballrooms and commonplace venues. Think "off the wall." If you're planning a party for the movie *Car Wash* where is the logical party location?

■ **Be tasteful.** Although there is a certain logic to holding a party for a horror movie in a mortuary or graveyard, think about it. Only the most morbid people are going to enjoy such a venue.

■ **Keep it simple.** Your budget line for parties is never very big so you're going to have to supply your own elbow grease and shoe leather.

Remember, your guests will be impressed just by being associated with your movie, you don't have to impress them with the food. Avoid expensive catering items. If it's an outdoor party—in a car wash, for example—then hot dogs and cokes are appropriate. Indoors, fresh vegetables, various types of crackers and a few hot items will satisfy most people and not destroy your budget.

Decorations should be imaginative and tie-in with the movie. You probably won't have the budget to hire a designer but you can enlist the help of high school or college students. (20th Century Fox may be able to build a replica of the spaceship in *Alien* for their promo party, but it's rare.) With the right motivation and supervision, volunteers can provide you with a valuable army of helpers. Just remember to invite them to the party!

■ **Hold your party as close to opening night as possible.** Parties, like most promotional events, should take place during the opening week of the movie. If you get media coverage, it will have the most impact at that time. Also, it's useless to have a promotional party before the public is primed by seeing your advertising campaign—and that's usually not until ten days to two weeks before opening.

■ **Invitations should be simple.** While your publicity department across the hall might be designing elaborate invitations for an opening night premiere party, your promotional party invites should be as simple as possible. Usually, a single card is appropriate. In fact, when you print the invitations for your national radio-promoted screenings, ask the art department to keep a couple thousand blanks on hand that can be printed with the promo-party information later.

33

DEALING WITH THE NATIONAL MEDIA—PRINT AND ELECTRONIC—PRIOR TO RELEASE

Release time is approaching. The film will be in the theaters soon and it's time to evaluate your campaign and plan the final most important push.

From Day One you've been conducting a publicity campaign which by now has developed public awareness for your film. But you can't stop now. The activity in the rest of the marketing and distribution offices is getting feverish and you're going to be getting a lot of pressure to produce even more publicity. It's as if the producers, the film production executives and any other creative person involved with the production of the film suddenly woke up and began to realize the importance of what you are doing. And like many creative types, they have a tendency to panic. Suddenly, the executive who never returned your calls is calling six times a day to find out if an article on his film is appearing in an opening week issue of *Time Magazine*. Some executives whom you've never heard of will now want to know about everything you've done since pre-production!

The spotlight is on you now and you'd better have a plan. Pre-release campaigns vary, depending on who's available for interviews and how much money's in the budget. Basically, there are four ways to approach the campaign at this point: **A**) continued media pitching from home base; **B**) a media tour to selected cities with available talent; **C**) an electronic press tour in LA or NYC which reaches different markets through satellite technology; or **D**) a press junket, sending journalists to a pre-arranged location for a screening and interviews.

Each plan is designed to get maximum use out of available talent. If you're working on a small independent film with no stars, a tour or junket is an enormous waste of time and money. Media interest will also be nil. In this case, go with plan A) – maintain your home base of operations and keep pitching. No one is going to be upset that you didn't conduct an elaborate media tour.

If you're working on the newest chapter in the *Ghostbusters* series and you're given only one week with the three stars—Bill Murray, Dan Aykroyd and Harold Ramis—then you have to consider a junket. It's an expensive proposition, but it's one of the simplest way of getting print and electronic exposure on a nationwide basis. And since it's *Ghostbusters* we're talking about, there should be money in the budget for a junket.

If the actors are available, but not enough journalists are free to travel, a satellite tour is a practical consideration. It also serves to maximize your available media time. More on satellites later.

Let's go through your campaign options and point out their advantages and disadvantages:

Plan A. The Basic No-Frills Approach: continued pitching from home base, local TV interviews, phone interviews, etc.

Not surprisingly, pre-release campaigns on most films opt for Plan A. It's the nature of the business. Fewer stars each year are available for publicity tours. There's seldom money in the budget for an elaborate junket. Sometimes, even a satellite tour is deemed too expensive. Money is being funnelled into the advertising campaign. The publicity and promotions department is expected to keep manufacturing miracles without spending any money.

There's plenty to do, including:

■ **Continue pitching actor and filmmaker interviews**. Now that we're in the pre-release period, you can forget about most of your magazine contacts. Their deadlines are well past. Aside from a few weeklies like *People* or *Time* and *Newsweek*, you should concentrate on your electronic and newspaper outlets. Assemble your actors and let them know that the pre-release interview process is beginning. Even the most uncooperative actor will do a few interviews now to support the picture. There are no givens, however. Some actors will simply not cooperate. Don't push it. Be sure to mention these facts to your producer and let him or her handle it. You should never take it upon yourself to force any personality to do an interview. It's not your job. Be persuasive, but let someone else be the authority figure.

Pitching continues in the same manner we discussed earlier in the book. Pitch letters with good angles, phone calls, press kits, follow-up, check off, interview. Keep up the pressure. You should never be idle. For a national campaign, there are simply too many outlets to cover.

If your actors are not based in Los Angeles, try to set up as many phone interviews as you can. The telephone can be an effective instrument for increased coverage. Even if Mr. Superstar is working on a new film in Sri Lanka, that doesn't mean he can't speak to the reporter at the *Los Angeles Times*. Many actors will cooperate while working on new projects. Don't hesitate to call the unit publicist on the new film and seek his or her cooperation. That publicist should be cooperative because every phoner could include information on the new project which makes him look good. And since you're doing all of the pitching and legwork, his job is simpler. His responsibility is getting the talent to the phone on time.

Satellite technology, which we will discuss in a moment, has also enabled actors to do television interviews from distant locations. Although it can be quite expensive, the technology is available to set up a dish next to virtually any location and broadcast the interview back to the States. It's truly amazing what you can do today if you have the budget and the actor's cooperation.

■ **Screen for critics**. Grab those quotes. Pitching interviews is only one of your pre-release period responsibilities. You still have to screen the finished film for critics which is, in itself, a full time job.

In a perfect world, the film will be finished two to three months before release and a print will be made available to you for critics screenings. In the real world, the film is completed three weeks before release and maybe, just maybe, a print is handed to you with two weeks to go.

Everyone suddenly wants review quotes for the opening day advertisements. "Two Thumbs Up," "Four Stars," "Highest Rating," "The Movie of the Decade," "Spectacular," "I Never Had So Much Fun"—blandishments that can help sway an opening day audience.

How do you get those quotes? First, the critic has to see the movie, and that is no easy task. I used to assume that if you rented the 1100 seat Academy of Motion Pictures theater on Wilshire in Los Angeles and invited every media person in town, you'd catch every important critic in one screening. Well, maybe if you're screening *The Last Emperor* or *Lawrence of Arabia*, but it's not the case for most films.

The fact of the matter is that when it comes to inviting film critics, every night is "a bad night." You may be screening the new Redford picture, but Critic A went to a play at the Mark Taper instead, Critic B had a cold and Critic C was invited to his wedding anniversary. You have to plan on chasing your top critics. In New York City, publicists plan 4-6 small screenings to catch as many critics as they can. It's not a bad idea to emulate that idea in Los Angeles. In LA, you're required to have at least one major industry screening to impress the producer's peers. You will invite every media person in town to the big screening, but since you won't hit *all* of your critics at this one, a few small screenings will be required.

■ **Continue to service all media with press kits, stills, color photos, etc.** Even though screenings are the best way to generate feature stories, many outlets will be able to give you some coverage from these materials alone. In some cases press kits will be all they get. There's always the possibility that you won't have a movie to screen in time, or, your producers won't let you screen the movie, period.

How can a media outlet cover the film without having seen it? You'd be surprised at how many do just that. There are dozens of radio and TV outlets, smaller papers and weekly magazines, and freelancers who are looking to bolster their coverage on new movies. They can't physically see every movie, but if they receive the proper materials on time, you have a good shot at getting some good "awareness building" coverage in their outlets.

That's why it's always important to have a good supply of publicity materials on hand. During the release period, you don't want to run out of press kits, color sets or video press kits. They're worth their weight in awareness.

Some publicity departments can get particularly stingy when it comes to color slide sets. I'm not. I usually have 50-60 sets available during the release period (and that's after I've already serviced another 50 to the long-lead magazines). Sure they cost money, but more and more newspaper outlets are using color and I don't want them shortchanged. Color is also utilized as graphic background material for TV coverage.

Always order more press kits than you need. You'd be surprised how many people suddenly begin to call about press kit availability. This usually happens during the last two weeks prior to release when journalists and critics begin to spot your television advertising spots and realize that your film is imminent. Excess press kits can always be sent over to your international department and video companies will always need them in quantity for their own media campaigns.

- **Remember to report on your activities.** Always keep your superiors informed with memos, progress reports, verbal updates and copies of all breaks. In the heat of publicity battle, don't neglect to keep the generals up-to-date on how the war is going.

You're in the spotlight now and important people are looking to you for results. The importance of your breaks will rise dramatically and everything you accomplish will be considered a boon for the production. Take advantage of this opportunity to show off: If you have the breaks, flaunt them.

Every time I obtain a break during the pre-release period— newspaper, magazine, television or radio—I have a photocopy of the article or transcript made and sent to my superiors. Don't send them one at a time, put them in batches and copy every possible executive who has a hand in the campaign.

It's not surprising to have up to twenty people receiving your batch of breaks. You should copy all of your key company executives, the producers of the film, the publicists who represent the individual actors, marketing and advertising consultants, etc.

Once your first *reviews* appear, copy them to everyone immediately. Positive reviews are the most eagerly awaited publicity item. They can single-handedly turn around the tenor of an entire campaign. Producers start to shout "Hit," advertising executives begin to plan their opening day ads with a big quoted review headline, production company executives start to think optimistically. And who is bringing these review quotes to their attention? You!

During the heat of a review campaign, your photocopied reviews are like important dispatches sent to a general in battle. You suddenly feel very important, and you should be. People are starting to pay attention to the work you've done on the production. All those pitch letters, all the phone calls, all the critic chasing and screenings—they're paying off. When such and such critic gives you a "10 out of 10" review, you can take pride in the accomplishment. Without you, there would have been no review.

While publicity breaks can be circulated to everyone, be careful about circulating reviews. Check with your superior before you circulate any review. Different companies have different policies. Normally, negative reviews are kept under wraps. Positive reviews are circulated. If a film receives nothing but negative reviews, then they become a file-and-forget item.

Negative reviews like movies that fail to generate box office interest, are soon forgotten. It's time to move on to another project. You'd also be surprised at how quickly a bad movie campaign is forgotten (especially if there are other film projects to work on).

Plan B.   The Actor's Publicity Tour. I remember a scene in *Damn Yankees* where comical Jean Stapleton is taking her girlfriend down to the train station in Hannibal, Missouri to see Gregory Peck get off the train. For her, and probably the whole town, the chance to see a movie star in person was unbelievably exciting.

Even though the public is being fed enormous amounts of entertainment news, "infotainment" on network news shows and in special shows like *Entertainment Tonight,* there is still a great excitement about seeing celebrities up close and in person. Catching Elizabeth Taylor's interview on *Sixty Minutes* is one thing, seeing her walk into your television studio in Kansas City is quite another.

The celebrity tour has been with us since the days of roving minstrels and religious fairs. When the first Popes went to visit their constituencies, they were on more or less a publicity tour. My guess is that they traveled with an entourage, they were protected by security, they had a strict itinerary that was followed to the T. At each stop, they were greeted by a host that took care of their every need. They greeted local dignitaries and in certain cases, they were interviewed. The interviewer may not have been equipped with video or audio recording tape, but it's certainly true that he or she remembered the Pope's words so that they could be repeated. And as those words were repeated from person to person, the full effect of the Pope's visit was felt.

Today, entertainment figures can generate the same kind of interest and excitement from the masses that Popes and Kings once did. They're the Popes and Kings of today's culture.

When the studio system was thriving, actors went on regular publicity and personal appearance tours. Before television and satellite interviews, the only way to spread the word was to physically go—either by plane, train or automobile—and meet the press and the public on their own turf.

And the publicists of that era squeezed every ounce of media value out of those tours. Newspaper editors, magazine editors, radio interviewers, local dignitaries, local photographers, wire service photographers, magazine photographers, school newspaper editors, everyone who could write a story about a new movie and its stars was alerted to greet the star.

That's why Gregory Peck's arrival was so exciting—his arrival in Hannibal, Missouri was fueled by the publicists and their media contacts. Royalty was coming to town.

Unfortunately, once the studio system began to falter in the late 1960s and actors began to develop a great deal of independence, and the importance of the media centers began to increase, the concept of the cross country publicity tour began to die. Without the studios and the contracts and the demanding executives, actors were free to choose what they wanted to do or not do. For most actors—especially ones who had not worked under the studio system—the time consuming publicity tours were just a "chore" and a "headache" rather than an accepted responsibility of their job. And as a new breed of personal publicist began to appear on the scene, catering to the whims and needs of the true stars, they fostered a new type of relationship between the star and the studio. Rather than the movie's box office success being the goal of everyone concerned, the actors began to put their own career first.

I don't want to say that all actors are like this. Many will put themselves on the firing line when a new project is ready for release. They will support it without hesitation. However, their numbers are dwindling over the years. Too many young actors today want all the success of their predecessors but don't want to get their hands dirty. I can't tell you how many times I've been told by teen stars that they want nothing to do with the teen magazines. Or that they won't do anything to help promote the movie they've just shot because they don't like their performance in it.

As much as I love what the satellite companies have provided—that fascinating capability of completing a concentrated number of national interviews in a small period of time, without leaving one's home town—they've also spoiled today's talent. There are actors today who really believe that Jay Leno and *The Today Show* are the be-all of publicity.

Many actors today don't know the hard work of promoting their movies: "If I get on Jay Leno or *The Today Show* it'll be all of the exposure we need," they'll say. Or, "Let's do a satellite tour. I'll give you a morning in some TV studio. You'll get talk show interviews in all your top markets and I'll be done with promoting the movie." Or, "Okay, I'll do publicity! I've got a day free in November, and you can have me the whole day."

I like satellite tours, but I'm concerned about two things: do they reach the right market and do they generate any excitement about the movie? For $11,000, I can put Mr. Superstar on television talk shows in 20 markets. But is my prime audience watching these talk shows? What about the people who like to read? Satellite coverage doesn't generate any print coverage. Or radio penetration, or the possibility of local photographers picking up on a story. There's no event that can be built around a star coming to town. Gregory Peck isn't getting off the train in Hannibal. He's sitting in a sterile studio in Century City or Manhattan, talking to a little voice in his ear.

I have to admit that I think the days of taking a star on a cross-country tour to 20-30 markets are over. They're too expensive and take to much of the star's valuable time. You can't do 20-30 markets in two weeks and that's about all any actor can afford to give these days.

Given the reality of time and budget limitations, what sort of publicity tours can we put together that will generate the kind of public awareness and excitement that are critical to any film's success?

■ **Determining the scope.** As I said, the days of 20-30 market tours are over. You can also forget about putting your actor in a chartered bus, or even a rental car. Any actor who has enough celebrity status to generate excitement on a tour, travels in an airplane. And they like to travel first class.

Actor publicity tours can last anywhere from one day to the previously mentioned two week limit. A very short "tour" means bringing your star to Los Angeles or New York. If the project is interesting enough, and the actor is a bit of a name, it shouldn't be difficult to put together enough interviews to fill a one, two, or even three day schedule.

When you plan your tour, think like an advertising executive. Pick "markets" that will reach the largest number of potential moviegoers for your film. If your star gives you two weeks, pick out your top 10 ADIs (Area of Dominant Influence). In selling television advertising, the agencies over the course of time have simply divided the U.S. map into ADI configurations. For the publicist, anything beyond the top 50 markets is superfluous because 1-50 represent the bulk of your core movie-going audience. For a publicity tour, your concern should be limited to Markets 1-20, and for a two week tour, which is about all you'll get, Markets 1-10.

The scope of your tour may also depend on the audience for the film. If you have a strong youth oriented action film, you may want to concentrate in large urban areas like LA, NY, Chicago, Philadelphia, Detroit. Look at your available top 20 markets and research the demographics of those cities. Sometimes the information can be very significant.

Will a youth-oriented film play in senior citizen heavy Miami? Will an upscale human drama play well in minority heavy, action-oriented Detroit? Will a baseball comedy play in Tampa which doesn't have a baseball team? There are usually no concrete answers to questions like this, but you should analyze your film's target audience and compare it to available demographic information on your potential tour markets.

Media interest will also determine whether you even enter that market. If at the last minute, you find that both Detroit daily newspapers have turned down your interview subject, then it's time to cancel that market and move on. Daily newspaper interviews are intrinsic to a tour's success. They reach the most people in the hinterlands and should be a serious barometer for the tour.

■ **Working with the local ad agencies.** Setting up the interviews. Unless you're forced to handle the tour entirely on your own, which isn't a good idea, you will receive support from local advertising agencies ("the field") that are in charge of buying local ads and providing publicity support. Technically, they can do everything for you. They can pitch the local media, send out the press kits, screen the picture, determine the interest and plan the itinerary. They can secure the hotel rooms, arrange the transportation to the appointments, even collect video copies, transcripts and xeroxes for your files. In the best case scenario, the top agencies can do this.

However, reality says that you should be prepared to take over on any level of the tour. The advantage of having local support, is that they are supposed to know their market. They know the entertainment editor of the local paper—most likely on a first name basis—a luxury you don't have. They know whether a local talk show does a movie feature, or whether the top local radio station will feature a celebrity guest, or whether the 4 or 5 local entertainment papers will feature an actor interview, non-exclusively. They also might know whether important public appearance opportunities exist in the town during the course of the tour. If 25,000 people are going to be attending a celebrity fund raiser for the local diabetes charity, then your local agency contact should be able to tell you whether your actor can become a part of the event.

But don't count on the local agencies too much. They vary in creativity and ability to help you out. In some cases, you'll be lucky to get a few interviews scheduled on time. Develop your own check list and if you're not getting the support you need, step right in.

- **The Tour Publicist**. Can you survive without one? Can you imagine the Pope arriving in Memphis without his entourage? Can you picture Wayne Newton driving himself to an interview with a Kansas City paper? Can you see Frank Sinatra dashing to the phone after running over-time on a radio interview to let the next disc jockey know that he'll be late? It's not that it's impossible to send anyone out on his or her own, it's just not the right thing to do. Sure, if it comes down to the fact that you don't have any money in your budget for a tour publicist, then you have no choice but to put the actor in the local agency's hands. But I wouldn't do it. In most cases, the actor knows you, not an agency in Omaha. The problems that could possibly occur in an interview situation should be problems you should solve, not a third party.

  Either go yourself, or send someone along who is familiar with the actor or the project. Someone who can follow a logistical plan without wavering, someone who remembers to phone ahead if the actor is going to be late, someone who can problem solve on their feet. Tour publicists can be perceived as nothing but "hand holders," but in point of fact they're your insurance policy that everything is going to work out as efficiently as possible.

  Actors are notoriously absent-minded, I wouldn't trust them to tie their shoes in the morning. If an actor is required to walk from his hotel room to the lobby for an interview, I would not guarantee that the task will be completed. Actors always have other things on their minds, millions of other things. Other than your old-time professionals, who seem to have an incredible respect for everyone and everything they do, today's actors can be preoccupied and immature. My point here is that you should always be prepared for the worst case scenario. Picture your actor floating in the East River, then make sure it doesn't happen.

  Who should go? If you're not incredibly busy, you should go. Otherwise, send your assistant if you have one. Or hire a professional for a part time assignment. Don't send a secretary who happens to work in your department, or your brother-in-law who happens to live in the tour city. Find a responsible publicity person and team him or her up with the celebrity.

- **Conducting the tour**. Some logistical tips. You've got a full schedule to accomplish in a very short time, but remember you're dealing with human beings. Realize that the actor can only be cooperative if he eats regularly, gets enough sleep and is given enough time to get from appointment to appointment. Research the actor's needs. If there's a question as to whether the actor will fly coach or not, contact his own publicist, agent or business manager. Don't embarrass yourself by asking the actor if he will fly coach. Frankly, provided there is some money in the budget, I always fly my actors first class, I book them into the best possible hotels, I make sure that they have enough money to eat out at fine restaurants.

An actor who feels like he's being treated with respect, even deference, will be more inclined to be cooperative and cordial to the press. The last thing you want is an actor who feels like you or the production company is taking advantage of him. The tour will be horrible, I guarantee it.

Your media contacts also deserve to be treated with respect. If there are delays, or timing problems, they need to be alerted. A journalist who is mistreated or abused during the interview process can turn into a time bomb that could sink the tour, the movie, even the star's career.

I always treat journalists like royalty, like they're doing me the biggest favor in the world for coming over. The smarter actors will do the same. Don't try to patronize, don't offer phoney comments or salutations. Just treat everyone with the utmost courtesy and respect—and try to keep everyone happy.

The best way to a journalist's good side is to get his or her interview done on schedule. Always give an actor plenty of time to get ready in the morning. If possible don't schedule interviews before 9:00 a.m., especially if you have to travel beyond the hotel lobby. Pre-determine the distance between appointments before finalizing your schedule. Allow plenty of time for travel difficulties. The last thing you want to do is schedule appointments too close together. Murphy's Law will seep into your schedule and you'll find yourself late for every appointment. Being a couple minutes late can be forgiven once or twice, *unless* your appointment is a live television or radio interview. A missed live interview could jeopardize your whole tour, not to mention your own career.

Book a limousine in Manhattan, if you have a lot of running around to do. The actor will enjoy the privacy and the royal treatment, and the availability of a car phone and a knowledgeable driver will help you make your appointments on time.

Well in advance of arriving in any tour city, type up an itinerary and give it to all concerned, especially the actor(s). Learn the names of your media contacts and call them by their first names. Make sure that every media contact on the list has a phone number. If delays or changes in schedule occur, you must have a way of getting through to that outlet.

Always carry a supply of cash and credit cards with you. You never know when you're going to need to buy something unusual, including last minute plane tickets if a foul-up has occurred.

Keep a supply of business cards with you and give them to your media contacts. Take advantage of what may be your first in-person meeting with key contacts. These people are responsible for getting you tapes, transcripts and photocopies. They also may be someone you will need to turn to for help in the future.

If possible, schedule print interviews in the actor's hotel. If the actor has a suite, it will probably be the most suitably private arena for an interview. If the actor doesn't want the interview conducted in the suite, shift it to a quiet corner of the lobby or the restaurant.

If the actor is traveling with a spouse or friend of the opposite sex, don't assume that that person should be invited to each interview. Consult the actor and find out how he or she wants to handle it. Sometimes this can be a sensitive issue. If the actor is recently divorced and she's traveling with a new companion, she may want to keep that person far away from any press. By anticipating sensitive situations, you can avoid potential problems.

Remember to bring some publicity photos, press kits, soundtrack cassettes, etc. with you to media appointments. They make great gifts at strategic moments. The fact that you have them and that you bring them out at all the right times, will impress the actor. It will also make him or her aware of how very important it is to be ready for any situation with a plan.

As much as you want to give the press everything they will need to prepare a positive story, remember that your first priority is the actor. If he signals you that it's time to wrap up the interview, don't encourage him to continue any further. He's reached his capacity, and the journalist will simply have to understand.

You don't want the actor to start thinking of you or your tour publicist as anything but a trusted friend. Admittedly, there are times when a journalist can squeeze a few more questions out of an actor, but for the most part help wrap up the interview as neatly as possible.

Should you or the tour publicist sit with the actor and print journalist during an interview? It used to be a sensitive question, but today I find that very few, if any, journalists object to interviews that include the publicist. Enjoy yourself, keep your mouth shut and let the actor do the talking.

Prioritize your media appointments. Some are more important than others. Sometimes sickness or exhaustion will make it necessary to cancel or re-schedule a few appointments. But be very protective of appointments that are critical to the tour! If *The Today Show* can only take you on Monday morning, then you should only cancel if there's an emergency. The fact that Actor B is having a tummy ache this morning should be cause for concern, but offer some words of sympathy, break out the stomach antacids and get everyone into the limousine ASAP.

However, if the first interview is with the teenage journalist from a local high school paper, don't hesitate to cancel. The actor will surely hate you if you don't, and you can always re-schedule the high school media. Let them work around your schedule, not the opposite.

- **Local press conferences for smaller media**. It depends on the project and the star, but there will be situations that require the actor to entertain the press in a conference format. Press conferences are particularly advantageous for servicing smaller but still vital media outlets.

For instance, in New York City, you may want to invite the editors of all the top teenage publications to Mr. Young Superstar's hotel suite for a press conference. You might throw in some high school or college reporters as well.

Press conferences are important when you know you don't have enough time in town to set up individual interviews. They also work when you're dealing with a group of speciality publications.

The basic conference is a Q and A format, just like a presidential press conference. Make sure the room is large enough, well lit and there are plenty of seats. Order a pitcher of water and make sure the actor has access to it. Depending on the size of the room, determine whether you will need a microphone. In most cases, it won't be necessary. The journalists will not be that far away from the speaker.

Conferences should last about an hour. Keep an eye on the actor and see whether he or she is enjoying the experience. If the questions are awful, the actor will begin to tire of the process quickly. Then you must begin thinking about ending the conference and putting the actor out of his misery. But if there's some good rapport between the actor and the press audience, you could extend the conference for a few minutes.

Press conferences, especially those that involve teen or fan magazines, usually attract photographers as well. Make sure that at the end of the conference, the actor is available for photo opportunities. It's a pain, but the journalists will be grateful. Try to pre-determine a spot for the photo. Sometimes the bare walls of a suite or conference room are not proper backgrounds for publicity photos. If it's a nice, non-windy day, you might be able to find a garden spot with a touch of privacy where photogs can shoot a few rolls. Keep the photo session short though, a maximum of five minutes. Nothing tires an actor out faster than posing for a battery of press photographers.

- **Personal appearances**. Don't worry too much about this one. The days when actors were available to open new supermarkets or movie houses are over. Consider yourself lucky if all of your media appointments are made without a problem. Anything else is icing on the cake.

Personal appearances only happen with lots of advance planning. You need to do a lot of research to find out about events which are going to happen within the tour cities. If Mr. Superstar is promoting a new political movie in a city where a political party is holding their national convention, you might be able to coordinate with the convention publicity people to get a personal appearance for your actor. An opportunity like this could be seen by millions of television viewers and should never be overlooked.

Every city has its own special seasonal rituals that have the potential to become a part of your itinerary. Try to tap into those rituals and find out whether a personal appearance could be valuable.

Personal appearances are effective publicity opportunities, but you're going to have to do some leg work to be able to exploit them. Political figures always seem to show up at new construction sites where they can help turn the first shovelful with the owners as the cameras click. Why, because their campaign managers and publicists research situations that could benefit the candidate's image.

■ **Wrapping up the tour.** When the tour is finished, get your actor home. That is your first priority. Get him on a plane back to his home base. If he needs a ride from the airport to his house, arrange for it. Your tour is completed when your actor is safe in his own bed.

Documenting the tour's success should be easy. You already have your media breaks listed on your tour itinerary. You can embellish upon these in an "after action" report.

Remember to keep all of your receipts. If you're smart, you've requested an expense advance which should have covered all of your out of pocket costs (tips, restaurant charges, special gifts, emergency costs, etc.). If you've had to tap into your own wallet, make sure you have all of your expense receipts and then type up an expense report so that you can get paid for those expenses. And don't wait too long. You should have an expense report on the desk of your financial officer the day after you arrive back in the office.

Keep in touch with your local ad representatives, and the media outlets. Your after action report should be followed by a report containing transcripts and/or xerox copies of the stories that appear in the local city papers. Your local ad agency is responsible for sending you copies of all your local breaks. Usually they will fax you the break as soon as they get it, but request the original or "hard copy" as well. You need them for your permanent files, and faxes are notorious for being hard to photocopy.

Plan C.   The Satellite Press Tour—A Viable Alternative. In a perfect world, actors would go on regular multi-city publicity tours and they would like it. The fact of the matter is that fewer and fewer name personalities are willing to travel and those that do are cutting their tours shorter every day.

Enter the age of satellites. We've come a long way from Sputnik and Telstar. Being a baseball fan, I first started to realize the effectiveness of satellite transmission when my local television sports reporter began to feature the video results of other league games on his daily telecasts. In the old days, being a Los Angeles resident, I would get a Dodger replay and an Angel replay and the scores from around the country, and that was it. Then in the mid 1980s I began to see diamond action in New York, Chicago, Baltimore, Cleveland and every other city with a major league baseball franchise. And how was this material coming to the newsroom? By satellite!

Satellites are a newsroom staple. Each network has their own satellite, and so do the independents. Local news reports of national consequence are video taped and then transmitted on the satellite (the "uplink" procedure). Member stations then determine whether they want to record the signal and prepare their equipment accordingly (the "downlink" procedure). In reality, the entire planet is now linked with satellite stations. Hence, Bryant Gumbal of *The Today Show* can conduct a live interview with a reporter standing on Red Square in Moscow; or Ted Koppel can interview several people at once on his *Nightline* show; or CBS Sports can feature Sunday half-time football results of several games that are still in progress.

Satellite transmission has revolutionized television broadcasting and it was just a matter of time before some enterprising publicists realized the potential benefit of a satellite press tour.

Although it is possible to contact a satellite company directly, purchase transmission time, and rent a studio, cameras and technical personnel, it is considerably easier to simply hire a satellite publicity company to put together your whole tour package.

A satellite publicity company provides a number of important services. In addition to taking complete control of the technical end of the satellite tour, they also publicize the interview subject to their various outlets, determining local interest. In other words, they perform as publicists, pitching your talent. Setting up a satellite tour follows the same pattern of a physical tour—you still have to interest the media in a story.

Your top satellite publicity companies maintain teams of publicists who contact virtually every possible TV outlet that would be interested in the interview or "feed." While it's true that I could contact the ABC affiliate station in Buffalo myself, the satellite publicity company has usually developed a more ongoing relationship with them. They can talk "turkey" to one another—passing on technical jargon and that sort of thing—much better than I. Plus, the top satellite publicity companies are pitching stories every day. So I let them do the pitching. If anyone can get the ABC station in Buffalo to take a Meryl Streep interview, they can.

Once you've decided to organize a satellite publicity tour, here are some tips on making it a pleasant, profitable experience:

- **Go directly to one of the top companies**. You can shop around for a "deal," but you'll find that charges are pretty standardized. The cost of a tour depends on the number of markets you want to cover.

In my experience, you can cover around 20 markets in two and a half hours for about $11,000 (1992 dollars). The costs go up after that. But you also have to be concerned about your actor's ability to hold up over a long satellite interview series. To keep someone confined in a small television studio, talking to someone he can't see for more than four hours could be a major problem. And one thing you must keep in mind at all times is that you're not doing this just out of convenience. You want to present your regional television audiences with a quality interview that will inspire them to go see the movie.

Sometimes, you get so caught up in the technical thrill of conducting a 20 city tour in four hours, that you forget that your actor is mumbling his words, he looks out of synch and he's getting grouchy. Not only will that type of interview turn off the audience, but the program director on the other end may kill the interview altogether. Even though they take the downlink, there is nothing to compel the local station to run the interview.

Working with a top company guarantees that you will be surrounded by people who conduct satellite interviews every day and will be able to tell you if your actor is starting to lose it. If you feel uncomfortable dealing with the actor about his posture, or his communications ability, these satellite people will be more than happy to drop a helpful hint. They want your business, but they also want to present top quality product to their television station program directors. It behooves them to make sure your talent comes off in a sparkling manner.

■ **Give the satellite company your wish list of stations and let them run with it.** Once you determine the length and cost of your tour, discuss your basic station needs with the satellite representative. It's pretty simple, actually. If you're opening the film nationally, you're probably going to want stations in the top 20 markets. You don't have to prioritize which stations, the satellite company will automatically pitch the top stations in each market—network affiliate and independent.

However, if you're not opening the entire country, you should make sure that the stations they choose conform to your opening markets. As they get "turn-downs" from various stations, the satellite publicists might suggest that you go with a Market #30 station to make up for the #19 who passed. It's a judgement call. You want twenty stations, they can only provide 19 in the top 20, and after going down the list, they know that market 30 is very interested. So you go along with them. A top satellite publicity company will get you the best possible tour. They're not going to sell you on a station unless it's enthusiastic about the movie.

Once you've established the guidelines for the tour, you can simply leave the satellite publicists to do their job. They'll report back to you on their progress and eventually they'll fax over a list of stations and the times the interviews will take place.

Some of the interviews will be live, some will be taped during the downlink and then broadcast during the film's opening week. If your satellite is taking place on opening week, then you must request a majority of live interviews. This story is breaking now, you don't want them to tape something that is going to be old news after Friday. Many stations are capable of taking live downlinks. They're equipped to handle live conversation—especially on many of the morning shows—and it's not a big problem. If your satellite is taking place weeks or even months prior to opening (which can be the case if you know that your actor is going to be out of the country at release time), then you will specify that all shows be taped for future airing. A live interview two months before release is a waste of time. Only the immediacy of a film's opening makes a televised interview effective.

- **Lock in your time and get your actor alerted and confirmed**. As soon as you've determined that the satellite is a viable alternative, contact your actor and make sure that he or she is available on a specific day. Thousands of dollars are riding on this appointment, so it should be checked and confirmed as soon as possible.

When should you have a satellite tour? It, of course, depends on the availability of your actors. If they're available opening week, then you should plan your tour opening week. Have you ever noticed that guests on the top morning shows—*The Today Show*, *Good Morning America* and *CBS This Morning*—always come on to plug their films during opening week. That's no accident. The film is opening this Friday, it's time to alert the masses. Given any more time than a few days to decide, the public will forget and go on to something else.

Hit them now, when your television ads are already blitzing the airwaves, when radio promotions are in place, when your print stories are breaking in newspapers and magazines.

If your actors are not available, then you have to "bank" the interviews. If Mr. Superstar is leaving for Bolivia in July and your film opens in August, then there's no reason why you can't contact the satellite publicity company early and set up a tour in which all of the interviews are taped for future airing. With a star of such magnitude, there is an excellent chance that all of the interviews will be aired.

With an actor unavailable to support the picture at a crucial time—a fact of life these days—the satellite tour does provide a necessary backup system.

- **Tour day: coping with a technological experience**. Satellite tours are very neat operations. When you work with the top companies, they take care of everything, down to the bagels and cream cheese and fresh orange juice.

If you're uplinking out of Los Angeles, figure an 8:00 a.m. start. East coast tours begin toward late morning. Have your talent picked up by limousine. Never, repeat never, allow them to make their own transportation plans. With a limousine, you have the capability of telephoning the driver and determining if there is a problem.

Since you're on a tight time schedule, your actor must arrive with time to spare. Arrival time is usually at least 30 minutes prior to the first interview. A makeup person is hired for the satellite tour—it's included in the fee you pay.

A satellite tour takes place in a mini-studio with a television camera, a set, a chair, and earphones. It's pretty basic. The satellite personnel direct the interviews from a control booth, just like any television broadcasting facility.

The process is actually quite fascinating. Your actor is seated in the studio set. An audio person hooks up an earphone through which the actor will hear his interview questions. He is then told to look directly into the camera to answer the questions.

Although it's a little unsatisfying to be unable to see the person asking the questions, it usually isn't a problem. It's just like conducting a telephone interview. The technical director will be in constant communication with the actor, and there are usually some cue cards present identifying the person on the other end of the line, his station and city.

It moves pretty quickly. At 8:00 a.m., you're on live with Tampa. "Hello, Tampa, how's the weather down there." The interview goes on for approximately ten minutes, they say their goodbyes, and suddenly it's "Hello, Washington D.C. how's Congress doing today?" Ten more minutes, then comes WWOR in New York, etc.

This will then continue for four hours. The actor can usually take a tiny break to visit the rest room or the buffet table, but there are no lunch periods or major interruptions. You have a lot of markets to cover.

Like any mass interview process, the actor must maintain his enthusiasm and salesmanship level. He's out there selling a product. Keep his spirits up. Some of the questions are going to be pretty basic and he's going to hear them twenty times, but he must maintain a good enthusiasm level. It's the key to the success of the satellite.

What you're looking for is a sense of magic—what you look for in any interview—a few seconds where the actor is actually having fun with the questions. Those precious few seconds can send a deep-rooted signal to the home viewer that "hey, maybe this is the type of movie I want to see. The actor's having fun, maybe I'll have fun too."

Interviewers are always looking for humorous or unusual anecdotes as well. It depends on the project, of course. If you have a very serious actor describing a very serious film, he'll probably address the salient reasons the film was made in the first place. He'll talk about the subject matter and its relevance to today's world. And this will be fine—a more academic approach, but the information will be useful to the home audience.

Comedies and adventure films lend themselves better to a more upbeat, often comical interview experience. It also depends on the actor's personality. Some actors could sit down on a pin cushion and still talk in a slow, pedantic boring monotone. Other actors are difficult to keep in the chair, let alone on one train of thought. Can you imagine what Robin Williams must be like on a satellite, or Bill Murray?

One major word of caution. Make sure your satellite publicity people fully brief their TV contacts on the actor's film and background. Usually, full video and editorial press kits are sent to the stations prior to the interview. On live interviews, the clips are dropped right into the interview segment. Taped interviews will be integrated with clip material at a later date.

Actors like to think that the people interviewing them are knowledgeable about their backgrounds and the project being discussed. No actor wants to hear the question, "How did you get into the business?" In a ten minute interview, when a film needs to be discussed, the actor doesn't have time to speak an essay about his film background—information that has already been summarized neatly in the press kit.

Unfortunately, due to the pressure under which most news and interview people work under, there are times when they can only give a cursory glance to the available press information. "Winging it" becomes their philosophy, and sometimes this can have disastrous consequences.

Beware of live mics. Technically, the control room should only turn the actor's headphone on when the on-air talent is ready to conduct the interview. But they're not always perfect, and sometimes what they hear is not what they're supposed to be hearing. It can work on the back end as well. After the interview is completed, the mic might remain on and the on-air talent might make a comment about the interview which the actor might also hear. So be very careful.

Once the satellite tour is completed, your actor's earphone will be removed and he will be free to go. Sometimes, if I'm smart, I will schedule some additional interviews in the studio with other journalists who need to speak to the actor. If an actor is going to give up his full morning or afternoon for satellite interviews, he'll probably be amenable to additional interviews on the premises.

■ **Wrapping up the satellite tour experience.** Once the satellite tour has been completed, you will receive some important paper work from the satellite publicity company. If the tour was live, in about a week to ten days, you'll get a summary print-out which will mention each outlet and, based on the ratings for that hour, the number of homes the interview reached.

Satellite company after action reports are usually very concise and can be shown directly to your superiors. If the interviews were taped, such information will be available down the line, shortly after the actual broadcast. The satellite publicity company is supposed to maintain ongoing communication with you about the upcoming broadcasts.

If you haven't already supplied them with film clips, they will ask for the clips when they become available. Their involvement with your project is not finished until their final after action or "usage" report is submitted.

Satellite publicity tours are now a common facet of the motion picture exploitation process and they will continue to gain importance in the future—especially as technology brings the downlink dish to other media entities—print and electronic.

Plan D. Junkets—Bringing the Mountain to Mohammed. The fourth and most expensive campaign plan for release period publicity is the press junket. You invite press from around the country to a central location to see the finished film and conduct interviews. It's like a convention. The journalists are wined and dined over a period of two-three days (usually over a weekend), they're provided with press materials and some promotional items, and they are methodically exposed to all available talent.

Putting on a major press junket is like organizing a smaller version of the annual Super Bowl football game. The journalists form one team, the talent another, and the field or arena must be organized to accommodate everyone's needs. Referees are needed in quantity, rest periods are a given, food and drink requirements are paramount. Everyone has to feel like they're in the midst of a carefully organized process. Once the organization breaks down, the whole process can backfire. It's an exercise for the detail-oriented. One missing detail can bring the whole game to a halt.

But it is the expense that is usually the most daunting element of a press junket. You have to provide travel arrangements and accommodations for a large number of journalists who must also be fed in a certain impressive style. Additionally, in this day and age, you'll be catering to a number of electronic journalists who will need to take their interviews back with them on video tape. Thus, you must hire an electronic publicity outfit to provide a video crew to tape interviews for the whole junket. Hotel convention rooms, suites, additional manpower, shuttle services, promotional items—all of this adds up to a rather large sum. Because of the high price tag, the press junket is usually the province of the major studios.

Like the Satellite Press Tour, the junket is influenced by the actor's availability. If the film has three major actors and you discover that they only have three common days of availability, then a junket becomes vital to take advantage of their time.

Junkets, by the way, are best suited to films with a number of stars, including well-known directors. You would never go to the expense of a major press junket if you did not have the star power to work with. First, the journalists would not come to such an event, and secondly if they did come, they would be suitably unimpressed by what you have to offer.

Some journalists treat the junket as a breach of ethics. By accepting your hospitality, they claim they can lose their story objectivity. After all, if Columbia Pictures is inviting me out to the Coast to see *Ghostbusters II*, what are they going to think if I trash the film in a feature story and review? Most studio executives will claim that they are not so much concerned with any particular review or story, it's quantity that matters. If the studio thinks the movie has a box office chance, they'll take the opportunity to help spread the word-of-mouth on the film by inviting as many top journalists to the junket as possible.

If a journalist trashes the picture, will he be invited back for another junket? Probably. There is a specific criteria for choosing journalists for junkets. If you're going to the expense of inviting them, you had better choose reporters who regularly report or critique new movies in all media. And since these journalists are the "kingpins" of their particular region, it's likely that they will be candidates in the future, simply because of the power they possess in their local markets.

For many journalists, the junket becomes their only opportunity to meet stars face to face. Fewer stars are taking publicity tours, satellite press tours are increasing, there really is no alternative for the journalist who wants a story based on an interview conducted in person.

Let's talk about organizing a major junket. Keep in mind that these details can be applied to any size junket—from 2 people to 200. The criteria is the same.

■ **Determining the scope of the junket**. Your budget will immediately tell you what you can and cannot do. One thing to consider is whether you can work another film into the same junket. It's common for the major studios to offer two, three, and even four films for the visiting journalist to cover. The additional films add a talent mix that can be very appealing to the journalist. It also allows the studio to spread the cost over more than one picture.

If a full junket costs $100,000 (for 50 national journalists), then $25,000 each for four pictures is a very reasonable cost. Even $50,000 each for two pictures could be termed reasonable, if it's the only way you can guarantee national press coverage on your film.

If these figures seem way beyond what is reasonable, remember that a studio may spend $10 million on advertising alone to open a picture. The average advertising expenditure for national openings these days is anywhere from 9 to 25 million dollars, depending on the scope of the film. Thus, $50,000 for a national junket is very reasonable. So consider piggybacking your projects, if you can.

- **How many press people are you going to invite?** When you plan a satellite publicity tour, you take into account "top markets" which will get you the best coverage most efficiently. The same is true of junkets. If you're opening a film nationally, then you want to be sure that journalists from the top 20 markets are invited to your junket. After that, you can work your way down through the markets as far as your budget will allow.

Within those top 20 markets, you may invite one newspaper writer, one television reporter, a top columnist, even a radio personality. It all depends on how deep the market is in terms of media talent. I like to give journalists attending my junkets a sense of "exclusivity." It's not a good idea to invite every paper and every TV station from any given market. Journalists are going to be more excited if they know that their story isn't going to be printed in every other paper in town, or broadcast on every other station.

A typical large junket for a major studio consists of a group of 25 print journalists and 25 electronic journalists. You can have more or less, depending on how much coverage you want, and, of course, the journalist's interest in your story. What would happen if you gave a junket and nobody came? It's happened.

You have to pitch a junket just like everything else. Sometimes you will get an interested response, sometimes you will get "No thanks." Journalists have lots of complications which dictate whether they say yes to attending your junket: work schedules, vacation time, the availability of competitive news stories, junkets by other studios, even ethical considerations. However, with a compelling pitch from you, a good mix of actors, a film which captures the imagination, most journalists will be more than happy to accept your invitation.

- **When is the best time to hold your junket?** Once again, you have to deal with everyone's availabilities. Journalists like to junket on weekends. If they can fly out on Friday and return Sunday night or Monday morning, they don't lose any real work time. It's the perfect vacation for them. As for the stars, you have to contact them and anchor their schedule. At these prices, you don't want any no shows.

Unlike the satellite press tour which can get your material on the screen quickly, the press junket needs more breathing time, especially since a good proportion of your visitors are print journalists.

I would give yourself a good three to four weeks out from release. Of course, you do hear about studios junketing in journalists a week before opening. I think that's cutting it a bit close. If the journalist suddenly develops a problem and can't make it, it's really too late to assign a replacement or go to another media outlet in the market.

A week out rushes the print journalist and virtually prevents him or her from putting together a feature story—and features are the expected result of junketing. Although there is no guarantee of a journalist reporting anything, most will try to put together some sort of feature piece on your film after being given the deluxe junket treatment. But if your schedule doesn't allow enough time, the features are not going to get written, no matter how much the writer loved your junket.

Thus, planning a junket 3-4 weeks out gives the journalist time to assemble his priorities and perhaps prepare that Sunday-before-Friday-opening piece which is so important to your opening. Why is it so important? Because usually in regions outside LA/NYC/CHI, a Sunday paper will include only one major movie feature. If it's your film he's covering that Sunday, then you're one leg up on the competition.

Marketing executives, your superiors, also like to receive Sunday feature copies on their desk. They begin to feel that the junket was justifiable.

As for time of year, there used to be pre-Summer and pre-Christmas junkets to cover all of the product being released during those vacation periods, but as release patterns have changed, the whole calendar is now available for junkets. It just depends on when your films are ready. You have to be able to screen the picture for your visiting journalists. Otherwise, the junket is a waste of time. Availability of screening prints will thus influence your junket time. You're going to have to sit on your production department and get a very specific time for print availability.

■ **Budgeting**. Here are some budget items that you will have to include in any junket:

$ Air Travel. Round trip coach fares for every journalist. No, they can't bring their wives and girlfriends. You don't have the budget. Occasionally you may want to fly some VIP journalists first class, but I try not to. The last thing you want is to put Journalist A in first and find out that Journalist B in coach saw her through the cabin curtain. Horrible!

$ Accommodations. Try to make a package deal with a nice local hotel where you can get a special rate. Since you'll also be using their banquet facilities for interviews, party, etc, you should be able to strike a good deal. Don't get chintzy at this point. The last thing you want is the journalist to feel like a second class citizen. In Los Angeles, the studios use the top hotels for junkets—Mondrian, Bel Age, Century Plaza, Four Seasons.

Assemble a welcome packet for each journalist. It should contain a personalized welcome note, a complete itinerary for the junket, some promotional items (if they're available), even a basket of fruit. Treat your journalists like dignitaries.

It's also a good idea to book the stars into the same hotel for the entire weekend. Having them close at hand will make it easier on them to be available for all the events planned for the weekend, and make it easier for them to get away too. After a full day of interviews, it's nice when they can go right up to their room and change clothes, take it easy, pop on the television, and just relax.

Some of your guests may decide to take advantage of the free air fare and stay over a few extra days. "No problem" as far as you're concerned as long as they take care of their own accommodations after the junket is over.

$ Shuttling. Once the journalist arrives at the airport, his movements are entirely within your responsibility. You have to provide shuttle service to and from the hotel, to and from the screening facility and to any other outside area (including restaurants, etc.). For this reason, you should plan on hiring some mini-buses for the entire weekend. How many buses depends on the number of journalists. Those same buses will be available for any shuttling throughout their stay.

However, if a journalist wants to do some traveling on his own, outside your aegis, he will have to provide his own transportation. You're not in the sightseeing business.

$ Meals. Meals should be planned with military precision. Since many junkets are under specific time constraints, it's best to plan catered meals. A buffet breakfast, a sit-down dinner. Lunch is tricky. If you have a full day of interviews planned, you may have to set up a lunch buffet somewhere in the hotel and let the journalists know they can lunch at their convenience.

During the daytime hours, your number one priority is to get those interviews finished. Although you must provide your actors with good catered meals, the journalists can be a little more flexible.

Let's look at a typical Friday in, Sunday out schedule for a single movie. Normally, you would plan for everyone to arrive in town on late Friday afternoon. A sit-down welcome dinner or a cocktail party and buffet would be planned for that evening, and a screening would follow. Remember that the journalists have to see the film before they conduct the interviews. After the first round of interviews are completed on Saturday, a second sit-down dinner should be planned. Sunday is then reserved for a final run of interviews, with everyone flying out Sunday night or Monday morning. A Sunday night sit-down dinner is optional.

Treat the sit-downs like any catered affair, but don't think that just because you're a film company you have to put caviar and Dom Perignon on every table. It is correct to ask visiting journalists if they have any specific dietary requirements. For sit-down dinners, beer and wine can be served, but I generally don't offer anything stronger, especially if I'm screening after dinner.

Alternatively, you may want to screen early and then follow with a dinner. This, however, may work better on the second night when your journalists have all arrived and are settled in.

$ Video Crew. Since half of your visiting journalists are going to be television reporters, you're going to have to set up some "video suites" for taped interviews. I usually go to the same company that handles satellite press tours or electronic press kits. They have the capability of hiring enough video crews and setting up everything for you.

You're going to need one crew and one suite for every interview subject. Each suite will contain a camera and an operator, a support person to help direct the interview segment, and the appropriate "set" (a nice plush chair and a plant will do).

Once your video suites are set up, the process is pretty easy to follow. If there are four suites, you set up a schedule which gives every video journalist a few minutes with each of the four stars. A specific time schedule should be part of the welcome packet for each video journalist. Figure a minimum of 15 minutes for each interview. This can be adjusted by determining the number of actors and the number of journalists. Like the satellite press tour, a four hour interview period is about average. If your budget limits you to two video suites, you must adjust your interview schedule to accommodate all needs.

Print interviewers do not have the luxury of a one on one interview with the actor. Their interviews are usually conducted in a "round-robin" fashion, with an actor seated at a table surrounded by 4 or 5 journalists.

$ Booking rooms. Discuss your room requirements with the hotel manager when you're making reservations. You'll need some suites for video taping and some larger rooms, often a banquet room with partitions or conference rooms for the round robin interviews.

$ Speciality Items. Typical movie promotional items—T-shirts, sweatshirts, pins, stickers, etc.—should be available to your journalists. Remember to keep some money in your budget for these. If your promotions department has designed a special item for your movie, the journalists are going to know about it and expect one for themselves. So be prepared.

$ Additional items. You should establish a policy for dealing with the journalist's incidental hotel expenses. If you don't have a policy, you're leaving yourself wide open for someone calling her boyfriend in Hawaii 31 times. A typical expense policy would pick up the first $25.00 of incidentals per day. Anything above that is the journalist's own responsibility. Incidental expenses cover things like room service snacks, liquor, telephone calls, an extra toothbrush, etc.

You may need to hire some additional publicists for the junket, although secretaries and assistants can be recruited for the weekend to help coordinate the events. You should discuss this arrangement well in advance with your personnel department.

You should also allow some funds in your budget for decorations. Centerpieces for the banquet tables, wall decorations, signs, etc. are nice touches, especially if they are done with some creativity and they relate to the theme of the movie.

■ **Keeping the press and your talent happy.** Junketing is really a three day party and you're the host. Talent, journalists, video crew, hotel representatives, studio employees assisting with the event are all part of the mix and everyone should have the best time possible. Granted, the party is business related and the bottom line is completing the interview process, but some thought must be given to making the process enjoyable. If you go out of your way to make someone comfortable, they'll remember you when they're writing their story back home. Of course, there are no guarantees. Many times in my career I maintained a fabulous relationship with a visiting journalist only to see a lukewarm story appear in their publication or show.

Here are some suggestions for keeping your visiting journalists as happy as possible:

✔ Treat them as individuals. Don't fall into the trap of being so intent on getting all the interviews accomplished that you push everyone around like a herd of cattle. Get to know your visiting journalists. Know their names and their needs. Converse with them. Find out a little about their publications, what they like to cover, what movies have particularly impressed them of late, what they plan on covering in the future.

If I were really organized, I would have a little computerized database cross-referencing film journalists with their specialities and interests. It would be extremely valuable to be able to chart the whole country and know how many film journalists are horror movie fans; how many love Woody Allen-type comedies; how many cannot stomach violent films. The publicist who does this research and puts together a "journalist interest database" will be a step ahead of everyone else in town.

✔ Create a "hospitality suite." Somewhere in the hotel, close to the interview process and any other activities you are planning, you should arrange a hospitality suite. It's a place where journalists can congregate between interviews; where they can catch their breath and prepare for their next task. It's also a good place to set up a snack table (or if possible a luncheon buffet.)

Someone from your staff should be present at all times to answer questions and assist in any way possible. Light refreshments are nice, but no liquor. You don't want to serve anything that could interfere with the work at hand.

The hospitality suite also gives journalists a place to socialize. They're away from home, without friends and family and will welcome a place to relax and swap stories with their associates. You don't have to become the recreation director on a cruise ship, but it is your responsibility to make sure that your media flock is comfortable and happy.

✔ A Party. A cocktail party on the night they arrive is always a good idea. It's an even better idea when you can get some of your talent to show. What better opportunity for the journalists to get comfortable with their interview subjects. A cocktail party with hot hors d'œurves or cold-cuts is less expensive than a formal sit-down dinner (which can be planned for the following night). It also gives you an opportunity to take some time and personally meet each of your guests. If you wait until the interview process, then any form of interaction will be rushed. Here, you can take your time and greet everyone, you can make a welcome speech, you can even attempt to get your stars to say a few words.

In terms of the liquor selection, determine with the input of your executives whether you want a full bar, or beer and wine only. I am inclined to lean towards a more limited selection of spirits.

✔ Go the extra yard. Through the welcoming party, the screenings, the dinners, and the interview process, keep up your duties as host. At every opportunity, find out whether your guests—both journalists and talent—are in need of anything. If your journalist from Minnesota drops a hint that she has an article appearing in the Vogue Magazine which just hit the newsstands, but she hasn't been able to get out to buy a copy, send one of your assistants out to get it. Little touches are often remembered the most and in the public relations game, being remembered is everything.

But don't hesitate to draw the line either. If your television reporter from Tampa has to see the new elephant exhibit at the LA County Zoo, you simply have to say that there's no time, that your support personnel are busy and that you can't afford to distract them from their job at hand.

As you become more familiar with the junket procedure, you'll realize that every journalist has his or her own needs and priorities. Accommodate them if you can, but realize that as important as it is to make your guests comfortable, your number one priority is to provide them with screenings and interviews.

34

THE REVIEW PRESS—SHEPHERDING YOUR QUOTES AS THEY BREAK

Quoted endorsements are a popular marketing tool in practically every industry. In some cases, corporations will pay millions of dollars for a celebrity spokesperson to endorse or represent their product. Michael Jackson dances his way through a Pepsi Cola commercial; Paula Abdul sings a Diet-Coke commercial jingle; Karl Malden sells the country on the merits of American Express traveler's checks; Michael Jordan sails through the air for Nike tennis shoes.

For the movie industry, celebrity endorsements, however, are unknown. Paul Newman will never go on national television and tell someone to go see someone else's movie. His name will never appear in print or in commercials as an endorsement. Even for his own projects, his only form of endorsement will be the interviews he grants to the entertainment press.

In the movie business, the only endorsing entity is the film critic. A quote from a reviewer for a nationally known publication (or TV show) is a common feature of most newspaper advertising campaigns. You've seen them a thousand times—huge blaring headlines with every adjective in the book: "Astounding," "Unbelievable," "Unforgettable," "A 10 out of 10," "The Best Movie of the Year," "The Movie of the Decade," "The Best Science Fiction Film since E.T," "The Best Acting of the Year," "It Made Me Sing," "It Made Me Laugh Till I Cried," "An Emotional Roller Coaster."

As it is on Broadway—or in the art world—on television, the review can be utilized to help sell a motion picture. It's an acceptable process with a few rules. Some publications will not permit an "advance quote." In other words, if Vincent Canby's review in the New York Times is published on Friday (the day you open your film), you cannot call Vincent up on the previous Monday and ask for an advance peek—a line or two you can use in your opening day ads.

Farming your potential reviews is very serious business. Although it's arguable that a film's box office fate does not rest on the quality of its reviews, many films can derive immeasurable benefit from positive notices. It doesn't hurt to have two TV film critics announce to a national audience that your film rates "two thumbs up." Millions of people are going to see that review. Whether they make up their minds or not at that point, they're probably going to remember the reviewer's opinion.

A Successful Opening Day Review Campaign.

Putting together an opening day review campaign is a very time-consuming complex job. It involves a great deal of phone work, screenings, personal relationships and luck. A successful review campaign can be worth millions of dollars in positive word-of-mouth—and those reviews can be used by other ancillary markets—video, commercial and pay TV, international, etc.

How do you put together a review campaign. Let's look at the steps:

- **Screen, Screen, Screen.** In order to review a film, a critic must first see it. There was a time when you invited a film critic to your main "all media" screening and he or she came. You didn't have to worry about scheduling another screening. These days, arranging for all the right critics to see your movie is a little like a "greased pig" contest and the critics, dare I say, are the little "piggies."

I always assume that if a critic has anything at all to do on the evening you hold your screening, he or she will probably stay away. So I'm beginning to adopt the strategy of East Coast public relations companies—schedule several screenings. How many? In addition to one "all media" screening at one of the big theatres, schedule one of the smaller screening rooms for two or three daytime screenings, say, two at 11:00 a.m. and one at 1:00 p.m. Then schedule a couple of additional weeknight screenings (7:30 p.m. or 8:00 p.m.) in the same smaller screening room. With this many opportunities, it will be hard for any critic to miss seeing your film.

When you're printing your invitations, don't forget to include a "review date." Why? Because, technically, it prevents a reviewer from breaking an early review. Actually, a review date is aimed specifically at the Hollywood trade papers, *Variety* and the *Hollywood Reporter*. If given a review date, they will usually honor it. And it's important for the trade papers to honor your date. If you have, say, a marginal film that could be trashed by the critics, then you don't want that trade review breaking before "Opening Day."

If you don't set a review date, and, let's say, *Variety* breaks on the Monday before your Friday opening, other reviewers may be compelled to also print their reviews early. Printing "Review Date is Opening Day" on your invitations is simply a good safeguard to follow. It will not adversely affect your ability to secure advance review quotes from the critics who will give them, and it could save you from early reviews that could harm the film's box office take.

■ **Farming early reviews: the magazines**. As your film project heads for release, your production and marketing executives are going to start asking about the potential of review quotes. Two to three months out, your first stop is going to be the magazine critic.

Magazine critics are your toughest catch. With their 3-4 month deadlines, the odds are slim that you're going to have a film ready for their screening needs. However, if you are lucky to have a finished film ready, then they're your first objective.

Magazine critic screenings fall into a special category and should not be budgeted with your normal run of release period screenings. Make a list of the national magazines that feature film critics—*Cosmopolitan*, *Glamour*, *Vogue*, etc.—and create a chart of their availabilities. Once you've contacted every critic, you can then set up a screening schedule (most likely, in New York) and invite them. They're going to be difficult to nail down, especially if you're screening something other than a blockbuster with huge stars.

Even though a critic RSVPs for a screening, that's no guarantee that he'll come. Keep up the pressure and provide as many opportunities as your budget will support. If you have a great film that appears to have excellent review potential, then your screening budget should be increased accordingly. Your superiors must understand that it takes time to get your critics in.

Once the critic has seen the film, you need to find out what he thought of it. It's bad etiquette to badger your guests as they walk out of your screening, so I just stand in the lobby and chat. If the critic found the film to be a positive experience, she or he won't mind telling you they liked it. You, of course, have to break out the mental tape recorder and remember every word you hear because there are dozens of people waiting back at your office for a reaction. Sometimes even a tiny whispered positive reaction can give filmmakers a glimmer of hope that perhaps they have a hit on their hands.

On the following day, get on the telephone and try to reach the magazine critics who attended your screening. If you get through, ask: A) What they thought about the film; and B) if it was positive, would they mind offering an advance review quote. Some critics will react positively but state that they can't offer a quote until they write their review. Thus, you might have to wait a few weeks. Since they're supposedly on a three to four month deadline, you should still have a quote in plenty of time for the release of your film.

A potential problem with any review, but it seems especially true with long-lead outlets like magazines, is that a promised review might not get printed. Some critics will offer you a quote only if the review is actually printed in the magazine. Since, the critic will sometimes submit more reviews than space permits, this could be a problem if yours is the unfortunate review that is cut.

As you make your follow up calls, some critics will give you the typical runaround: Call back in a few days, call back after my vacation, let me think about it a little while, call back next month, I can't give out a quote, etc.

Of course, some critics will not like your film and will tell you so. Don't argue with them. Trying to ply a semi-sweet quote out of a film critic who didn't like your film is a tacky, low-class tactic. You'll have enough work just getting a quote out of the positive reviewers.

Keep up the pressure. Be prepared to show your superiors exactly where each of your key magazine critics stands on the quote situation. Don't give up until you: A) get your quote; or B) the critic indicates that it's impossible to give you one at this time. If you get the latter response, put a note on your calendar to maintain contact as you get closer to the release of the film. That magazine critic who couldn't offer you a magazine review quote in June, might have written a newspaper review in August and could have an available quote.

■ **Pre-opening day quotes—the TV and radio press**. Once you've exhausted your magazine critics, your next target is the electronic arena—TV and Radio. Even busier than your print critics, electronic journalists have to be pitched on advance screenings, just as they are pitched on story ideas. My standard pitch is, "I have a film that I really would like to show you at your earliest convenience, how does your schedule look next week?" Keep it low key. Don't start to hype the critic on how great you think the film is, you're just trying to get the critic into the screening room. A standard reply is, "I'll see the film opening week." Which is fine, but it eliminates the possibility of an advance quote.

Booking your film into one of the national review shows (e.g. Siskel & Ebert) is extremely competitive and difficult. Start by contacting the show's producer and mentioning that the film is now available for screening. What will generally happen is that the producer will look at the schedule for the week that your film is opening and find out whether there is an opening on the show. This doesn't necessarily cancel out the possibility of an advance quote, because the shows are all taped in advance. If your film is approved for the show, then you have to make the print available to their critics. This sometimes involves screening in different cities, depending on where the critic's home base is located. Don't hesitate to work your schedule around that of the national critic's. If he or she suddenly needs a print sent to Boston, try to cooperate. You could lose a major national review quote by failing to ship a print on time.

Once the show is taped, the producer will generally provide you with a faxed transcript from which you can pull your quotes. And since the taping usually occurs at least a week before your Friday opening, there's still time to prepare opening day review ads.

Radio reviewers, of which there are a limited number, should be treated in similar fashion. Even though their deadlines can be equally frenetic, I find the radio press easier to deal with and more open to screening possibilities. Don't slight them. A positive review quote from a Westwood One or NBC Radio could be extremely useful in your review campaign.

Do readers pay attention to the source of review quotes? No official studies have been done, but it is unlikely that the average filmgoer can tell the difference between Kevin Thomas of the *Los Angeles Times* and Vincent Canby of the *New York Times*. When the headline reads "Astounding" who cares who said it?

I remember a rather silly but effective campaign for the time-travel comedy, *Bill and Ted's Excellent Adventure* which spoofed the importance of review quotes. Some creative mind in the advertising department made up fantastic superlatives and attributed them to historical figures. (The historical figure angle tied in with the plot of the movie.) "Astounding," said Socrates. "Unbelievable," said Napoleon. "Riveting," observed Beethoven. The film went on to be a major hit at the box office and the campaign was deemed a success.

- **Opening day reviews: culling your quotes**. Opening day is long and busy for me. I try to get to my office in Los Angeles early because East Coast reviews are already arriving via the fax machine. As each review arrives, I read it, searching for positive sentences—the stuff of great quotes. Using a highlighting marker, I'll isolate the positive sentences and send them over, usually in batches, to my marketing department superior.

Who breaks the news to the filmmaker? It's usually me. Since I'm the collector of reviews, I can usually flip through them quickly and find the positive comments that filmmakers yearn for. I find myself spending what seems like hours on the phone reading these choice morsels to the director, writer, producer, star, etc. Actually, you might receive a call from virtually anyone on the production, including the production designer, special effects supervisor, even the stunt coordinator. Have your reading material ready.

Once you've received all of your reviews, and the positive sentences have been culled and highlighted, you can start to prepare a review advertisement with your advertising department.

- **Preparing the review ad**. There's nothing mystical about a review ad. It's simply a collection of your best quotes with the most positive adjectives printed in huge blaring headline type. When their films are particularly well reviewed, it's not uncommon for the major studios to pay for two page advertisements which are a virtual who's who of critical comments.

It always helps when you get early review quotes. Advertising executives like to have a positive quote for their first ads—usually the Sunday before the Friday opening. Unfortunately, most of your reviews are not going to be available before opening day. Your first opportunity to utilize the quotes is going to be in Saturday's paper which is, unfortunately, still one of your smaller ads of the week.

If they've been culled on opening day, your review ad will probably make its biggest impact in the second week of advertising. Hopefully, your film has some box office legs and can hang in there that long. If word-of-mouth is indeed trickling forth, the review ad can only help your campaign. If the movie is dead in the water, even the President of the United States' positive comment won't save it.

Positive reviews can be utilized in other mediums as well. Your advertising department can put them into a television commercial, mixing the typical preview with the positive comments. It becomes a "review spot."

They can even combine the "review spot" with a "testimonial spot" where theatergoers are interviewed outside the theater and talk about how much they loved the film. These kind of advertising devices help built positive word-of-mouth on a film and are fueled by great opening day reviews.

Even if the film bombs, those reviews will still be valuable to the video company that markets the cassette, plus all of the other ancillary avenues the film will take. Keep a supply of the positive reviews available for all parties. As to the fate of your negative reviews, keep them in a dark place, far from your filmmaker's eyes. Don't throw them away. If the film does $100 million in U.S. domestic box office gross, he will probably call you up and ask you to send the negative reviews over to his house for ersatz bathroom wallpaper use. He may also want to send a sweet letter to each critic that slammed the picture.

Your involvement as a publicist in the determination and viability of review ads will vary from company to company. In independent circles, you may have direct involvement. In the major companies, you may be simply the errand boy getting the quotes to the ad department.

However you are involved, remember not only how important those reviews are to the campaign, but that you were the one who coordinated their appearance in the first place. This is another arena where diligent, knowledgeable publicists are worth their weight in box office gold.

35

Continuing Your Media Campaign Through Opening Day

Like the space shuttle, publicity campaigns get extremely exciting prior to launch. If you've been doing your job, there should be a great deal of anticipation in the air. Certainly with the advertising department kicking in with its trailers, television spots and opening day newspaper ads, there is awareness being generated.

You're literally in a horse race and because of the work that you've done, your horse has a reputation. When you started working on the publicity campaign no one knew about your film. It was up to you to educate the media and the public. Now that the film is about to be released, your efforts have produced public awareness and hopefully everyone perceives it as a "sure winner."

What's happening at this stage in your department? You're beginning to wind down. You've completed your press and promotional screenings. Your key press have their editorial press kits in hand. Feature stories are breaking in newspapers and magazines. Video press kits are airing on broadcast and cable outlets. Critics are preparing their reviews. The feverish pace that has been your department's lot the past few months is being transferred over to the advertising department where final ads are being prepared—some of which may contain quotes from the reviews you have helped generate. Don't quite relax yet. You still have final chores to perform.

For instance:

■ **Additional interviews**. If you've got the troops, the interview process can continue up until opening day. Every interview is important for creating awareness and excitement about the imminent release of the film. Since print lead times have passed, you'll be concentrating on last minute electronic media interviews—television and radio.

If you're fortunate, your leading actor will be speaking on one of the "morning shows." If you're even more fortunate, you'll have more than one actor on those shows. It, of course, depends on the film, the stature of the actors, and how persuasive you can be when talking to the talent booker.

Persistence, even at this late date, pays off. Sometimes even your stodgiest film journalist will suddenly be receptive to your pitch. The fact that the film is opening in two days has something to do with it. This is probably the journalist who has continually said, "Call me back closer to release time."

With release imminent, the trade papers—*Hollywood Reporter* and *Daily Variety*—are always on the lookout for a good behind-the-scenes piece. Give them a hook, though. Just the fact that the film is opening on Friday isn't enough.

■ **Dispensing last minute press kits and other materials**. You'd be amazed at how many people come out of the woodwork at the last minute and ask for press materials.

As a rule, I try to keep at least 100 kits in the office for general purpose use. I also like to have a good supply of color transparencies on hand, plus some additional black and white stills beyond those I've chosen for the press kit key set. The last thing you want to do at this late date is go through the re-order process.

Requests come from all sides and in all varieties. Your Denver field agency calls and says the *Denver Post* wants to run a specific color shot on the cover of their Sunday magazine, do you have anything beyond the key set? You go back into your slide book and find the right shot. If there isn't enough time to make a dupe, do you send the original?

Letting original art out of your possession is a risky business, but there are times when the risk is worth it. Let's say the paper wants a specific shot of Dustin Hoffman throwing a baseball. They're doing a special feature on sports themes in current films. You flip through your book(s) of slides and discover just the shot they're looking for. In fact, you see that there are several of the same kind (usually, if the photographer is good, his motor drive was cranking out a series.) If, you have similar shots available, I wouldn't hesitate to send an original slide to a media outlet (for last minute usage). It's not something you should get into the habit of doing, but as long as you label the shot as an original and mention in a cover letter that you would like to have it returned, it should be okay.

Remember, after the release of the picture, most of your materials will be sitting in a closet collecting dust until the video and international releases are scheduled. Even then, those publicity entities have already asked for your own key set as an initial guideline—there being an excellent chance that your original selections will eventually be utilized in all media. Be very possessive about original art, but don't miss a publicity opportunity because you don't have time to get a dupe made.

Although I try to accommodate all media requests, occasionally you have a right to be stingy. You'll get calls from the third cousin of the fifth lead actor requesting a press kit for her collection. Answer: "Sorry, you can eventually make a copy from one in the collection of the Academy of Motion Pictures." You'll get calls from video magazines. Answer: "Contact the video company, they'll be happy to take care of you."

Regarding international press, technically your international department should be handling their requests. However, I have found that on films that are about to enter domestic release, the international departments still haven't begun to set up their campaigns. Since international requests are usually limited to a few calls, I will supply them with kits and color (as long as I have a supply). There is always the possibility that the international rights to your film haven't even been sold yet, so it could be literally months before the international press has a proper contact who can handle international requests.

Be aware of advertising materials—especially "title treatments" (the method in which the title of the film is rendered). Occasionally, publications will request the title treatment for use in the story layout. You should have a contact in your art department who can supply you with a quantity of title treatments. It's a legitimate supply item.

You're also going to get calls for actual advertising materials—known as the "slicks" (because they're printed on glossy paper). I usually refer those calls to the advertising department, although it's always a good idea to have a slick on hand for reference.

It's a good idea to have posters on hand. Those requests will come from many different directions—theaters, journalists, the stars and key behind-the-scenes people, etc. This supply is in addition to the quantity you're using as part of your promotion fulfillment.

T-shirts are great, but I generally find that as soon as the promotions are fulfilled, I quickly run out of shirts. (You should keep a quantity for your top 50 media contacts—they're great "thank you" gifts.)

Keep a good supply of reviews and press clippings on hand. I make photocopied bundles which I can send out easily as the requests come in.

Be aware of musical materials like cassette copies of the soundtrack album or singles, and keep a supply on hand. They also make great thank you gifts for your top media contacts.

■ **Reporting box office figures to the appropriate outlets.** Finally, after many months of preparation, the film opens. You spend the weekend combing the theaters, determining the public reaction to the film you've been publicizing and promoting for the last eight months.

You're on the phone to your superiors, letting them know what you saw, felt, heard. And then Monday morning you're besieged by reporters asking for actual box office figures. What do you do?

First, you should have developed a policy beforehand. There was a time when box office performance was a secret business fact known only by a handful of top level film executives. If you scan the trades of the Fifties and Sixties, there are no box office stats.

Today box office performance is one of the most pervasive forms of motion picture industry news—especially in the Hollywood trade papers where Tuesday is box office news day. In both the *Hollywood Reporter* and *Daily Variety*, the weekend box office performance of virtually every motion picture in release is detailed in a chart and accompanying news story. Each listing includes: the film's title; its studio or independent releasing company; the number of theaters in its release pattern (known as "screens"); the per screen average weekend box office figure (how much money the film made from Friday to Sunday); and the cumulative box office total for that film. The films are ranked in terms of their weekend box office performance.

There are probably many executives who would prefer to keep performance figures secret, but unfortunately the rule these days is full disclosure, often down to the penny. If a studio tries to fudge the box office results on a film that opens badly, the trade journalists will be able to spot the error.

How? Because they most likely subscribe to a national report published by Entertainment Data, which provides a weekly sampling of the national box office performance of top films. If the report, plus the journalist's own estimates of total box office do not coincide with the studio or independent company's reported figure, they will cry foul. Many an embarrassed publicist has read a testy article in the Tuesday trades describing his company's attempt to "cover-up" the truly miserable performance of a certain film.

Let's get back to policy. If you immediately eliminate the idea of distributing falsified figures (as unprofessional and stupid), there are two ways to deal with box office reporting: either provide the figures as soon as they're available, or don't provide them.

Never, repeat never, disperse box office information without the approval of your superior (or the head of the company). In many ways, box office performance is the most sensitive information you can provide to a journalist.

If your movie is looking like a "bomb," the producer may opt for not disclosing any box office figures. So, what do you say to the *Variety* reporter who calls asking for figures? The standard response is, "Sorry, our computer broke down and we can't get our figures today." Every journalist in town knows that's a "cop out," but they have no other choice but to look you up in the Entertainment Data report and estimate numbers on their own.

Non-disclosure is more common with independent companies than the major studios. Whether the movie is a big success or a big fizzle, the majors are inclined to be forthright with their figures. The fact that they're public companies is probably one reason, the other being that they have so many releases, they expect to release a bomb every once in a while. It's the nature of their business.

When your superior leaves it up to you to determine whether to release figures, vote for the computer malfunction. What's interesting about box office results is that only a day or so after the weekly box office report, the story is old business and no longer newsworthy. You also find that the trade papers do not play up the fact that figures were not reported. Generally, they only object when you report the wrong figures.

It's tragic, but nine months of publicity and promotion on your part can sometimes translate into "the film that never was" (at least in terms of box office reporting).

If your film's a smash, then you have the world of possibilities to turn your box office story into a major feature around the country. You might suggest that the trade papers interview your head of distribution. The same executive could be interviewed by other nationally distributed newspaper correspondents: *USA Today*, the *New York Times*, *Wall Street Journal*. Everyone loves a success story and for the time being you're going to be on the top of everyone's entertainment news priority list. Enjoy it while it lasts.

■ **Preparing for renewed interest in the film.** All publicists hope for a smash at the box office. It's not only the natural inclination to pull for a winner. A success at the box office is a natural reward for a long, difficult publicity campaign.

There's an old oft-quoted phrase in Hollywood that success has many parents, but failure is an orphan. That's particularly true of the publicity and promotions department. No matter how much time is involved in a particular campaign, if the movie bombs on its first weekend it's a forgotten entity on Tuesday. It's shocking, but it's the truth.

If your film flops, move on to the next project. A winner, though, begins to produce immediate dividends. It's nice to get a call from *People* magazine, telling you how excited they are for the success of your movie and wondering whether key cast members would be available for a cover photo session—one of those "look what's hot" covers.

Reporters who cover the movie business scene—the same writers who chart box office business—will call and ask for an interview with your marketing or distribution chief. Everyone loves a winner, and Hollywood journalists are particularly interested in what went right.

It's the type of media exposure that everyone prays for. The "post release glow." Take advantage of it. You shouldn't have any problems booking key interviews for your top executives. If your movie is a success at the box office, the journalists will be looking for a story, or they'll be very interested in your pitch.

Post-release publicity on a box office winner is particularly effective for smaller independent films that have opened in limited engagements. In order to increase the all-important word-of-mouth, the smaller films count on those post-release feature stories and interviews. Without the sizable advertising budgets and promotional tie-ins that are common to their big studio brothers, the smaller independents have to seize every opportunity to exploit their success—publicity paves that way.

For the smaller films without the recognizable names and "high concept" plots, a publicist's job often doesn't get into full swing until the post-release period. Keep your eye on the box office results, week to week. Slight percentage drops are common, but if there is a major drop off, then the fate of your film is sealed. Your film could be out of release just as your publicity starts to break.

You're not responsible for box office performance. Don't take it personally if the film bombs. Your job is to take advantage of every possible media break. If the press was not returning your phone calls before release, now is the time to hit them hard. The film is out there, it's been reviewed, it's doing good business, the public is enjoying the experience. We have a story here.

Keep your actors working the talk show circuit. An actor who has a film in general release that is doing business is a far better interview subject because the public can relate to his or her film. If they're intrigued by the interview, they can run out and see the movie right now. Talk show talent bookers can still pass on your interview subject—no matter how well the film is doing. But there's no question that you have a better chance now. Go for it.

If the film's success is tied to a specific location, organization or theme, take advantage of the publicity value in the post-release period. If Chevy Chase's new hit movie is about a specific orphanage in Des Moines, take Chevy back to the home with a photographer. Take one of those post-release celebration photos. Or get a local photographer from AP, UPI or Reuters to snap the photo. It's newsworthy.

Get your actors on the telephone to the nation's columnists. Let them talk about what it's like to bask in the success of their film. Again, everyone loves a winner. If your producer is already talking about a sequel, let him mention it in the columns. It's timely news.

Prepare a new national press release, detailing the cast and crew's reaction to the success of the film. Attach a new photograph (perhaps the "Chevy Chase at the orphanage" shot). The news magazines may pick up on this. *Time Magazine* might schedule a short feature on the film's success—especially if they can tie it to a pop cultural trend. *Entertainment Tonight* might join you at the orphanage for a post-release celebration feature. Whatever you do, enjoy the post release glow. It doesn't come very often.

36

REVIEWING YOUR PUBLICITY AND PROMOTIONS CAMPAIGN

As I mentioned in the previous chapter, once a motion picture bombs at the box office, it's quickly forgotten. Although there are exceptions like *Ishtar* and *Heaven's Gate*—costly failures that had hundreds of stories written about who was responsible and how it could have been done differently—the majority of films simply die quietly—to be resurrected on video cassette.

How does a failure at the box office affect your department? If you've done your job, you have nothing to be ashamed of. Lots of publicity can't hurt a good movie and it can certainly help a bad one.

There are those who believe that hype of the wrong kind *can* hurt a film's chances with the public. A few years ago, Warner Bros. released *The Right Stuff*—a spectacular look at the early days of NASA and the Astronaut training program. Somehow, a great deal of press was generated about Senator John Glenn and how his political campaign was benefitting from the release of the movie. Although director Philip Kaufman's offbeat study of the early days of Project Mercury was apolitical, all the political stories about Senator Glenn may have turned off some potential audiences.

Producer Jack Schwartzman told me another story about publicity which took a negative turn. When Sean Connery was promoting his last James Bond movie, *Never Say Never Again* in 1983, he did his interviews the way he likes to do them—sans toupee. Schwartzman pointed out that in the markets where Connery was particularly visible, the box office actually went down. Why? Young people—the core movie-going audience 12-24 year-olds saw an older, balding 52-year-old man and said, "Who is this old man playing James Bond?" and stayed away in droves.

These are isolated cases, showing that publicity sometimes can affect box office adversely. But in general, publicity doesn't create impressions, either positive or negative, it simply builds awareness. A good P.R. campaign doesn't motivate a person to actually go to the cinema. The subject matter of the movie, the star appeal, the critical reactions, word-of-mouth recommendations are what influence people to line up at the box office.

Probably because most executives don't think of publicity as being a major player in the success or failure of their film, they seldom ask you for a report evaluating how your campaign worked, and didn't work. However, I have gotten into the habit of sending key executives a little good-bye present of newspaper and magazine clippings and TV transcripts and, on occasion, a typed list of all breaks.

Again, if you feel strongly about your campaign, you have nothing to worry about, even if the film bombed. Job security? That can be a problem even if the film is a success. Experts say that job security doesn't exist in the entertainment business. I maintain that if you're secure in your career performance, you will always work, regardless of how many companies change management. You may not be working for the same company, but good publicity and promotions executives are always in demand.

If you decide to work in movies, don't be surprised if your company suddenly makes a change in its ranks—in other words, you're laid off, fired, let go, canned—whatever euphemism you like. Like major league baseball teams, new top level management executives like to clean house. The fact that you're fired may have absolutely nothing to do with your performance—and it probably doesn't. The President simply likes to work with an old friend in public relations who is going to take your job. It's not right, it's not logical—but it's an accepted practice.

Whether or not the fate of the film affects your job security, you should always keep in the back of your mind a set of post release evaluation criteria so that you, yourself, can evaluate your performance. You never know when a new generation of top level executives will come and demand post-release evaluation reports, oral and written, as if they've always existed.

Let's look at some of the questions you might ask yourself to evaluate all of your hard work. The success or failure of your film really doesn't matter, what you need to evaluate is your individual performance.

■ Did you contact all appropriate media and provide them with the correct materials? You should have been keeping detailed check lists so you know at a glance who has been contacted and who hasn't. Earlier in the book I discussed how absolutely vital it is to contact everyone on your list. The publicist's nightmare is to be asked by your superior for a reaction from a certain media person which you've forgotten to contact at all! It's perfectly acceptable to say you haven't had any response from an important journalist. You could lose your job, though, if you say you forgot to contact her.

Another nice thing about check lists is that you can easily turn them into a post-release publicity evaluation. You simply transfer the names to a new list and add notes on the progress of each contact (whether the story broke; whether they passed; whether it's pending, etc.).

And don't fudge it. Be prepared to discuss virtually every contact on the list. If you say you've contacted *Time Magazine* and your superior discovers that you haven't, again, start looking for a new line of work.

■ Did your available talent accomplish all they could—media wise? Another checklist should be kept of your available talent and how they helped the campaign. It's doubtful that your superior will ever ask you whether you utilized your talent to the best of their availability, but you should be prepared, anyway.

You also don't want to be caught in a situation where a certain individual informs your superior that he was available for interviews, but nobody called him. That can be as embarrassing as forgetting to call *Time Magazine*.

Most of the time actors will not come back to haunt you. Publicity is not their most favorite activity and if you don't contact them, they're more likely to thank you than complain.

■ Were you able to create some excitement about the film? Instinctively, you'll know whether this is true. It's a case of adding everything up in your head—breaks, stunts, promotions, media interest in the film, discussion on the street, awareness. Excitement is a relative term which can have virtually no effect on box office. *Ishtar* was one film that had a very exciting publicity campaign. The Columbia Pictures publicity department had a lock on virtually every major magazine cover and Dustin Hoffman and Warren Beatty (certainly not known for their high media profile) were featured on television programs coast to coast. Was there any box office excitement? After moviegoers had their first taste the first weekend, word-of-mouth dowsed any further excitement.

During an effective publicity campaign, events happen every day. Column items break, stories are pitched and there's interest, a TV show is going to feature a piece the following day, a promotion comes through, a stunt's working, more column breaks—all of this begins to add up to "excitement" as you close in on the release date. Even your boss is getting excited as you wear out the rug coming into his office with more publicity reports. It's up to you to spread the word every time something breaks. Memo everyone about upcoming publicity breaks. More memos means more excitement. In the cosmic scheme, a Page 12 story in *Teen Dream* may not be the biggest event, but in the universe of your publicity campaign it's another little bit of news that fuels your excitement machine.

■ How difficult is it to establish the effectiveness of your publicity campaign? In reality, it's very difficult. If the advertising department purchases a 30-second spot on a top rated network television show, they have a formula for determining the number of people who watched that spot. They can justify the huge expense by quoting numbers. Advertising is a numbers game.

Publicity and promotion is not a numbers game. Yes, you can supply your superiors with the rating of a show which featured one of your stars. You can type up lists of all your breaks, but in the long run publicity evaluation is purely subjective. It's your boss' feeling about whether your campaign had enough breaks or not, or whether the publicity you generated was of the right kind, or if you "busted your buns" hard enough.

Your own assessment of the job you did is just as important as anyone else's. Your post-production review, even if it's just for yourself, should be honest and should document everything you did—even those things that didn't work so well. Getting into the habit of doing a rigorous postmortem will do almost as much good for your career as getting that lucky blockbuster.

There's no question in my mind that if you cover your bases, contact the media, develop the breaks and report the progress to your superior on a continual basis, then you will receive a positive evaluation. Whether you ever work again depends, of course, on how you market yourself. The professional publicist always keeps track of his media successes and the campaigns that worked.

In a business where experience is everything, the ability to name drop film titles and the idiosyncrasies of their publicity campaigns is a valuable asset.

37

THE FUTURE OF MOTION PICTURE PUBLICITY AND PROMOTION

Gaining The Respect We Deserve.

Why is it that every year the cost of advertising rises and the number of available publicity jobs appears to fall? Why is it that a field which should have strong acceptance and be included in *every* motion picture campaign is often struggling for respect?

One reason could be the gradual transformation in the movie business in the last twenty-five years from a showman's medium to a businessman's medium. In the days of the big studios, the moguls were showmen. Of course they knew they had to show a profit, they had to show a good reason to make a picture, but they also were well aware of how their films could be turned into events, how their actors could become stars and how much a well-oiled publicity machine was vital to their success.

Today, many, but not all, studio executives and producers come from a different background. Many are trained lawyers, MBA graduates, agents, deal makers—they understand the business end of show business—but they've forgotten how to be showmen.

Putting a movie deal together is simply a collecting process for today's studio execs. They collect a director here, a star there, a cameraman, etc. Someone points out to them that they need a publicist and they say, "Oh, yeah" and they hire one.

Publicity is difficult to understand if you're used to plugging figures into spreadsheets and staring at the bottom line. How do you gauge the success of a publicity campaign in terms of dollars and cents? There are statistics to show how many movie-goers are being "delivered" for every advertising dollar spent. But how do you count heads in a publicity campaign? Because of this difficulty in quantifying the effectiveness of publicity, many studio execs today fail to give the publicity department the same kind of respect they give to an advertising department or a media buying department.

Can we change this attitude? Yes! To get more respect, we need to start thinking of ourselves and our jobs in a more professional way. Too many times, unqualified film publicists are hired onto a job. They fail to do their work properly and they give the profession a bad name.

For many years, publicity jobs were an opportunity for a free ride—a chance to play in the film business, to do a minimum amount of work and get paid good sums for it. Publicity jobs were plentiful then and there were enough top quality professionals doing their job to disguise the fact that there were some n'er-do-wells in the mix.

With fewer jobs available today, there's no room for the unprofessional. It's simple, really. If a producer feels that a publicist is doing a great job of supporting the picture, he'll be apt to hire that publicist again. Good work is rewarded in the movie business. If the publicist performs poorly, the consequences not only hurt that publicist's chances for work, but that of the entire profession.

There are producers out there who feel they can get along without a publicity arm. They may eventually hire an agency to represent the film during its release period, but they'll seldom hire a a unit publicist or turn to a publicity expert to help keep the film alive during post-production.

This may seem like a tirade against attitudes or an oversimplification of circumstances, but I've worked with many producers who have no respect for the publicity and promotion department. Their attitude is probably based on experience; they may have never worked with a publicist who bothered to show them that publicity really counts.

We can help solve this perception problem. We can be publicity activists and make our job "high profile." We can't be scared rabbits anymore, fearful of our jobs and afraid to speak our piece. A low-profile publicist keeps in the background sending out an occasional press release, feeding an occasional column item and scheduling an occasional interview. Publicity requires the cooperation of producers, actors and many other people involved in a production. A low profile publicist doesn't want to appear aggressive lest that all important cooperation should disappear.

That's one way of looking at it. The other way is to realize that you have a big job to do and that you're going to have to "bother" a lot of people if you're going to get your job done.

Becoming more high profile means doing things which get you noticed by other departments. Get involved in the marketing process early. When you do early photo sessions, think of special shots which might be useful in an advertising campaign later. Always try to develop high profile publicity opportunities: pitch ideas that could turn into cover stories, not just column pieces.

Being high profile requires that you work hard and *produce* good publicity. The more tasks you accomplish during any aspect of the campaign—pre-production to pre-release—the more opportunities you have to call attention to your job. If publicity reports are regularly crossing a producers desk, he or she will at the very least become curious about all your activity. A little curiosity can lead to understanding more about what you do to earn your salary. And understanding will certainly lead to respect as long as you do your job well.

Computerization.

Computers are already having a strong impact on today's publicity campaigns. Computers and "word processing" make writing, and rewriting much easier than it used to be in the days of the typewriter. In the old days, if a producer didn't like the way a press release was composed, he would suggest changes, then more changes, and more changes. The poor publicist would present his or her release, listen to those changes and return to the typewriter to re-type the whole release—sometimes needing to change only a word or two. Today, thanks to computers, publicists can make the required revisions and reprint the whole document in record time. Also these days, publicists are beginning to share information "on disk" as well as in the traditional hard copy format. For instance, it is now routine for unit publicists to turn in their production press kits on disk. If you've ever re-typed a 35 page press kit, you know how valuable computers can be.

Computers are also marvelous for mailing list management. Although gathering a list and keeping it current can be a full-time job, the computer makes sorting, organizing, changing and printing out things like lists and mailing labels a simple operation, rather than an impossible task. What formerly took dozens of hours at the typewriter can now be accomplished with a few keystrokes.

Computers also allow you to send out letters to hundreds of media people that sound personalized without having to actually type each one. Any good word processing program will let you merge name and address information and little tidbits of personal information into the body of a form letter. Again, a few keystrokes and you have "personal" letters tumbling out of your laser printer. I like to use my computer and a laser printer even if every letter is exactly the same, addressed to "Dear Member of the Music Branch of the Motion Picture Academy." Laser printers are fast and the output usually looks better than running your letterhead through the photocopier.

A caveat to the computer novice. You must pay attention to the new and strange ways computers "think." For instance when you're printing a form letter with a different name on each one, you have to *tell* the computer to change the salutation each time it changes the name. It's quite the faux pas to have a letter addressed to Joe Smith with a salutation: Dear Mary Anne.

In the future, computers will become even more helpful to the publicist. Modems, which connect computers via the telephone lines, will offer publicists direct access to the computers of journalists, editors and producers of talk shows. Imagine a unit publicist operating a portable computer out of a camper on location in the Amazon jungle, being able to send messages, press releases and pitch letters directly into a journalist or editor's computer. Not only will this type of communication come to replace fax machines, it will actually change the relationship between the publicist and the journalist. If your words and ideas are already in the computer of the person you want to write a story for you, won't it be much easier for them to "cut and paste" your ideas into a story, put their name on it and send it along (again via modem) to a newspaper, magazine or TV show?

Direct Mail.

As we finish out the 20th Century, the motion picture business' use of direct mail is still in its infancy. How often do you, as a private citizen, receive material on upcoming movies? Probably not very often. But direct mail promotions are being used by more and more businesses. You receive catalogues from department stores, newsletters from utility companies, petitions from animal rights organizations, even telephone numbers and delivery information from the local pizzeria. It is only a matter of time before movie companies and local movie houses team up for direct mail campaigns to their customers. As information becomes more and more computerized, it will be relatively simple to target an audience—say people who purchased more than $50 worth of movie tickets—and send promotional pieces about your movies directly to their homes.

Up until now direct mail has taken a back seat to all other forms of promotion. Advertising executives have felt that television advertisements, although more expensive, were worth it because of their strong visual impact. However, television's advantage will be diluted as direct mail can reach really targeted audiences. A mailing piece to a target audience who you know will be receptive could be more cost effective than a TV commercial which is broadcast to millions.

As computerized mailing lists which target frequent filmgoers are made available, sometimes being able to isolate things like *all the teenagers in Philadelphia who saw Boyz N The Hood*, studios and theatre owners will be able to do joint promotions which key off the interests of a particular audience. They'll offer preview information, opening dates, key cast and crew members, photographs, games, film clubs, even promotional items. Being able to share promotional costs with theatres will make direct mail especially attractive.

If a prominent credit card company has information in its computer banks that isolates all card holders that purchased golf equipment last year, there's no reason why a studio can't produce a mailing list that isolates frequent filmgoers—the type of audience that could respond to a direct mail campaign. Direct mail campaigns will become a staple of all future movie marketing campaigns. The publicity and promotional possibilities are endless.

The Future of Video Promotion.

While computers have revolutionized communication in America, the video tape recorder has revolutionized home entertainment. Publicists have already discovered the value of a video press kit when dealing with the entertainment-oriented shows like *ET* and E! Entertainment Channel. But some of these tapes, copied onto VHS format are also finding their way to print journalists who can watch them on their home video machines. It's an electronic pitch and the price of the tape and duplication is low enough to justify a special mailing to "key" journalists.

Watching behind-the-scenes footage and interviews may spark a print journalist to set up his own set visit or interview. Video is simply another ace in the publicist's pitch deck.

Given the proliferation of home video players, certain entrepreneurial individuals are already developing video products that can be used in a direct mail campaign or a point of purchase promotion. These video "magazines" are often financed by third party companies that insert their commercials onto the actual program.

Since the American filmgoer is so visually oriented, the idea of monthly video magazines is not that far-fetched. *Playboy Magazine* pioneered the idea with their *Playboy Video* series which is sold in your local video store just like a magazine. *National Geographic* also markets a video series of their top specials. Even behind-the-scenes documentaries on top movies often get individual video marketing campaigns simply because the shows are so interesting.

If the tapes can be produced, duplicated and marketed inexpensively enough, they also make great premium items. A national auto parts retailing chain may purchase 50,000 video documentaries on the making of a new auto racing movie and then give them away to their top customers.

Satellite Distribution.

You don't have to be a science fiction writer to envision publicists of the future sending information via satellite from movie sets directly to television stations around the world. The technology already exists and is employed every day by news trucks that are equipped with satellite dishes. How long before miniature dishes will make direct satellite transmission feasible for movie studios and even individual publicists?

Whereas it's always been difficult to pitch canned pieces to the major TV news networks, the number of entertainment outlets has increased dramatically in recent years, providing more outlets for your video materials. Morning and afternoon talk and "infotainment" shows, cable movie channels, MTV and other speciality outlets are constantly in need of up-to-the-minute entertainment news. The satellite dish can be that source.

Kiosks at the Shopping Mall.

The shopping mall is a natural venue for spreading movie news. Studio marketing departments haven't been blind to the fact that the mall has replaced the corner drug store as the meeting ground of today's youth and frequent filmgoer. Movie companies have already tried to reach this crowd with various promotional ideas. One of the most common is a video kiosk that simply plays trailers from upcoming films. Universal Pictures used them effectively a few years ago in the Westwood area of Los Angeles—where frequent filmgoers congregate. And similar kiosks have been placed in malls around the country.

Ideally, if an arrangement can be made with a local mall, a kiosk should become a permanent exposition in the top 25 markets. It can be the focal point for all types of movie promotions. Giveaways, interviews, surveys and promotional events can all be conducted around the kiosk.

The viability of a permanent film promotion kiosk depends on the future relationship between studio marketing departments and the exhibition community. The theater owner has already established a foothold in the mall and is probably responsible for a majority of the mall's foot traffic. It's up to the studio to capitalize on that relationship.

The Publicist as Catalyst.

You can talk about the whiz bang applications of future computers, videos, satellite dishes and kiosks, but the true future of publicity depends on one thing—the publicist.

A new generation of outspoken, adventurous and determined publicists is needed. They will generate new ideas. Some will recall the high-spirited hustling of the early movie moguls, some will be strictly 21st Century. But they will share one thing in common—a strong ongoing desire to be a part of the creative process of movie-marketing.

We need them. We need creative thinkers and doers. People who love movies and who will go to great lengths to guarantee them the exposure they need. People who aren't afraid of rejection, who will circulate a dozen ideas to get one of them moving. People who realize that there are no rules in the publicity business and that every idea has merit.

Where will these future publicists come from? Probably not from film schools. They're too busy turning out the writers and directors of the future. It's too bad, because our film schools desperately need a marketing discipline.

Many of them will come from the P.R. agency battlegrounds where vital publicity disciplines are learned on the firing line. Others will wander in by accident and stay because they like the work.

As the movie business gets more and more business-like, publicity and promotion still requires showmanship. P.T. Barnum was a huckster and a great promoter. Those with a little Barnum hucksterism in their personalities will succeed dramatically in a publicity career. You can make a living by doing the job, staying out of the spotlight and trying to keep your superiors happy. Or you can make a career out of making the impossible happen with fresh ideas. Be bold, be dynamic, be informed and you will be successful. Opportunity awaits!

APPENDIX

The following pages show samples of publicity materials. These few examples by no means represent *all* the different letters, press releases, memos and pitch letters publicists write on a daily basis, but they do illustrate many of the types of written communication discussed in the book. Also there are some photos of actual publicity events staged by the author.

"SPACEHUNTER: ADVENTURES IN THE FORBIDDEN ZONE"

Production Information

Outer-space travel and planetary adventure make a stunning 3-D debut in "Spacehunter: Adventures in the Forbidden Zone," a sci-fi fantasy thriller directed by Lamont Johnson and starring Peter Strauss and Molly Ringwald. With spectacular 3-D images, in space and on the surface of a devastated world of the 22nd Century, "Spacehunter" takes a quantum leap beyond all previous 3-D experiences.

Although this $12-million space saga emphasizes vigorous action, featuring hordes of alien creatures and mutant humanoids, director Lamont Johnson also introduces a surprisingly strong human story about two space tramps who form an uneasy partnership. The story of how these two fiercely independent loners, Captain Wolff (Strauss) and Niki (Ringwald), grow to respect and care for one another shapes the real backbone of "Spacehunter."

Equally startling is the fact that 3-D is used subtly in the film. Unlike the glut of exploitation films that have used the third dimension to continually assault audiences with spears, knives, fire balls and anything else they can throw at the camera, "Spacehunter" emphasizes story, not effects. Consequently, the 3-D element adds a realistic dimension to the film. Audiences will be transported through outer space to the surface of the plague-infested planet Terra Eleven.

-more-

"SPACEHUNTER" - Production Information...-2-

"Spacehunter: Adventures in the Forbidden Zone" is an Ivan
Reitman Production of a Lamont Johnson Film, produced by Don
Carmody, John Dunning and Andre Link. Ivan Reitman is executive
producer. Directed by Lamont Johnson, the screenplay is by Edith
Rey & David Preston and Dan Goldberg & Len Blum based on an original
story idea by Stewart Harding and Jean Lafleur.

About the Story...

Wolff, a wily salvage pilot, responds quickly and decisively
to a galactic distress signal from the shipwrecked spacecraft,
the Eridani Princess. Onboard are three lovely space maidens who
become marooned on the plague-infested planet Terra Eleven.
Reaching the planet, Wolff goes in search and is joined by Niki,
the orphaned survivor of an abortive medical rescue mission that
took place years earlier. Desperate for food and shelter, Niki
offers to lead Wolff into the Forbidden Zone, a region infested
with strange creatures and wandering bands of plague-carrying
mutants.

Joining Wolff and Niki on their trek to the Zone are
Washington (Ernie Hudson), the Terra Sector Chief and an old
space buddy of Wolff's; Chalmers (Andrea Marcovicci), Wolff's
comely and resourceful chief engineer; and the Patterson brothers,
Duster (Patrick Rowe) and Jarrett (Paul Boretski), two courageous
Techno-cyclists.

Ruling over this wasteland is the tyrannical Overdog (Michael
Ironside), a renegade Earth scientist who came to power by hoarding
the desperately needed plague serum. Dying of plague himself,

-more-

"SPACEHUNTER" - Production Information...-3-

Overdog lives in the Graveyard City, an eerie metropolis built upon the scavenged hulks of rotting spaceships and smashed industrial technology. Kept alive in a life-support pod that has reduced him to half-man/half-machine, Overdog is tended to by a legion of followers, including the nefarious Chemist (Hrant Alianak), another plague victim who eventually captures the three space maidens: Nova (Cali Timmins), Meagan (Deborah Pratt) and Reena (Aleisa Shirley).

Using Niki's skills as a guide, Wolff journeys across the planet, encountering numerous deadly adversaries, including the Trike gladiators who travel on three-wheel war chariots; the flying Vultures; the strange mutant children of the Junkyard; the swamp-dwelling, Amazon-like Barracuda Women; the ravenous, grossly corpulant Bat People; and, finally, the ragtag mercenary soldiers of the Overdog himself. Against this miserable army, Wolff leads a formidable convoy of armored vehicles, including the Scrambler, a rocket-equipped, all-terrain assault jeep; the Ramrod, a steam-roller-like mobile battering ram; and the roll-cycles, strange canopied motorcycles equipped with revolving laser cannons.

About the Cast...

In his first feature film role since rocketing to fame on television, PETER STRAUSS takes an unorthodox step in his distinguished acting career by portraying the brave and daring space pilot, Wolff. A native New Yorker, Strauss rose to stardom as Rudy Jordache in the immensely popular television series, "Rich Man, Poor Man." Yet it was his portrait of Rain Murphy, a convicted

-more-

Two views of the *Born American* parade, held on Hollywood Blvd. on opening day in August 1986. Costumes added realism to the event which was billed as a "Soviet Invasion of Hollywood, California." Wire photos circulated throughout the Southwest, while TV coverage helped spur excitement over the LA opening.

"PORKY'S II: THE NEXT DAY"

Production Information

The most successful movie comedy of 1982 has a sibling:
Bob Clark's continuing comedy of juvenile misadventure,
"Porky's II: The Next Day," a 20th Century-Fox release of
a Simon/Reeves/Landsburg Productions and Astral Bellevue
Pathe Inc. presentation.

Thanks to director/co-writer/co-producer Bob Clark,
whose "Porky's" turned a $4.5 million investment into a
$110 million plus boxoffice smash, the boys from mythical
Angel Beach High are back in action, turning their town
and school upside down. Having eliminated Porky Wallace's
infamous Everglades nightclub, they're now introduced to
their latest nemesis -- fiery, backwoods bigot Reverend
Bubba Flavel. His targets: the school's Shakespeare Festival
and a young Seminole Indian boy essaying Romeo. The innocent
tribute soon explodes in a townwide controversy that threatens
to engulf our heroes -- until they strike back with an ex-
plosively comic scheme.

Meanwhile, the raunchy pranks that made "Porky's" a
household word in America last year, continue in the sequel.
Determined to impress his new girlfriend Wendy Williams
(KAKI HUNTER), as well as the lusty appetites of his com-
panions, bumbling Peewee Morris (DAN MONAHAN) continues his
search for the experienced woman who can satisfy everyone.

(More)

"PORKY'S II: THE NEXT DAY"...Production Information   -2-

Simultaneously, Tommy (WYATT KNIGHT) whose wrenching shower
room encounter in the first film miserably backfired, finds
himself once more matching wits with the humorless physical
education instructor, Beula Balbricker (NANCY PARSONS).

The rest of the Angel Beach gang -- Tim (CYRIL O'REILLY),
Mickey (ROGER WILSON), Anthony "Meat" (TONY GANIOS), Billy
(MARK HERRIER) and Brian (SCOTT COLOMBY) -- tangle with
lecherous politicians, corrupt officials, carnival sirens
and, above all, their own youthful urges.

Also reprising their original roles are ART HINDLE, as
a bemused police officer; ERIC CHRISTMAS, as the embattled
high school principal; ROD BALL as Steve, whose masquerade
as a drunken ghoul in the town's graveyard is one of the film's
wacky moments; JACK MULCAHY as Frank whose "frog" jokes bounded
through the original and ILSA EARL who expands her role as
Peewee's drama teacher mother.

Representing the new team members are JOSEPH RUNNING FOX
(a real-life Pueblo Indian, portraying a Seminole in "Porky's
II"), who stars as the determined young acting student who
runs afoul of the local segregationists; BILL WILEY, as the
teenagers' new antagonist, Bubba Flavel; CISSE CAMERON, the
lovely carnival stripper who, in an elaborate prank perpe-
trated against Peewee, becomes "Graveyard Gloria"; and
finally, ED WINTER, the corrupt city commissioner who makes
a costly political mistake when he turns traitor and supports
the anti-Shakespeare coalition.

Bob Clark's unique brand of nostalgia, in the 1950'S,
once again pervades the second chapter in the "Porky's" saga.

(More)

"PORKY'S II: THE NEXT DAY"...Production Information   -3-

It is still 1954. The kids continue to hangout at Deadbeat's
Drive-in on the beach. Women's liberation, rock music and
sexual freedom are unheard of. And nothing comes quite easy
for the kids from Angel Beach, even in the quiet, in between
times of the Eisenhower Era.

Perhaps the key to his success with these young actors
is the pure simplicity that Clark brings to his story. In
"Porky's II: The Next Day," good and evil remain easily dis-
cernible, and even as both sides clash, the results are pretty
harmless.

In the latest story though, the comedy is delivered on
a more spectacular level, reminiscent of the pranks in '30s
screwball comedies, when shots were taken at the hypocritical
society of the period.

"Actually," says Clark, "the first film was more of a
farce and if there were any social comments, they were very
subliminal. 'Porky's II' is just as ribald in nature, but has
an expanded view of society. Rather than just another 'rites
of passage' story chronicling the emergence of young manhood
depicted in the first film, we now explore their attitudes
towards the society which surrounds them. In doing so, we
can make some comments about the hypocritical social con-
sciousness present at that time."

Taking advantage of the tranquil, tropical locations in
South Florida, Clark broadens the scope of the "Porky's" saga.
Reverend Flavel's anti-Shakespearean rally is recreated in
full blown splendor, utilizing hundreds of extras, who portray
the embattled townspeople of Angel Beach and the pious "Righteous

(More)

"PORKY'S II : THE NEXT DAY"...Production Information   -4-

Flock" of rabble rousers.

Additionally, Clark and his able casting directors have assembled a large body of Seminole Indians from various regions of Florida, who get their just revenge on their adversaries during a comical sequence in the school gymnasium. Other stand-out moments in "Porky's II: The Next Day," include a frolic through the town graveyard, a moment of retribution in Miss Balbricker's school restroom and a Shakespearean costume festival that presents various members of the youthful acting troupe in an entirely novel light.

Whomever the character, wherever the action, Bob Clark's "Porky's" saga steamrolls its way forward in its second chapter, bringing together all of the humorous elements that guaranteed the first "Porky's" its unprecedented boxoffice success, and to its players the adoration of a hero hungry American public.

*

Simon/Reeves/Landsburg Productions and Astral Bellevue Pathe Inc. present Bob Clark's "Porky's II: The Next Day," a 20th Century-Fox release starring Dan Monahan, Wyatt Knight, Mark Herrier, Roger Wilson, Cyril O'Reilly, Tony Ganios, Kaki Hunter, Scott Colomby, Nancy Parsons, Edward Winter and Art Hindle. Bob Clark directs from a screenplay by Roger E. Swaybill, Alan Ormsby and himself. The film is produced by Don Carmody and Bob Clark.

The 1987 *Witchboard* promotion at the Hollywood Wax Museum. The giant Ouija board was an oversized duplicate of the "killer board" which was the real star of the movie. The "haunted" Hollywood Wax Museum proved to be the ideal location for an opening day publicity stunt which featured stars from the film, costumed witches and a board game where dollar amounts were hidden under the letters and numbers.

The 1986 *Rad* Promotional Tour involved a 9,000mile tour with an enthusiastic group of acrobatic bicyclists in a convoy of vans which were painted and equipped with video display units. Media coverage was the main goal, but in addition to many talk show appearances, the bicyclists were featured at major sporting events, including NBA basketball gamed, NASCAR automobile races and shopping malls.

ENDANGERED SPECIES

Mankind is the "Endangered Species" in writer/director Alan Rudolph's dark thriller for MGM about an investigation into one of this decade's greatest unsolved mysteries. The film marks television superstar Robert Urich's motion picture debut as Ruben Castle, a tough, cynical ex-New York detective whose retirement in rural Colorado is jolted by a bizarre plague of cattle mutilations. Urich is teamed with JoBeth Williams, who portrays a stalwart Colorado sheriff whose own investigation is stonewalled by local intrigue and government red tape. Together, these two law enforcement officers enter a tangled, perplexing web of fear and destruction that threatens their lives -- and perhaps the fate of the entire planet.

The fourteen year old mystery of cattle mutilation provides the mysterious background to this suspenseful story by Judson Klinger and Richard Woods, with a screenplay by Alan Rudolph and John Binder, emphasizing human relationships that undergo profound changes as the mystery is unraveled. "Endangered Species" is filled with mysterious, troubled, people like cattleman Ben Morgan (HOYT AXTON) who holds the tiny town of Buffalo, Colorado in an iron grip; Joe Hiatt (PAUL DOOLEY) a New York newspaperman/turned local journalist who is investigating a major exposé story; teenager Mac Castle (MARIN KANTER) a precociously "tough" young woman looking for a home and a father to

-2-

love; and Boyd Emmer (HARRY CAREY JR.), a local veternarian who finds the mutilated cattle the most perplexing case in his career.

What these characters eventually find is a story stranger than Three Mile Island, that turns their quiet town into a battleground of confusion. What happens to the citizens of tiny Buffalo, Colorado could eventually be unleashed to destroy every living being on Earth.

"Endangered Species" weaves a story as fresh as today's television news commentary; its special brand of fear is as real as a nuclear power disaster or an exploding volcano. But, while there are visible clues to the causes of these disasters, "Endangered Species" offers a deeper, more complex mystery.

Filmed entirely on location in the natural wonderlands of Wyoming and Colorado, "Endangered Species" is the second feature film collaboration for producer Carolyn Pfeiffer and Director Alan Rudolph. Under the Alive Enterprises banner, they previously teamed on the contemporary musical comedy, "Roadie." "Endangered Species," is released in the United States and Canada by MGM/UA Entertainment Co.

Based on actual events, the film was researched by a team of professional journalists who conducted interviews throughout the Western United States, culling material on the mutilation plagues from newspaper files, news documentaries, and numerous magazine articles. Every facet of the mystery has been documented.

THE MYSTERY

In the Fall of 1967, an Alamosa, Colorado rancher found a two year old gelding named "Snippy" out on the range, its body

A CAPSULE HISTORY OF 3-D

Since the very beginning of motion picture history, pioneer filmmakers and studio entrepreneurs have tried to create an artistically interesting and commercially viable 3-D film process. With its stunning dimensional images, in outer space and on the surface of a plague-ravaged world of the 22nd Century, Columbia Pictures' "Spacehunter: Adventures in the Forbidden Zone" takes an ambitious and spectacular quantum leap over all previous 3-D ventures. Its "state of the art" technology, engineered and refined by 3-D expert Ernest McNabb, is the product of nearly a century of research and experimentation in the 3-D field.

Interest in dimensional art forms actually dates back to the ancient Greeks, Romans and Egyptians, who utilized "interposition" to obtain depth and perspective in their magnificent sculptings. In that ancient world, the Sphinx, the Colossus of Rhodes and the Temple of Zeus were the 3-D creations of their day, designed to impress the public with an outsized portrait of reality.

A continual fascination with dimensional art proceeded down through the ages, advanced by such masters as Michelangelo and Da Vinci, and it was only a matter of time before such creativity could be applied to more complex mediums.

Interest in 3-D began to build following the birth of modern photography techniques in the mid-19th Century (Mathew Brady and daguerreotype). Three-dimensional images were first introduced in

-more-

CAPSULE HISTORY OF 3-D...-2-

film form in 1838 when Englishman Sir Charles Wheatstone invented
the stereoscope, a viewing apparatus in which individual "slides"
were presented in three dimensions through a prism technique.
Brought to America as the "Stereoptican," this device was greeted
enthusiastically by the public and, right up to the 1950s, the
3-D viewer was a popular item among school children.

Beginning in the early 1900s, several attempts were made to
create 3-D motion picture films. One of the earliest was that of
William Friese-Greene, the British motion picture pioneer, who
patented a 3-D movie process that used two films projected side
by side on the screen. The viewer had to use an actual stereoptican
to see the depth, at that time making it impractical for theatrical
use. Many of the 3-D experiments completed in the early 1900s were
similarly clumsy and ill-suited for mass-market exploitation.

The first major breakthrough came in 1921 when pioneer stereog-
rapher Jacob Leventhal, with the aid of Billy Bitzer (D.W. Griffith's
cameraman), introduced the "Plastigrams," the first of the "anaglyphic"
3-D movies. This method utilized two cameras photographing separate
images, which were then projected through red and green color filters.
To unscramble the image, the patron was given the first 3-D glasses,
each lens coated with a similar red and green filter. When the
eye looks through the corresponding colors in the glasses, the
images separate and the one eye sees only red images and the other
eye, green images. Presto! 3-D movies.

Abandoning the purely documentary approaches to 3-D films,
feature films began to appear in U.S. theaters, the first being
"The Power of Love," which opened at the Ambassador Theater in
Los Angeles on September 27, 1922, to favorable reviews.

-more-

CAPSULE HISTORY OF 3-D...-3-

Throughout the 1920s and 1930s, filmmakers experimented with various 3-D systems. In addition to the "anaglyphs," there was the "Teleview" system in which each theater seat was equipped with motor-driven viewing devices synchronized with the projector, which alternately blocked the left and right eyes. The "parallax stereogram," developed by the Russian Semyon Ivanov, projected double images on a specially constructed grid screen made up of 36,000 copper wires radiating in three directions. Although the expense of constructing the Ivanov screen was enormous, the system eliminated the need for glasses. Finally, the "Polarized" system began appearing in Europe in the late 1930s.

In 1932, while still an undergraduate at Harvard, Edwin H. Land developed a light-polarizing material that could be manufactured economically. The principle of "polarizing" filters had long been understood, but Land was the first to find a way to make polarizing material in quantity. Basically, the polarizing filter acts as a comb that allows light to pass through only if its waves are oriented in the same direction as the lines on the filter. Two filters placed across each other at right angles effectively block out all light. Polarizing filters could be made to do what anaglyph filters had done before: block out one of two images projected on a motion picture screen, with the added advantage that they caused no color distortion. Polarized light at last allowed the projection of full-color, three-dimensional films.

The polarization breakthrough was first exploited by German filmmakers in 1937. "You Can Nearly Touch It" (utilizing polarized viewers made by the Zeiss Company) became the first color 3-D feature

-more-

CAPSULE HISTORY OF 3-D...-4-

(with sound). American filmmaker John Norling then followed with a 15-minute short about the construction of a Chrysler motor car which had a spectacular debut at the New York World's Fair in 1939.

The outbreak of World War II temporarily halted the expanding tide of three-dimensional films. Between 1939 and 1951, the "polarized filter" system was refined, but it wasn't until 1952 that a shrewd Hollywood showman engineered the first commercial film blockbuster to take advantage of "state of the art" 3-D technology.

Timing was everything for ex-radio writer turned film producer Arch Oboler. In 1952, the motion picture industry was battling television in an ever-expanding war for audiences. The public was staying home to watch the little magic box, and studio executives were growing desperate to fill their dwindling number of theaters. In stepped Oboler with a little jungle exploitation film called "Bwana Devil." The film, which co-starred Robert Stack and Barbara Britton (the ad lines read, "A lion in your lap! A lover in your arms!"), was filmed in the "Natural Vision" process, a polarized system refined by Milton L. Gunzburg, his brother Julian, an eye specialist, and Friend Baker, a Hollywood camera engineer.

The novelty of good-quality 3-D presented in "Bwana Devil" was immediately accepted by an eager public. Though featuring a thin story line, the film was, nonetheless, a major boxoffice bonanza because of its extraordinary 3-D photography.

Thus, in the greatest revolution since the coming of sound, Hollywood began to make 3-D movies in earnest. Ironically, the 3-D revolution lasted just a little over a year. Between the end

-more-

CAPSULE HISTORY OF 3-D...-5-

of 1952 and the beginning of 1954, over 100 features and short subjects were produced, utilizing the basic "polarized filter" film format. Some of the more memorable were "House of Wax," "Dial M for Murder," "Kiss Me Kate," "The Creature From the Black Lagoon," "The Charge at Feather River" and "It Came From Outer Space." However, most others were cheaply made exploitation films that did little to advance the artistic quality of 3-D. Once the audience got their taste of these travesties, the excitement of 3-D began to wane.

Coupled with the overall quality problems was a lack of creative control in projection. Since most of the films were run on twin projectors, there was a constant need to maintain synchronization of the twin images. Eyestrain would result once an image got out of sync. Unfamiliar with the new technology, many projectionists were incapable of projecting the film correctly. Simultaneously, exhibitors continually fought with the studios over the extra prices of specialty lenses, 3-D glasses and exorbitant sales commissions.

Disabled on two fronts, with bad product and bad publicity, the crowning blow to 3-D came when Twentieth Century-Fox debuted its wide-screen CinemaScope format. This system, which utilized a single lens attached to normal theater projectors, was touted as the real revolution in film technology. Taking the line of least resistance, the major studios abandoned their planned 3-D productions and began to produce their own variations of the wide-screen format. Many films shot in the two-camera 3-D format were released "flat," and by the mid-1950s 3-D was all but forgotten.

Since 1955, when Universal released the last of the initial wave of 3-D films, "Revenge of the Creature," there have been only

-more-

CAPSULE HISTORY OF 3-D...-6-

a handful of major 3-D film releases. In 1962, United Producers
released the soft-core "The Bellboy and the Playgirls," which
featured 3-D sequences in both the polarized and anaglyphic formats.
(The director was a newcomer, Francis Ford Coppola.) In 1969, the
fledgling Stereovision Company released another soft-core entry,
"The Stewardesses," the most successful 3-D film of its time (it
grossed $26 million). Other topical and mildly successful 3-D films
of the 1960s and early 1970s include Arch Oboler's "Fantastic
Invasion of Planet Earth" (1966), Andy Warhol's "Frankenstein"
(1974), "Lollipop Girls in Hard Candy" (1976) and "Sea Dream," a
remarkable documentary film completed in 1978 as part of a Marineland
exhibit in Florida. (Ernest McNabb of "Spacehunter" helped design
its camera system.)

Three-dimensional films received a shot in the arm in 1981
with "Comin' at Ya," a collage of 3-D effects produced by former
Xerox salesmen Gene Quintano and Marshall Lupo and actor Tony
Anthony. In their recent book, Amazing 3-D, writers Hal Morgan
and Dan Symmes explain the source of "Comin' at Ya's" effect:
"Every three minutes something is thrown at or dumped on the
audience: beans, bats, arrows, even a baby half-way through a
diaper change..."

Several of the mechanical problems that hampered 3-D films
of the 1950s have been solved recently by the newly developed
technology. Most importantly, 3-D films can now be screened on
a single projector, eliminating the need for constant readjustment
and synchronization. Like the CinemaScope films of the 1950s,
theater owners need only use a single lens for 3-D conversion.
Audiences must still use polarized glasses, but even the design

-more-

CAPSULE HISTORY OF 3-D...-7-

of the glasses has been refined and improved, eliminating the
threat of eye strain. In terms of camera technology, the work
of Canadian Ernest McNabb has certainly benefited the cause of
Columbia Pictures' entry in the 3-D race, "Spacehunter: Adventures
in the Forbidden Zone." "State of the art" Panavision equipment
can now be used in the 3-D system designed by McNabb. Additionally,
special high-speed cameras can film space effects and miniatures
in 3-D for the first time.

     Repeating the same tired, uninteresting, exploitation ele-
ments that originally killed the 3-D films of the fifties, many
of the recent three-dimensional films like "Parasite," "Friday
the 13th, Part III" and "Treasure of the Four Crowns" have still
proved profitable and popular among audiences searching for a
new Saturday night thrill that will rescue them from their video
games and mega-channel cable-TV.

     How they will greet "Spacehunter," which emphasizes story
over 3-D exploitation, will be determined on May 20, 1983. Another
revolution could be waiting in the wings...

                          * * *

Unit publicity work can sometimes border on the ridiculous. Here in the industrial swamp sequence created for *Spacehunter* in 1983, I can be seen in the foreground obtaining biographical information from one of the "barracuda women." Peter Strauss' scrambler truck, which I later transported cross-country for a national promotional tour, can be seen in the background.

Supervising the video press kit crew is one of the publicist's most important responsibilities during production. Here the crew and I gather footage outside the *Desert Bloom* house in Tucson in 1984. Actress Ellen Barkin can be partially seen to the right of the Panavision camera.

ABOUT THE "DIRTY HALF-DOZEN"....

Ohio native DAN MONAHAN returns in PORKY'S II...THE NEXT DAY
as the chronically frustrated Peewee Morris, whose failure to
provide sexual relief for his overheated circle of friends gets him
into constant hot water. This time out, Peewee develops a budding
relationship with Wendy (KAKI HUNTER), a romantic interlude that
balances his comical appearance as "Puck," in the Shakespeare Festival.

One of four sons born to Thomas and Carol Monahan of Olmstead
Falls, Ohio (about twenty minutes outside Cleveland), Dan Monahan
was quite the smart-aleck when he attended high school. "I guess
you could say I was the typical class clown," he admits. "Some
of those high school experiences were helpful when it came time to
play Peewee, but life in Cleveland was quite a bit different than
it was in Angel Beach." Though he studied business at Ohio University,
contemplating law school, financial considerations drew him away
from a legal career.

A drama stand-out in high school, especially in such productions
as "Twelve Angry Men" (as the foreman), and "Second Fiddle" (as the
lawyer), it wasn't until a friend talked him into trying out for Michael
Weller's "Moon Children," at Ohio U. that he began to seriously
consider an acting career.

Ironically, his first major stage role was that of Michael, the
smart-aleck in Weller's warmly allegorical story. Dan shined in the
part, and soon divided his studies between business courses (he still
has a good head for numbers, which is valuable in the business of film),

and acting.

Majoring in "offbeat," Dan starred in college adaptations of "The
Fantastics" (as the Indian), "Twelfth Night" (as the fanciful Fabian),
"Tilly" (as an alcoholic clown), and "The Tingleberry Bird" (a children'
play in which he portrayed a sixty-eight year old man with a black wife)

His professional career began in 1977 when in arrived in New
York and immediately began working in commercials, his first being
a spot for Safeguard Soap, which earned him his SAG card.

He was quickly signed to appear opposite Cliff Robertson and
Brooke Shields in "Morning, Winter and Night," a drama based on a
Maxwell Anderson short story, which unfortunately for all concerned,
ran out of money before production could be completed.

It was a good experience, though, that brought Dan to the attention
of NBC, then casting its television dramatization of the "Adventures
of Huckleberry Finn. He was hired to portray good old boy, Tom Sawyer
in the Americana classic which aired in the Fall of 1977. A series of
television appearances followed, including "The Terrible Secret,"
an ABC Afternoon Special, and guest roles on "Eight is Enough,"
the McLane Stephenson Show, "In the Beginning..." and "How the West Was
Won."

A major break came in early 1979 when he appeared as the page in
a Broadway production of Richard III which starred Al Pacino. During
the course of the play, he was able to understudy some of ther other
characters, and appeared on stage as Dorset several times.

Beginning in mid-1979, Dan joined actress Gail Garnett in New
York and spent over a year working with her improvisational troupe,
before he found himself at the Mayflower Hotel one winter's morning

in 1980, auditioning for PORKY'S I.

"I thought I was very unimpressive that first day," he recalled. "But Bob Clark called me back for a screen test and I ended up working on a scene with Mark Herrier and Roger Wilson. I heard the good news a week later, and before I knew it I was in Miami for three months, which was great because I was hurting for money. You don't get wealthy doing improv for a year."

As the bumbling Peewee, Dan firmly establishes himself as a top character talent, who repeats all of that nervous energy in PORKY'S II...THE NEXT DAY.

Californian <u>MARK HERRIER</u> reprises his role in PORKY'S II...THE NEXT DAY as lanky Midwesterner Billy McCarty, the conservative member of the "Dirty Half Dozen," who is nonetheless an ardent prankster and enthusiastic pleasure seeker."

During the Shakespearean sequences, Mark utilized his own stage experience to help director Clark choreograph a realistic sword fight between Hamlet and McDuff. He also contributed ideas to the script based on a series of humorous high school drama recollections. Throughout the staged tribute, Mark was the most comfortable in the Shakespearean wardrobe and makeup.

For this talented actor, whose mannerisms and versatility remind one of a young Jimmy Stewart, it all started back in Lompoc (pronounced like cowpoke) California, a small coastal hamlet in Central California where he grew up and attended high school. The second son of Wilbur and Trudy Herrier, he was born October 6, 1954. Though he claims today that acting was an original constitution of his blood, he readily admits that the discovery did not come until age 10, when his mother took him to a local double feature, where Disney's "The Painted Desert," was playing opposite "The Music Man" with Robert Preston.

Whereas the former left him high, dry and thirsty, "The Music Man" enthralled him. "I nearly jumped out of my seat during the production numbers," he remembers. "And I loved Robert Preston. He was incredible. There was something magical about him prancing around, something I will never forget."

An acting opportunity came soon after, when the drama teacher at his elementary school cast the lanky fourth grader in the children's classic, "The Musicians of Bremen," an allegory about a trio of animals on their way to a German musical festival who save a peasant woman's house from burglars.

Recalls Mark, "The qualifications for acting in those days were not great. In fact if you could yell on cue, then you generally got the part. I was a pretty shy kid, but that little play really opened things up for me. I was playing the donkey in the show, and during one comical scene, I had to pick up a revolver and look down the barrel. I can still remember the kids howling with laughter. For a quiet guy like me, that was quite a moment. I then realized that there was an entirely different world on stage."

Following that success with starring roles in "Scrooge" and "The Pirates of Penzance," he segued to nearby Lompoc Senior High School where he was eventually placed in an honor's program. In major school drama productions like "Camelot," and "Teahouse of the August Moon," Mark was featured in starring roles. While maintaining an A-minus grade average, he jumped around from acting to basketball, to public speaking (he won several awards), and eventually tried politics when he ran for several student body offices.

Graduating Lompoc in 1972, he was actually considering a scholarship to USC and a pre-law degree when he opted for nearby Alan Hancock Junior College in Santa Maria, California, home of the reputable Pacific Conservatory for the Performing Arts. Mark cut his actor's teeth on such plays as "The Time of Your Life" (as Harry the hoofer), "Midsummer Night's Dream" (as Lysander), "Romeo and Juliet" (as Benvolio), "Thieves Carnival" (as Gustave) and many other popular shows. In 1975, he applied to the University of Washington's Drama program where he sought to fine tune his craft.

In 1978, he got his first break when acting instructor Duncan Ross cast him as Ragner in Ibsen's "The Master Builder." Mark's first professional appearance was directed by future Tony winner, Vivian Matalon, a creative force who would later hire him to appear on Broadway in"Brigadoon."

After "The Master Builder," he left for Los Angeles where he spent eighteen months with the Improvisational Theater Project, an experience that improved his acting and netted him his future wife, actress Becky Gonzalez. In the New York stage production of "Brigadoon," Mark was signed to play the American bartender, a small part which was his first stage role. When "Brigadoon," finished its New York run,

he spent three months traveling with the road company. He
was finishing up the tour in the Winter of 1980 when he joined
college friend Boyd Gaines at the PORKY'S auditions in New York City.
Director Bob Clark later admitted that Mark was a bonus for the
casting search that he could not pass up.

Says fellow actor Wyatt Knight, "Mark is the funniest guy on the
set. You wouldn't know it at times, and on screen he plays it pretty
straight, but during the filming of both PORKY'S, he would always
come up with a gag or a joke that would break up the whole crew."

Once the original PORKY'S wrapped, Mark returned to California
and was immediately signed to portray Arthur in the South Coast
Repertory Company's production of "Ah Wilderness." The New York
stage soon beckoned him and he appeared on Broadway in "Macbeth"
(as Donalbain), and segued to the critically acclaimed Christopher
Durang play, "Sister Mary Ignatius Explains It All To You." Director
Bob Clark then grabbed him to reprise Billy McCarty in PORKY'S II...
THE NEXT DAY.

WYATT KNIGHT once again appears in the PORKY'S saga as prankster
Tommy Turner, whose wrenching encounter with Miss Balbricker (NANCY
PARSONS) in the first PORKY'S, was one of the comical highlights
of that film. This time out, he gets his revenge, when he cleverly
plants a water snake in Balbricker's toilet.

The oldest son of John and Joyce Knight, Wyatt was born January
20, 1955 in Mojave, California where his Air Force officer father was
stationed. He grew up on a series of military outposts until his

<u>Director Alan Rudolph</u> is the son of Oscar Rudolph, a prominent American television director of the 1950's and '60's. Rudolph was born in Los Angeles and grew up on the backlots of Hollywood, often appearing in his father's productions. In 1951, at the age of eight, he accompanied his family to New York, and for a year, while his father completed several live television shows, young Rudolph was able to view a large number of cynical English films of the period -- dark, compelling studies of people under stress which would forever influence his later film work.

Back in California, he attended Birmingham High School, and started writing in his spare time. Rather than join his father in the television industry, Rudolph gravitated towards a more independent existence, at one time considering a career in business. However, he could never get films entirely out of his blood, and in his early twenties, he began picking up odd jobs at local studios, including a stint in the Paramount Studios Mail Room. In 1969, he was accepted to the prestigious Assistant Director's Training Program sponsored by the Director's Guild, an experience which doubled his interest in a motion picture career. Working with directors Joseph Sargent, and later with Robert Altman, Rudolph continued writing.

After an association with Altman on "California Split" and "The Long Goodbye," for which he served as assistant director, he joined his mentor on "Buffalo Bill and the Indians" as co-writer. Rudolph was encouraged to pursue independent projects, the first

of which was the unusual 1977 romantic film, "Welcome to LA"
which won the director plaudits from many critics, followed
by his second feature, "Remember My Name."

In 1978, Rudolph joined forces with producer Carolyn
Pfeiffer on the musical comedy, "Roadie," which starred music
star Meatloaf. "I want the audience to reach out and grasp an
idea from the film," says Rudolph, and "they will reach if you
entice them enough. In this way, people come away from the
film experience with a new thought."

Rudolph is quick to point out that, although "Endangered
Species" features a mystery brimming with action and violence,
it is more a character study than anything else. "It is also
a protest film, a warning to us all that we are flirting with
the annihilation of our planet."

An early example of video usage in mall promotions was demonstrated in Washington DC during the *Spacehunter* promotional tour. The combination of video materials promoting the upcoming film and working props on display proved to be a popular crowd attraction as well as a starting point for the all-important local media coverage.

The 1983 *Spacehunter* National Promotional Tour involved transporting huge working props. Here the scrambler truck is parked in front of the White House. Although the truck was not considered roadworthy (no license plates, turn signals, gas gauge, headlights, mirrors or any type of registration), it did not prevent me from "stealing" it from its static display for jaunts like this to various local monuments.

Dear Susan,

I'm sorry I missed your call last week. I haven't had a chance
to speak to you since we had that nice chat on DESERT BLOOM (which
has been pushed back to a February release). Speaking of
February releases, I'm currently working on another one. It's
called PRETTY IN PINK, and it's the latest teen fable from the
prolific John Hughes.

There are a number of interesting angles, Susan. I've attached
some production notes that should fill you in on the story, but
in a nutshell, it features a girl from the other side of the tracks
(MOLLY RINGWALD) who falls in love with one of her rich high school
mates (ANDREW MCCARTHY), while avoiding the interest of her fellow
"zoid" (JON CRYER). Between the freethinking "zoids" and the
"richies", PRETTY IN PINK has a strong touch of ROMEO AND JULIET
and WEST SIDE STORY, with a nice love-triangle thrown in for measure.

First time director, and ex-music video maker Howard Deutch has given
the look of the film an interesting style that covers music, fashion,
makeup, production design-all in tune with Hughes' interesting
dialogue. The result will probably be the most sophisticated teen
pic in years-a mature adult approach to teen romance which is certainly
Hughes' strongpoint.

Is there a chance one of your LA freelancers might be interested
in visiting our set over the last three weeks of filming? I'd love
to nail Deutch down on his stylistic approach to the film and how
music will play an important part in the narrative. Although there's
been enough said about young actors these days (I think they're
now calling it "Brat Pack" fever), we do have another collection
of young talent (Ringwald, McCarthy, Jon Cryer (who is wonderful),
James Spader, Dweezil Zappa (in a cute bit).

Page 2

Anyways, that about covers it. I'll call you this week and
perhaps we can coordinate an interesting feature.

As always, thanks for your time.

Best,

Steve Rubin
Unit Publicist
PRETTY IN PINK
(213) 468-5507

I THINK WE'RE
IN FOR SOME
SERIOUS
COMPETITION
NEXT SUMMER,
C-THREEPIO!!

NOW IN POST-PRODUCTION

COME ON PETER! IS THIS ANY WAY TO CELEBRATE??

JAWS III EAT YOUR HEART OUT!

CRAFT SERVICE FIGURES REPORTED

CRAFT SERVICE chief JOANNE "I keep it pouring" RYAN has announced the results of the 1st TERRA ELEVEN craft service survey. During the three month shoot, she reported the crew consumed 52,987 glazed donuts, 349,345 carrot sticks, 45,678 gallons of coffee, 5 million sugar cubes, 3407 bananas and enough luncheon meat to feed the island of Maui for the entire month of June.

SOLAR SYSTEM BUSINESS WEEK
Aug. 14, 1984   50¢

Is Kraft Trying To Monopolize The Cheese On The Moon!

"You'll Never Believe Where They Want Me To Relocate!" by a panicky Underwood Typewriter Salesman

Captains Wolff and Washington split 3000 megs for rescue of Space Valley Girls

FORD'S NEW EXPANSION PLAN TO OTHER PLANETS: When They Tell You To See Your "Mercury" Dealer . . . They'll Really Mean It!

CAN WE PEACEFULLY ORGANIZE SATURN'S LABOR FORCE WITHOUT THEM EATING US? by Walter Reuther

VANCOUVER VICE SQUAD INVESTIGATING STRANGE REPORT FROM ZONE SET

INVESTIGATING officers from the Vancouver Vice Squad were called to the set yesterday when it was reported that Chalmers had been violated by an unknown assailant. Rumors that the A Camera Team were guilty of a little too much afternoon delight were unfounded. However, ace first assistant ROD "I keep'em" PRIDY had quite a grin on his face throughout the late afternoon.

FINAL SMILE OF THE WEEK AWARD

GOES TO craft service assistant TANA "They Need More What?" TOCHER who has really pitched in the last two weeks. TANA a North Vancouverite is the daughter of seafarer GEORDIE TOCHER, who once sailed a 50 foot Haida Indian style canoe/outrigger from Vancouver to Hawaii. TANA is also an able sea person, who teaches wind surfing during the Sunny months. She's also a darn good cook. We will definitely miss her smile.

WRAP PARTY WRAP PARTY WRAP

It's all set everyone. The First Ever SPACEHUNTER WRAP PARTY, with publicity copy by STEWART "GoGo" HARDING will take place tomorrow night at 8:30 PM at the Miramar. Last minute plans were being made by WARREN "I'm sick of these wordisms on my name" CARR to invite several of the top Davie Street madames to spice up the entertainment.

DOES ED JOHNSON HAVE A WOODEN LEFT LEG?

Crew insiders were beginning to wonder yesterday when it was rumored that ace prop shop elf ED "I'm proud to be an Italian American" JOHNSON actually has a wooden left leg. The story surfaced when MOLLY "GOLLY" RINGWALD discovered that Ed's family is part owner of the Evinrude Lawn Mower Company of Minneapolis, and that when Eddie was a baby he actually was swallowed by a giant industrial mower which spit him out, but ate his left limb. Johnson however denied the rumor stating that he has full motor capabilities. Whether those capabilities are courtesy of PERRY "The Mad Electronic Doctor" MCLAMB has yet to be determined.

HERE COMES MOLLY!!!!!!!

HEY tube watchers, look for our own very capable MOLLY RINGWALD on Monday February 7th at 9:00 PM in PACKIN' IT IN with Dick Benjamin and Paula Prentiss. This Television film on CBS focuses on a scavenging young teenager who spends the whole two hours trying to squeeze her sleeping bag into the glove compartment of the family car. Sound familiar? Just kidding, it's a fun film and we're already looking forward to MOLLY'S FUTURE TRIUMPH. Good luck at the Golden Globes Saturday Night, Kid!

STRANGE GOINGS ON IN THE GRAVEYARD CITY

(OVERDOGLAND)-Fear ran rampant through the Graveyard last night when orders tripling guard strength on the prisoner cages were announced. Both the Herman Goering and Panzer Lehr crack divisions have been recalled from Terra 10. Insiders are hoping they will arrive in time. Infiltrations are increasing, and strange rumors are filling the area about renegade Earthers on the March. ***Morale remains low due to the small number of females present in the city. With a ratio of 6 men to every women, times aredefinitely tough. **Several Zoners complained last week when the admission price to the Maze Games was raised to five nuts (as in bolts). However, the presence of popcorn a delicasy, was greeted with approval. The Lord Overdog announced yesterday that Season Seats for the 1984 games will be postponed until after the Earther Chicks have been drained of energy. Population increased last week to 345,000. There were 58 births, and 48 decapitations. A food drop is scheduled for Monday. Cargo jets from the Sirius Megatherium will be dumping Asteroid Candy into the Zone. The 21st day of Halloweeen will be celebrated on May 1st this year.

Football fever swept through the crew last week as Prop elve WAYNE "Too Tall" ZAVOSKY walked away with two big 250.00 prizes in one pool (the Washington Minnesota game) and Shop Steward BEN RUSS1 napped 500 big ones. As of press time, ERIK "The Bear" NELSON announced that the following people were still liable for their payment on big board squares: The A Camera Syndicate, Duster and Jarrett, Bob Bowe, Walter Scott, George Erschebamer, Steel and Neufeld, Carole McDonald, Rod Pridy and Tucker. Pay soon everybody or your squares are forfeited. The countdown continues to Superbowl Sunday on Terra Eleven. Chief Engineer Chalmers of the Junk Bat is still fixing the antenna guys, so let's pray for good reception.

FOOTBALL PICKS

Last week I was 3 for 4, missing the Raiders Jets game. But I certainly liked Miami, didn't I, as I do again this weekend. Give 1½ and take the Dolphins And Take the Redskins over the Cowboys. A dynasty is about to be dethroned.

SPACE POLICE RAID CHEMIST LAIR/ELVES CAUGHT IN THE BLACK LIGHT OF THE LAW

It was like a scene out of a 1960's psychadelic movie. There in the darkness of the Prop shop, ROBERT "Lord of the Rings" JOYCE was sprinkling silver sparkles onto a moistened black light while PERRY "The Mad Electronic Doctor" MCLAMB was putting together another one of his marvels, an electric light bubble maker. Hoisting a much needed beer, ED "Big Mac" JOHNSON was running madly through the scene philosphizing about its meaning, while WAYNE "Too Tall" ZAVOSKY was overdosing on too much color control. In stepped JACK "THANK the lord for the nighttime" DEGOVIA surveying the magic quality of the moment, which sent shivers up the spine, harking back to the black laboratories of Lucretia Borgia and UNcle Fester. But it all ended at 3:00 AM when galactic space police broke up the scene and turned off the blacklights. Judge Overdog's sentence: Everyone is to be locked in a room for one year, and forced to listen to Groucho Marx sing Maurice Chevalier songs...

SCRIPT SUPERVISOR'S TRAINING COURSE
Students will apprentice on a professional film.
SARAH GRAHAME

PATRICK "EAT MY DUSTER" ROWE and PAUL "I'm Singin in the Rain" BORETSKI modeling umbrellas for the Travelers Insurance Company, back in the good old Moab days...

SPACEHUNTER HOURGLASS EMPTYING RAPIDLY

Vancouver-Drama appears to be building on the set of SPACEHUNTER as we enter our last week of principal photography. Crew members stationed at the Miramar were already reported to have dusted off their suit cases, preparing their civilian clothes and accoutrements. A Wrap party to end all wrap parties is scheduled for next Saturday Night. Caterer MARY PENHALL of "A Perfect Affair" Caterers has announced that a truly incredible riposte will be awaiting attendees. Penhall and her co-catering persons, DOUG "I Cut the Meat that Makes the Young Girls Cry" Russell and MARY FENSKI are already preparing hor doeurves for that night. A site has yet to be determined. On Sunday morning, members of the Vancouver Art Community will be coming down to perhaps purchase pieces of our set (the sculptings) in the first ever SPACEHUNTER ART AND CHARITY SALE. Following that, we have the SUPER BOWL, and that is going to be true drama for some lucky crew member and syndicate. Next weeks issue, our last, will carry farewell greetings and remembrances from especially vocal Zoners.

INTERSTELLAR POSTAL FLASH GREEN CODE 9876-091k1

(First Word from the Space Chicks) This post card was found in a beer bottle floating through Crab Nebula...

Dearest Mom,

Galactic greetings. Sorry its been so long but this is really the first time we had to get a few words off. Right now the girls and I have been hanging around, checking out the "local color." We got picked up by this guy named Chemist. (Reena attracts the wierdest men). He tried to be sweet but god what a sleeze. Anyway, he fixed us up with a friend of his named Overdog who's got the hots for Nova. He likes blondes. He's kind of cute in his own way but a trip to Nautilus would really put him in touch with his body. I'm going to recommend Spiralina Vitamins. Well, gotta go there seems to be some big gatherings at the local club, "The Maze." Everyone will be there. Haven't a thing to wear. We'll try and get home soon but as I said we're really hung up. Having a great time, wish you were here. Love Meagan. Ps. Nova and Reena send kisses.

SPOTLIGHT ON THE WARDROBE DEPARTMENT

Replacing our "Smile of the Week" column is a special tribute to the especially creative SPACEHUNTER wardrobe department which has been outfiting a veritable army of zoners, creeps, guards, slaves and assorted wierdos this week in the Graveyard World of Overdog. Leading that team of "Magic Fingers" is GAIL "Needles and Pins" FILMAN who works costumes like Gretsky works the puck. Joining her in these endeavors is MONIQUE "I live on a sailboat with Alois" PRUDHOMME. By the way that sailboat is named the Signet 5, which "rings" a bell. PATRICIAN "Tish the Dish" MONAGHAN is a Vancouver nativewho is half Irish and half Austrian, although shes never been to Austria. Her mother is married to a priest so be civil. JANE "I spell it with an "E" GROSE announces that she is "mated." She also has 15 years experience in movies. including GREY FOX with Frank "I'M Not Very Tidy". LINDA LEE "Lovey" LANGDON is the daughter of a Salmon Fisherman who just got through working on Running Brave with Robby Benson. Her favorite color is purple. Rounding out this lovely group of female pulchritude is JEAN CAUSEY who is a wonderful addition to any team.

Two shots of the scrambler truck en röute to the White House. Local police were not too happy to see an unregistered vehicle on the highway, but I was able to talk my way out of any unpleasant situations. The most common question was, "What the &*#% is it?".

"RAD: THE MOVIE"
PUBLICITY PROGRESS REPORT #1 (September 17, 1985)

We are now half-way through principal photography, beginning our
fourth week of production. A mood of excitement surrounds the picture,
especially after the completion of our "Helltrack" action exteriors.
The acrobatic dexterity of the BMX professional rider has to be seen
to believed, and film audiences are going to get plenty of that in
"RAD." Still photographer Doug Curren and videographer John
Schwartzman have been getting excellent coverage of the shoot, some
of which is already being distributed to our national media outlets.

Thus far, actor Bill Allen has been a real plus for the film. He's
photogenic, easy going, and has a wonderful screen presence, especially
in his scenes with lovely Lori Loughlin. The supporting cast has also
been a plus. Winsome Jamie Clarke, a local lad playing "Luke," has
had some funny moments and has become the darling of the local press.
New York actress Marta Kober, with her laugh and offbeat personality is
also a crew favorite. Laura Jacoby (from the Jacoby acting family) has
also stolen some scenes. All of the above will make good angles for
the teen magazines.

We're also getting as much coverage as we can with Talia Shire, and
we're just starting to work with Ray Walston and Jack Weston. Stunt
rider Eddie Fiola, one of the top BMX freestylists in the world, is
another excellent angle for coverage-and he's inspired me to begin
thinking about field promotions for next February and March. A
written concept for a field promotional team will be on your desk in
the next two weeks.

Of all our personalities, though, director Hal Needham is the prince.
He's the perfect centerpiece for "RAD," and his gift of gab makes him
a good spokesman. I'm going to continue to get him on the phone and
in front of the cameras as often as possible. More than anyone else,
he appears to be having a great time on this picture.

Herewith, some breakdown on current publicity activity:

1. ENTERTAINMENT TONIGHT visited the Helltrack set on Saturday September
14th. Through Pete Hammond in Hollywood, they've utilized a Calgary
video crew headed by local man, Lou Schizas, an ex-New Yorker with good
interview skills. During the course of the afternoon, he interviewed
Hal Needham, Robert Levy, Sam Bernard, Bill Allen, Lori Loughlin,
Marta Kober, Laura Jacoby, H.B. Haggerty and the Hayes Twins. Lou is
also coming back today to interview Talia Shire on the set.

2. CABLE NEWS NETWORK is also interested in a location piece and they
are going to use local man, Lou Schizas as well. He's bringing his
crew out to the set today (9/17) and will interview Needham, Allen,
Loughlin, etc. He will interview Talia for both ET and CNN.
I spoke to Kendall Baldwin in Los Angeles and she's very excited about
the piece (she'll also do stories on the project down the line as well,
which is ET's promise as well).

-1-

RAD PUBLICITY PROGRESS/2

3. Frank Swertlow of the DAILY NEWS (San Fernando Valley), interviewed Hal on the telephone for his Hollywood Freeway column on Wednesday September 11th. That piece was supposed to run on Friday September 13th. I'm awaiting clips. I'm also going to interest staff writer Bruce Cook in a feature piece.

4. As previously noted, Jerry Pam has set up telephone interviews between Talia Shire and Army Archerd which made the September 5th DAILY VARIETY column. Talia also recently did an interview with MARILYN BECK, a clip of which we are awaiting.

5. Tom Huff and Chris Phoenix who are creating the new TEEN SCENE which makes its Southern California debut this November as a glossy magazine, paid their own way up to Calgary to cover the Helltrack racing. What turned out to be a plus was the fact that Chris is a pro BMX racer, and Hal put him in the actual race. "How I Survived Helltrack" will be a cute feature in his new magazine, and Tom promises a number of plugs up until release. I'm also going to put Chris in touch with Donna Myrow of the YOUTH NEWS SERVICE, which sends location pieces on motion pictures to major newspapers. The angle is that the pieces have to be written by teens, which is great because Chris is 17.

6. Wendy Osborne, the editor of BMX ACTION MAGAZINE, and a close friend of our stunt rider, Eddie Fiola, also paid her own way up here. We're giving her magazine, which is by far the biggest and best of the BMX magazines (they also publish "FreeStyle"), an exclusive on set visit material. She'll do a number of features on the film in her magazine up until release time. She's also interested in promotional tie-ins. (Her magazine is already featured on screen). Managing editor Don Toshach also mentioned that he doesn't mind us sending editorial and picture material to the other BMX Magazines-BMX PLUS and SUPER BMX, as long as they don't come to set. Eddie Fiola said that their readership is duplicated by BMX Action Magazine, anyways.

By the way, I'm collecting the names, ages, addresses, and phone numbers of all the BMX pros racing at Helltrack. They may become valuable during any promotional campaign for "RAD." They're all eager to help the film in any way.

7. I'm going to get freelance special photographer ALAN MARKFIELD up to Calgary for the bicycle dancing sequences. Alan, a New Yorker, has excellent contacts through his Sygma Agency, and he can service photo materials internationally. Per Jerry Pam, Alan will be charging us for plane fare and hotel only.

8. I'm also getting in touch with the morning shows, GOOD MORNING AMERICA and THE TODAY SHOW about sending a crew up to cover the bicycle dancing sequence. This is a very promotable concept. I was on the phone with a magazine editor the other day and she told me that this type of dancing was mentioned in a San Francisco Chronicle article as "Break Bicycling." It wouldn't hurt to be the first movie to feature "Break Bicycling.

RAD PUBLICITY PROGRESS/3

9. Kathy Levinski of MTV-NEWS, is definitely interested in behind the scenes video coverage of our break-bicycling sequence. She also mentioned that their other subscriber service, VH-1, might be interested as well. I'm going to get John Schwartzman to provide that feed.

10. Speaking of John, his Los Angeles office is assembling a list of television stations throughout the United States who might be interested in our video press materials. They've already had good response.

11. Barbara Hoffman of TEEN MAGAZINE in Los Angeles is interested in pictures of Bill and Lori for their March issue. She also wants some Bart Conner material. I'm also going to get a list of the teen magazines published in New York city and send them material as well. Bill could be the next teen heart-throb.

12. Jeff Liederman, who publishes the FAST TIMES newspaper which goes to California high school students will publish a RAD picture in his February issue and do a story in his March issue. We are supplying him with photographs, and we'll set up some interviews with Bill Allen in Los Angeles.

13. Since Bill is a native of Dallas, Texas, I'm also going to set up some interviews with the Texas newspapers when he arrives back home for a visit after wrap. Bill currently lives in Los Angeles.

14. One of the top teen magazines in the country at the moment is Howard Weiss' TEEN SET. Howard prefers to cover films on location, and I mentioned if there is room in our budget towards the end of the shoot, there might be a possibility of bringing him up. It could be the difference between four stories all the way up to release, or one or two pictures and items. Weiss is also friends with our little star, Laura Jacoby.

15. Robin Green of CALIFORNIA MAGAZINE will take a cute picture from RAD, but isn't interested in a feature article. The Magazine concentrates on "how they got started in the business" profiles. Hal Needham might be a good angle. I'll have more on this later.

16. I'm going to be supplying items and pics to US MAGAZINE, PEOPLE, TIME, and NEWSWEEK. I want to save our break bicycling pictures for "newsmakers" column in NEWSWEEK or the "people page" in TIME. I'm also going to pitch them on feature stories on the BMX magazine phenomenon. I know a sports editor at Newsweek named J.D. Reed who might be interested in the angle.

17. Items and pics will also be circulated to the "out-takes" column of the Sunday LOS ANGELES TIMES CALENDAR (Pat Broeske), and Gregg Kilday's column at the LOS ANGELES HERALD EXAMINER. Gregg called up here during the first week of production, looking for items.

18. We also want to do something big with USA TODAY. We've got the best possible angle because our leads are all paper boys for USA Today, thanks

RAD PUBLICITY PROGRESS/4

to prop master Lou Fleming. I'm already having some color and black
and white material sent to the Washington D.C. head office. I'm also
going to contact LA bureau writer, Jack Curry, about a story idea.

19. Karen McGee, national assignments editor for PM MAGAZINE is
currently ruminating over a RAD feature. I will have some more news
on this later.

20. Columnist Bill Harris of SHOWTIME is interested in some RAD pictures,
preferably of Talia and Hal. I am sending him some.

21. Lauri Smith of MOVIELINE MAGAZINE is also interested in a location
piece on RAD. She doesn't have a Canadian writer, though, but I will
possibly refer her to Chris Phoenix of Teen Scene who may have enough
material for ten articles after this experience.

22. Jim Steranko, who publishes the glossy PREVIEW MAGAZINE, and who is
a personal friend, will also mention RAD in a number of items through
the release period.

23. Dick Crew of "The Hollywood Insider," which is a movie clip show
that runs on the USA Network (3 times a week) is interested in behind
the scenes coverage on RAD. I am supplying his producer Steve Bronstein
with some of John Schwartzman's feed.

24. I pitched RAD to Larry Van Gelder at the NEW YORK TIMES, but he
wasn't interested in a location story. He was very nice though, and
mentioned that he seldom sends writers out of the U.S. for production
stories anymore.

25. Pamela Hughes of HOLLYWOOD CLOSEUP, out of KABC in Hollywood, is
also interested in video materials on RAD. This will come, once again,
from the John Schwartzman video package.

26. Speaking of the John Schwartzman video package, there has been some
talk among us about the viability of a 1/2 hour program about BMX racing
which would tie-in with RAD. John's team has some contact with the SFM
Network in New York, which syndicates programming. We should seriously
think about this, because a half-hour program will alter, somewhat,
John's approach to the filming.

27. One of our most interesting stuntmen is Jose Yanez, who performs
a back flip on a bicycle for the cameras. He's a Phoenix resident,
and the ARIZONA REPUBLIC is already interested in a feature on him.
I spoke to their entertainment editor Mike McKay and I will be coordinating
this upon Jose's return from Canada.

28. One of the reasons this report was delayed for a week was because I
have had to muster the local media in Calgary to support our Helltrack
crowd needs. Fortunately, they helped a great deal and we had approximately
4500 people our there for the two weekend days. Please note the
outlets in which we've had multiple breaks:

RAD PUBLICITY PROGRESS/5

Calgary Herald
Calgary Sun
CFCN-TV
CBC-TV
CFAC-TV
CJAY Radio
CKO Radio
AM 106 Radio (7 breaks)
QR-Radio
Cable 10 Television
CKRY Country Radio

29) Jeff Adams of the CANADIAN PRESS (the Associated Press of Canada) also came to our set one day and is doing a national feature for his outfit. I am supplying him with photographs.

30) I also got in touch with producer Herb Dudnick of the new NBC/ Bryant Gumbal kid's show "Mainstreet" which debuts shortly. He is interested in seeing some material on RAD for a possible story segment.

That's about all for now. I'm continuing to contact the 90 or so outlets which received our advance production notes. I'll have another report prior to our wrap.

Steve Rubin
Unit Publicist
RAD

One of the joys of production publicity work is meeting the many people who grace a typical film set, including the colorful array of supporting actors. On *Rad* in Calgary in 1985, I spent some enjoyable time with ex-wrestler H.B. (Hard Boiled) Haggerty who had a wealth of stories. On a slow-moving film set, you remember happy times like this.

Having completed a twenty city national satellite tour from a Century City office tower for *Eddie and the Cruisers II*, actor Michael Pare and myself take time for a quick snapshot. After a grueling morning interview session breaks like this were welcome.

REEL EXPOSURE

February 6, 1987

To: Field Agencies

From: Steve Rubin, National Publicity and Promotional Director
      Cinema Group

Re: "WITCHBOARD"-(Opening March 13th, nationwide)

By now I will have spoken to all of you individually in regards
to the release of "WITCHBOARD" which hits your territory on
March 13 (Friday the 13th, what a coincidence!)

I've attached a press kit so that you can become more familiar
with the project. I would like to stress that "WITCHBOARD" is
not another slasher movie. It has strong romantic elements and
the love triangle between the three main characters should draw
females (we hope).

In terms of names, the only actor with some recognizability is
Stephen Nichols, the star of the Daytime soap, "Days of Our Lives."
He will be available in LA for phone interviews, but I am probably
not going to tour him. We're currently trying to nail down an
expert on the occult to talk about the colorful history of
ouija boards. This is one phone interview which should cross over
to the lifestyle page, and we should get some good feature response
tieing the film with the occult and the Friday the 13th opening
day.

We will be supplying you with black t-shirts (with the red
Witchboard logo), plus a supply of ouija boards for the radio
station promos. I would think the disc jockeys would have some
fun with these.

In terms of that fun, you should think in terms of any local
retailers who would like to tie-in. The easiest game I can think
of is that since a ouija board features a number of letters and
numbers, the call-in contestants could pick a letter or number and
there could be a prize under each. They can be small prizes, but
the interaction between the guest and the witchboard would be
perfect.

All of you utilize local nightclubs for possible promotions. Please
feel free to extend the radio promo to a club for a Witchboard
night on the Thursday night before we open (or Friday if you prefer).
This nightclub event could take place after the Thursday night
radio promoted screenings.

I am budgeting for a theater for the Thursday night screening.
Although we are not giving local critics a lot of lead time, we
will allow them to see the movie that night, so in a sense we are
screening it for them. If ouija board stories don't appear until
the following week, that's still okay. And please invite

"WITCHBOARD"
Page 2

lifestyle editors and reporters to the Thursday night screening. They must see the film to get the ouija board impact.

Let me know if you have a special expert on the occult available in your local market. Since we're not touring on this picture, that occult expert may want to go on the air and discuss the colorful history of witchboards. I will still try to find a national expert for phoners.

We will most likely have a radio buy in each of your markets. Edie Keller in Los Angeles will be giving you the details of the buy.

I have recorded your needs in terms of press kits and video clips, and these will be going out in the next two weeks. You should have them on or before the 1st of March. Those of you with special needs and deadlines, please let me know and we'll treat those requests individually.

T-shirts and boards will also be delivered around the 1st.

In terms of the radio station for the promotion, I would like to hit 12-24 year olds, but, as always, I'm interested in a promotional conscious station that likes to have fun with movie tie-ins. The 18-34 young male audience is also important to this picture. Use your best judgement and keep me posted so that I can compile my radio station list ASAP. I can then relay this information to Edie for the buy.

I will be back in touch with you once you receive your kits.

Best,

Front

Back

NEW CENTURY/VISTA FILM CO.

cordially invites you
and a guest to a
special advance screening of

Lady in White

Thursday, March 17, 1988
at 7:30 P.M.

AMC 14 Theatres
10250 Santa Monica Blvd.
Century City
Los Angeles, CA 90067

Please R.S.V.P. to
(213) 556-8962

Free Parking

REVIEW DATE: APRIL 22, 1988

SPECIAL EDITION Los Angeles Herald

TODAY'S WEATHER
Hot performers and cool music coming tonight

COMBROS

Circulation : 1,896,430 Daily/ 3,548,822 Sunday | Friday, August 18, 1989 | Daily .50

EDDIE WILSON IS ALIVE!

Famed Rock Star of "Eddie and the Cruisers" Found Alive in Montreal – News Stuns World!

REACTIONS

SATIN RECORDS STOCK SKYROCKETS
New York

News of Eddie Wilson's reappearance in Montreal had an astounding effect on the stock of Satin Records, a Manhattan based record label that trades over the counter. The stock, listed at 1 1/2, jumped five points to 6 1/2 in heavy trading.

MUSIC TRADES PREDICT "CRUISERS" MUSIC WILL JUMP TO NO. 1
Los Angeles

Recovering from the initial shock of seeing a long deceased rock legend alive and well and performing for thousands, the editors of several top music trade publications, who refused to be identified, predict that the music of "Eddie and the Cruisers" will soon top all record charts. "The entire catalogue is going to be out of stock almost immediately," said one top executive with a weekly trade paper. "This is unprecedented. Even people who aren't rock and roll fans are fascinated by the return of a great legend in music, and they're going to buy records by the truckload."

TABLOID PAPERS SEND TOP REPORTERS TO MONTREAL

Teams of reporters, representing every tabloid newspaper in the world, were booking flights to Montreal last night after word of the Eddie Wilson reappearance was announced. Just where Eddie's entourage headed after the concert is a closely guarded secret, according to a public affairs officer with the Montreal Police Department which escorted the Wilson caravan out of the Conservatory of Arts parking lot at approximately 9:20 p.m. According to eyewitness accounts, Wilson and his band, known as "Rock Solid" and an unidentified caucasian female, rumored to be Eddie Wilson's girlfriend, were seen entering two limousines which headed south on Sherbrooke Avenue to an unknown destination. According to Lindsey Caputo, coordinator of the Montreal Music Festival where Eddie Wilson played, the limousines belonged to another featured band, but "due to extenuating circumstances and the need for appropriate privacy and security we commandeered them for Eddie's escape."

FORMER MEMBERS OF THE "CRUISERS" STUNNED BY WILSON NEWS

No one was more surprised about the reappearance of Eddie Wilson than members of his former band. Contacted at his home in Wildwood, New Jersey, former "Eddie and the Cruisers" keyboardist Frank Ridgeway (who now teaches high school English) thought reporters were pulling a fast one when they arrived early this morning. Once he was convinced that the stories were true, he said, "It's the best news I've heard in years. I always thought there was something strange about the accident. Now I hope I get the chance to meet him. We've got a lot to catch up on." Former "Cruisers" manager Doc Robbins who is a disc jockey at WRHE radio in Asbury Park, New Jersey, was admitted to the local emergency room suffering from shock after hearing the news about Eddie. Eddie's former girlfriend, Joanne Carlino, who is a dance choreographer in Atlantic City, was shocked and could offer no comments to reporters who visited her office. Ex-"Cruisers" drummer Kenny Hopkins, a blackjack dealer in Atlantic City, was the most vocal of former band members. "It's the greatest thing that's ever happened to the music world," he said. "People have been troubled for years by Eddie's death, now they can rest. A legend has returned." "Cruisers" bass player Sal Amato who has his own rock and roll revival band could not be reached for comment.

Former "Cruiser" Sal Amato

LIVE CONCERT AT MONTREAL MUSIC FESTIVAL IS AMAZING

MONTREAL

There were cheers, there were tears, there were the gasps of an absolutely stunned audience. Eddie Wilson, the legendary rock and roll star of "Eddie and the Cruisers" who was supposed to have died when his car jumped the Raritan Bridge in 1964, performed *LIVE* on the stage at the Montreal Music Festival last night.

The amazing event took place at 8:05 p.m. Eastern Standard Time at the Montreal Conservatory of the Arts Auditorium. Wilson, performing with a band that was identified in the festival program as "Rock Solid", began a forty-five minute set that had the audience rocking in the aisles. After the first song, a thumper called "Pride and Passion", Wilson took the microphone and quietly introduced the band, ending in an incredibly dramatic moment with his own admission - "I'm Eddie Wilson".

The feeling at first, among fans and press alike, was that this was another stunt pulled by Satin Records which has been selling a lot of Eddie Wilson albums lately with its massive "Eddie Lives" publicity campaign. But when the gentleman in question stepped forward on stage and began to sing, there was no doubt that this was the real Eddie. If only Elvis and Jim Morrison could come back in such a manner.

Lindsey Caputo, the executive in charge of the Festival, who has been besieged by worldwide press attention, could shed little light on the phenomenon. She did mention that following the concert, Wilson and his entourage left in a caravan of vehicles, escorted by the Montreal Police to protect them from the huge throng that waited outside for the band.

Caputo confirmed that the "Rock Solid" band had been scouted for the last few months and was chosen as the festival's opening act after a successful audition last July 1st. "I thought he looked a little like Eddie Wilson," Caputo explained, "and I even told the lead guitarist of the band that we could probably exploit that in light of all these 'Eddie Lives' rumors but I never figured that he would really be Eddie. This is amazing." Caputo mentioned that in the band's contract, Wilson used the name Joe West.

Worldwide reaction has been nothing short of astonishing. Newspaper presses from Burbank to Bangkok were stopped to include the miraculous news that one of the legends of rock was alive. Crowds began lining up outside

THE FACT
A very live Eddie Wilson performs at the Montreal Music Festival.

THE FANTASY
N.J. State Police pull Eddie's Convertible out of the Raritan River in 1964.

the Satin Records office in Manhattan early this morning, demanding information on Eddie Wilson and the mystery tapes that have been heavily hyped for the last few months.

Lew Eisen, President of Satin Records, was expected to hold a press conference this morning at 10:00 a.m.

Dave Pagent, senior vice president of promotion for the label, was in the hospital supposedly recovering form a fight with an irate fan at the Montreal concert. Reports that Eisen and Pagent were at the concert indicate that Satin Records may have known about Eddie prior to last night.

THE NEW MUSIC OF EDDIE WILSON

by Casey Rogers, Los Angeles Herald special music correspondent

Eddie Wilson's new music is like Eddie Wilson. It's alive. The forty-five minute concert at the Conservatory of Arts last night ran the gamut from the hard-driving, pulse pounding beat of "Pride and Passion" to the soulful strands of the ballad, "Just a Matter of Time". The pace never let up, even after Eddie introduced himself, which will go down as the most dramatic moment in rock history. Everything clicked.

Eddie's vocals are still top drawer and his presence, despite the gap of many years, is still electrifying. At a time when rock artists are going for gimmicks to thrill the audience, Eddie just gives them the music. You believe the lyrics, you believe him.

The legend returns.

I particularly enjoyed a ballad called "NYC Song" which carried me back to the easy going South Jersey sound I enjoyed as a kid. Eddie Wilson was a hero in my community. The local record shop always had a huge poster of Eddie in the window and his album was a strong seller for years - in fact it's still selling. The radio station always treated him with a reverance afforded few rock artists. Eddie Wilson, Elvis, Chuck Berry.

They were legends.

It's unimaginable that Eddie is alive. Where has he been all these years? What has he been doing? What are his plans? Why did he choose the Montreal Music Festival for his comeback? I'm sure these questions will be answered soon. Meanwhile, I was just blown away by the music. Satin Records has a platinum on its hands with this new album if they can get the rights to it. Considering the stormy original relationship between Eddie and Lew Eisen, it's doubtful.

Eddie's band was also a definite plus. Hilton Overstreet's saxophone was smooth and added a key dimension to several of the songs. Rick DeSal's lead guitar was understated and correct, Charley Tansey's drumming consistent and in the pocket, Quinn Quinley's bass was on target and Stewart Fairbanks' keyboards lent a classic air to some songs, including "Mary a". Presence

Satin Records To Make Announcement At A.M. Press Conference

NEW YORK

Satin Records, the company that owns the rights to Eddie Wilson's two previous albums, will host a press conference of Elvis Presley and Jim Morrison could have been more dramatic than the return of Eddie Wilson." Riley will be present this morning with Satin Records

Historical Look at the Accident

SPECIAL TO THE LOS ANGELES HERALD

MONTREAL

Eddie Wilson of "Eddie and the Cruisers came to life last night, shocking the world. The mysterious rock star who was rapidly approaching superstardom back in 1964 supposedly drowned when his car jumped the Raritan Bridge at 3:07 a.m. March 15, 1964. However, his body was never found and for two decades, many people have wondered whether Eddie was alive.

Richard Edward Bass, chief investigator for the Somerset County Sheriff's office, was a rookie cop and the first on the scene that cold March night in 1964, when Eddie's green 1957 Chevrolet was found floating upside down in the Raritan River.

Bass' then superior, J. Wallace Morrison, conducted the investigation and after a week-long dredging effort, Eddie's body was not recovered. According to the county coroner the official cause of death was then listed as "presumed drowned". Obviously, events have changed that.

Eddie Wilson and his band, "Eddie and the Cruisers" were hot as a pistol back in 1963. After appearing in club dates throughout New Jersey and Maryland, the band signed a contract with Satin Records. Their first album, "Tender Years" was a number one hit in 1963. A single off that album, "On the Dark Side", also reached the top of the charts. However, from that point misfortune struck the group hard. Saxophone player Wendell Newton, one of Eddie Wilson's best friends died suddenly in August 1963 and the groups second album, "Season in Hell" was rejected by the record label. These events forced the band to regroup and it was at this point that Eddie stopped touring. His demise on the Raritan Bridge was thought to have been caused by his depression over the sad events.

Says music historian, Marian Jansen, "Eddie Wilson was one of the brightest stars in rock 'n' roll back in '64. His music was perhaps a little ahead of its time, but its roots were in the great tradition of Chuck Berry, Elvis and Little Richard. Today's South Jersey sound, reflected in the music of John

---

REEL EXPOSURE